The Goodliest Place in Middlesex

being a history of the ancient parish of Ruislip which comprised Ruislip, Northwood, Eastcote, Ruislip Manor and South Ruislip

by

Eileen M. Bowlt

HILLINGDON BOROUGH LIBRARIES
1989

© Eileen M. Bowlt

Published by Hillingdon Borough Libraries, 1989
ISBN 0-907869-11-4
Designed by Stephen Barnes
Printed by Echo Press (1983) Ltd.,
for Hillingdon Borough Libraries,
High Street, Uxbridge, Middlesex.

CONTENTS

Title Explanation		4
Illustrations		5
Maps		6
Acknowledgements		7
Abbreviations used		8
Table of weights and measures		8
Introduction		9
Chapter 1.	The Parish of Ruislip and its Church	11
Chapter 2.	The Manor of Ruislip (from Domesday to 1087)	35
Chapter 3.	Ruislip under the Abbey of Bec c. 1087-1404	43
Chapter 4.	The Manor of Ruislip 1404-1451	69
Chapter 5.	St Catherine's Manor and Southcote	75
Chapter 6.	The Manor of Ruislip and King's College	97
Chapter 7.	The Hawtreys, Rogers and Deanes, of Eastcote House	125
Chapter 8.	Life in 17th Century and 18th Century Ruislip	151
Chapter 9.	The care of the poor	169
Chapter 10.	Enclosure in Ruislip Parish	193
Chapter 11.	Growth of Estates in the 19th century and their eventual break-up	213
Chapter 12.	The present century	247
Index		266

References are listed at the end of each chapter.

"THE GOODLIEST PLACE IN MIDDLESEX"

The title of this book was inspired by a phrase in a letter from Dr Richard Neile, Sir Robert Cecil's chaplain, to Sir Robert.

"1601. I have sent to your honour the letters expected from Dr Goode, but I have not yet heard from the gentlemen of Cambridgeshire. The Doctor shall perhaps seem to stand too much upon some nice times with you, but you will please to remember that the letter is to be shown to the now tenant who should conceive that, in this business the college good is chiefly regarded. It were convenient if you should send for both the father and son from Hatfield while you are at London. The motions I have made to Mr Assheby (Ashby) the son were then there. Either you honour to give him 100 L present to surrender his lease reserving to him for his time as much his 8 years, to give him 10 years, or to give him 1,000 L for his whole interest in the lease. Your honour shall seem willing to stay the time that the College may make a sufficient lease to you, only you should engage them, if they depart with this interest that you should have the first refusal of it.

If Mr Asshby (sic) the father, to you, it may please you to offer him composition of his lease, if the great ward of Ruislip, which is a third thing from the site and demisses of Ruislip, which his son hath, and from the park, which M. Garret and Hawtrey have. The whole thing, if it might be compassed together, would be one of the goodliest things in Middlesex."

(The final paragraph of this letter does not refer to Ruislip and has been omitted. See Hatfield House MSS for the complete text).

ILLUSTRATIONS

Interior of St Martin's Church, Ruislip	12
Reverend Thomas Marsh-Everett, Vicar 1878-1900	22
Ruislip Vicarage, Bury Street	24
St Mary's Church, South Ruislip. Opened 1959	31
St Martin's 1935	34
The Park. The embankment.	37
The Abbey of Bec Cloister	44
The Great Barn showing the original main framing	50
The Great Barn Detail	50
The Abbey of Bec. St Nicholas Tower	65
Rawedge	68
Field End Farm	71
Youngwood Farm	81
The Mill House, Bury Street, Ruislip	112
Ramin, Eastcote High Road	113
White Cottage, Harlyn Drive	118
Ralph Hawtrey, 1570-1638	130
Mary Hawtrey, d. 1647	131
Eastcote House, originally "Hopkyttes"	136
Eastcote House (1935) The Cromwell Room	147
Hill Farm, Orchard Close	160
Laurel Cottage, Primrose Cottage, Tudor Cottage – Wood Lane	162
Bury Farm	162
Old House, Bury Street	163
Ducks Hill Farm	163
Hayden Hall	165
Harker's House	171
Mr Casemore, Verger at St Martin's Church	177
Jeremiah Bright's bread cupboard	180
The Workhouse, Ruislip Common	186
The cottages in front of the Old Shooting Box	193
Entrance to Poors Field	202
Ruislip Reservoir	204
New Pond Farm	208
Little New Pond alias Old Pond Farm	209
Priors Farm	210
Hayden Hall	229
The Grange	237
Reverend W. A. G. Gray	249
The Manor Homes built by George Ball	260

LIST OF MAPS

Ruislip and adjoining parishes in North-West Middlesex	10
Land allotted to the Vicar at the Ruislip Enclosure 1806	26
Modern Parishes	30
Ruislip Park Wood, ancient and later Medieval	39
Earthworks at Manor Farm	40
Possible site of Grange at Bourne	48
Place names derived from surnames found in the Customal	56
Outposts of other Manors within Ruislip	72
St Catherine's Manor 14th-15th Century	74
Site of Southcote Manor Moat	76
Mad Bess Wood, showing embankments	78
Rocque's map 1754 – St Catherine's Manor	83
From Ruislip Enclosure map 1806	84
Ownership of St Catherine's Manor after the sale of 1873	86
Breakspear Road Triangle	87
St. Catherine's – 20th Century ownership	91
The Demesne 1565	102
Doharty's map of the enclosed meadows of Manor Farm 1750	104
Distribution of dwellings 1565	109
Plans of High Street 1565 and 1986	114
The Common Fields and Wood of Ruislip	116
Bourne Farm, South Ruislip	140
Northwood Farm	142
New Pond Farm	143
Ruislip Workhouse	170
The Almshouses, Ruislip	173
King's End Farm	197
Ruislip Park House Estate	215
Eastcote Cottage	217
Myrtle Cottage, Joel Street	220
Field End House Farm	222
Mistletoe Farm, Eastcote	224
Bury House	226
Hayden Hall 1883	228
Eastcote Lodge and surrounds 1896	231
Highgrove, Eastcote	233
The Grange, Northwood	235
The Grange Estate	235
The Eastbury Estate 1857	239
Northwood Hall and Northwood Park Estate	243
Sales of land for suburban development in the south of the Parish	253

ACKNOWLEDGEMENTS

Any local historian working on Ruislip must owe a great debt of gratitude to the late Laurence E. Morris (1910-73) who amassed a great collection of notes and transcribed documents and wrote so many illuminating articles . the Journals of the Ruislip and District Natural History Society and the Ruislip, Northwood and Eastcote Local History Society; the L.A.M.A.S. Transactions and a book *The History of Ruislip*. All his papers were generously made available to me by his widow, Ella, during her lifetime and since her death have been lodged in Ruislip Library.

    I should like to thank all those archivists and librarians who have helped me during my researches. Miss Margaret Hoare and the staff of Ruislip Library; Miss Mary Pearce and Mrs Carolynne Cotton, Uxbridge Library; Mr Guy Allen, Civic Centre; Mr A. E. B. Owen, King's College Cambridge; Mrs Holmes, St. George's, Windsor; Mr Samways and the staff of the Greater London Record Office; the vicar and churchwardens of St. Martins. I am also grateful to those Ruislip residents who have allowed me to peruse their house deeds and personal collections of letters and memorabilia, especially Stanley and the late Helen Hoare and those who have shared with me their memories of life in Ruislip in the early years of this century, in particular Mrs Alice Hood (nee Weedon) and Miss Rene Twitchen.

    Members of the Research Group of Ruislip, Northwood and Eastcote Local History Society; Colleen Cox, Denise Shackell, Celia Cartwright, Irene Furbank, Karen Spink, Susan Toms, George Camp and Jean Brown and members of my Extra-Mural classes 1976-86 have been of great assistance to me over many years, in extracting information from parish registers, census records and local newspapers, sorting and indexing it and discussing its implications. Len and Elizabeth Krause, Chairman and Secretary of R.N.E. L.H.S. have constantly encouraged and assisted the publication of local studies.

    Above all I wish to acknowledge the assistance of James McBean who has copied out and made available to me, many documents including 17th century wills and 19th century Rate Books and has delved into the family affairs of many of the large local landowners and their tenants, making plain much which was formerly obscure in the inheritance of estates. He has drawn and prepared for publication all the plans and maps which appear in this book for which I am ever grateful.

    Finally I thank Miss Margaret Hoare for preparing the splendid comprehensive index, which completes this book.

    Dedication To my husband Colin and children, Gerard, Helen, Ursula and Dominic who have cheerfully allowed me to spend 95% of my time (their estimation and grossly exaggerated) on local history.

ABBREVIATIONS

C.P.O.   COMPULSORY PURCHASE ORDER
G.L.R.O.   GREATER LONDON RECORD OFFICE
L.B.H.   LONDON BOROUGH OF HILLINGDON
M.C.C.   MIDDLESEX COUNTY COUNCIL
P.C.C.   PAROCHIAL CHURCH COUNCIL
P.R.O.   PUBLIC RECORD OFFICE
R.N.E.L.H.S. RUISLIP, NORTHWOOD & EASTCOTE LOCAL HISTORY SOCIETY
R.N.U.D.C.   RUISLIP-NORTHWOOD URBAN DISTRICT COUNCIL

Tables of weights and measures

Weight
16 oz = 1 lb
14 lb = 1 st
2 st = 1 qr
8 st = 1 cwt
20 cwt = 1 ton

Linear
12 in = 1 ft
3 ft = 1 yd
5½ yds = 1 pole
22 yds = 1 chain
10 chains = 1 furlong
8 furlongs = 1 mile

Square measure
40 poles = 1 rood
4 roods = 1 acre
4840 sq yds = 1 acre

Money
12 d = 1 shilling
20 s = £1

INTRODUCTION

In this book I have attempted to relate the history of the ancient parish of Ruislip from the time the name first appears in a written record, (in the Domesday Book – exactly 900 years ago) until its metamorphosis into the modern suburbs of Ruislip, Northwood and Eastcote in recent times.

It is the story of one tract of land (6500 acres) and how it has been used, ploughed, laid waste, deforested, grazed, made into hay-fields and built upon by varying numbers of landowners and inhabitants in an ever-changing pattern over the centuries.

The skeleton of the ancient lanes and field boundaries lies very close to the surface and has dictated the shape and layout of modern housing estates. It can be seen when the large trees of an ancient boundary rise between modern gardens (as in Green Walk, Ruislip) or where the main road carrying heavy traffic through old Eastcote winds around the ancient park and along the one-time marshy banks of the Pinn and turns sharply as it joins the old road, Cheyney Street, whose north-eastern section is now called Cuckoo Hill. Green Lane, Northwood still ends at the old entrance to Gate Hill Farm.

In concentrating upon the last 900 years I do not wish to imply that Ruislip was an empty quarter before the Saxons came. Scarcely anything is known about the original settlers, but they left traces of their existence and clues to their life-style with the potsherds and implements dug from the soil, and the ditches and embankments still running across the landscape.

Flint flakes, arrow heads, scrapers and knives have all been found in gardens along the Pinn Valley and in Park Wood in recent years. These artifacts date from the Mesolithic and Neolithic periods and the Bronze Age and indicate settlement along the alluvial deposits of the Pinn, perhaps made by migrants from the more densely settled Colne Valley. The archaeology of the area has been chronicled by Derricourt in R.N.E. L.H.S. Occasional Paper No. 1 and by Cotton, Mills & Clegg in the *Archaeology of West Middlesex*. I have contented myself by gleaning my story from what men and women committed to parchment or paper and the objects, be they houses, or hedgerows, which they left above the ground.

Eileen M. Bowlt
1986

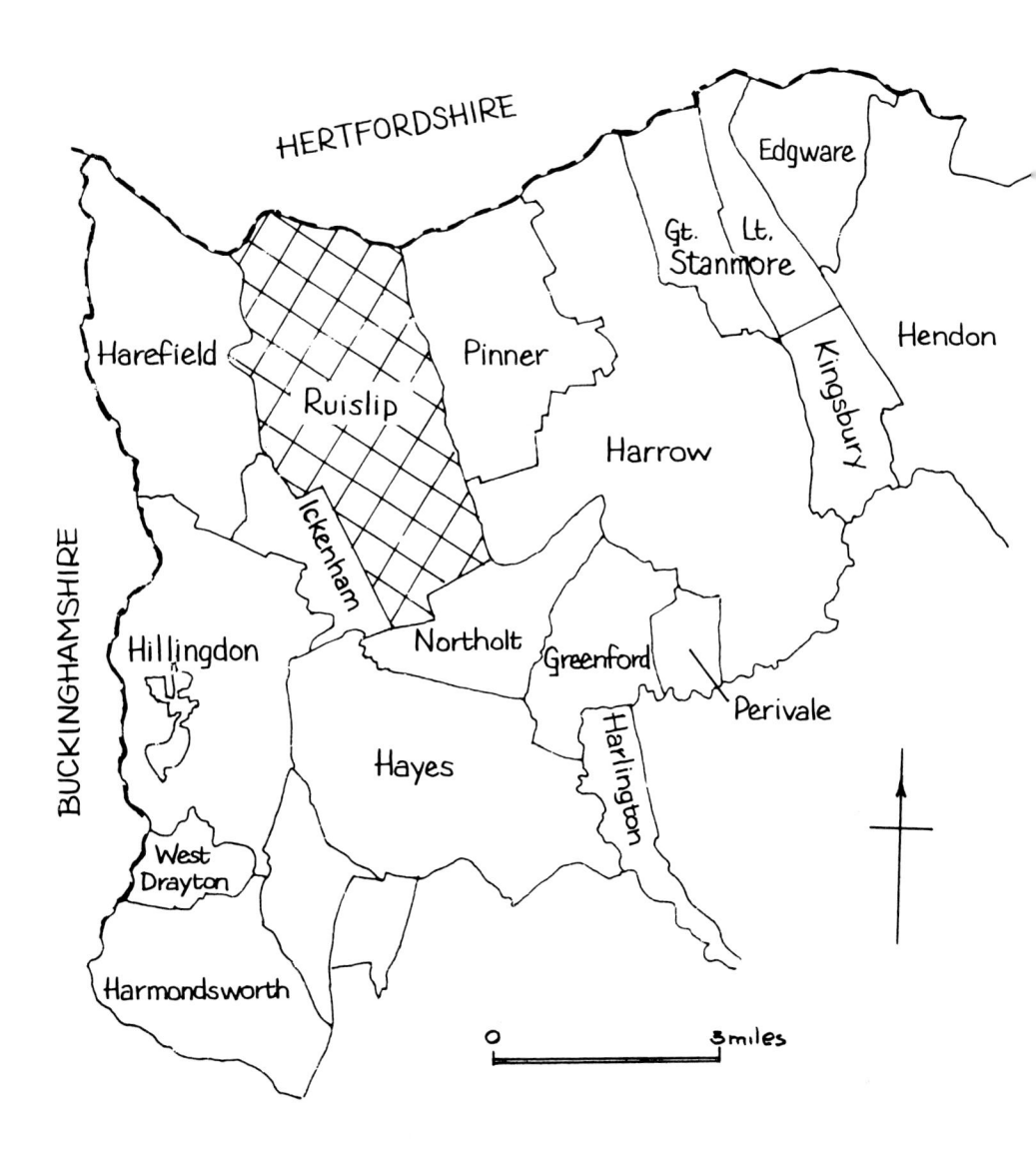

Ruislip and adjoining parishes in North-West Middlesex

Chapter One

The Parish of Ruislip and its Church

The Parish

The ancient parish of Ruislip covered modern Ruislip, Northwood, Eastcote, Ruislip Manor and South Ruislip. Bounded by the parishes of Rickmansworth, Watford, Harefield, Ickenham, Northolt and Pinner, it was in the hundred of Elthorne and the county of Middlesex. Hundreds were ancient divisions of counties, dating from the Saxon period. A parish was the area served by a church, in this case St. Martin's. All inhabitants within it received spiritual care from the parish priest or parson (i.e. the person of the parish) and in return paid tithes towards his maintenance. The boundaries of Ruislip like those of many old English parishes were formed in Saxon times and remained unchanged until in the 19th century an increasing population in Northwood almost four miles distant from the church led to the formation of Holy Trinity parish in 1854. Suburban development in the past eighty years caused many more new parishes to be created within the old boundaries. (See page 30).

Early parishes were ecclesiastical and spiritual in nature. Practical matters like maintaining the church fabric were managed by the priest and a body of lay-people called the vestry after the room in which meetings were usually held.

Vestries emerged in the 14th century and varied in composition from place to place. Unfortunately no documents survive to tell us of a Ruislip vestry in the medieval period but one must have existed. At the Easter vestry it was normal for two churchwardens to be elected, who assisted by other members were responsible for the upkeep of the nave (the part of the church which sheltered the parishioners) and the provision of furniture and vessels for public worship, for which purposes they were empowered to raise a rate. The chancel which covered the altar was repaired by the priest or those who appointed him. At that early time secular affairs were governed by the manor court.

Gradually the power of the manor court declined and the regular vestry meeting was its natural successor, becoming by the end of the 16th century the administrative centre of the parish in civil as well as church matters. Sixteenth century parliamentary legislation heaped responsibility upon the vestry and increased its powers at the same time. The provision of arms for soldiers; the relief of maimed soldiers; the appointment of overseers of highways and the levying of a highway rate all fell to the vestry's lot. The Elizabethan Poor Law of 1601 authorised overseers of the poor appointed by the vestry to levy a compulsory poor rate for a purely civil purpose. In Ruislip the ecclesiastical and civil parish were coterminous. After 1854 Holy Trinity had an ecclesiastical vestry but Northwood civil affairs continued to be governed by Ruislip vestry.

Interior of St Martin's Church, Ruislip

St. Martin's Church

At the centre of Ruislip parish, physically and figuratively, stood St. Martin's church. None of the Domesday entries for Middlesex makes any mention of a church but there are 17 references to priests holding land. Ruislip had a priest with half a hide of land (40-60 acres) and by inference a church of some kind.

A stone with chevron markings apparently of the Norman period, discovered in the south aisle during restoration work on wall paintings in summer 1986, suggests that a stone-built church already stood in Ruislip in the late 12th or early 13th century, but the present building with walls of flint rubble, dressing of Reigate and Tottenhoe stone at the corners and around the windows, and a roof covered with tiles and lead dates from the mid-13th century.[1] The nave has two

The Parish of Ruislip and its Church

arcades, the south being built c. 1240 and the north sometime later. The tower at the west end was added in stages in the 15th century and in the second half of that century the chancel and the south aisle were rebuilt and a vestry was extended from the north wall of the chancel. About 1500 the north aisle was rebuilt, the bell-chamber added to the tower and the south aisle extended east to form a south chapel, an arch being inserted between it and the chancel. The tower staircase was built early in the 17th century. The church was restored by Gilbert Scott in 1870 and the west porch is modern.

It is clear from the above brief summary that Ruislip church underwent a major reconstruction in the 13th century and another in the 15th century. Were these undertaken simply to improve and beautify the church or to repair it? It is necessary to look at those responsible for the church in order to assess the reasons for rebuilding.

The Norman lord of Ruislip, Ernulf de Hesdin probably granted the church of Ruislip along with the manor to the Abbey of Bec in 1087 and Bishops of London from the time of Richard Fitz Neal (1189-98) confirmed the appropriation to Bec until the late 13th century.[2] William de Guineville, a vigorous and able man, became Proctor – General of Bec in 1242 at which time Ruislip was an important centre of administration for Bec's English lands, being the venue for the central audit (see Ch. 2). De Guineville's main residence in England was probably the priory in the present Manor Farm area. Stewards and other officials of the various manors must have foregathered in Ruislip and although the priory had a small chapel, no doubt attended St. Martin's. A customal[3] (list of manorial practices) written about 1245 indicates that the population had increased three-fold since 1086. Consequently a larger church may have been needed for accommodation and a beautiful stone-built one for prestige. One of the men named in the customal, Ralph Truler may have been a mason as his name suggests and living in Ruislip because he was working on the church.

The Abbey of Bec became an alien priory in the 14th century, was crippled with heavy taxes and lost its English lands in 1404 so it would not be surprising to find the church out of repair at the end of that period. John of Lancaster, later Duke of Bedford, jointly with Thomas Langley, later Bishop of Durham and William de St. Vaast, Prior of Ogbourne received Ruislip and other Bec lands in 1404. In 1422, by which time he was in sole possession, the Duke of Bedford granted the spiritualities of all his churches to the Warden and Canons of Windsor, who were to pray for him before and after his death.[4] The Dean and Canons of St. George's have been patrons of Ruislip ever since. If the church was in a poor state in 1422 they did not rush to repair it. By the time the chancel was rebuilt some 50 years later the Dean and Canons were farming the rectory, that is leasing out the right to collect tithes, and the responsibility for rebuilding may have fallen on the lessee, John Walleston.[5]

Some idea of the appearance of the church interior is revealed by 15th century wills. It must have been bright with the coloured statues of saints, with candles and stained glass. William Livinge in 1453 left 6d for a light to burn in front of St. Michael's statue. John Edlin in 1473 left two sheep to have a light in front of St. Mary's statue and a heifer for one to burn before the image of All Saints and a sheep apiece for St. Zita and Holy Trinity. Other statues and images mentioned are of St. Erasmus and the Holy Rood, the great crucifix with Our Lady and St. John beside it, standing high above the screen which separated the chancel from the nave.[6]

The Goodliest Place in Middlesex

The walls at that time were decorated with paintings some of which we can still trace today. After several centuries of being hidden under whitewash, they came to light in 1851 when workmen accidentally uncovered coloured patches which were recognised as important by the schoolmaster/organist who was present and who recommended their preservation. The most easily distinguished mural near the door to the rood loft shows St. Michael weighing a soul with a small devil sitting on one scale pan trying to secure the soul for hell and Our Lady standing to his left and touching the other pan to help it into heaven. Below is a figure with an architectural setting, said to be St. Lawrence with his gridiron. Clive Rouse FSA worked on the wall paintings in 1937 and discovered the Corporal Works of Mercy above the south arcade, corresponding with the Seven Deadly Sins on the north side, both of 15th century date, the former overpainted with the figure of a man wearing dress of period c. 1530. Further restoration in summer 1986 by Ann Ballantyne reveals that the man is seated at a table but his identity is unknown.[7]

The only piece of old glass left in the church is in the north west window in the north aisle, part of a roundel with a shield bearing the letter M. Thomas Ferne in 1521 asked to be buried in front of the window of St. Martin and St. George. The dedication of the church to St. Martin of Tours is probably original. The earliest mention of it found so far occurs incidentally in the 1245 customal where Randolph Coke is said to have a house "in front of St. Martin's". Other documents simply refer to Ruislip Church.

Many will-makers left small amounts of money toward the repair of the church fabric and Thomas Bettz in 1463 left £26.13s.4d for mending the bells.[8]

Chantries were established at St. Martin's, perhaps with their own altars, for occasional references occur to chantry priests. Gilbard Crosyer in 1494 provided in his will for "an honest preste to syng for my soulle in the said chirche a hoole yere for his salary 106s.8d"[9] and Sir Richard, described as Chantry Priest of Ruislip, baptised a child at St. Giles, Ickenham in 1540.[10] All chantries were suppressed in 1547.

The religious changes of the 16th and 17th centuries altered the appearance of churches by a series of decrees which must have affected St. Martin's, although no specific record is left. A Bible in Latin and English had to be set up in every chancel before 1st August 1537. Most images were removed during the reign of Edward VI (1546-54). Nicholas Ridley, Bishop of London ordered altars to be removed from churches in the London diocese by Whit Week 1550 and replaced by a simple table. Under Elizabeth crucifixes and tapers were forbidden. The pulpit came to be the focal point of a church as the emphasis moved from the sacrifice of the mass on the altar to the preaching of the word. The pulpit in St. Martin's is Jacobean.

Most of the seating in St. Martin's is modern and of pine except for some oak benches at the west end of the nave with moulded top rails and ends and a pew on the north side of the chancel with linen-fold panelling, which date from about 1500. At one time some box pews were introduced. A faculty still exists permitting one 17 feet long to be erected in the chancel in 1631 by Lady Alice, Dowager Countess of Derby for the accommodation of the residents of Hayden Hall. There was at least one other for Eastcote House.[11]

Two prints dated 1795 show the exterior of St. Martin's on both the north and south sides. Dormer windows let light into the nave; the vestry on the north side of the chancel can just be seen and a timber and lath and plaster porch appears at the west end. Lysons gives a good description of the church monuments in his *Environs of London* (1800), but does not speak of the state of the church. Sperling in *Church Walks in Middlesex* (1848) says it was in "a disgraceful state of neglect and dilapidation". A major restoration was undertaken during 1869-70, directed by Gilbert Scott. Today the church with the altar the main centre of interest and statues restored probably resembles its medieval state more nearly that at any time since the Reformation, only lacking the rood screen and the bright colours which the walls must once have had.

Rectors and Vicars

As Christianity spread in England in the 7th century a tradition grew of wealthy laymen founding churches and appointing the priest. Economic provision was made for the clergyman by allotting him a share in the village arable (glebe land) and by making offerings and voluntarily paying tithes. By the 11th century priests were instituted by bishops but often appointed by the lay-patron. They were secure against dispossession but still economically dependent upon agreement with the lord, until tithes were universally imposed by the Lateran Council in 1179. In the 12th century the patron presented his chosen candidate to the bishop who, having checked the suitability of his learning, virtue and age (25 minimum) then inducted him into the Spiritualities (pastoral rights over his flock) and the Temporalities (civil law rights over the material possessions of the benefice). A parish priest who received all the tithes and farmed all the glebe was termed a rector. If the rector (Latin for ruler) was absent for any reason a vicar was appointed in his stead and the tithes were split into great tithes (corn, hay, wood, etc.) for the rector and little tithes (minor produce – milk, eggs, etc.) for the vicar.

There was a tendency for lay-patrons to endow religious houses with all rights in the churches they or their predecessors had founded, in return for prayers for the good of their souls. This is precisely what happened in Ruislip when Ernulf de Hesdin granted the church to the Abbey of Bec in the late 11th century and again in 1422 when John, Duke of Bedford gave it to the Dean and Canons of Windsor.

Lay-rectors leased the Rectory (the right to collect tithes) from Windsor from 1476 onwards. Those first recorded were members of the Walleston family, who were succeeded as rectors in 1532 by Ralph Hawtrey, a relation by marriage.[12] The letting of tithes was a common practice, particularly to London merchants, among whom were probably numbered the Wallestons.

The Hawtreys and their descendants, Rogers and Deanes continued to lease the Rectory until 1867,[13] when all Windsor's ecclesiastical estates passed to the Ecclesiastical Commissioners.[14]

Although monks from Bec were resident in Ruislip it is unlikely that they acted as parish priests, and they probably appointed vicars instead. A man called Augustine, vicar of Ruislip witnessed a deed concerning land in Harefield in the 13th century,[15] but nothing else is known of early vicars. The recorded list starts in 1327 when William de Berminton resigned and John de Lekford was appointed to the living.

The Goodliest Place in Middlesex

LIST OF RECORDED VICARS OF RUISLIP

Name	Appointed	Vacates
William de Berminton		1327 res.
John de Lekford	1327	
Thomas Sely	1338	
Robert de Bokeworth or Bikkenworth	1361	1386 d.
Philip Hughelat or Howlet	1386	1400 d.
John Prest	1400	1431 res.
Richard Lucas	1431	1437 ced.
Thomas Suthill	1437	1440 d.
William Pychford	1440	1479 d.
Thomas Blake	1479	1483 ced.
George Percy alias Gard	1483	1492 ex.
Thomas Machey	1492	1497 res.
Robert Tomson	1497	
Richard Wytston or Whetton		1515 d.
Hugh Gifford	1516	1522 res.
Henry Hanley or Hawley	1522	
George Whitehorne		1554 dep.
Robert Peerson	1554	1559
George Whitehorne		1565 d.
Thomas Smith	1565	1615
Edmund Nuthall	1615	1616 d.
Daniel Collins	1617	1633 res.
John Ellys	1633	1639 d.
Daniel Collins	1640	1641 res.
William Dring	1641	
Nathaniel Giles	1648	
Robert Cresswell		
Thomas Bright	1662	
John Maximilian de Langley	1674	1682 ced.
Robert Rowsell	1682	
John Shorediche	1708	1714
William Bowles	1715	1743 d.
Robert Carr	1743	1755 ced.
Henry Duckworth	1755	1778 res.
Weldon Champneys	1778	1794 res.
John Gibbons	1794	1797 d.
Daniel Carter Lewis	1797	1834 d.
Christopher Packe	1834	1878 d.
Thomas Marsh Everett	1878	1900 d.
William Arthur Gordon Grey	1900	1923 ex.
Edward Cornwall-Jones	1923	1938 d.
George Derek Barnsley	1938	1943 d.
Ernest Clement Mortimer	1943	1952 ex.
Ronald Dupre Grange-Bennett	1952	1962 res.
Christopher Byron	1962	1970 res.
Kenneth Toovey	1970	1981 res.
Richard Fenwick	1983	

d. = died   res. = resigned   ced. = ceded   ex. = exchanged   dep. = deprived

Little is known about the Ruislip vicars except what can be gleaned from the 18th century *Newcourt's Repertorium* and the revised and extended edition called the *Novum Repertorium* produced by George Hennessey in 1896. With the exception of John Shorediche (1708-14) a younger son of Richard Shorediche, Lord of the Manor of Ickenham, the vicars do not appear to have local connections. Daniel Collins who was vicar twice (1617-33 and 1640-1) was not one of the Ruislip Collins but son of Baldwin Collins, Vice-Provost of Eton. He was one of several vicars who held other appointments being at the same time Canon of Windsor, Fellow of Eton and Rector of Cowley.

Pluralism (holding several benefices at the same time) was a great evil as the income from the Church was concentrated in a few hands and some parishes never saw their incumbent, while in others the Cure of Souls was left to an ill-paid curate. Pluralists on a grand scale like Cardinal Wolsey (two bishoprics, one archbishopric and an abbacy) were motivated by greed and self-aggrandisement, but many ordinary clergymen were so poverty-stricken that they required several appointments to achieve an adequate income.

Many of Ruislip's vicars were minor canons of Windsor. The constitution of St. George's defined by statutes in 1352 was 13 canons including the Dean, 13 priest vicars, 4 secular clerks and 6 chorister boys. The priest vicars were intended as resident deputies for the canons, ready to attend daily service as required. They were to have skill in music, to sing and chant the services well. Minor canons replaced priest vicars during the 16th century and perpetual residence ceased to be a requirement. They numbered seven from 1563-1849 and four thereafter. When a living within the gift of the Dean and Canons such as Ruislip fell vacant it was customary for it to be offered to the minor canons in order of seniority.

The two periods of greatest upheaval in the Church were the Reformation in the 16th century and the rise of Puritanism and the Civil Wars and their aftermath in the 17th century. The Ruislip incumbent during the Reformation was George Whitehorne who became vicar at an unknown date after 1522, was deposed in 1554 and was again vicar after 1559, dying in office in 1565. It must be supposed that he accepted the alterations made in the Church during Edward VI's reign, but was not willing to restore the mass under Mary (1554-8) and was replaced by Robert Peerson, being restored again under Elizabeth. There is no evidence of popular opposition to any of the religious changes in the parish. Conformity at all times seems to have been the rule among the villagers of rural Ruislip, docilely following the lead of the Hawtreys of Eastcote House. Some centres of religious rebellion existed among influential families in neighbouring parishes. The Bellamy family made Uxendon Manor House at Wembley a refuge for Catholic priests from the beginning of the Jesuit Mission to England in 1580. The Pagets of West Drayton remained Catholic and Sebastian Newdigate, one of the 17 children of John and Amphilisia Newdigate of Harefield, was one of the monks of Charterhouse who suffered martyrdom at Tyburn in 1535. Moorcroft in Uxbridge sheltered Catholic priests after the passing of the Recusancy Act in 1581 and four suspected Papists from Ruislip were presented at Quarter-Sessions for non-attendance at the Parish Church.[16] These were Elizabeth, wife of John Eden, and Catherine Eden spinster, and John and Maria Wylchen. There are no other references to Catholicism in the parish until the 20th century. Protestantism and Non-conformity flourished among the urban population of Uxbridge, where three Protestants, brought from Buckinghamshire, were burnt at the Lynch in 1555 as an example, during the Marian persecutions.

The quality of Ruislip's post-Reformation vicars is not generally known, but at the Bishop's Visitation in 1586, 27 clergy of the Middlesex deanery *"were enjoined to gyve their attendance for their exercises in the scriptures"*. Thomas Smith (1565-1615), Vicar of Ruislip was pronounced *"tollerable"*, which was better than Henry Kendall of Ickenham who was described as *"simple"* and Thomas Matthew of Cowley who was *"old and ignorant"* while Samuel Hawkinsby of Hillingdon failed to attend for his examination![17]

The Puritan movement growing in the Church during the early 17th century, particularly demanded a preaching, and consequently teaching, clergy. There was a lack of well-educated incumbents capable of fulfilling these demands which may be partly because able men were not attracted to such a relatively poverty-stricken profession.

For the remedying of any deficiencies among the beneficed clergy the House of Commons voted in September 1641 *"it shall be lawful for the Parishioners of any Parish...to set up a lecture, and to maintain an orthodox minister at their own charge to preach every Lord's Day where there is no preaching..."*. We know little of affairs at Ruislip Church at this period. Walker's *"Suffering of the Clergy"* (Oxford 1948) says that Nathaniel Giles came here in 1644 and was *"to this day a proverb in the parish for his litigiousness. He used to preach, it is said, with a pistol about him, which most commonly hung at his neck"*. Presumably the former vicar, William Dring had been ejected by Parliament as a "scandalous minister". Mr Giles, pistol and all moved to Steeple Deeping, Wiltshire in 1648. Presentments made by the jurors of the hundreds of Isleworth, Elthorne and Spelthorne on 8th June 1649 say of Ruislip that the vicarage was possessed by Robert Cresswell *"our present and constant preaching minister"*[18] and that there was one church *"sufficient to receive all our parishioners without the help of any Chapell,"* which sounds as though the parishioners of Ruislip at that time were happy enough with their vicar. This fortunate state of affairs seems to have continued, because later in the century the books of Bishop's Visitation show that Thomas Bright, the Restoration vicar was considered *"competant"*.

The Bishop of London sent a circular letter to his parish clergy in April 1706 requesting information about Papists. This inquiry resulted from the Privy Council's disquiet at several instances of *"very great boldness and presumption of the Romish priests and Papists in this Kingdom"*. Robert Rowswell of Ruislip replied more fully than many of his brother clergymen, many of whom scribbled curt replies on the back of the Bishop's letter. He wrote: *"In obedience to your lordship's command I have made as strict a scrutiny as possibly I could into the principles and practices of the inhabitants of my parish and my lord, I find prophaneness and imorality doth to much increase and I have to many practical Atheists and I am afraid some speculative ones tho they conceal their principles as much as possible. My Lord as for Papists or reputed Papists I know none within my precincts..."*.[19] Were the practical atheists simply parishioners unwilling to attend church?

A late 18th century Visitation Book gives the first intimation of Methodism in the area. After stating that a service was held twice every Sunday, that the Sacraments were given out four times a year to between 30 and 40 communicants and that children were usually catechised in Lent, it continued: *"There are no Papists and Methodists have decreased of late years."*[20]

The Parish of Ruislip and its Church

Only three vicars covered the 19th century at St. Martin's. The value of the living greatly increased after the enclosure of Ruislip's waste and common fields between 1806 and 1814 and by 1834 it was worth £462 per annum. The flood of letters of application written to the Dean and Canons of Windsor in 1834 and 1878 when the Ruislip incumbency fell vacant is probably a reflection of both its desirability and the indigence of clergymen trying to support the appearance of gentlemen on low incomes. There was little hope of anyone other than a minor canon receiving the post and there was competition even among them, but many others tried their luck. After the death of Daniel Carter Lewis on 21st March 1834 Christopher Packe applied for the living even though he was not the most senior minor canon. Hearing that a Mr Champris had declined the post early in July he wrote again and was eventually appointed to Ruislip in the late autumn. He was to remain for the rest of his long life. He died in 1878 aged 86.

Christopher Packe was born in Edinburgh in 1792, the son of Dr Herbert Packe. He matriculated from Worcester College, Oxford in May 1810, thus qualifying to proceed to a bachelor's degree which he obtained in 1814, becoming a deacon the same year. Two years later he was ordained by the Archbishop of Canterbury and began his career in the Church of England Ministry. His appointments were as follows:

1817–35 Minor Canon of St. Pauls
1833–78 Junior Cardinal of St. Pauls
1821–67 Minor Canon of St. George's Chapel, Windsor. From the time of his resignation in 1867 until his death he received a pension of £115 per annum from the Dean and Chapter.
1821 Preacher-in-Ordinary to Queen Caroline
1821 Priest-in-Ordinary to the King
1821–35 Rector of St. Michael Bassishaw
1834–78 Vicar of Ruislip and
Priest-in-Ordinary of St. James.

It will be noted that the dates of several of the posts overlap. He wrote in July 1834 to the Dean and Canons of Windsor: *"I have upon various occasions...been assailed as a great Pluralist. I grant that I am such. But...believe me that nothing but my necessities have urged me to become such"*.[21]

He had married, probably in 1821, which may account for his acquiring several posts in that year. A rapidly expanding, but alas sickly family brought mounting expenses and personal tragedy. His letter continued *"And I most solemnly declare and will show from my books that until this last twelve months my income (after my annual average bill for medical attendance has been discharged) has never amounted to £400 a year"*. He continues *"That I should feel most anxious for a home in the country you gentlemen, who are aware of the numerous losses I have sustained in my family during the eight years I have lived in my present residence in London cannot feel surprised. Five children have been snatched from me during that period and of the two remaining little ones the infant only of nine months has enjoyed health. My other little girl has been three times on the brink of the grave within the last year. But beyond all this, gentlemen, I have at the moment a sister whose safety requires that she should be in confinement, did not my poverty exclude the possibility of my placing her there"*.

"In my present situation...the approach of summer which the Almighty seems to have appointed as a season of rejoicing for all nature, by me is

regarded with anticipation of misery which many years experience has proved not to be groundless. I long, God knows how I long for the pure air of the country".

Mr Packe's cri de coeur illustrates the difficulties faced by a married clergyman striving to support a wife and family (he had 14 children altogether) on tithes and glebe allotted in medieval times for the maintenance of a celibate clergyman. Tithes originally paid in kind had been largely commuted to money payments during the 16th century and had failed to rise during periods of inflation. Incumbents who received tithes in kind were better off than those who received a fixed sum of money. It is unfortunate that no one was thoughtful enough to write down the method of tithe collection in Ruislip for the delectation of future historians. There is one oblique reference in James Ewer's Diary dated October 1778 the year when Mr Weldon Champneys became vicar: *"Whereas a despute arises between the Present Minister and the Parish concerning the prive tiths and so he wold take it in kind. I mesuard the firs pail and there was nine pints. Joseph Vincon Witness,"*[22] which suggests that money payments had been the usual practice in the parish. Christopher Packe's family, compiled from baptismal registers of St. Martin's, graves (Nos. 82 and 83 graveyard survey, Ruislip Library), a monument in the north aisle of the church and the censuses of 1851, 1861 and 1871, appears to have been as follows:

Five children who died young before July 1834

Herbert	born 1822	died November 1871
Christopher	born 1824	died February 1851
Mary Elizabeth	born 1832	died 1870
Julia	born 1833	
Rosa	born 1835	died 1934
Charles Lewis	born 1837	
Ellen Maria	born June 1838	died November 1841
Francis	born July 1840	(but not baptised until May 1841)
Elizabeth Frances	born May 1842	

It is difficult to assess the character of Christopher Packe. He showed a spirit of Christian resignation in the face of his bereavements. The family monument in the church says *"The Lord gave and the Lord hath taken away. Blessed is the name of the Lord".* His wife died in 1874 and only two of his children seem to have survived him.

Several references in vestry minutes suggest that in common with many clergymen, he regarded drunkenness as a great evil. In 1835 he suggested that someone should patrol the ale houses and report the names of all paupers (i.e. those receiving parish relief) found tippling in public houses. Four years later he referred in the vestry meeting to the immoralities of drunkenness and gambling with other prophaneness on the Sabbath Day.[23]

He was probably zealous in his ministry. He headed a petition for a chapel-of-ease to be set up in Northwood in 1837, stating that *"very few if any of the labouring part of the population attend any church at all"* as St. Martin's was four miles distant by road. He trusted that a new place of worship would promote *"the efficacy and stability of the established church and the Salvation of Souls may thereby be promoted."*[24] He was prepared to set aside £10 per annum chargeable upon Glebe lands for a repairing fund.

Methodism was a threat to the established church at the time and the Northwood Chapel may have been intended to stem its tide. Adam Clarke at

Hayden Hall was sowing the seeds in Eastcote and a chapel was opened at the bottom of Field End Road in 1848.[25] The chapel at Ruislip Common opened in 1852.

Towards the end of his long life (86 years – the grave says 88!) he became unfit for the business of the parish and the Rev. J. J. Roumieu, his curate from 1870, was virtually in sole charge. Lady Hume-Campbell of Highgrove referred in a letter to *"our poor old vicar Mr Packe."*[26] The local paper reporting his funeral, which took place in June 1878, said that he had kept his house for the last four years because of ill health, but had been much respected and was spoken of in a kind manner in the neighbourhood.

Once again Windsor was beset with applications from all parts of the country from clergy whose wives had been advised by their doctors to live only in a country parish with pure air etc., etc. An added complication was the number of letters from local gentry trying to influence the Dean and Canons.

The Hume-Campbells of Highgrove favoured the existing Curate for the post. Lady Juliana Hume-Campbell wrote on 16 June 1878 that it was *"the strong wish of many of the parishioners, myself and Sir Hugh.... that Mr Roumieu should remain with us.... He has been most zealous in his Ministry and his kindness to the Poor as well as that of his wife has endeared him to many a cottage household.... In these days of ritual and schisms it is very desirable (especially here where there are many Dissenters) to have a Clergyman of sound and moderate views."*[27] In order to press her point Lady Hume-Campbell also sought an introduction to Mr Wellesley, Dean of Windsor through the good offices of his sister, Lady Ebury of Moor Park.

Lady Ebury was unwilling to oblige and instead wrote to her brother enclosing Lady Hume-Campbell's letter to herself and one each from Sir Hugh Hume-Campbell and Lady Hume-Campbell to the Dean. No doubt Lady Ebury was frequently the subject of similar applications. In her own letter to her brother she writes *"I have not given the letter of introduction which would have been too great a bore to you.... I believe Mr R is a good man. He has done duty once or twice at Northwood. I don't know him and I suppose "sound and moderate" is a good description, so many people think the best that can be given.... Lady Hume-Campbell is a great Lady in these parts – a good woman I believe but I know her very slightly."*[28]

Francis Deane of Eastcote House, lessee of the Rectory wrote to Lord Ebury soliciting his support for his brother the Rev. Charles Deane *"as you are nearly connected with the Dean of Windsor."* Lord Ebury sent this letter on to Windsor with a rather cool covering note.[29] Charles Deane wrote on his own behalf pointing out his connection with Ruislip. *"My family having been lessees of the Rectory for about 400 years.... My brother Francis apart from other members of the family contributed £300 to the late Church Restoration and all my blood that I have known have been laid in Ruislip Churchyard."*[30]

H. Kingsmill, Manager of the British Linen Bank and probably a member of the family living at 4 Field End Villas, Eastcote wrote to Windsor twice opposing Mr Roumieu's application and implying that he was disliked by the labouring classes. He stated his preference for another minor canon.[31] He was to have one. Thomas Marsh-Everett was appointed. He was the second son of James Everett of Wold, Northants and was 34 when he took up his Ruislip appointment. He married Miss Edith Baker daughter of L. J. Baker of Hayden Hall in October 1882.[32] New lighting was put in the church as a wedding gift.[33]

Reverend Thomas Marsh-Everett, Vicar 1878-1900

He established a tradition of musical concerts in the parish at which he was a frequent performer and played a large part in civic affairs. He died in 1900 and was commemorated by the lych-gate in Eastcote Road.

Mr Marsh-Everett's place was taken by W. A. G. Gray who played a diplomatic role in local affairs during the establishment of the R.N.U.D.C. in 1904. (See Chapter 11). He exchanged the living with Mr Cornwall-Jones for that of Aboyne, Deeside in 1923. Mr Cornwall-Jones had been born at Holyhead in 1869 and educated at University and Richmond Colleges (Non-Conformist College) and maintained a friendly relationship between St. Martin's and the Methodist Church during his time in Ruislip. *Outlook*, the parish magazine which continues to be published, was his brainchild. He was keenly interested in the social problems of the industrial areas of the metropolis and had worked in

The Parish of Ruislip and its Church

Tottenham in his early years. He found work in Ruislip for a number of young Welsh girls who came into service in the houses springing up in King Edward's and similar roads. He suffered a grave illness in 1936 and died in November 1937.[34] During Mr Cornwall-Jones' last illness Dean Quainton came to assist at St. Martin's and stayed on after his death, although unwell himself. The Dean was a great preacher and filled the church to overflowing with his simple but uplifting sermons, so that forms and chairs had to be borrowed to accommodate people who crowded the church. His last sermon was delivered only two days before his death in February 1938, while he was in great pain and could only maintain an upright position by wedging himself into the pulpit.[35]

Mr George Derek Barnsley was the new vicar appointed in 1938. He made some changes in the ceremonial, introducing candles and images, which caused some disquiet among members of the Parochial Church Council in 1939. He met an untimely death in 1943 by falling from a tree at Beaconsfield while helping his brother to cut some branches.[36]

His successor Mr Mortimer went to Minehead in 1952. While considering whether to accept Mr Grange-Bennett then vicar of Minehead in exchange, the P.C.C. noted *"The main problem for any Vicar of St. Martin's is to minister to people of different traditions under the one roof of the parish church without rough treatment of anybody....and without resorting to an insipid compromise."* Mr Grange-Bennett made a favourable impression upon the churchwardens and was invited to become vicar.[37]

He obtained a number of faculties (authorisations from the bishop) which affected the appearance of the church interior: one for an aumbry for the reservation of the Blessed Sacrament in 1953; for St. Michael's Chapel in 1956; St. Martin's Statue and the Rood and Calvary Cross in memory of Mrs Gower in 1957; new altar rails with gates in memory of Mrs Dorothy Russell in 1958 and a new sanctuary lamp and statue of Our Lady in 1960.[38]

Father Byron (1962) and then Father Toovey (1970-81) followed in the same tradition. From November 1981-May 1983 St. Martin's was without a vicar and cared for by two curates – Father Fenwick was appointed vicar by the Bishop of London in 1983, asserting his right to do so as the Dean and Canons of Windsor had defaulted.

The Vicarage House

The vicar of Ruislip had a house on the west side of Bury Street, north of the Pinn from before 1391 to the autumn of 1981. The earliest reference occurs in a Court Roll of Harmondsworth when the Forester of that manor held a field between Sitheclack Mill (end of Clack Lane) and the Vicar's House.[39] Excavations on the south side of the latest house on the site (built 1881) in spring 1982 revealed stratified remains of occupation dating back to c. 1300 (sherds of Middlesex – Hertfordshire grey ware), though whether clerical or not could not be proved. The site is somewhat distant from the Church. Indeed it is closer to what was the Abbey of Bec's Priory in the 14th century. The Terrier (land roll) of 1565 names the building in Bury Street as a vicarage for the first time.[40]

How many houses have stood on that site is not known for certain. A map of Park Wood dated 1633 depicts the vicarage as a low building with two gables standing end on to Bury Street, while on Doharty's map (1750) it appears as a long building facing the Street and end on to the Pinn. Whether either of these

23

The Goodliest Place in Middlesex

should be taken as accurate drawings or merely as indications of a house, is uncertain.[41] The Enclosure Map (1806) has the first reliable ground plan and a glebe terrier dated 1810 describes it as built partly with brick and partly with lath and plaster covered in tiles, having a stable and adjoining offices also wood covered with tiles.[42] The brick portion was a new wing added in the late 18th century. It seems to have served Christopher Packe, but Thomas Marsh-Everett built a new house (now the Old Vicarage) immediately north of the existing building. The earlier vicarage was demolished without any painting, drawing or written record to tell us what it was like, but the "new wing" was left and is now a separate house called the Vicarage Cottage.

Mr Marsh-Everett wrote to the Ecclesiastical Commissioners hoping to obtain a grant towards the cost of the new vicarage saying that he would have £500 dilapidation money and would give £200 from his own pocket to start the subscription list. *"I must then see what I can get from friends and parishioners and borrow the rest from Queen Anne's Bounty.... Perhaps my kind Patrons will be kind enough to give me a little for I feel sure that their name on my list would be a great help to me and encouragement to others to contribute."*[43]

The vicarage which he built still stands but was converted into flats Spring 1985. It is built of a pleasant red brick, with gables, a tiled roof and interesting chimneys owing something perhaps to the architectural "cottage

Ruislip Vicarage, Bury Street showing original main door

style" employed by George and Peto on the Hayden Hall estate of Marsh-Everett's father-in-law L. J. Baker. The architect of the vicarage is not known, but as H. A. Peto was related by marriage to the Bakers, he and his partner Earnest George may have been employed by Mr Marsh Everett. The front door was in the south front facing the Pinn with a carriage sweep from Bury Street leading to it. Mr Barnsley extended the vicarage in 1938 and moved the main door to the east side, making a double sweep and improving the entrance from the road.

Later vicars found the house too large. Mr Mortimer exchanged the benefice with Mr Grange-Bennett of Minehead in 1952 because of his private need for a smaller labour-saving vicarage. When Father Toovey moved in November 1981 the vicarage was sold to a private developer. The new vicar, inducted in May 1983, moved into a detached house in Eastcote Road, opposite the church, which was built as an ordinary family home in 1925.

The presence of other buildings near the vicarage – a stable and former cow byre (later a scout hut demolished in 1984) – serve to remind us that earlier vicars had agricultural interests and brings us to the question of the vicar's glebe in the next section.

One wonders where the curates lived. There is evidence in the 16th century that curates who served an absentee vicar simply leased the vicarage from him. Mr Harland in the 1860's lived in Eastcote Cottage, Wiltshire Lane and J. J. Roumieu in the 1870's also lived in Eastcote. In a large parish it may have been good policy to have the vicar in Ruislip and the curate in Eastcote to maintain a clerical presence.

The Glebe

The Domesday Priest had half a hide of land (40-60 acres). No full description of the glebe occurs until the 1565 Terrier was drawn up. The vicar's land then consisted of 36½ selions scattered through the common fields of Westcote, 3 selions in the fields of Eastcote and 2 acres of land in Northwood.

In addition there were 2½ acres enclosed land around the vicarage. The total acreage approximates to the Domesday half hide provided that the hyde in Ruislip was only 80 acres. (See Chapter 6). The vicar had grazing rights on the common pastures and waste of the manor along with the other tenants. His income was supplemented by the collection of the small tithes.

A dispute over wood tithes arose in 1577 while Thomas Smith was vicar. Normally, when a parish had both rector and vicar, the tithes of corn, hay and wood (the coppiced hornbeam which was cut on rotation in local woods) constituted the Great or Rectorial Tithes but the wood tithes were not always collected in Ruislip. John Hawtrey, Lessee of the Rectory, probably claimed or attempted to claim the tithe wood after a long lapse and Mr Wold of Weybridge who had leased the wood and underwood in Ruislip Park from King's College refused to pay it. Five elderly residents of Ruislip made depositions on Mr Wold's behalf. The first John Smith, 67 who lived at Manor Farm (then called Ruislip Court) had been born in Brastead and was one-time Fellow of King's College. He had lived in Ruislip for 32 years and had known it for 12 years before that. The others were Thomas Fern, 68, labouring man; John Lyvinge, 60, husbandman; Stephen Wheeler, 67, labourer and wood dealer; Thomas Lyon, 74, carpenter.[44]

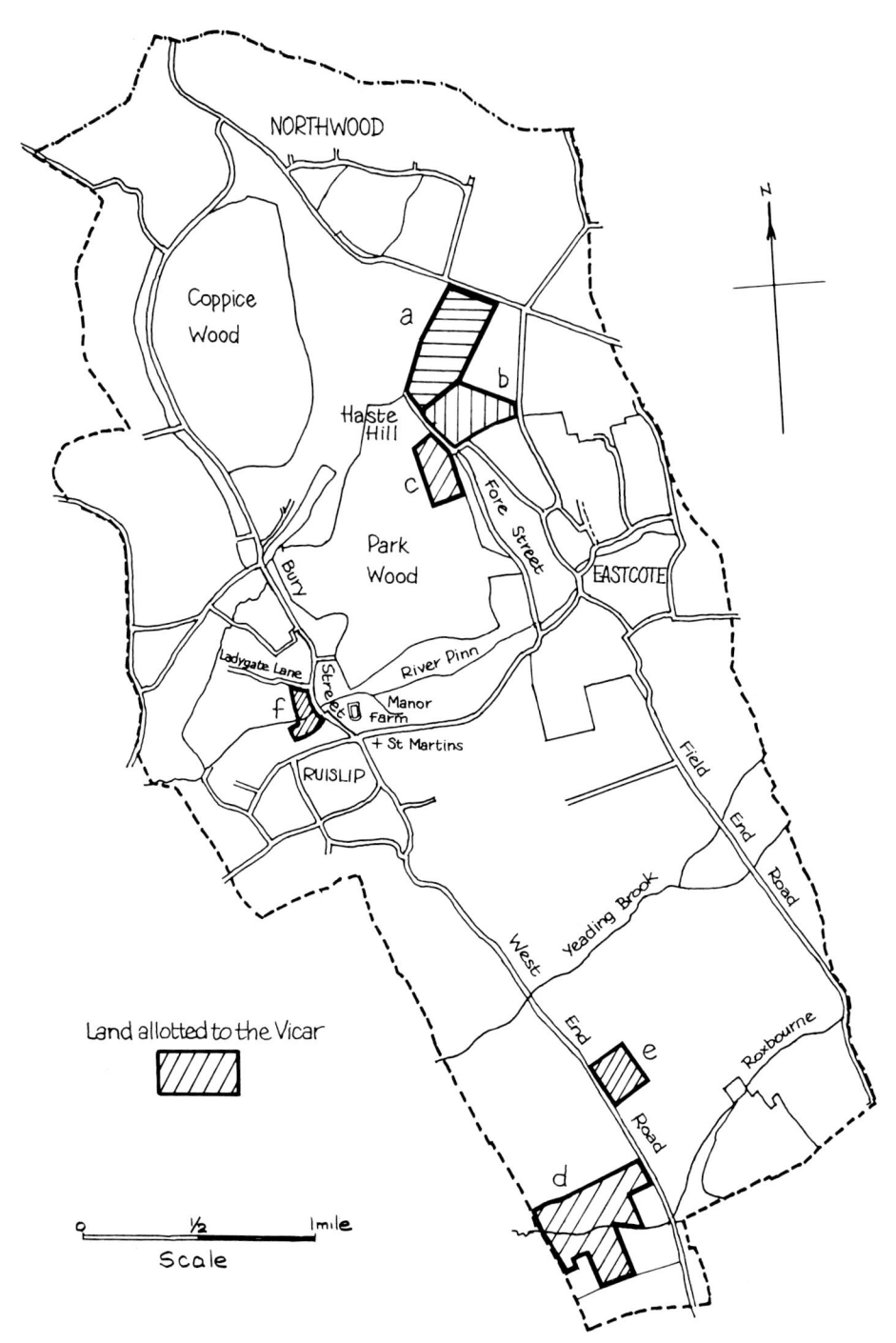

Land allotted to the Vicar at the Ruislip Enclosure 1806

All agreed that the farmers of the Parsonage, i.e. the Rectory lessees never received any tithes but corn and hay and that the vicars until 20-30 years previously (1547-57) had received 20 loads of wood for their fires. Thomas Lyon's deposition runs as follows:

"He says that he has heard of his father when this deponent was but young and also of other old men in the parish of Ruislip that time out of mind there was an old custom in the same parish that there was no tithe wood paid in the same parish, but that in recompense of the tithe wood of the whole parish the vicar of Ruislip ought to have 20 loads of wood yearly only of the Lord's wood, and ever since that time hitherto the common voice and speech hath been in Ruislip that the vicar should so have as before he hath declared.

And about 40 years past or more there was one Sir Richard Gamlyn* vicar of Ruislip who for his time received the same 20 loads and this deponent had an uncle named James Osmond which as he hath told this deponent did help to carry the same wood for parson Gamlyn divers times, and one Jeffrey and one Thom Hore did use to take the same wood forth, and he hath also seen the same wood otherwhiles carried home to the vicarage out of the Lords manor wood, and seen those men fall and dress the same wood for the vicar as he had had occasion to come by that way, and till within those 20 years he never heard or understood otherwise but the vicar there had those 20 loads yearly, and he never knew or heard any tithe wood neither claimed or paid any way in all this time otherwise than the loads aforesaid and yet he hath seen much wood in his time felled in that parish. He says that for all his time he hath seen the farmer of the parsonage there receive and take tithe corn and hay there and no other tithes, and almost 60 years past he dwelt with one Mr Wallaston farmer of the same parsonage about 2 years, and at that time he saw Mr Wallaston receive the same corn and hay and no other tithes and if any other had been due he thinks he would have had it but all other tithes (except of wood) the vicars there have accustomably received the same."

John Hawtrey and his successors seem to have allowed the matter to lie dormant and not claimed wood tithes. The vicar, however, having been reminded of his rights claimed his firewood. The 20 loads a year was not always readily given by the College Bailiff and Thomas Smith, vicar 1565-1615, was compelled to write to King's College in 1590 requesting an order under the College Seal for the Bailiff to point out yearly a sufficient plot in the Common Wood of Ruislip *"whereof the vicar may take 20 loads of wood"*, between All Saint's (1 Nov) and St. Andrew's (30 Nov).[45] This matter does not crop up again in any surviving documents so perhaps the College fulfilled Mr Smith's request.

A major re-allocation of glebe took place at Enclosure in 1806. Tithes were extinguished on the new enclosures and the vicar was given land in compensation for loss of tithes in addition to land equivalent to his Common Field glebe. The vicarial allotments were as follows:
a. 61a. 1r 32p north-east of Park Wood – for tithes
b. 50a at the top of Haste Hill
c. 25a out of the north-east side of Park Wood – for fuel rights
d. 72a. Or 18p. on the west side of West End Road – tithes and glebe
e. 30a 3r 17p. on the east side of West End Road – tithes
f. Old Enclosures around the Vicarage House from the Pinn to Ladygate Lane and in Sharps Lane totalling nearly 13a.

*Richard Gamlyn does not appear in the recorded list of vicars.

The Goodliest Place in Middlesex

The grand total was roughly 250a which placed the vicar high in the order of landowners.

The 200 acres or so in lieu of tithes and fuel rights was potentially much more valuable than the former tithes, for it could be let at an agricultural rent. This practice must account for the increased value of the living in Christopher Packe's time. In 1837 he was letting the 25 acres of Park Wood (which had been cleared and become pasture) to Thomas Collet; the 50 acres pasture on Haste Hill to Edward Long; and 40 acres of the remainder, which had become arable to Daniel Kirby. The 72 acres in South Ruislip was meadow land let to James Welch and the 30 acres there was also meadow and let to John Gurney.[46]

Late in the 19th century when the development of Northwood began, following the opening of the Metropolitan Railway Station in 1887, Mr Marsh-Everett began to plan the development of the Northwood glebeland. The former parcel of Park Wood was let on a 99 year building lease to Charles W. Millar in September 1892 at £30 per acre. One suitable dwellinghouse with outbuildings was permitted. It was to be constructed of the best materials and to cost not less than £1,000. The house called Ruislip Holt was built in 1893.[47] Mr Millar paid £1,200 to have his leasehold converted into freehold in 1900. St. Vincent's Cripples Home moved there in 1911 and the house still stands as part of St. Vincent's Orthopaedic Hospital.

In 1898 12 acres on the opposite side of the road (part of the 50 acres) was leased to John Robert Cooper of Ventham, Bull & Cooper *"who must build a dwellinghouse costing not less than £2,000 within two years."*[48] That house also still stands and is now part of St. Vincent's along with land to the south including that upon which the Spastic Day Centre was built in 1970. As for the rest of the 50 acres, Headstone Manor & Estates Limited of Watford bought 31 acres in 1933.[49] Rochester, Lincoln, Cranbourne and Winchester Roads are now built on it.

Most of the 61 acre parcel was acquired by Ruislip-Northwood Urban District Council and much is open space. It encompasses part of Haste Hill Golf Course (1913) the Recreation Ground and Allotment Gardens (1913 and 1931), Northwood Cemetery, a Council Depot and houses fronting Pinner Road. A strip of land was sold to the Metropolitan Railway Co. and the railway line cuts across this land.

The 72 acres in West End Road was exchanged for Little Manor Farm with Sir Charles Mills in 1877 (see Chapter 5) and subsequently had Glebe Farm built on it in 1882. Most of it was taken into Northolt Aerodrome in 1915, reducing Glebe Farm to 17 acres. Western Avenue was built across the southern section of this in 1935 and Glebe Avenue now occupies the north section. However, the farmhouse still stands behind the Polish War Memorial with a remnant of land. For the subsequent development of Little Manor Farm and Clack Farm which became glebe in 1877 see Chapter 5 on St. Catherine's Manor.

The 30 acres in West End Road is now bounded by Cavendish Avenue and Station Approach. About three acres (now Acol Crescent) was sold to the Middlesex County Council in 1931 and the rest to Davis Estates Limited in 1936.[50]

The Sharps Lane land was sold for building in 1932. Vicarage Close was built on the enclosed land north of the vicarage in 1965 and the vicarage and garden was sold to Ruddy Developments in 1982.

SUB-DIVISION OF THE ANCIENT PARISH
A Church for Northwood

The first sub-division of the ancient parish occurred in 1854 when Holy Trinity was built in Northwood. In the mid-19th century Northwood was described by Robert Bayne in *Moor Park* as *"a destitute area near Moor Park"* and in the words of Mrs Soames of Northwood House (now The Grange) was *"an accidental aggregation of houses far from Church or School."*[51] Her husband Nathaniel Soames offered one acre of land and £100 for a chapel in 1837. Christopher Packe's petition to the Dean and Canons of Windsor for sanctioning the proposed building mentioned a population of about 200. A licence to perform divine service and administer the sacrament in a chapel at Northwood was granted in June 1839 and states that the chapel was situated near Northwood House and was capable of holding 150 people.[52] This chapel seems to have been an old timber-framed building on the East side of Northwood House, now called Green Close and attached to the Grange. Old maps show that until as late as 1864 Green Close was divided from the main house (now the Grange) by an open space. The entrance to Green Close is through an ecclesiastical type porch in Gothic style which has a cross on the gable. It is likely that Nathaniel Soames built this in 1838-9 while converting the building into a chapel. When Holy Trinity was opened, the building became a cottage and is referred to as such with *"late chapel"* written beside it in the 1855 Rate Books.

Lord Robert Grosvenor, later Baron Ebury, 3rd son of the Marquis of Westminster, inherited Moor Park in 1846. He was a moral and ecclesiastical reformer well-known for his evangelical views on religion and he established new churches at Croxley Green, West Hyde and Northwood. Writing to the Dean and Canons of Windsor on 15 February 1851 he said.... *"We do contemplate building a church at Norwood and constituting it if possible, a new district for which its position is favourable. I intend giving a site, a thousand pounds and a small endowment upon condition that I have the patronage."*[53] A letter of appeal was circulated in September 1852 seeking £2000 for the church, £1000 for the Parsonage House and £300 for Architect's Commission and Sundries. £1350 had already been subscribed: £1000 Lord Robert Grosvenor; £200 Nathaniel Soames; £100 Daniel Norton of Northwood Hall (now Denville Hall); £50 Mrs Marsh of Eastbury (now HMS Warrior).[54]

The new Ecclesiastical District was formed from three parishes, Batchworth Heath out of Rickmansworth; Eastbury out of Watford and Northwood out of Ruislip and was in two dioceses London and Rochester. The land given for the church was 3r 8p of Barn Mead, parcel of Kewferry Farm which had been added to the Moor Park Estate about 1830. S. S. Teulon the well-regarded Victorian church architect designed Holy Trinity in an Early English style with a nave and chancel, using flint as his main material. The foundation stone was laid on 20 October 1852 and the church consecrated by the Bishop of London on 14 January 1854, the ceremony nearly having to be cancelled because of a blizzard which blocked the roads. Sir Robert's tenants cleared the snow.[55]

A different architect William Burns was employed for the Parsonage House. It was built on the north side of the church, a six bedroomed-house with stables adjoining completed in May 1857. All that now remains of what appears

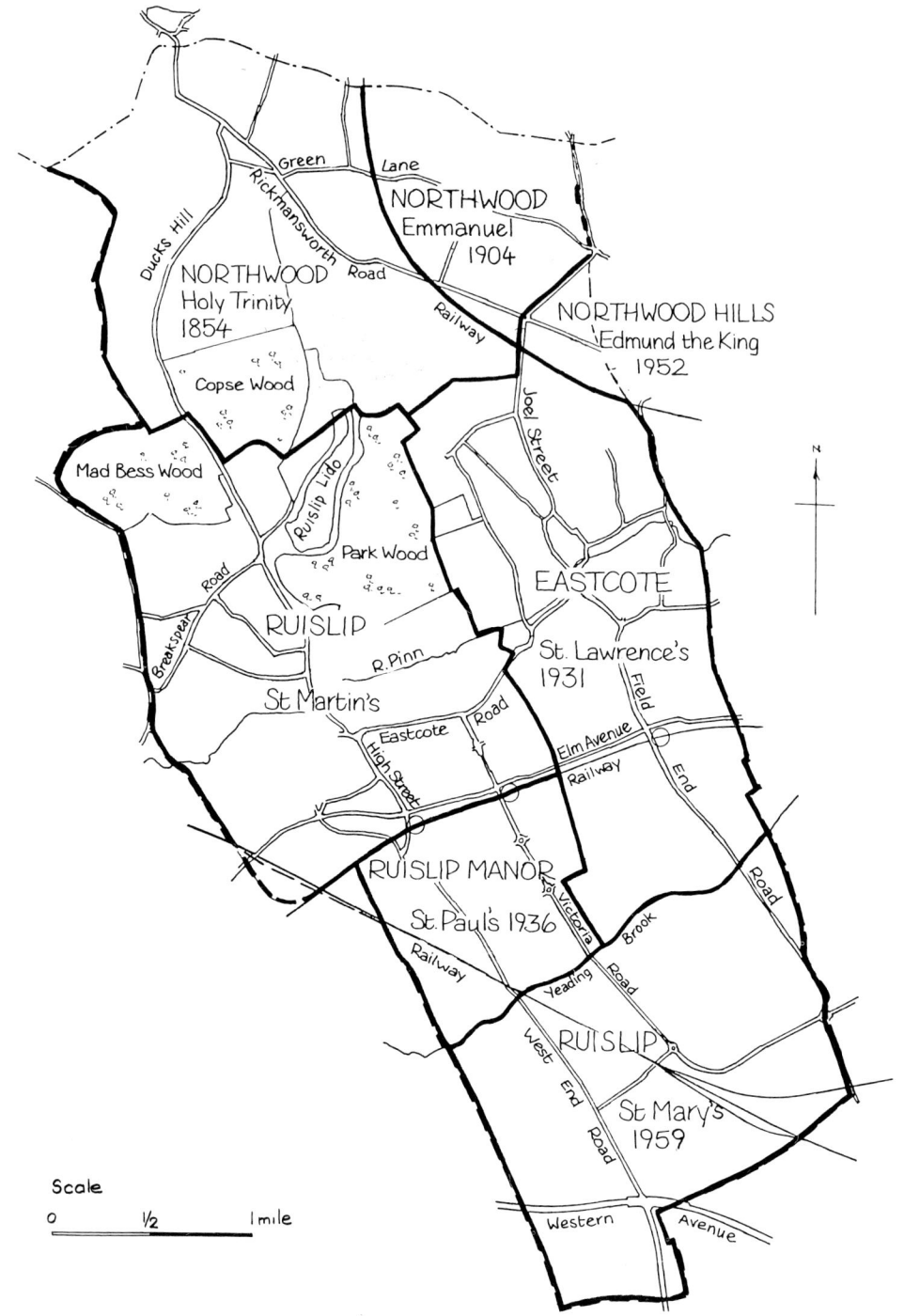

Modern Parishes (now within the Deanery of Hillingdon) created within the ancient parish of St Martin's, Ruislip

from the plans and elevation to have been an imposing building is a cedar in the middle of Gateway Close.

Some of the church windows are of interest. One with two angel figures on it was designed by Sir Edward Burne Jones in 1887 and commemorates Thomas George Grosvenor who died at St. Petersburg in 1886 and was brought back to Northwood for burial.

Northwood's population began to increase rapidly after the opening of the Metropolitan Railway Station in 1887 and the sale of land for building, which made a larger church a necessity. A north aisle was built on by Messrs Fassnidge of Uxbridge and consecrated in October 1895. The nave was extended to include a bapistry and the south aisle added in 1928 as yet more accommodation was required, but by that time Northwood parish, like Ruislip before it, had been subdivided.

Emmanuel Church designed by Sir Frank Elgood was opened in July 1904, the permanent church replacing the Church Mission Room (a tin hut) which had been serving the Half Mile Lane (now High Street) end of the parish since 1895.[56]

Another mission church, St. Edmund the King, was established in Northwood Hills to serve the new houses built there following the opening of Northwood Hills Station in 1934. The present Church was opened in 1968 in Pinner Road, adjoining the site of the temporary building.[57]

St Mary's Church, South Ruislip. Opened 1959

The Church in Eastcote

The suburban development of Eastcote began after 1906 when a halt was opened there on the Metropolitan Railway. By 1913 it was thought that the population warranted a church of its own and an acre of land at Field End was purchased from Ralph Hawtrey Deane, who gave a second acre in 1921. A temporary corrugated iron church was opened in December 1920 and called St. Lawrence. Much of the money for the church was raised by Mr Kenneth Goschen of Sigers.[58] The permanent church on the same site was opened on 21 October 1933. Sir Charles Nicholson was the architect. The church built of red brick consists of a nave and two aisles and has a short gabled tower.

Ruislip Manor and South Ruislip

Building operations south of the railway line progressed from 1933 onwards and included St. Paul's Church in Thurlstone Road opened in 1936.

The area around Northolt Junction (now South Ruislip Station) began to develop before the First World War. A wooden hall was used for services from 1931 and the present Church of St. Mary's in The Fairway, opened in 1959. It was designed by Laurance Edward King OBE; FRIBA; FSA who was responsible for a number of churches in new suburban areas. The church is built of brick and concrete with a lofty nave and narrow windows of full height in the north and south walls. There are a series of gables to the shallow clerestory windows, a stumpy spire and a huge modern figure of Christ crucified on the outside of the tall full width west window.[59]

The mother parish now covers a greatly reduced area, three square miles instead of the original twelve square miles, but within its circumscribed bounds serves 22,000 souls, an hundredfold increase over the inhabitants of the far flung parish cared for by those nameless priests of the 11th century.

REFERENCES
1. L. E. Morris *"Ruislip Parish Church: History and Guide"*
2. St. George's, Windsor: XI.G.6; 7; 51; 52; 64
3. *Select Documents of the English Lands of the Abbey of Bec* Camden Third Series, Vol LXIII, Royal Historical Society 1951
4. St. George's, Windsor X.4.1
5. Ibid. XV.31.65
6. W. W. Druett: *"Ruislip-Northwood through the ages"* 1957 – Chapter XIII
7. V. J. E. Cowley – private communication
8. W. W. Druett: op cit
9. Ibid
10. Ickenham Parish Registers G.L.R.O. DRO 27 A1/1
11. G.L.R.O. Acc. 249/764
12. St. George's, Windsor XV 31.65 – 73
13. Ibid XVI. 1.58 – 80
14. Information from Church Commissioners
15. L. E. Morris: op cit
16. G.L.R.O. S.R. 231/10
17. Guildhall MS 9537/6

18. Lambeth Palace: Commonwealth Records XIIa/12/188-9
19. Guildhall MS 9800
20. Ibid 9557
21. St. George's, Windsor: XVII 38 8
22. G.L.R.O. Acc. 538/1st Dep./8/11
23. G.L.R.O. DRO 19 C1/6
24. St. George's, Windsor: XVI.1.81
25. Programme for opening ceremony
26. St. George's, Windsor 111.k.3
27. Ibid
28. Ibid
29. Ibid
30. Ibid
31. Ibid
32. Harrow Civic Centre Library: Supplement to Harrow Gazette
33. Ruislip Library: Report in local paper
34. G.L.R.O. DRO 19 D1/1
35. Ibid
36. Ibid
37. Ibid
38. Ibid
39. G.L.R.O. Acc. 446/L1/14
40. King's College: R.36
41. Photocopies of maps at Ruislip Library
42. G.L.R.O. DRO 19 C1/7
43. St. George's, Windsor XVII 38 8
44. King's College: Q. 23
45. King's College: Q. 24
46. G.L.R.O. DRO 19 E3/2
47. St. George's, Windsor: 111.K.3
48. Ibid
49. G.L.R.O. Middlesex Deeds Registry
50. Ibid
51. St. George's, Windsor: 1051, 2, 3, 4 (22b)
52. Guildhall MS 9532-11
53. St. George's, Windsor: 1051, 2, 3, 4 (22b)
54. Ibid
55. Ruislip Library: Holy Trinity Centenary Booklet
56. W. Kemp *"Story of Northwood and Northwood Hills"*
57. V.C.H. Middlesex Vol. IV
58. R.N.L.H.S. *"A Pictorial History of Eastcote"*
59. Ruislip Library: James McBean – Notes on South Ruislip

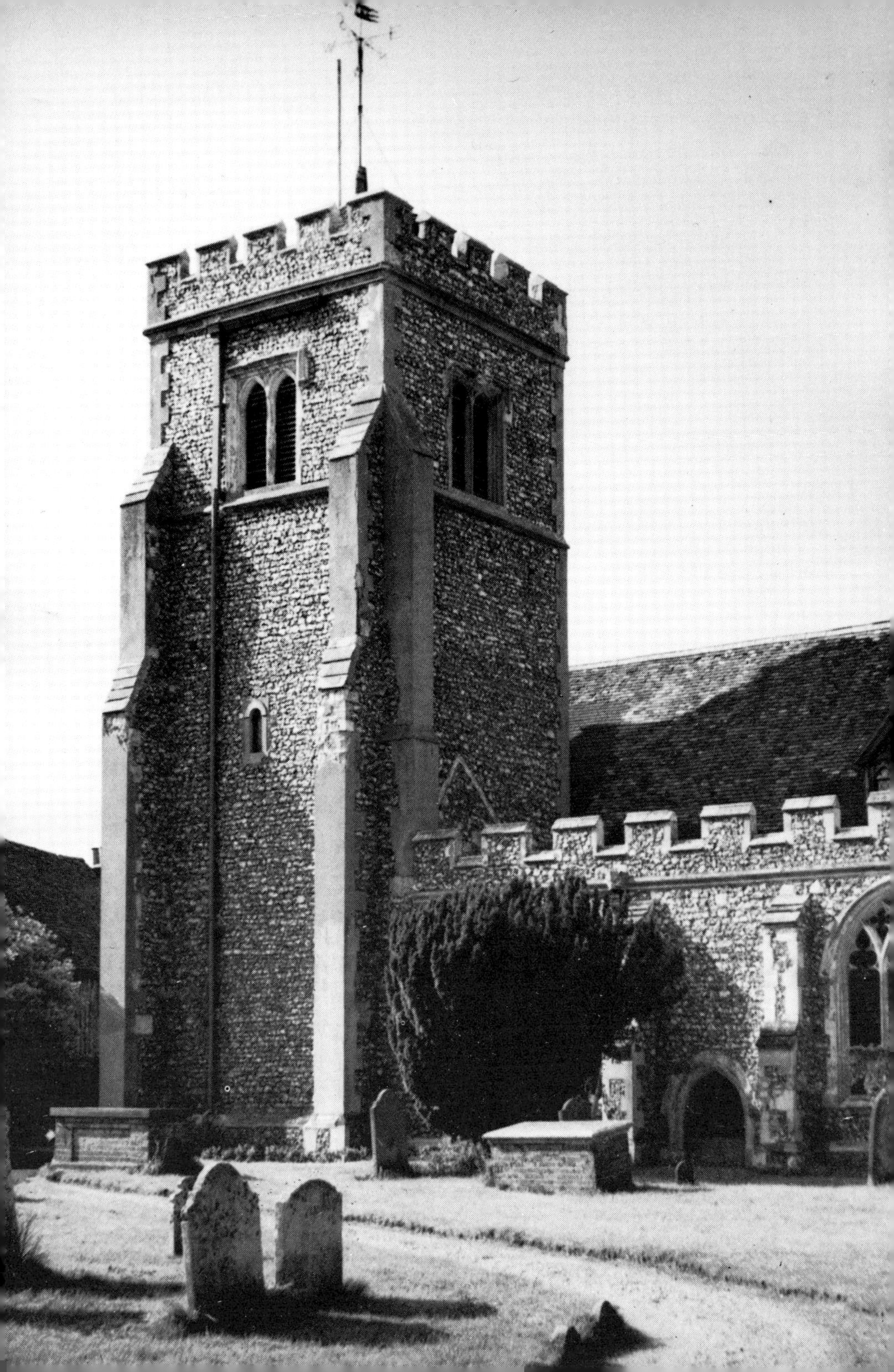

Chapter Two

The Manor of Ruislip (From Domesday to 1087)

The Domesday Book Entry for Ruislip
The Manor of Ruislip is mentioned for the first time in 1086 in Domesday Book. Manor, a word meaning mansion or dwelling is not found in Old English documents, but was introduced into England by Norman clerks after the Conquest. They used it to describe an infinite variety of pre-Conquest estates, their only common feature being a lord's house. [In a few rare cases the Domesday Survey explains that a manor has no lord's hall as if its absence needs to be stated and explained]. Some manors were very large including many dependent villages, hamlets and farms, others small having only a hall and a few acres. The boundaries of some manors coincided with the area of a single village community, but in other cases villages were divided between the manors of several lords. As the Domesday Survey refers only once to Ruislip, showing that the village area was not divided between several owners in 1086, we can assume that the village area and manor were the same and had been so since before 1066 when Wlward Wit was the only Saxon landowner connected with it. This is in contrast with the neighbouring village of Ickenham which had three lords in 1086, Earl Roger, Geoffrey de Mandeville and Roger Fafiton and had been divided between five lords (one being Wlward Wit) in the time of King Edward. Undivided villages like Ruislip conformed more nearly to the rule in Middlesex.
       Domesday Book was written in abbreviated Latin. An extended transcript of the Ruislip entry appears below, together with an English translation.

Extended transcript – Ruislip
TERRA ERNULFI DE HESDING HELETHORNE HUNDREDUM

M *Ernulfus de Hesding tenet Rislepe, pro xxx hidis se defendebat. Terra est xx carucis. In dominio xi hidae et ibi sunt iii carucae. Inter francigenas et villanos sunt xii carucae et v adhuc possunt fieri. Ibi presbyter dimidia hida*
   et ii villani de l hida
   et xvii villani quisque l virga
   et x villani quisque dimidia virga
   et vii bordarii quisque iiii acris
   et viii cotarii
   et iiii servi
   et iiii francigenae de iii hidis et i virga

The Goodliest Place in Middlesex

*Pastura ad pecuniam villae
Parcus est ibi ferarum silvaticarum
Silva mille et quingentis porcis
et xx denarii
In totis valentibus valet xx libras
Quando recepit xii libras
Tempore Regis Edwardi xxx libras
Hoc manerium tenuit Wluuard Wit teignus
Regis Edwardi potuit vendere cui voluit*

Translation
Manor. LAND OF ERNULF DE HESDIN IN ELTHORN HUNDRED.
Ernulf de Hesdin holds Ruislip. It was assessed for 30 hides.
There is land for 20 ploughs. In demesne there are 11 hides and 3 ploughs. Among the Frenchmen and the villeins there are 12 ploughs and 5 more are possible.
There is a priest with half a hide
and two villeins with 1 hide
and 17 villeins with 1 virgate each
and 10 villeins with half a virgate each
and 7 bordars with 4 acres each
and 8 cottars
and 4 slaves
and 4 Frenchmen with 3 hides and 1 virgate
(There is) pasture for the livestock of the vill.
There is a Park for Woodland beasts. Wood for 1500 pigs and (rendering) 20d.
In total value, it is worth £20.
When received £12.
In the time of King Edward £30.
Wlward Wit a thegn of King Edward held this manor. He could sell to whom he wished.

The Land
The manor of Ruislip thus described probably covered much the same area as the late Ruislip-Northwood Urban District, for the county boundary was already established by the 11th century and the places adjoining Ruislip: Ickenham, Harefield, Harrow (the Pinner and Roxeth portions) and Northolt are also mentioned in the Domesday Book. It consisted of 6500 acres.
    The picture of Ruislip emerging from the Domesday Survey reveals a village landscape with much arable land, some pastureland on which livestock was raised and a considerable stretch of woodland measured as elsewhere in this county by the number of pigs it could support, but the proportions of the different types of land use cannot be worked out exactly. The hide was notionally the amount of land which could be ploughed by one ox-team in a year and support a family. It came to be recognised as a measurement varying in size from 80-120 acres. A virgate was a quarter of a hide. However in Domesday Book, the hides for which places were assessed, in the case of Ruislip 30 hides, were Geld-hides, that is units of taxation, not measurements and it would not be safe to assume that the landholdings given in hides and virgates were actual measured acres either.

The Manor of Ruislip (from Domesday to 1087)

Extrapolating back from 13th century surveys it can probably be said that between a third and a half of the land was arable, pasture or meadow and the rest was woodland, uncleared and uncultivated. The arable probably lay south of Eastcote Road on the flatter areas where the soil was mainly London clay. The meadow would have been along the banks of streams and the wooded area was left on the northern uplands where there was more sand and gravel and the land was more difficult to plough. It appears that rather more than half of the cultivated land was in demesne, that is, it was held directly by the lord, being attached to his hall and worked by his servants, perhaps assisted by the tenants.

The Park. The embankment

The Park

A most interesting feature of Ruislip in 1086 was the park for woodland beasts, as only one other existed in Middlesex, at Enfield on the other side of the county. Parks were used as game reserves and as larders for storing food on the hoof. Ruislip's park was an enclosure of about 300 acres within a vast tract of woodland which stretched across the northern uplands of Middlesex. It was oval in shape and situated in the southern half of the present Park Wood and the area bounded by Bury Street, Eastcote Road and Fore Street (which takes its name from its position at the front of the park).

Massive earthbanks with an external ditch (30-35ft total width) can still be traced through the middle of Park Wood from near the western entrance in

Broadwood Avenue, curving round to the footpath by Grangewood School in Fore Street. As late as the 1920s, before the widening of Bury Street and extensive building on the Manor Farm estate, the western and southern earthbanks could still be seen as well. The age of the earthbanks cannot be ascertained until some archaeological investigation can be carried out, but they seem to pre-date the three roads, which all follow their curves. For the moment all that can be said for certain is that the park is earlier than 1086. The banks were topped with palings. There is a reference to stocking the park with five live deer from the Archbishop of Canterbury's Harrow Wood in 1270 and to repairing the palings in 1436.[1]

The lord's hall appears to have been built inside the south-western boundary of the park, possibly in the late Saxon period and another deep ditch and earthwork now seen at the northern end of Manor Farm orchard might have been made at the same time in order to protect it.

Hugh Braun who visited Ruislip from c. 1918 onwards and studied the earthworks when they were clearer on the ground, believed that the Manor Farm ditch was part of a rampart surrounding the medieval village centre. He also found evidence of a small Roman building, where the garden of 1 St. Martin's Approach is now.[2]

In later medieval times the southern portion of the park was altered in character. Land along the Pinn became meadows attached to the hall and about 12 acres north of the Pinn became enclosed pasture called Harrys Croft. On the east, houses built at the lower end of Fore Street, took land out of the park. Perhaps in compensation it was extended northwards to a stream (which now feeds the reservoir). This additional area was enclosed with slightly less massive earthbanks (20-25ft) now best viewed along the Fore Street edge of Park Wood.

The wooded area outside the park which stretched across what is now Haste Hill, the Golf Course, Poors Field and Northwood Hills was known as either the Outwood or the Common Wood.

The People

The priest and his glebe suggests that Ruislip already had a church. The 53 people mentioned, with the exception of the four slaves, are likely to have been heads of households and families. A precise estimate of population is impossible, but there were probably about 250 men, women and children living in about 50 houses. By the same computation Ickenham would have had about 150 people in 30 houses and Harefield 120 people in 24 houses.

The classification of the tenants as villani, bordarii, cotarii and servi had no legal definition and was the attempt of foreign clerks to categorise English society without understanding the subtle differences that existed between a lord's tenants in pre-conquest days. The villani were the largest class in Middlesex (1141) and in Ruislip (29). It is a fluid term now thought to be best translated as villagers. The pre-conquest villagers were probably freemen holding their land by agreement with the lord, perhaps paying both rent and labour services, but not tied to their land. Villani translated as villein did not come to have the stricter meaning of an unfree, though not necessarily poor man, tied to his lord until the 12th and 13th centuries.

Bordarii of whom there were 342 in Middlesex and seven in Ruislip were small-holders with a cottage and about five acres. The cotarii (464 in Middlesex and eight in Ruislip) had a cottage and less than five acres, often no land at all. Slaves had no property and probably belonged to the households of

The Manor of Ruislip (from Domesday to 1087)

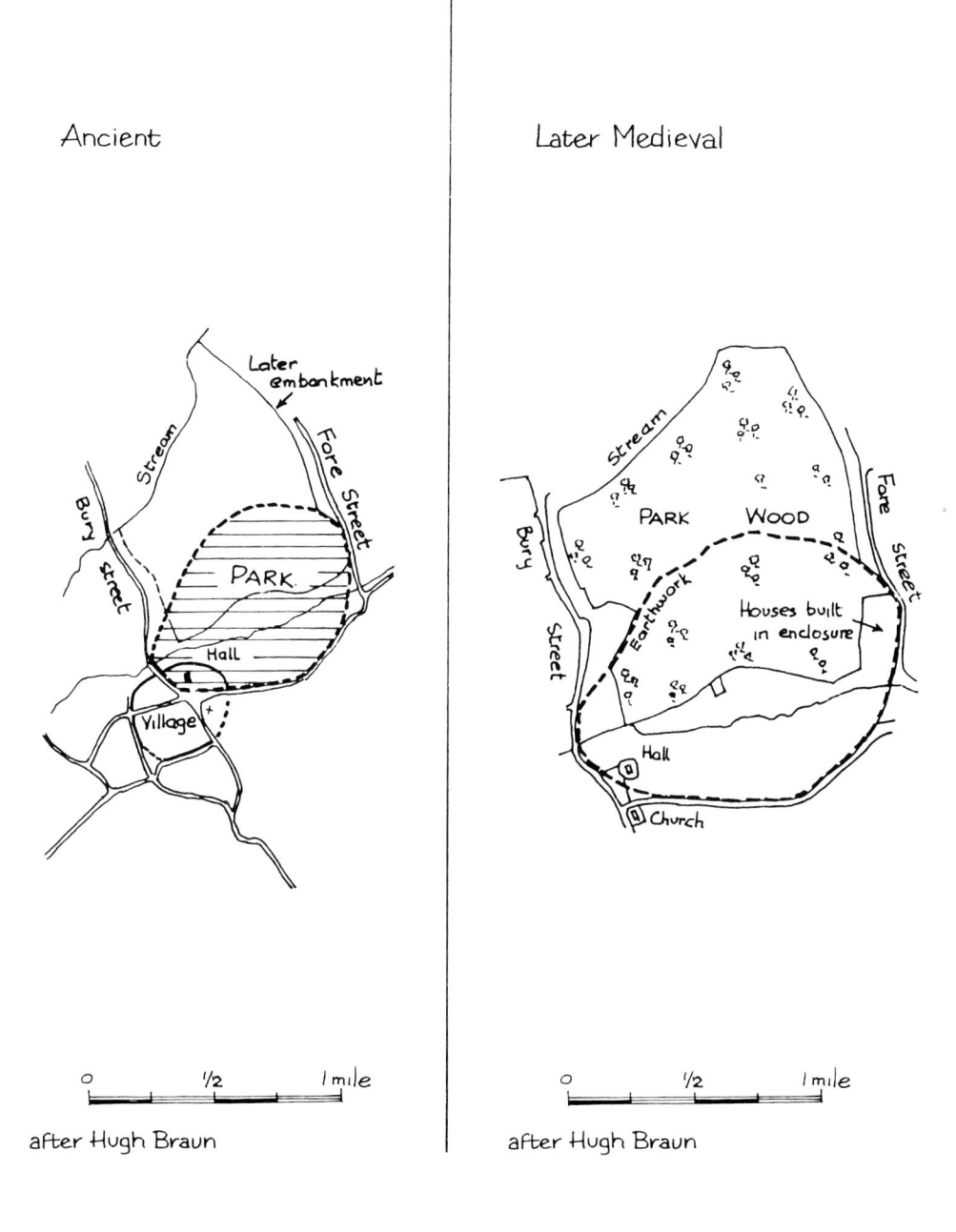

Ruislip Park Wood, ancient and later medieval

39

The Goodliest Place in Middlesex

larger landowners. Slavery was an accepted status in all the codes of law given out by Saxon kings, and slaves had been an important English export to the Continent in pre-Conquest times.

The church in the care of the priest most likely stood where St. Martin's is now, some of the houses no doubt clustered round it, while others would have been scattered in lanes leading into the fields and up to the wood pasture north of the park.

The Saxon lord of Ruislip, Wlward Wit, had held land in eleven counties, his most extensive estates being in Somerset and Buckinghamshire. In Middlesex he had Ruislip, Kempton, Kingsbury and two hides in Ickenham held by his man Aelmer. He lost most of his land at the Conquest but was of sufficient stature to retain some of his Somerset estates.[3]

Ernulf de Hesdin, probably connected with Hesdin in Picardy, was granted many of Wlward's lands in Oxfordshire, Gloucestershire, Berkshire, Bedfordshire and Middlesex where he succeeded to Ruislip and Kingsbury, but not to Kempton and Ickenham. He also held land as tenant-in-chief in Hampshire, Wiltshire, Dorset, Somerset, Huntingdonshire and as an under-tenant in Kent and Staffordshire.[4]

We have no means of knowing how either of these earliest known owners viewed Ruislip. Whether they visited it much or ever lived here is doubtful. Ernulf de Hesdin's principal residence is thought to have been in Wiltshire.

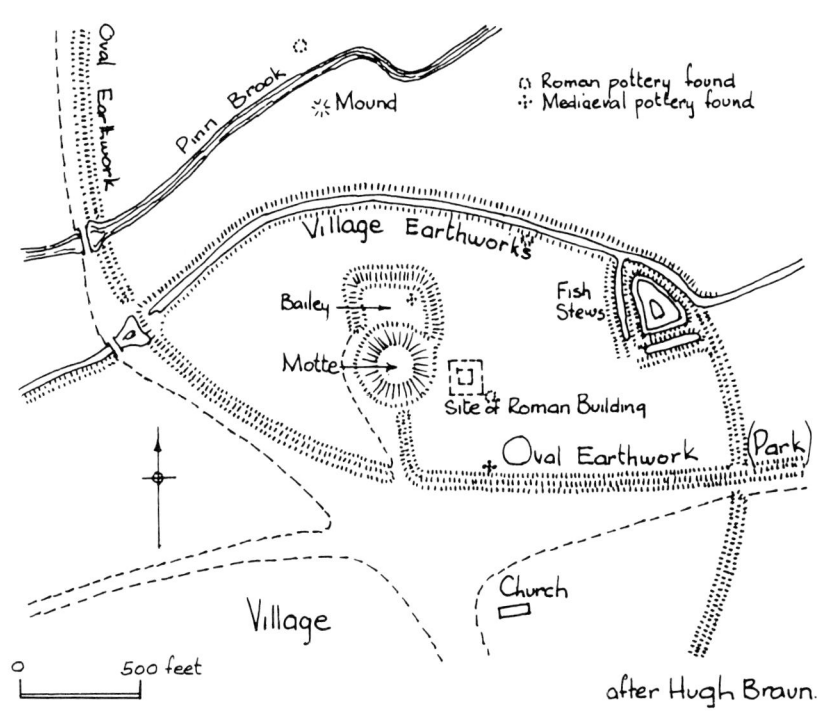

Earthworks at Manor Farm

The Lord's Hall

The moated area at Manor Farm is an ancient monument, scheduled as the site of a motte-bailey castle, the motte being thought to be the artificial mound south of the house, now a private garden and the bailey (courtyard) the area where the house and flower-beds are. The northern section of the oval shaped moat, filled in by H. J. Ewer in 1888, is clearly denoted by the sharp dip in the ground at the beginning of the orchard.[5] The motte was probably originally encircled by a moat, which was extended to surround the bailey as well. No proper archaeological excavation has ever been carried out so the castle theory has yet to be proved or disproved. However, oval-shaped moats often belong to the 11th century and usually denote a fortification of sorts and the name Bury Street might have some significance. Bury sometimes means a fortification.

The Saxon hall was almost certainly in this position as it is on high ground near to the Pinn, but above its flood plain. From Pinn Way or near the running track in the Pinn Fields, Manor Farm can be seen standing on an eminence and rising above its modern neighbours in St. Martin's Approach. Early 11th century Middlesex was reasonably peaceful, making fortification unnecessary for the Saxon house. As the valuation of Ruislip was reduced from £30 in the time of King Edward to £12 when received by Ernulf de Hesdin (1067-70) it would seem that the place had been ravaged in some way by the Normans, perhaps by being stripped of crops to supply food for a column on the march. Geographically Ruislip lies in a line of vills; Hampton, Bedfont, Stanwell, Harmondsworth, Hayes, Northolt, which all declined in value at that period and may have been the route of a Norman troop. It is certainly possible that Ernulf de Hesdin caused a small wooden castle to be built in Ruislip, for fear of Saxon reprisal. Among the inhabitants listed, the four Frenchmen deserve special notice as they were scattered thinly on the ground in Middlesex (four in Ruislip, two in Hillingdon, two in Tottenham, and an unspecified number in Fulham and Isleworth). Sir Frank Stenton suggests in *English Fuedalism* that they were probably lesser followers of the Conqueror, household officials, knights and squires whose services were rewarded with small grants of land. The four in Ruislip had 3 hides and 1 virgate between them, the two in Hillingdon had 1½ hides, the two in Tottenham 1 hide and 3 virgates. It is difficult to say how they fitted into English society. Since they held land which must have been taken from the original community they were probably unpopular and indeed are usually found in groups. The Ruislip Frenchmen may have lived at the Manor House or Castle and maintained order among the tenants on Ernulf de Hesdin's behalf.

Ernulf de Hesdin

Ernulf de Hesdin himself received a good character from William of Malmesbury, an English Chronicler, in his *Gesta Pontificum* written in the early 12th century. He was charitable to the poor, prompt in his payment of tithes, and skilled at farming. Balm from the tomb of St. Aldhelm cured him of a disease which had paralysed his hands. In thanksgiving he set out on a pilgrimage to Jerusalem and died on the journey. The other source for his life story, *Liber Monasterii de Hyda* agrees that he died in the Holy Land, but offers a different explanation. Having been wrongfully accused of implication in the 1095 plot to replace William Rufus with Stephen of Aumâle he was forced to undergo ordeal by battle. His champion

The Goodliest Place in Middlesex

won, but he wisely removed himself from England by joining Duke Robert of Normandy's 1095 Crusade. He died before the walls of Antioch. Some years before he left for whatever reason, he granted Ruislip to the Abbey of Bec in Normandy. The exact date of his gift is unknown, but it was confirmed in a charter of the Abbey dated between June 1086 and September 1087 and must have been after the compilation of Domesday Book in Autumn 1086.[6] The Charter of confirmation specifically excluded one hide of land in Ruislip which was held by the Abbey of Holy Trinity at Rouen. The Domesday entry makes no reference to Holy Trinity holding land in Ruislip which suggests that Ernulf de Hesdin perhaps gave the land to Holy Trinity about the same time as he granted the rest of Ruislip to the Abbey of Bec.

The land in question was a tract of wooded waste lying west of Bury Street and Ducks Hill, now Mad Bess Wood and land to the south, long known as St. Catherine's, The Little Manor or Catherine's End. (See Chapter 5). All the rest of the parish of Ruislip was owned by the Abbey of Bec for the next 327 years.

REFERENCES
1. P.R.O. S.C. 6/917/27: Transcript Ruislip Library – L. E. Morris Collection
2. Hugh Braun "Earliest Ruislip": LAMAS Transactions VII, 99-123
3. V.C.H. Middlesex Vol. I p. 101
4. Ibid p. 114
5. Reminiscences: Ruislip Library
6. V.C.H. Middlesex Vol. I p. 202

Chapter Three
Ruislip under the Abbey of Bec c. 1087-1404

Abbey of Bec
Herlwyn (or Herluin) a Norman vassal of Gilbert de Brionne, receiving divine inspiration at the age of 37, sought his overlord's permission to withdraw from his service. He built a chapel at Bonneville-Appetot in 1034 and became a monk the following year. Finding that the site was frequently flooded, he begged Count Gilbert for a corner of the forest of Brionne and was granted land near the confluence of the Bec and Risle rivers. He removed there in 1040.[1]

Herlwyn placed his foundation under the Rule of St. Benedict, written by that saint in the sixth century, a way of life intended for ordinary western men of ordinary spiritual attainments, as opposed to the excessively ascetic lives lived by early eastern hermits. Monks were to spend a balanced day divided between manual labour, reading and the liturgy. Monasteries should be in the country and self supporting, with farms, gardens, workshops, barns and a mill. Monks were to live a communal life under an abbot, never singly. Each monastery was to be independent, owing allegiance to the Holy See. All Benedictines were to wear black habits.

The second half of the 11th century saw a vigorous monastic revival in Normandy. Bec became famous for the piety of Herlwyn and his companions and attracted such foreign scholars as the Italian, Lanfranc to its cloisters. Under his teaching a renowned "School of Bec" developed which became a spiritual and intellectual centre and seminary for bishops and abbots. Lanfranc was summoned by William the Conqueror to be Archbishop of Canterbury and St. Anselm, who became Abbot of Bec upon Herlwyn's death in 1077, followed Lanfranc at Canterbury in 1092.

Many Normans, spiritually influenced by Bec, endowed it with a portion of their newly acquired English lands.[2] Chief among these lay benefactors were the Clares, descendants of Herlwyn's overlord, Gilbert de Brionne. Four conventual priories where the full choral office was sung, were founded by them, at St. Neots, Hunts; Stoke-by-Clare, Suffolk; Cowick, Devon and Goldcliffe, Mons. In addition Bec had received 24 manors spread across 14 counties before 1100. Among these were Ruislip given by Ernulf de Hesdin and Combe (Hants) by his wife Emmelina.

The administration of these manors presented a problem to the Abbot of Bec. Very small cells with one or two monks only were probably established on the manors in the 12th century. Ruislip certainly had a small priory at that period. Monks so isolated and constantly concerned in commercial administration found the monastic rule difficult to follow. St. Anselm commended his monks to the spiritual care of local bishops, who made visitations

The Abbey of Bec Cloister. Note the distinctive white habit worn by monks of Bec since the early 13th century

from time to time. Even so the difficulties persisted. Statutes for the Reform of Monastic Life were promulgated at a General Chapter held in 1219. From that time documents speak of an "Order of Bec" and all monks dependent upon Bec wore a distinctive white habit. Abbot Ymerius in 1304 ordered that all monks in English Priories should be recalled to Bec every six years and must bring their Priory accounts and a certificate of good conduct with them.[3]

During the 13th century the Abbot of Bec caused 24 of the English manors to be grouped into the Bailiwick of Ogbourne which was administered by only two priories, Ogbourne and Ruislip. All other small cells were closed. The two priors appear to have divided the Bailiwick between them at first, but later there was only one Proctor-General who probably made Ruislip his headquarters. The centralised audit was certainly held there.[4]

The common lordship united the widespread manors as the Proctor/Prior himself and other officials moved from one to another, holding courts and transacting other business. Services exacted from some tenants included providing horses and hospitality for the Prior and his servants when they were on their travels. For instance, Eustace FitzWilliam of East Wretham, Norfolk, had to collect and carry the lord's revenue at Ruislip and elsewhere; attend the monks and servants of Bec and bring bread as maintenance; and to provide gifts and aid for the Abbots of Bec when they came to visit their English lands.[5] At the same time (c. 1245) Gilbert Aldred and several other Ruislip tenants could be asked to undertake journeys on behalf of the monks.[6]

Many visits had to be made to London where the Proctor owned a Townhouse in Castle Lane (Baynards Castle) between the Thames and Blackfriars, which had been purchased by Richard de Coleville, Prior of Ruislip in the late 12th century.[7]

Originally the revenues of Ogbourne had been intended to supply the Monks' Wardrobe. By the beginning of the 13th century the following objects had to be sent to Bec annually:

Michaelmas: 2 leather garments and a blanket for the Abbot.
Feast of St. John the Baptist: 2 marks and knives for the convent.
(a mark = 13.4d or ⅔ of £1)
20 lengths of woollen cloth
30 leather garments
32 weys of cheese[8]

The tenants of the various manors came in contact with one another and sometimes moved their place of residence from one manor to another. A man called Peter de Swyncombe was one of the larger landowners in Ruislip in 1245. At the same time John the Shepherd, a Swyncombe resident was expected to act as a drover at Ruislip and Ogbourne.[9]

The Demesne under the Abbey of Bec

During the long periods of intemittent warfare between England and France in the late 13th and 14th centuries, the possessions of French Abbeys were classed as "Alien Priories" and seized by the Crown. On such occasions Extents (inventories) were made. Three Extents dated 1294, 1324 and 1336 have survived for Ruislip.[10] In 1294 and 1324 Ruislip remained in the King's hands for only a short time but after 1336/7 when the Hundred Years War had begun, it remained more or less continuously in his hands. Priors were allowed to remain in Ruislip as administrators, however, until 1404 when the Bec connection was severed by the death of William de St. Vaast the last Prior.

Below are some extracts from the 1294 Extent.

Belonging to the Abbot of Bec	£.	s.	d.
1 palfrey (a riding horse)	2.	13.	4
6 cart-horses each 13s.4d.	4.	0.	0
1 horse for the mill		6.	8
30 oxen, each 5s.	7.	10.	0
3 steers and 3 foals	2.	0.	0
In the park, 4 steers, 4 foals, 1 mule, 1 ass	1.	2.	0
63 oxen each 8s.	25.	4.	0
25 cows each 6s.8d.	8.	6.	8
Item 60 bull calves, each 1s.		15.	0 (sic)
89 sheep, each 10d.	3.	14.	2
18 goats each 10d.		15.	0
1 lamb			6
50 pigs each 1s. 4d.	3.	6.	8
60 piglets each 10d.	2.	10.	0
11 suckling pigs each 4d.		3.	8
2 swans each 3s.		6.	0

The Goodliest Place in Middlesex

	£.	s.	d.
17 peacocks each 1s.		17.	0
Ornaments in the chapel	2.	13.	4
Fields sown with wheat, 330 acres, 3s. per acre	49.	10.	0
Fields sown with barley, 15 acres, 3s. per acre	2.	5.	0
Fields sown with oats, 330 acres, 20d. per acre	27.	10.	0
45 acres mowing grass, 18d. per acre	3.	7.	6
TOTAL	157.	16.6 (sic)	

Extent of the same Manor

	£.	s.	d.
The jurors say that the commodities & easements belonging to the court are valued per annum at		16.	0
Rents of free tenants	2.	7.	6
Rents & services of customary tenants as could be estimated for certain	26.	17.	0½
Value of 807 acres of arable land in demesne 4d. per acre	13.	9.	0
Value of 45 acres of meadow in demesne 2s. per acre	4.	10.	0
14 acres of separate pasture 18d. acre	1.	1.	0
80 acres of pasture in the park 4d. acre	1.	6.	8
Pannage of pigs, "foreign & domestic"	5.	0.	0
1 windmill & 1 watermill	2.	0.	0
○ Profits & perquisites with fines on land & with tallage of bondsmen	6.	0.	0
Tithes of the church in Ruislip	16.	13.	4
Certain tithes in Hayes		8.	1
TOTAL	81.	6.6½ (sic)	

+ For a breviary	13s	4d.
For boots and shoes for the boys	6s	2d.
× Carrying of writs for Sheriff's tourn	1s	4d.
For mail	18s	6d.
Livery made to Walter de Rokesle	£20. 0.	0d.
Livery made to the Lord	£23. 0.	0d.
And so from all accounts and allowances	£5.	2s6½d.

to the said bailiff which the lord owed him from the last account the bailiff now owes the lord, £5.3s.3d. Afterwards he paid upon account 3s.3d. and so he owes to the lord, clear £5.

Dorse (the back)
Rislep Outgoings of the barns per annum.
   Of *wheat* 961 quarters 5 bushels
   Of which for seed 101 quarters
   For house bread per annum 418 quarters, 2 bushels
   For brewing, 47 quarters
= For liveries to the farm servants, 168 quarters
   (Lost?) in threshing and winnowing 23 quarters 7 bushels
   Sold 202 quarters

Ruislip under the Abbey of Bec c 1087-1404

In gifts.... of the lord 1½ quarters
Of *barley* 6½ quarters
All sold
of *beans and peas* 190 quarters 3 bushels
Of which seed 19 quarters 7 bushels
For bread 20 quarters
In alms, 29 quarters 6 bushels
☐ In pottage 6 quarters 1 bushel
In pig feed 50 quarters 1 bushel
In provender for the horses 13 quarters
Sold 10 quarters
In gifts 1½ quarters
Remaining in the granary 40 quarters
Of *oats* 912 quarters 5 bushels
Of which for seed 212 quarters 6 bushels
for brewing 220 quarters
For potage 16 quarters
For provender for horses and oxen 453 quarters 7 bushels
For geese and hens 6 quarters
For gifts 4 quarters

TOTAL 2,074 quarters 1 bushel

○ Tallage was a tax levied at Michaelmas on unfree tenants – probably at the rate of 4d. per tenant as there were about 150 tenants at the time.
+ A book containing the Divine Office.
× The Sheriff attended the Manor Court once or twice a year (usually at Easter and Michaelmas) to oversee the View of Frankpledge. That means that he inspected the Tithings (groups of ten men who were mutually responsible for good behaviour).
☐ Pottage is soup. Notice that the monks and their servants ate soup made from peas and beans which must have been the same as the pease pottage of the nursery rhyme.
= A livery was an allowance of food.

    The 1293 Extent shows that growing crops was more important and of greater value in Ruislip than rearing animals – unlike the Abbey of Bec's manors in Wiltshire and Oxfordshire where sheep rearing was the main source of income. There were 807 acres of arable land in the demesne but only 675 acres sown with crops: therefore 132 acres were lying fallow. The demesne covered about one third of the manor. The rest of the land was occupied by the tenants.
    Wheat and oats were the most important crops grown that year, with a little barley, but crops were grown in rotation and in some years peas and beans were grown as shown by the quantity stored in the granary.
    Wheat, oats, barley, beans and peas were measured *by volume* in a *Bushel* measure. 8 Bushels = 1 Quarter
    The weight varied according to density –
        A bushel of *Wheat* = 63 lb.
        A quarter of *Wheat* = 504 lb.
        A bushell of *Oats* = 42 lb.
        A quarter of *Oats* = 336 lb.

The Goodliest Place in Middlesex

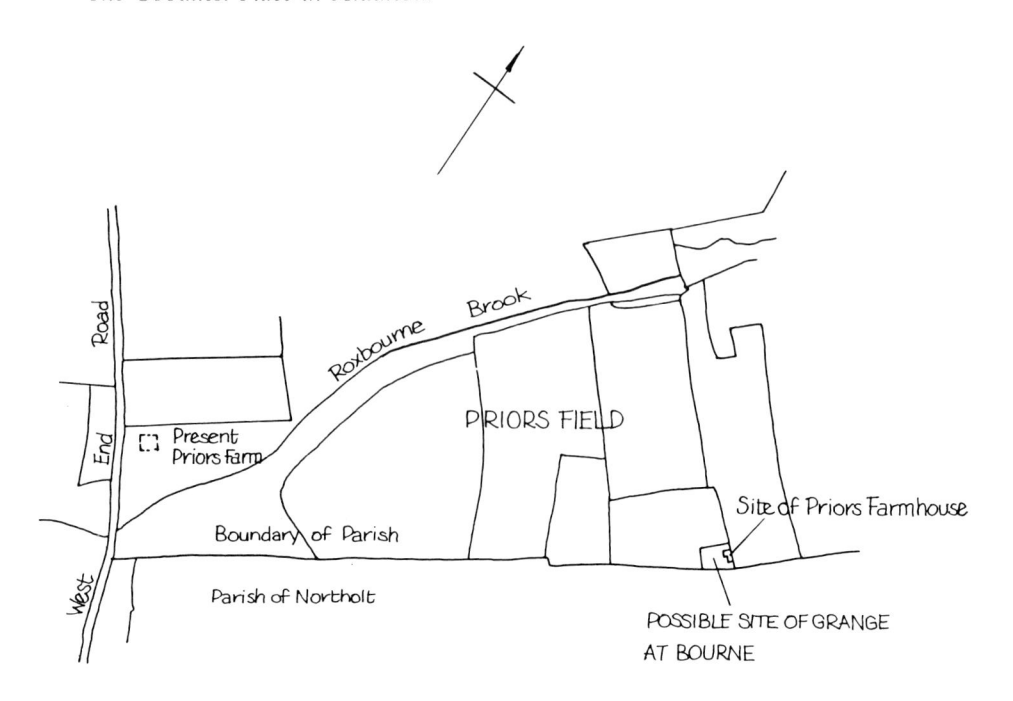

LOCATION PLAN

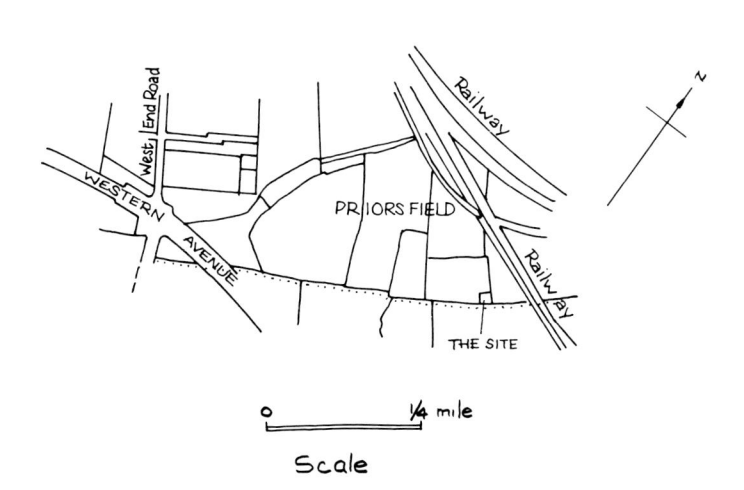

Possible site of Grange at Bourne

The yield, 961 quarters 5 bushels wheat from 330 acres = approx. 13 cwt (hundredweights) to the acre, not very different from that obtained in the early 20th century.

Before the Second World War, English farmers expected an average of 15 cwts. to the acre. Since the war productivity has increased –
1955 – the average yield was 2 tons (40 cwts) to the acre
1987 – the average yield is 3 tons (60 cwts) to the acre

A really progressive farmer aims at 4 tons to the acre (10 tons a hectare).[11] The very high yield nowadays is due to improved strains of wheat introduced since 1955. Agricultural improvements (fertilisation and drainage) in the 18th and 19th centuries only marginally improved the yield per acre, but did increase the area of land on which crops could be grown, by making a fallow year unnecessary.

The arable acreage in 1293 seems extraordinarily large as the 1336 Extent gives it as only 561 acres and by 1565 when the arable lay in open fields south of Manor Farm it amounted to 519 acres. The extra ploughland may have been in Northwood where there was a Grange, which was probably leased out by 1336. This outlying house is first mentioned in 1300 when a kitchen boy there received 2s 6d a year wages.[12] In 1324 six ploughmen lived at Northwood Grange with one maidservant who made the pottage. The earliest lease of Northwood that is extant is in 1384 when John Saint George and Joan his wife paid 5 marks a year for the house and parcel of land which Roger Redinge had formerly.[13] The Northwood Grange was probably near the site of the present Grange in Rickmansworth Road.

Another Grange which had a barn and at one time a boy to look after the oxen (plough animals) was situated at Bourne.[14] Its exact site has not yet been determined. The open field called Bourne Field ran south from the Yeading Brook down the centre of the manor. South of that between the Roxbourne brook and the parish boundary there was a field called Priors Field which was enclosed from the open fields at an early but unknown date. By the 18th century that land had become Priors Farm with a farm house which was still standing in 1806 when the Enclosure Map was drawn. The present Priors Farm built after enclosure of the common fields incorporated the old enclosed land and replaced the old building. The present farmer Mr Val Jones has seen very large flints dug out of the ground where the old house stood, which suggests that it was an early medieval building standing on a flint sill. This could be the site of the Grange at Bourne. (See map).

The Extents give some idea of the Priory and buildings within the old moated area at the centre of the manor. The Priory had a chapel with ornaments worth £2.13s.4d in 1294. In 1324 the hall (aula) and rooms (camerae) were in need of repair. There was a Guest House and 3 barns, one which was said to lie northwards and southwards might have been the Great Barn, dated by Cecil Hewitt, on evidence of carpentry techniques to c. 1280. The Great Barn is of superior craftsmanship and was built while the power of the Priory was at its height and shortly before the long period of decline when Ruislip was an Alien Priory.

Inside the Priory were thirteen dishes worth £9.12s; twelve salt cellars worth 40s; six silver cups worth £3.12s; one cup made of a nut with a silver foot worth 5s and two cups of maplewood worth 5s. Brass pots, brass mortars and

The Goodliest Place in Middlesex

A general view of the Great Barn showing the original main framing

The Great Barn. Detail showing the junction of main post no. 7 with one of the original cill plates. Note assembly marks

iron pestles were to be found in the kitchen, reminding us of the amount of grinding and pounding of herbs which was an integral part of medieval cooking. Two swans at 3d each and seventeen peacocks at 1s. each, mentioned in 1294 were probably destined for the table.

In 1324 the servants included a reeve, 14 ploughmen, a swineherd, cowherd, two men to look after the Prior's horses, a carpenter to mend ploughs, harrows, *"and other necessary things in the same manor"* a smith, a woodward (to look after the woods which are rather strangely not otherwise mentioned) and a hayward who was responsible for fences. A tiler had been hired with his servant for seven days to do roofing work which suggests that tiles were already being made locally and proves that some roofs were tiled, probably the hall and the Great Barn.

Ruislip had two mills, a watermill somewhere along the Pinn probably near Clack Lane and a windmill which almost certainly stood near the modern Windmill Hill. No further references occur to either mill beyond the early 15th century.

An earlier list of servants for the year 1300, listed, in addition to the above, two shepherds, two carters and boy, seven drovers and three kitchen boys (one at Northwood, one at Bourne and one at the Manor) a gooseherd, a goatherd, a miller. At harvest time only, wages were paid to two stackmakers, two tithe collectors and two pitchers into carts.[15]

Customal c. 1245

A glimpse of life in 13th century Ruislip for the Abbot of Bec's tenants is revealed in a Customal[16] dating from c. 1245, which lists all their names, states the amount of land which they held, the rent they had to pay and the labour services which they were obliged to perform for the Prior and monks. It is a long document covering all Bec's manors in the eastern region and was drawn up a few years after William de Guineville became Proctor-General (1242).

The Ruislip section of the Customal lists 117 tenants and several more names have been obliterated by damp. There were possibly 150 in all. If we assume five people to each household we arrive at an estimated population of 750, a threefold increase since the estimated population of 250 for 1086. Such a rise could only occur during a period of expansion when ever larger areas of land were being brought under cultivation. It was an increase entirely in line with that of the population of England as a whole which increased from about 2 million to 6⅓ million between 1086-1265.[17] The Customal gives evidence of new land being brought under cultivation for Richard Brun, William Slipere, Robert Croys all had a virgate of land "with an increase" (cum augmento).

Land Holdings

The Customal gives very little information about the layout of the parish, but it is reasonable to suppose that the arable lay in open fields south of Eastcote Road, as it is shown to have done later by 14th, 15th and 16th century documents. Tenants' holdings in the open fields are given as hides, half hides, virgates and half virgates, that is as fractions of a hide. By the mid-13th century the hide can be accepted as measuring between 80 and 120 acres, which means that the half hide is *about* 50 acres, the virgate *about* 25 acres and a half virgate *about* 12½ acres.

The Goodliest Place in Middlesex

The men who had a share of the village arable were equivalent to the villani of Domesday Book. Their houses were situated in the northern part of the manor and the land holdings were divided into sellions (strips) and scattered throughout the common fields in the southern area.

Not all the tenants had a share in the village arable. Their holdings were given either as crofts (variable) or as "half an acre", 2 acres etc.

Crofts were enclosures usually surrounding or close to a dwelling. The holders of crofts were similar to the cottars and bordars of 1086. The crofts were often pasture capable of supporting an animal or two when taken in conjunction with grazing available on the common waste, which in Ruislip was the woodland lying north and east of the park, now Poors Field, Copse Wood, Haste Hill and Northwood Hills. Smaller stretches of waste lay along the unfenced and unmade roads and at small greens at road junctions. A few crofters were probably craftsmen but most must have worked on the lands of the larger land-holders.

About half of the tenants were crofters, while the majority of those who held arable land were virgate holders. The Customals show that the virgate was a common peasant holding throughout the Abbey of Bec's English properties.

In Table 1 sizes of land holdings and the number of tenants with each, are given both for 1086 (Domesday Book) and c. 1245 (Customal). It can be seen that the crofters were the fastest growing class.

Table 1   Size of Landholdings

Size	No. of Holders 1086	%	No. of Holders 1245	%	Change in %
Hide	2	2.6	2	1.7	− 0.9
3 virgates	4	7.7	3	2.6	− 5.1
Half-hides	1	7.7	11	9.4	+ 1.7
1½ hides	0	0.0	3	2.6	+ 2.6
Virgates	17	43.6	32	27.4	−16.2
Half-virgate	10	25.6	4	3.4	−22.2
Croft	15	12.8	62	53.0	+40.2

Note: 4 landless slaves omitted from 1086 list.

The new crofts had almost certainly been cleared from the Common Wood or Outwood, up Bury Street and Fore Street and the other lanes leading north from Eastcote High Road. The settlements at Silver Street Green near The Plough, Bury Street, and Park Hearne (south of Reservoir Road), both produced late 13th century potsherds during recent building developments and from their positions must precede the extension northwards of the Domesday Park.

The Names

The Customal is the earliest document to name Ruislip tenants as opposed to simply enumerating them. It is written at a time when surnames were only just coming into general use as they had been unnecessary as a means of identification in a very small community. Most 13th century surnames referred to a man's occupation, to his father's Christian name, to his place of origin, to some

Ruislip under the Abbey of Bec c 1087-1404

topographical feature near which he lived, or were nicknames. Consequently men from the same family may well have borne completely different surnames. Indeed, in this list Roger Cook is described as the brother of Henry Carter. On the other hand some families seem to have had settled names as there were several de Hullas, Horsemans, Hardings and Cooks. Gradually each family acquired a specific surname.

Surname as in Customal	Christian Name	Translation
OCCUPATION		
BERKARIUS	William	Tanner (possibly Shepherd)
CAPELLANUS	Arthur	Chaplain
CARETARIUS	Henry	Carter
CLERICUS	William	Clerk
COCUS	Randolf	Cook
COK	Roger	Cook
COK	William	Cook
COK	Ysabella	Cook
le CORDER	Robert	Corder
la FUGELARE	Gonilda	Fowler
le FULIN	William	Fuller
le HAYWARD		Hayward
HORSEMAN	Richard	Horseman
HORSEMAN	Walter	Horseman
KOK	Roger	Cook
MARLEWARD	Richard	Marlward
MARLEWARD	William	Marlward
MOLENDINARIUS	Robert & Rose	Miller
PARKER	John	Parker
SLIPERE	William	Sharpener
le TAILLOR	Richard	Tailor
TECTOR	Geoffrey	Thatcher
le TRULER	Ralph	Mason
HONTE	Richard	Hunt
FATHER'S CHRISTIAN NAME		
FILIUS CLERICI	Berengarius	Clerkson
COK	Roger son of Robert Cook	Cookson
HUBERTI	Richard	Huberts
OSEBERTI	Alice	Osberts
FILIUS PETRI	Ralph	Peterson
FILIUS SACERDOTIS		Clerkson
FILIUS WALTERI		Walterson
ROBIN	Richard	Robins
PLACE OF ORIGIN		
de OCKEBURN	Thomas	Ogbourne
de PINNORE	Richard	Pinner
de PINNORE	William	Pinner
de SUTHCOTE	Roger & Avicia	Southcote
de SUYNCOMBE	Peter	Swyncombe

53

TOPOGRAPHICAL

de ARBORE	Hugo	Tree
de ASSARTO	Robert	Assart
iuxta BOSCUM		Bywood
BISUTHE	Gilbert	By the South
BLAKEMERE	Walter	Blackmere
del BROK	John	Brook
de BURNA	Agnes	Bourne
le BUT	Walter	Butt (of land)
de CAMPO	Hereward	Field
de FELDA	William	Field
de FONTE	Robert	Fountain
de FORDA	Hugo	Ford
de GRENA	Richard	Green
de la HACHE	Ralph	Hatch (gate to wood)
HARDING	William	Harding (hardland)
HARDING	Isabella	Harding (hardland)
de la HALE	Robert	Hale (nook)
de HULLA	John	Hill
de HULLA	Matil	Hill
de la HULLA	William	Hill
de MOLENDINO	Robert	Mill
de PONFRAYT	Richard	Brokenbridge
de PONTE	Alevona	Bridge
de PORTA	Robert	Gate
de RADDING	Robert	Reading (clearing)
RADDING	Emma	Reading
STRATA	Arturus	Street
de la STRETE	Hugo	Street

NICKNAMES

AGNUS	Gilbert	Lamb
ALBUS	William	White
ALDRED	Richard	Aldred (Noble Counsel)
ALFRED	Gilbert	Alfred (Noble Counsel)
BALDVYNE	William	Bold Friend
BRADEFER	John	Ironarm
BRUN	Richard	Brown
BRUNMAN	Richard	Brownman
CAPRA	Reginald	Goat
COLE	Ralph	Cole (Swarthy)
DRUET	Mabel	Druet (Little Sweetheart)
KING	Robert	King (King Like)
LEONARDUS	Lion	Leonard (Bold)
LONGUS	Gregory	Long
LONGUS	John	Long
LOVE	Richard	Love
PYEWIT	Richard	Magpie
SAVAGE	Alice	Savage
WYT	Richard	White
WYNES	Richard	Friend

MISCELLANEOUS

BALLE	Richard	Ball
BEYVIN	William	Bevin
BRUTEWINE	Richard	Brutewine
CAMULE	Richard	Camule
CANON	Roger	Canon
COYN	Richard	Coyn
CROYS	Robert	Croys
FIGE	John	Fige
FIGE	Thomas	Fige
FRAY		Fray
le GEST	Richard	Gest
HAMUND		Hammond
HEREWARD	John	Hereward (Army Guard)
IOVANT	Isabella	Jovant
LOFRED	Richard	Lofred
MALEHERE	Roger	Malehere
MALEVILE	Richard	Malevile
MESSUR	Stephen	Messur
NOTHEL	Geoffrey	Nothel
OGERE	John	Ogere
RAISUN	John	Raisun
SALVAGE	John	Salvage
SEEFUGEL		Seefugel
SIGAR	Walter	Sigar (Victory Spear)
STIKEWRICTE	Humphrey	Stikewricte
SUMWYLE	Alvona	Sumwile
VIGAR	Robert & Matelina	Vigar
soror PRESBYTERI		Priest's sister

Occupation: The occupation names are the common ones which might be expected to be found in a medieval village. The hayward looked after the fences and the marlward was in charge of the marl pits. Marl was sand and gravel used to lighten the heavy clay soil found in the Ruislip common fields, one of which was called Marl Pit Field. John Parker probably looked after the Park. The Cook family was well established. One of them had a messuage in front of St. Martin's church. The presence of Geoffrey Thatcher suggests that thatch as a roofing material was common in Ruislip. The earliest reference to tiles[18] is in the early 14th century and Tyler appears as a surname in the 15th century.[19] The only building at all likely to have been built of stone here, in the mid-13th century is the church. The present nave is believed to have been built about 1240. Perhaps Ralph Truler (Mason) was employed on this work when the Customal was written.

Several names suggest a clerical occupation. There was Arthur Chaplain, William Clerk, two Clerk's sons and the sister of a Priest. A clerk at that time would be in orders, but perhaps a deacon or sub deacon rather than an ordained priest. The lesser orders may have married as a matter of course and priestly celibacy may well have been the ideal rather than the rule. What is certain is that Priest, Prest, Priste was a common surname found in local records until well

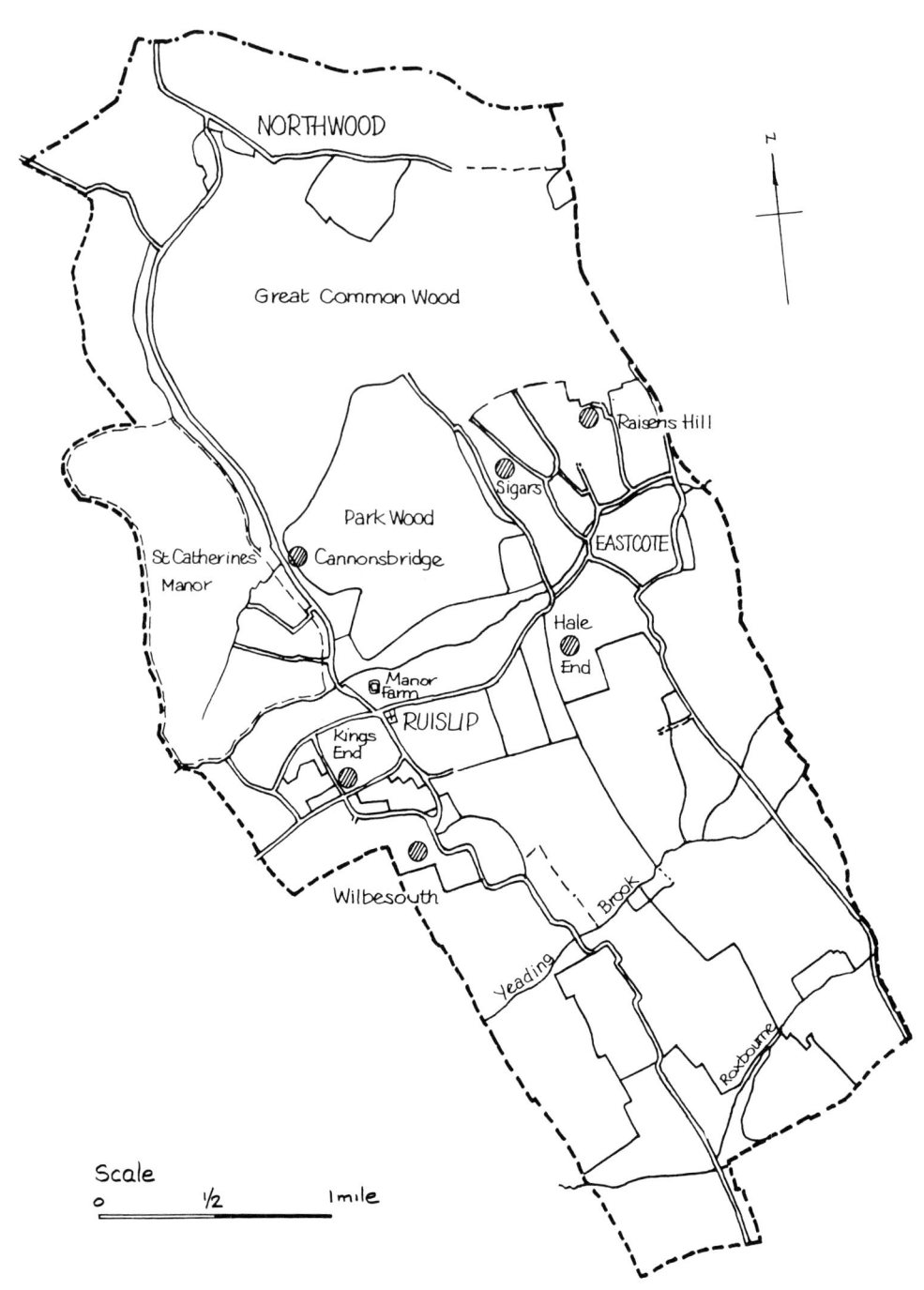

Place names derived from surnames found in the Customal

Ruislip under the Abbey of Bec c 1087-1404

into the 16th century. Whether Roger Canon whose family has given its name to Cannons Bridge, was a clerical canon is not known.

Place of Origin: Peter of Swyncombe and Thomas of Ogbourne were probably manorial officials and hailed from Swyncombe in Oxfordshire and Ogbourne in Wiltshire, both manors belonging to Bec. Peter acted as proctor for Bec in a legal action in 1245.

Topographical: Hugh le Tree (or de Arbore) who probably lived near the woods granted a piece of land called "Le Stocking"[20], a name which signifies former woodland, to the Abbey of Bec.

Most of the topographical names are prefixed by de, del or de la. Some of these names survived in the district for several centuries but dropped their prefixes. De la Strete and De la Hale had become plain Street and Hale by 1565. The Hale which means a nook or corner was at Highgrove which is at a corner of Eastcote Road. It is pleasing to see the old name retained in the modern Hale End Close. An assart was newly cleared land, in this area probably on the edge of the woods. De Campo and De Felda translates most easily as Field, but the Atlees (at field) were prolific in west Middlesex and could be the same family. Gilbert Bisuthe's land may have constituted the cottage and ground that stood just south of Ruislip Rugby Club. It was later called Willbesouths. Perhaps William was a descendant of Gilberts. The house was already in ruins by 1565, but the land called Willbesouths is still mentioned in late 17th century documents.

Nicknames: The Bradefer family appears in Minister's Accounts as Bras de fer "Arm of iron". The original Bradefer may have been a soldier. It is possible that Reginald Goat was a goat-herd rather than a goat-like person. Brown, Bronman and White probably refer to complexion or hair colour. Cole meaning swarthy or coal-black was commonly the name for a smith in some parts of England.

Surnames now found as place names within Ruislip: There are several parts of Ruislip today which are named after families who lived in the areas in the 13th century: King's End, Cannon's Bridge, Hale End, Sigars, Raisun's Hill are examples. If you look at these places on the modern street map you will see that 13th century Ruislip was not a nucleated village with the population clustered round the church, but a manor of widely-scattered hamlets spread across the northern upland area.

Saxon Names: The Customal was written about 180 years after the Conquest. It is interesting to note how few Saxon Christian names survive, showing how complete had been the Normanisation of this part of Middlesex. Those that did were mostly female names.

Christian Names	Emma
Hereward	Alvona
Gonilda	Aldiva
Alevona	Geoffrey

How the Manorial Tenants Lived

Seven tenants were freemen. They paid rent for their land and performed no labour services except on the special boon days. They were Peter de Swyncombe, Roger de Southcote and Avicia his wife, Sir Roger de la Dune, Randolf Coke, Randolf Truler, William Hill and Randolf Cole. Roger and Avicia had Southcote

Manor (see chapter 5). They had three virgates and a millpond called Sitteclack. The millpond was probably along the Pinn where Clack Lane (unfortunately now renamed Hills Lane) crosses it to join a footpath leading to Tile-Kiln. Clack is an onomatopaeic name suggesting the sound of a mill. A 1391 Court Roll of Harmondsworth mentions the mill in Southcote.[21] The mill may have lain within Southcote, as the Pinn is its southern boundary while the mill-pond was in the main manor of Ruislip. The Ruislip Enclosure Map 1806 shows an empty triangle of land at this point which may be the mill site. Sir Roger de la Dune who was Constable of the Tower and Lord of the Manor of Down Barnes was one of the two men who held a hide of land. Randolf Coke had 3 acres of land beside his house in front of the church and a virgate in the common fields as well. It is interesting to speculate just where his house stood at the corner of the High Street. Nos 1, 3 and 5 High Street were originally all one building, listed as 16th century with 19th century additions at the front, but the carved beam above the fire-place in No 5 looks earlier. No 7-15 are also 16th century buildings. Any of these may have replaced Randolf's house. Only three other houses are mentioned in the Customal, but with no clue to their positions.

The customary works of Gilbert Aldred, holder of half a hide are set out at the beginning of the Ruislip Customal as follows:

"Item from the feast of St. Peter ad Vincula to Michaelmas he must reap three days a week, with one man, wherever required, or do whatever other work the lord wishes him to do without maintenance. And if he carries for his work from the fields beyond the grange of Bourne he must carry a waggonload of corn or two cartloads, and if from the fields on this side of the said grange two waggonloads or four cartloads. He must also at the first boon day of harvest time find one man to reap and (he shall) have maintenance. And so at the second boon he must reap with all his family, except his wife and his herdsman. And he himself shall be present the whole day with a rod of authority to see that his family work well, and they shall have maintenance twice in the day, namely, about the hour of nine, corn bread, cheese, ale or cider, and in the evening corn bread, pottage...or ale or cider. Item, at the third boon day he must reap with one man, at his own payment, and about the hour of nine in the evening have...in common in the midst of the fields...two full pots of ale or cider and three tubs full of apples if the lord should have apples. Item, if it happens that the lord shall wish to send hams or other produce to Bec he has to find carriage to the Thames for that purpose. Item, if he should have pigs of his own rearing he must pay pannage for them, namely, for a pig of over a year old a penny, and less than a year old a halfpenny and in the same way he must pay pannage for all his pigs that are separated from the mother. Item, in Lent he must harrow for one day, if required, and have maintenance and carry for one day at harvest time and have maintenance. Item, in a year in which full work is worked he must work from Michaelmas to the feast of St. Peter ad Vincula three days a week wherever required, at whatever kind of work the lord may require, with one man, and for feast days falling within the aforesaid term he must make good the work on succeeding working days and in the same way must plough just as he ploughs when not fully working, but on the days on which he ploughs for the accustomed service of herbage two works must be remitted to him. He must also prepare a load of malt for Christmas and have fodder or firewood ready dried, with remittance of one work; and for Easter all in the same manner. Item, he must do carrying service to the neighbouring market, namely half a quarter of corn, and in the meantime be quit of one work, and if he goes to London he must collect a waggonload and be

quit of one work, and if to St. Neots quit of three days, likewise if to North Stoke of three days, likewise if to Swyncombe of two days. Item, if the monks go to distant parts he must find a baggage wagon for them and their equipment and other necessities and then three of his works must be remitted, and he must have maintenance for the journey, and if to near places so that it is possible to return the same day he must be quit of a single work only. Item, he must harrow as often as he may be instructed to, insuch wise that when the ploughs of the lord begin to plough he must harrow to the hour when they cease. He must also do sheep washing and shearing right up to the completion of the shearing, and he must scythe the meadows, make the hay, cart it and put it into cocks, until all is complete, and all alike shall receive a ram or twelvepence, and he must carry letters, drive animals, load manure and spread it on the fields, carry the folds of the lord from one place to another, prepare and mend the wattles, cut up wood for fencing and make it into fences, and he shall ditch and dig, and if he brews he shall give a penny of toll for one sester. Item, he is not to sell a horse or an ox of his own rearing without the licence of the lord, nor give his daughter in marriage. Item, for all dues and aid he must pay scot and lot, and after his death the lord shall have the best beast as a heriot, and if he dies intestate all his goods and chattels shall be at the disposal and will of the lord. And he must be reeve if the lord wishes it, and pay a toll on all things sold within the boundaries of the manor."

The feast of St. Peter ad Vincula (St. Peter in Chains) falls on 1st August and Michaelmas is the 29th September. Gilbert was required to work for the monks three days a week all the year round performing whatever jobs were in season, if required. These were known as week works. Boon days were special days, for example at harvest when all tenants even those free of labour services worked on the demesne as a boon or favour to the lord, in return for which they received a ration of food.

Pannage was a tax levied on pigs put into the woods to forage for acorns.

Herbage was the right to graze animals on the lord's grass, in return for which the tenant did two days' ploughing.

The neighbouring market was at Uxbridge. St. Neots, Huntingdonshire and Swyncombe, Oxfordshire were Bec manors and the tithes of North Stoke, Oxfordshire belonged to the Abbey.

Heriot was a death-duty. Usually the best beast of the deceased was paid to the lord.

At first sight Gilbert Aldred appears little better off than a slave, until we remember that as a half-hide holder he was one of the better-off members of the village community and could probably send a servant to perform his weekly works in his stead and that the wording of the above extract suggests that full works were only required in certain years, so that his services may not have been so onerous as they sound. We should also remember that at present many items cannot be sold without a licence, VAT has to be paid on many goods and our sons and daughters alike require licences, when contemplating matrimony.

The names of the other tenants follow Gilbert Aldred's. Their customs are not fully set out and nearly all relate in some way to those of Gilbert Aldred. Most of the half-hide and virgate-holders and half the crofters followed his customs. It is common to find virgate holders expected to perform week works, but very unusual to find crofters doing the same. Dr M. Chibnall who translated the Customal in *Select Pleas of the Abbey of Bec* has suggested that the

The Goodliest Place in Middlesex

scribe made a slip of the pen and that the 29 crofters said to follow Gilbert Aldred, actually followed the customs of some other Gilbert.

Everyone else owed much lighter labour services, either half works, or part works.

Gilbert Bisuthe, Gilbert Lamb and Robert Marlward were expected to represent the vill at the hundred and shire courts.

They were leading men in the community. All appear as pledges in the court rolls of the period and probably represented the three tithings within the manor, Ruislip, Ascot (Eastcote) and Northwood. Their full customs were set out as..."*he must plough on ploughing boon days as Gilbert Aldred and between the feast of St. Michael (29 September) and St. Martin (11 November) must plough an acre for custom of herbage and must receive the grain in his granary for sowing that acre, and must sow and harrow it. If there is need he must follow the county and hundred on behalf of the whole vill when it is summoned to hear the commands of the lord king. He must reap at harvest boon days as Gilbert Aldred, must pay pannage for his pigs. He may not sell his ox or horse or give his daughter in marriage without permission.*" These three men were practically free of agricultural duties except for boon works. The attendance at court was probably time consuming (as it is now for those on Jury Service). The meeting place of the hundred court of Elthorne has not been discovered. Hundred courts were generally held in the open air and had met monthly in Saxon times. The county courts under the Shire Reeve (Sheriff) and itinerant justices were held twice a year. The meeting place of the Middlesex court at this date is not known. 16th century courts were held at the Castle Tavern Clerkenwell and at Hicks Hall in St. John's Street a century later.[22]

Table 2 shows the relationship between common field holdings and labour services demanded.

Table 2 Relationship between common field holdings and labour services

	Hide	3 Virgates	Half Hide	1½ Virgate	Virgate	Half Virgate	Croft	Total
Free	1	2			1		3	7
Week works			4	2	30		29	65
Half works						4		4
Part works			7		1		30	38
Rep. at Courts	1	1		1	1			3

Many Ruislip tenants seem to have been allowed to choose whether to perform all the works required of them or to pay a higher rent instead.

Only four men, all half hide holders including Gilbert Aldred, paid no rent. In most other cases two rents, one much lower than the other, are given for each tenant. In the case of William White it is stated that he pays 3s.11d for his half hide when fully working and 7s.0½d when not. Three other half hide holders paid 3s.6d or 7s.0d depending upon whether they were working or not. The two levels of rent for the virgate holders are mostly 5d and 4s, those "with an increase"

60

paying slightly more, 7d and 4s.2d, though there are some discrepancies. Richard Horseman paid 3s and 2 hens or 6s.2d and 2 hens for his virgate plus 6d and 2 hens at Christmas for an assart (land newly brought into cultivation from the waste). The half virgate holders also seem to have been able to choose whether to work or pay higher rents. The four had variable rents:

Mabel Druett	2½d	or 2s.2d
Arthur Street	1s.8d	or 3s.6d
Richard Brunman	8½d	or 2s.8½d
Gonilda Fowler	1s.	or 2s.10d

Very few crofters and acre holders were given a choice. The most common rent was one shilling and a few gave hens and capons at Christmas.

The rents appear to be variations based on an initial standard of:
13s.4d for a hide
6s.8d for a ½ hide
3s.4d for a virgate
1s. for a croft

The commuting of services for rent was an important step toward the freeing of villeins from their manorial ties and seems to have continued in Ruislip as the 1324 Extent lists a large number of paid servants working on the demesne. The process was assisted throughout the country by the 14th century outbreaks of plague which greatly reduced the labour force, but it was well advanced on many Bec manors long before the first outbreak of pestilence in 1348-9. Gradually all the messuages and cottages and common field holdings which had been held of the lord of the manor in return for customary services evolved into copyholds. The tenant proved his ownership by holding a copy of the entry in the manor court roll and was known as a copyholder.

Rents comprised several customary payments, one being a Quit Rent to be quit of all services. An undated Rental (but early 15th century) lists 107 tenants. Since no services are mentioned it looks as if the freeing of the Ruislip villein was completed by then.

Manor Courts

Court rolls (accounts of proceedings in the manor courts) are often headed "Court Leet, General Court Baron and Customary Court" A court baron was held by every lord of the manor. It dealt with estate administration, agricultural and economic matters relating to the open fields, grazing rights and changes in tenancy. The court baron was held in theory for free tenants and a customary court (or halimote) for villeins. Ruislip had very few free tenants and the court baron and customary court were one and the same in practice. A court leet was held where special powers had been granted to certain lords of manors to try matters which would normally lie in the provenance of the King's court such as the maintenance of peace; the election of a constable and ale taster and trying criminal matters. During the 13th century and 14th century the King's lawyers held Quo Warranto Inquiries (By what warrant?) in an attempt to tabulate and legalise the work of manorial courts and prevent encroachment on the King's courts.

Courts leet and courts baron were synonymous so far as the Abbey of Bec's courts were concerned at least from 1244.[23] The Proctor-General, his Steward or an itinerant bailiff called the Steward of the Courts visited the Bec

The Goodliest Place in Middlesex

manors to hold courts twice a year. He went on circuit between Michaelmas and Christmas, again in May-June and occasionally in Lent.

Ruislip being an important administrative centre where the central audit was held as well as the main residence of the Proctor-General, had a large demesne and consequently much court business, which led to courts being held there frequently.

In 1290 courts were held on 22nd June, 16th July and 3rd August and in 1311-12 on 6th December, 12th March and 6th May.

The following extracts from Court Rolls (Maitland. Select pleas in Manorial Cts. Vol. I) give an insight into some aspects of Ruislip village life and illustrate the customs which appear to infringe personal liberties so seriously, working in practice.

Some men did not obtain the lord's licence before their daughters married. At a court held on the Saturday after Quasimodo Sunday (1st after Easter) 1280-1 it was recorded that Christina daughter of Richard Maleville had married at London without the Lord's licence. Perhaps she had eloped. Her father was fined 12d for his connivance or ignorance.

In 1296 John Robin offered the Lord a mark of silver for leave to retire from the office of Reeve. A mark was ⅔ of a pound i.e. 13s.4d, a considerable sum, but perhaps worthwhile to free John Robin from the time consuming office of Reeve.

On the Saturday after the Purification (2nd February) 1248 the roll runs:

"Walter Hulle gives 13s.4d for licence to dwell on the land of the Prior of Harmondsworth so long as he shall live and as a condition finds pledges, to wit, William Slipper, John Bishuthe, Gilbert Bisuthe, Hugh Tree, William John's son, John Hulle, who undertake that the said Walter shall do to the lord all the services and customs which he would do if he dwelt on the lord's land and that his heriot shall be secured to the lord in case he dies there (i.e. at Harmondsworth)."

The customary right of the lord to bind his tenants to his own manor was to protect himself against loss of taxes etc. Walter Hulle (possibly Hill) was probably removing not to Harmondsworth proper, but only to the area of Ruislip known as St. Catherine's which was a detached parcel of Harmondsworth. Since he was expected to continue to perform services on the demesne he must have retained land in the main manor thus becoming a landowner in both manors. As the commuting of labour services for money progressed it became much simpler for a man to be a tenant of several lords.

The court held on the Tuesday after the Ascension 1246 sheds several interesting sidelights on the lives of people named in the Customal.

"The Court presents that Nicholas Brakespear is not in a tithing and holds land. Therefore let him be distrained.

Breakers of the assize: Alice, Salvage's widow (fined 12d.), Agnotta the Shepherd's mistress, Roger Canon (fined 6d.), the wife of Richard Chayham, the widow of Peter Beyondgrove, the wife of Ralf Coke (fined 6d.), Ailwin (fined 6d.), John Shepherd (fined 6d.), Geoffrey Carpenter, Roise the Miller's wife (fined 6d.), William White, John Carpenter, John Bradif.

Roger Hamo's son gives 20 shillings to have seisin of the land which was his father's and to have an inquest of twelve as to a certain croft which Gilbert Bisuthe holds. Pledges, Gilbert Lamb, William John's son and Robert King.

Ruislip under the Abbey of Bec c 1087-1404

Isabella Peter's widow is in mercy for a trespass which her son John had committed in the lord's wood. Fine, 18d. Pledges, Gilbert Bisuthe and Richard Robin.

Richard Maleville is at his law against the lord to prove that he did not take from the lord's servants goods taken in distress to the damage and dishonour of his lord to the extent of 20s. Pledges, Gilbert Bisuthe and Richard Hubert.

Hugh Tree in mercy for his beasts caught in the lord's garden. Pledges, Walter Hill and William Slipper. Fine, 6d.

(The) twelve jurors say that Hugh Cross has right in the bank and hedge about which there was a dispute between him and William White. Therefore let him hold in peace and let William be distrained for his many trespasses. (Afterwards he made fine for 12d.) They say also that the hedge which is between the Widow Druet and William Slipper so far as the bank extends should be divided along the middle of the bank, so that the crest of the bank should be the boundary between them, for the crest was thrown up along the ancient boundary.

Ruislip was divided into 3 tithings by 1245, Westcote, Eastcote and Norwood. All men of a tithing were responsible for the good behaviour of the others and all male landowners over 12 years of age were supposed to be members of a tithing. The breakers of the assize were probably over-charging for their home-brewed ale or made it under strength and the ale-taster was an important manorial official. Ale played a much larger part in people's lives then, for in the absence of tea, coffee, orange squash, etc., everyone drank it. The tax on home-brewed ale was a useful part of the lord's income.

Parents like Isabella Peters were held responsible for their children's misbehaviour and fined accordingly. People then as now squabbled over boundaries and aired their differences in front of their neighbours in court.

On several occasions the rights of widows were upheld. For example in 1296:

"Henry White demands one acre of land which was holden by John his brother whose heir he is, as he says. And Cristina Trice comes and says that she has greater right to hold the said acre for her life than Henry to demand it, for she says the said John purchased the said acre after his marriage with her and according to the custom of the manor of Ruislip a wife after her husband's death should hold the whole of any purchase made by him after his marriage with her; and this she offers to verify by the court, and she gives the lord 6d to have an inquest.

And the inquest says that the custom of the manor is as Cristina pleads it, so that she has greater right to hold than Henry to demand the said land. Therefore it is considered that she do hold as she now holds and that Henry be in mercy etc; (i.e. fined) 3d."

Occasionally thefts and violence erupt in the Court rolls. 1280: *"Richard Maleville has drawn blood from Stephen Gest – Fined 2d."*

Most malefactors were fined, but occasionally physical punishments were imposed. In 1296 we read:

"Also it is presented that Walter Savage, John Blackmere, William Field, William Marleward, John ate Hatche, Robert Wrenche, Richard ate Forde, Amicia of Pinner, Juliana ate Hulle, Richard Sherewind, Richard Wheeler, William Edelot and Ralph Fountain levied the hue against the lord and his servants wrongfully and kept it up for a long time before the lord's gate and wrongfully. Therefore they are adjudged to the pillory and put in the stocks etc."

Lucy Mill who had committed adultery in 1280 had all her tenements seized into the lord's hands, which must have punished her husband as much as herself. No mention is made of her adulterous partner.

The end of the Abbey of Bec's Administration

Despite the confiscation of the Abbey's English lands by King Edward I in 1294, Edward II in 1324 and Edward III in 1336 – some money still found its way from England to Bec – to rebuild the abbey church after the church tower had fallen for example – and efficient estate administration continued on the English lands.[24] As the 14th century progressed, money from England dried up, some manors were handed over to lay farmers at the royal command and debts were incurred by the Proctor-General as regular amounts of money were exacted by the Royal Exchequer regardless of farming conditions. During Richard II's reign (1377-99) exactions were particularly heavy, causing many French monks to leave England, and a chapter held in 1379 decided to lease English properties to raise lump sums to ease the load of debt. Even then Ruislip, (perhaps because it was the residence of the Proctor-General) continued to be farmed in demesne. Money however, must have been in short supply and buildings may have become dilapidated. There is documentary evidence that barns and other buildings in some manors, Wilsford for example, were in a state of collapse. Ruislip has no such written evidence, but the main posts on the east side of the Great Barn present a very weather-beaten appearance near the top, suggesting that the barn was partly open to the elements for many years, long ago.

William de St. Vaast was Proctor-General from 1364 until his death in 1404. Shortly before his death, Henry IV granted to him, along with Thomas Langley, Dean of York, later Bishop of Durham, and John of Lancaster (later the Duke of Bedford), third son of the King, all the Bec property in the Bailiwick of Ogbourne for as long as the war with France should last.[25] Before peace came alien priories had been suppressed, so Ruislip's long connection with the Abbey of Bec ended with William de St. Vaast's death in 1404.

The memory of the monks of Bec lived on in Ruislip passed down by common report. Five deponents in a case heard in Chancery in 1577 (Hawtrey v Wold)[26] all make reference to "French Friars" in the time before King's College owned Ruislip.

One of them, Thomas Lyon, Carpenter, aged 74 "deposed" that he heard his father and his ancestors say when he was a child that there was a house of French friars in the place where Ruislip Court (Manor Farm) now is, and that it was the head house of the French friars and that one time when there was war between England and France those friars sent writing on to their country against the King of England and that thereupon they were put down and that a king of this land did afterwards give the manor of Ruislip to King's College Cambridge.

John Smyth, 67, the Demesne farmer another deponent reported the story as it was remembered in Cambridge:

"he says that when he was fellow of King's College in Cambridge which was about 40 years ago as he remembers or more, he heard it commonly talked in the college there that the same Ruislip Park with all the lordship of Ruislip was sometime before the creation of King's College articulate belonging to certain religious men being Frenchmen called Friars Ogborne which had their house in the

The Abbey of Bec. St Nicholas Tower

The Goodliest Place in Middlesex

same place where this deponent now dwelleth in Ruislip called Ruislip Court, and that when King Henry the fifth was at Agincourt Field in France those French Friars were commanded among other religious men of the realm to pray to God for the prosperous success of the same King Henry the fifth and because they would not so do therefore as it was said King Henry the fifth took occasion to put those Friars down and then King Henry the sixth when he built the King's College in Cambridge gave the same Ruislip Park with other temporal land in Ruislip belonging to the same friars unto the same college, and gave the parsonage to Windsor College."

The suggestion that the Abbey of Bec lost its English lands because the monks refused to pray for Henry V at Agincourt (25 October 1415) is an embroidery as the battle was a year later than the Suppression of Alien Priories. This is an example of the danger of relying upon personal reminiscences for historical facts. It is interesting, however, to speculate upon the relationship between the monks and the people of Ruislip. How visible were they in the village? Did they give alms to the poor at the Ladygate entrance to the Priory or is that a fanciful idea thought out by 20th century inhabitants to account for the ancient name Ladygate Lane? A 15th century lawsuit suggests that they did at times provide some kind of dole. Since there was a chapel in the Priory the monks would not be seen in St. Martin's at daily mass. They appointed vicars to Ruislip, but not from among their own number.

In the 13th century and early 14th century when the Ruislip Priory was the administrative centre for the Bailiwick of Ogbourne, Ruislip achieved an importance it has never since known. Monks, bailiffs and stewards from all over southern England attended for the audit, bringing news, colour and spectacle into the lives of the ordinary people of Ruislip. Many of the villeins, men like Gilbert Aldred, had their horizons enlarged by cross-country journeys on the monks' business to distant estates.

The influence of the monks lasted 300 years and prevented Ruislip from becoming a closed community. It is small wonder that their presence was remembered and that as John Lyvinge, 60 year-old husbandman said in 1577 "this speech hath remained long in the country thereabout."

REFERENCES
1. Et seq. Poree: Histoire de l'Abbaye du Bec.
2. Et seq. M. Morgan: *English Lands of the Abbey of Bec.* O.U.P. 1946
3. Ibid.
4. Ibid.
5. *'Select Documents of the Abbey of Bec'*. Camden Third Series, Vol LXIII, Royal Historical Society, 1951.
6. Ibid.
7. M. Morgan op cit
8. Ibid.
9. *'Select Documents of the Abbey of Bec'*. Camden Third Series, Vol LXIII, Royal Historical Society, 1951.
10. P.R.O. E 106/2 (1-6); S.C. 6/1126/5; C. 47/18/1/12.
11. Ex info John Dalton of Copthall Farm.
12. *'Select Documents of the Abbey of Bec'*. Camden Third Series, Vol LXIII, Royal Historical Society, 1951.
13. King's College Q.8.

14. 'Select Documents of the Abbey of Bec'. Camden Third Series, Vol LXIII, Royal Historical Society, 1951.
15. Ibid.
16. Ibid
17. H. E. Hallam: *Rural England 1066-1348* Fontana 1981.
18. P.R.O. SC6/1126/5.
19. King's College R.44.
20. King's College Q.7.
21. G.L.R.O. Acc 446/L1/14.
22. Radcliffe: *Middlesex:* New edition, Evans Brothers.
23. Et seq. M. Morgan: op cit
24. Ibid.
25. P.R.O. Cal Patent Rolls 6 Henry IV.
26. King's College Q.23.

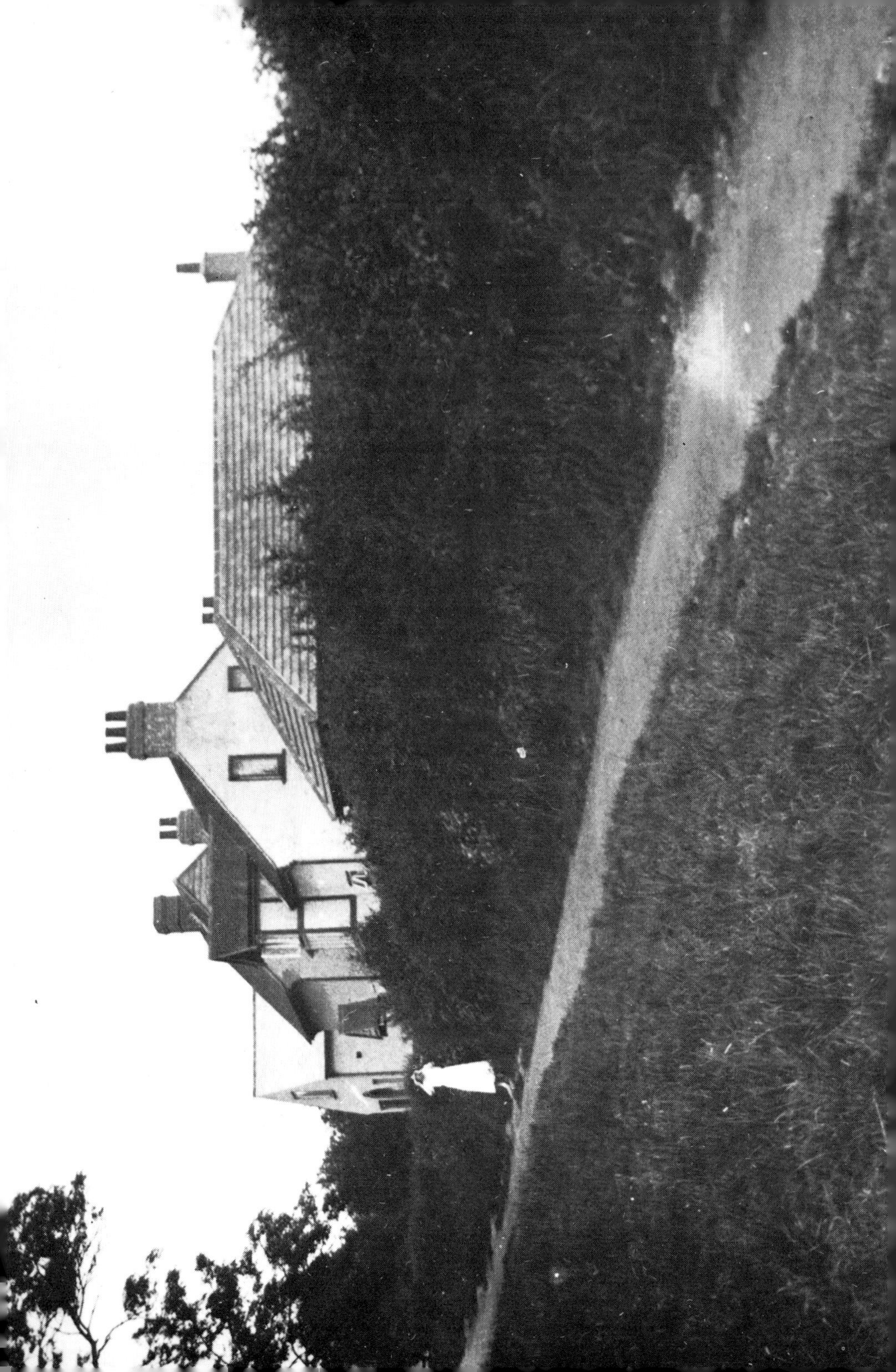

Chapter Four
The Manor of Ruislip
1404-1451

After William de St. Vaast's death in 1404 Thomas Langley exchanged his interest in Ruislip for other land, leaving John of Lancaster in sole possession. Prince John, third son of Henry IV and younger brother of Henry V, was created Duke of Bedford in 1414 and as such continued to be lord of Ruislip until his death in 1436.

As a Knight of the Garter, he had a special interest in St. George's, Windsor and granted the spiritualities of all the churches of which the Abbey had once been patron to the Dean and Canons in December 1422.[1] Since then the Dean and Canons of St. George's, Windsor have been Patrons of the Living of Ruislip.

Henry VI (the Duke of Bedford's nephew) assumed Ruislip and the other properties into his own hands in 1436. He granted the manor of Ruislip *"with a place called Northwood"* to John Somerset, his Chancellor, for life, in a letter patent dated 10 July 1437. The University of Cambridge was to have its reversion after Somerset's death.[2]

After 1440 a commission was appointed to settle the future ownership of alien priories. Eight, including Ruislip, were finally granted to the College of Our Blessed Lady and St. Nicholas at Cambridge (later known as King's College) which had been founded by Henry VI in 1441. Ruislip was confirmed to King's College in 1451, after complaints from Somerset (in a tedious Latin Lament) about the ingratitude of Cambridge and King's College.[3] *"The Councils did not grant Ruislip, they kept it as a security for you... When you stole it you took my livelihood by stealth... you seize wide and fertile estates by your craft, deceit etc. etc."*

King's College, as a Lancastrian foundation, suffered several years of insecurity when the Wars of the Roses ended with a Yorkist King on the throne. The uncertainty ended happily for the College in 1462 when Edward IV regranted Ruislip to the Provost and Scholars *"that they may pray for the good estate of the King and for the soul of the King after death and those of his father Richard, late Duke of York and Cicely his mother, his projenitors."*[4]

The Early 15th Century
Several rentals[5] dating from the period of John, Duke of Bedford's ownership of Ruislip, and Minister's Accounts 1434-6,[6] covering the period of his death, throw some light upon manorial administration in the 15th century and provide us with lists of names of Ruislip's inhabitants. About 107 names appear in the rentals, only 13 families being the same as those in the Customal. One or two items of topographical interest occur.

Rawedge – now Brickwall Lane

The Goodliest Place in Middlesex

Minister's Accounts show that the demesne was divided and let out to various farmers. A dairy and a garden outside the moat was let to William Leving. Could this have been the land on which Winston Churchill Hall now stands? A barn within the manor called the Tithing barn (almost certainly the Great Barn) and a small piece of garden land enclosing it was in Richard Bradefer's hands. The Manor House or former Priory is not mentioned as being let, but is inventoried under the heading "list of deadstock remaining in the Manor", which suggests an empty house. It contained:

Larder:	1 large trough, 2 small trestles, "1 dressing borde", 1 grate.
Kitchen:	1 watercanne with iron hoops, one piece of lead set in a mould.
Scullery:	12 quarters coal and wood
Aula (Hall)	1 trestle table, 3 trestles, 3 "tabuldormands", 2 benches
Chamber I:	1 mattress, 1 coverlet, 2 basins with ewer, 2 candlesticks, 2 tables, 3 benches, 3 small trestles, 1 counting board with an aumbry, 2 cathedra (official chairs) 1 old spoon mended.
Countinghouse:	2 boxes without wax and nails one small table with a whole set of chessmen to play on that table.
Bakehouse:	one large piece of lead set in a mould, 2 knedynge-troughs, 1 mouldingboard, 1 large marshfate, 1 small axe, 1 bushel one newly bought iron.
Chamber of the Prior:	1 small table, 1 small bench, 1 cupboard, 1 old box.
Chamber of the Lord:	1 trestle table of Estrychbord (wood from the Easterlyngs), 1 other table, 1 small trestle, 2 benches.
Chapel:	1 desk, 1 laverstock of lead (perhaps the support of a cistern).
Scullery:	1 dish of pewter, 4 dishes, 4 saucers, 1 candle-stick, 1 salt-seller of pewter old, 2 cloths "de erip" 1 large cistern of lead in the brewhouse.

1 large spoon mended in the room of the forester.

No branches had been cut for the lord's works that year and no oaks had been cut down for repairs to the Manor House, which further suggests that it was not inhabited at the time.

The Demesne farmer had land in Marlpit Field, Bencroft (Beancroft), Cophawe, Rawhedge, Bourbrigg, Horsemanhole, Rothwell and Windmylnhill. Marlpit Field stretched from the present Brickwall Lane to the Yeading Brook and took its name from the pit from which marl was dug. Marl was chalky gravel and sand used to dress the heavy London clay to make better arable. Rawedge lasted as the name of the northern edge of Marlpit Field until this century. It ran from where Brickwall Lane bends to meet Windmill Way. An elderly resident has told the present writer how before the First World War her mother used to send her from Field End Farm to Rawedge where her father was working to carry him his dinner. The same lady has spoken of White Butts where West End Road crosses the Yeading Brook near Ruislip Gardens Station. White Butts was let to John Haydon in 1435.

Windmylnhill has given its name to the modern Windmill Hill. The Windmill mentioned in the 1294 Extent almost certainly stood on the crest. Two fields Great and Little Windmill Field are marked on Doharty's 1750 map, which

Field End Farm, junction of Wood Lane/West End Road. Site of Barrengers, an outlier of Northolt Manor, demolished 1963

shows a square of apparently empty land thought to be the mill site. The other names did not survive and their whereabouts are unknown, through Bourbrigg was probably where West End Road crosses the Roxbourne stream.

Some other fields named Copwell Mead, Batescroft and Harry's Croft, also part of the demesne, were let out in 1435. Copwell Mead is now cut by Pinn Way and the entrance to Winston Churchill Hall, but remains a field. Bates Field west of Sharps Lane is now part of Ruislip Golf Course and Harry's Croft has Mead Way, part of Pinn Way and Numbers 92-118 Bury Street built in it. The Allotment Gardens between Park Avenue and Mead Way are the remnant of Harry's Croft.

The old Priory buildings were known as The Court because Manor Courts were held there and there are several references to vacant ridges of land at the Court gate. Somewhere nearby Thomas Smith was enlarging his forge by the church and having to pay 3s.4d extra in rent. At about the same period Emma Smith (almost certainly a widow) had a smithy near the Manor House Gate.[8]

Emma and Thomas may have been mother and son. Somewhere near the churchyard John Baldwyn had acquired *"a certain parcel of the lord's waste 12 feet wide and 20 feet long adjoining the cemetery there"*. His rent was 3d p.a. but nothing was paid "because the said John is dead without heirs".

Another interesting feature mentioned in the Minister's Accounts is the shop of Thomas Andrews *"near the Churchyard"*. Was it a shop in the accepted sense or an ale-shop?

Three tradesmen only appear in the rentals: John Berenger, a tiler, Richard Clere, a joiner; and Thomas Hall, a London Tailor, who presumably owned land here, while carrying on his business in London.

A section of the accounts headed Farm Works shows that the sale of customary works was now established at the rate 10s for a virgate holder and pro rata, a much more uniform system than the rather haphazard two tier rents of the Customal. The tied tenants of the mid-13th century had become copyholders.

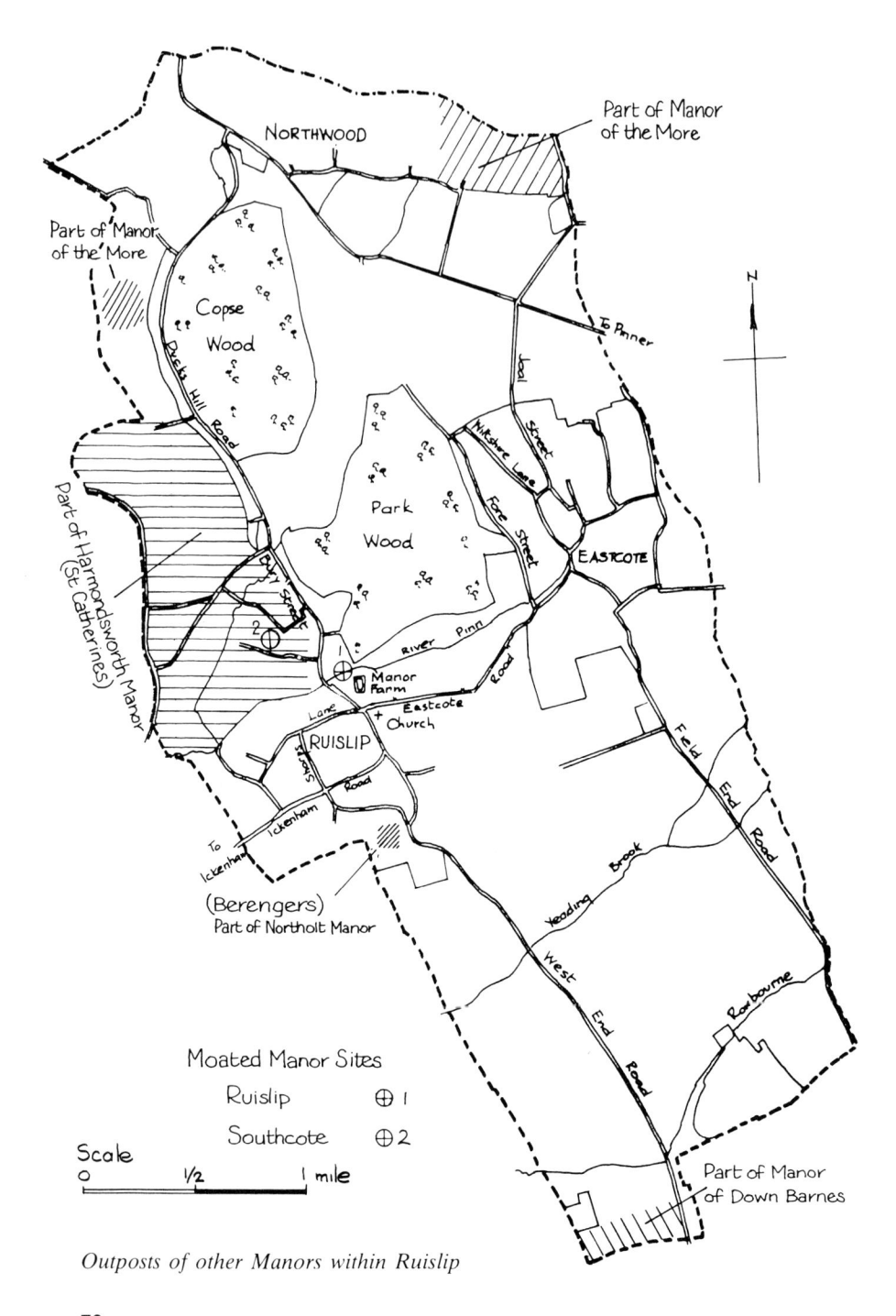

Outposts of other Manors within Ruislip

Outliers of Other Manors Within Ruislip Parish

By the time King's College received Ruislip in 1451 several other manors had outliers within the parish. The largest of these was St. Catherine's, the area west of Bury Street, which was a parcel of Harmondsworth. It is described in detail in Chapter 5.

Small outliers of three other manors lay within Ruislip parish in medieval times. Gate Hill Farm, Northwood with 90 acres of land, belonged to the manor of the More in Hertfordshire. A Ruislip court roll of 1428 records that the lord exercised his right to felon's goods by seizing three messuages in Northwood belonging to Guy atte Hill and 12 acres called Whiteslands, then Guy's property but formerly belonging to William White.[9] Guy atte Hill became corrupted over the years to Gyot Hill and later to Gate Hill. The Redinge family owned it in the 16th century and the Hawtreys[10] held it for much of the 17th century selling it to Sir Bartholmew Shower of Pinner Hill in 1695.[11] Manor of the More Court Rolls refer to two messuages called Guy atte Hill and Whytes lying in Ruislip in the 16th century and later.[12] A ten acre field called Hill Field on Ducks Hill, constantly crops up in the 18th century More Court Rolls and may be the former Whiteslands.[13] It was surrendered by James Nelham of Ruislip, Baker, to Simeon Howard owner of Ducks Hill Farm, becoming part of the farm in 1734.

The manor house of Down Barnes was situated in the moated site on Sharvel Lane immediately adjoining the south-west boundary of Ruislip. The moat is now within the land of Down Barnes Farm and the modern farmhouse stands on the Ruislip side of the boundary. In 1245 Roger de la Dune held a hide of land in the manor of Ruislip.[14] Northolt Manor adjoined Ruislip on its south-east boundary and had a tenement called Barrengers (or Berengers) at Field End, Ruislip (junction of Wood Lane and West End Road), with land in Ruislip common fields in the 15th and 16th centuries. This tenement was still part of the Manor of Northall (Northolt) in 1565 when Richard Cogges was the tenant.[15] The abuttals given in the 1565 Terrier show that it was Field End Farm (demolished to build Pond Green in 1963).

REFERENCES
1. St. George's, Windsor: X.4.1.
2. King's College: Q.11.
3. Ruislip Library: Transcript in L. E. Morris Collection.
4. P.R.O. Cal. Pat. 1461-7, 54.
5. King's College: R.39; 40; 41; 44.
6. P.R.O. S.C. 6/917/27; Ruislip Library Transcript: L. E. Morris Collection.
7. 'Select Documents of the Abbey of Bec'. Camden Third Series, Vol LXIII Royal Historical Society 1951.
8. King's College: R.39; 40.
9. King's College: Q.51.
10. Herts. R.O. D/EB 1841 M1: D/EB 513 T73/76.
11. National Register of Archives Catalogue – RNUDC 1953 p. 27.
12. Herts. R.O. D/EB 513 T.74.
13. Ibid 25452.
14. 'Select Documents of the Abbey of Bec'. Camden Third Series, Vol LXIII Royal Historical Society 1951.
15. King's College: R.36.

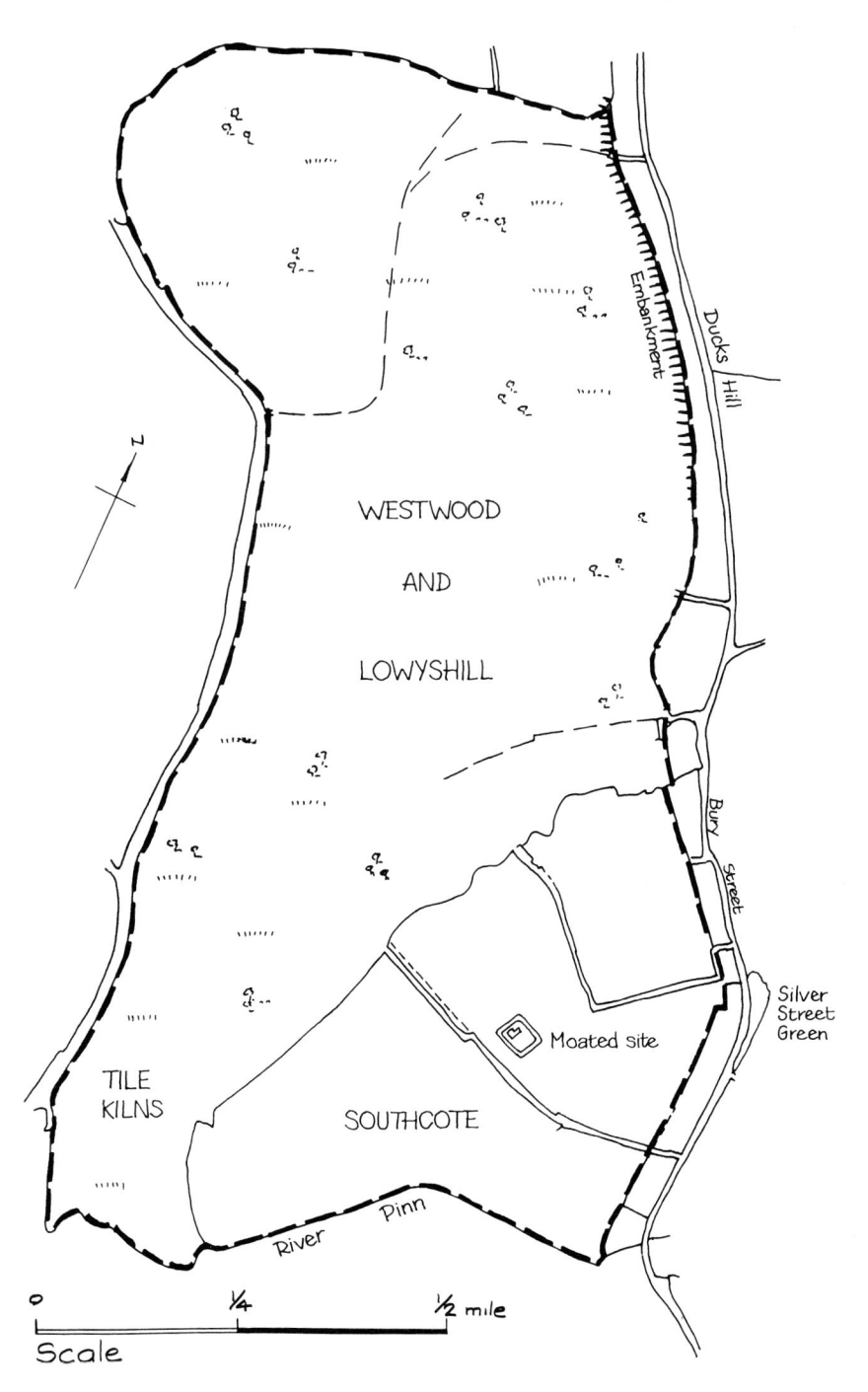

St Catherine's Manor 14th-15th Century

Chapter Five

St. Catherine's Manor and Southcote

The portion of Ruislip parish lying west of Bury Street and Ducks Hill from the northern boundary of Mad Bess Wood to the Pinn was long known as St. Catherine's Manor, Katherine End or the Little Manor. Ernulf de Hesdin's gift to the Abbey of Bec specifically excluded one hide of land within Ruislip already belonging to Holy Trinity at Rouen,[1] an abbey popularly known as St. Catherine's because of relics held there, and owner of Harmondsworth since 1069. Accordingly the affairs of this quarter of Ruislip are recorded in the Harmondsworth Court Rolls and papers. The boundaries of St. Catherine's are described in only the vaguest terms until the wastelands there were enclosed in 1769 and are not properly delineated on a map until the Ruislip Enclosure Map was drawn in 1806. In the 11th century it must have formed part of the great band of wooded waste lying north of Ruislip and was referred to as "Westwood and Lowyshill" the former name referring to its position west of the Common Wood in the Great Manor.[2]

The eastern boundary of St. Catherine's Manor exists as a large embankment topped with stubbed trees in Mad Bess Wood, but has practically disappeared further south in Bury Street.

Southcote
Within St. Catherine's there was a freehold estate called Southcote which took its name from a Harmondsworth family who had land called Southcote (thought to be between Heathrow and Perry Oaks). Roger and Avicia de Southcote as seen in Chapter 3 held land and a millpond called Sitheclack in Ruislip in 1245.[3] The de Southcotes were hereditary foresters of Harmondsworth in the 13th and 14th centuries and may have acquired the Ruislip estate because of its proximity to the wooded waste which made up most of Harmondsworth's Ruislip land.[4]

The division between Southcote and St. Catherine's is unknown, but the two remained in separate ownership until 1603. Southcote is often referred to as a manor and several cottages[5] at Silver Street Green, Bury Street, were said to be held freely from the Manor of Southcote in 1565, but the owner of Southcote never seems to have had such manorial prerogatives as the right to hold courts.
The Southcote lands spread far outside Ruislip parish. 14th century documents mention Southcote property in Ickenham, Harrow, Stanwell and Colnbrook as well.[6] In Richard II's time there were 80 acres in Eastcote.[7] It is just possible that St. Catherine's Farm in Catlins Lane, Eastcote, derives its name from this tenuous, connection with St. Catherine's through Southcote.

The Southcote family retained the property until 1341 when the reversion was sold to William and Isobel Pycot.[8] It passed through a number of

Site of Southcote Manor Moat

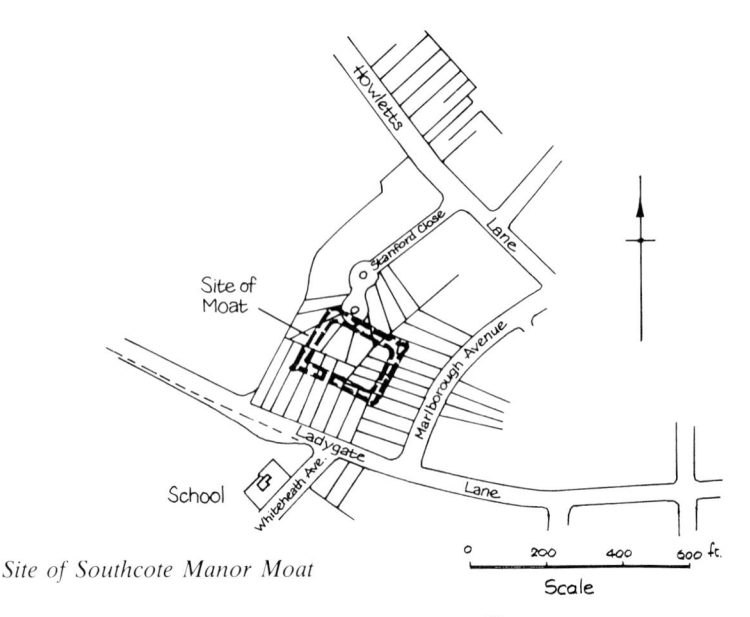

other hands until 1597 when Henry Clarke Esq.[9] bought it and six years later he purchased St. Catherine's thereby uniting the two.[10] The whereabouts of the 1597 conveyance is unknown, but extracts from it exist among the Hawtrey Papers. They are of little help in defining the Southcote estate precisely, but offer a clue to its position, placing it in the Ladygate Lane area and roughly in the southern portion of St. Catherine's Manor, but the lands were probably intermingled. The name lingered on in Southcote Farm which stood on land now occupied by Whiteheath Junior School.

In 1378, when Alice Perrers, Edward III's mistress, was owner, there was a manor site with a building said to be ruinous.[11] A rectangular moat north of Ladygate Lane shown on all maps until as recently as 1935 is believed to be the site of the Manor House. Buildings were shown within it in 1806 on the Ruislip Enclosure Map, but had gone by 1865 when the 25 inch Ordnance Survey map was drawn. The moated area was filled in and lies between Stanford Close and Marlborough Avenue.

It would appear from later surveys that Southcote Manor House was the principal dwelling in the whole of St. Catherine's and probably the only one to be a gentleman's residence.[12] In 1803, towards the end of its life it was described as a "large Mansion House, with offices of every description" and a walled garden.[13] John Lulham, Esq., was then the tenant. No known paintings or prints of it exist.

St. Catherine's

St. Catherine's was sold as a parcel of Harmondsworth in 1391 to William of Wykeham, the year when Holy Trinity (an alien priory like the Abbey of Bec) was licensed to sell its English possessions.[14] From 1391-1543 it formed part of the endowment of Winchester College, then passed into Henry VIII's hands in exchange for other lands in south and west Hampshire, Dorset and Gloucester.[15] Harmondsworth with Westwood and Lowyshill in Ruislip was

St Catherine's Manor and Southcote

granted to William Paget, later Lord Paget, who already owned West Drayton, in 1547.[16]

A Harmondsworth Survey dated 1549 includes a section headed "Rislypp."[17] It lists one free tenant, John Smythe, and twelve copyholders. The freehold property was the manor of Southcote. Its presence in the list shows that Southcote although spoken of as a manor was subordinate to Harmondsworth and that its owner owed suit of court and paid 18s 4d a year to the main manor. The copyholders had between them 1 messuage, 6 cottages (1 in ruins), diverse tenements, a "Tile House" and a "Tile Place". Their rents totalled 8s 11d.

William Paget died in 1563 and his son Henry in 1568. William's second son, Thomas, became the third Lord Paget. The family were Catholic. Thomas fled to Paris in 1583 at the time of the Throckmorton plot and was attainted in 1586 for his implication in the Babington Plot to put Mary, Queen of Scots on the English throne. Fortunately for those of us interested in the history of St. Catherine's, his lands were surveyed for the Crown. From the pages of the 1587 survey a fuller picture of St. Catherine's with Southcote begins to emerge.[18]

St. Catherine's Survey 1587

The survey was taken at Ruislip in May 1587 before three auditors of the Court of Exchequer: Jerome Halley, John Hill, Alexander King and two Commissioners: George Woodward Esq., and William Kerton, gentleman. Richard Reading, John Osmond, John Nash, George Tunbridge, Gregory Milward, Christopher Badger, John Kirton, Thomas Gowle and John Butler, tenants of the Manor, gave the information on oath, always referring to the area as St. Catherine's End.

There were nine free and 15 copyhold tenants (four common to both lists). The freehold property consisted of a messuage and 88 acres belonging to Moseley, gentleman (15s 4d rent); two tenements, one with 1 rod of orchard and one with a garden (halfpence each); several parcels of meadow and pasture and 12 acres arable called North Redding, (a name suggesting newly cleared land). The freely held land probably made up the Manor of Southcote.

The copyholders had eight cottages, five tenements and three tile houses between them. They paid 9s 1½d. They held at least 36 acres, but precise measurements are not given for some holdings.

The rest of the land was 160 acres of common called Westwood, where the wood and soil belonged to the Lord of the Manor, but the tenants could pasture cattle and swine. The Pagets had just begun to enclose parcels of woodland from the waste: 10 acres "lately enclosed" and another 26 acres in 1586. These enclosures formed part of the wood now known as Mad Bess. Some of the banks and ditches dividing the woodland today date from this time. 124 acres were woodland waste. The enclosed parcels are an example of a lord of the manor infringing the common rights of the tenants as pasture rights must have been extinguished in the newly-fenced woodlands. On this occasion no outcry is heard from the tenants and the enclosures may not have meant much on the whole for 160 acres is still designated common as late as 1769.[19]

360 "good oak fit for timber worth by estimation 6s 8d a tree" were growing in the enclosed woods and timber trees "whose number is not known" worth £120 on the unenclosed waste. 68 acres were not growing with wood, (i.e. coppice).

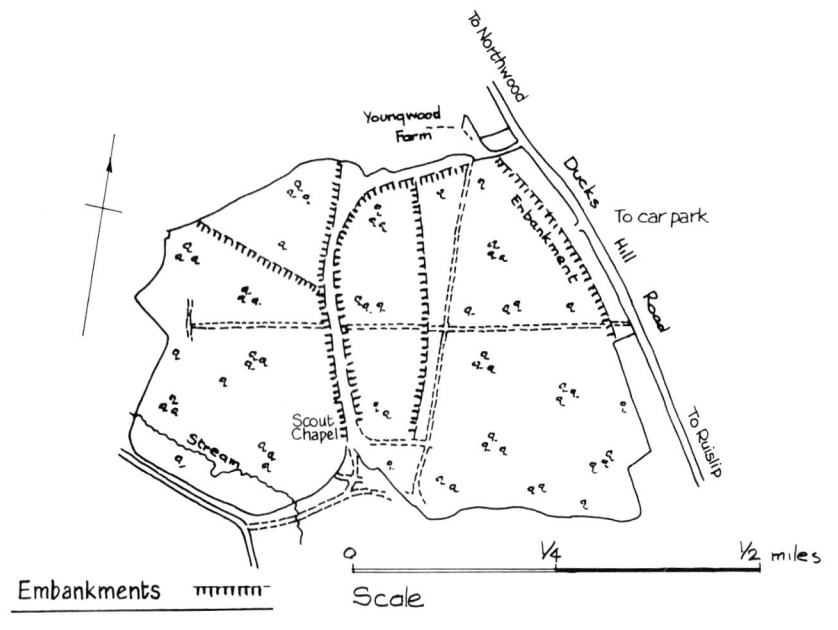

Mad Bess Wood, showing embankments

      This Ruislip woodland was a valuable source of timber for the Pagets in the 1580s. Ten acres were felled in 1585 and 12 acres in 1586, leaving 30 acres of 50 years growth and 40 acres of 40 years growth. Apart from the oak grown for timber, Westwood supplied underwood, probably hornbeam which was coppiced on a 7-12 year rotation to supply poles for hurdles, bean and pea sticks and kindlewood. Trees were coppiced by being cut fairly close to the ground, leaving a stool which was allowed to regenerate naturally.

      Oak of 50 years' growth was suitable for the studding and rafters of timber-framed buildings, though not for the main posts and joists, and therefore found a ready market. The felling of relatively young oaks was common practice in the Ruislip area, so it is not surprising to find that the ancient woodland of Westwood Common contained nothing older than 50 years and does not mean that the woodland had only been planted 50 years earlier. The natural woodland had been managed by felling certain sections and allowed by natural regeneration to restock itself.

      The right to coppice certain areas was sold to woodmen for £6 an acre, in 1586.

      Tilemaking was associated with the southern area of St. Catherine's called Tile Kilns (now Tile Kiln Lane) from 1448 until the beginning of Queen Victoria's reign.[20] Clay suitable for tilemaking was ready to hand on Westwood Common. The whole of St. Catherine's is on either London clay or Reading clay. In the words of the Survey *"The tenants of this hamlet are to have loam and clay for their necessary uses in and upon the said Westwood Common"*. The clay was not entirely free. *"Every tenant of this Manor which keepeth a tile kiln must pay to the lord every year when he diggeth earth upon the said common and maketh brick or tile therewith in respect of the said earth one thousand of tiles besides his rent renewed"*.

      One other interesting piece of information from the Survey is that *"The Lady Paget did grant about two years since to Thomas Gold her Bailiff and*

Woodward of this hamlet two acres of ground out of the said common for to build a house upon. Upon which grant he felled so much wood as amounted to eight loads of tallwood (wood cut into uniform length for fuel and tied in bundles) worth 3s 4d the load and 3 old scrubbed oaks worth by estimation 10 shillings and built thereupon a tenement for which he payeth yearly 4d".

One would dearly love to know where Thomas Gold's tenement was built and if it still stands. Eight houses dating from the 16th century are to be found in St. Catherine's today – Youngwood Farm just within the boundary, isolated from the rest of the manor by the woods, is the most likely candidate for Gold's tenement. Breakspear Garage (an example of unsympathetic treatment of an ancient building), Brill Cottage and Rose Cottage stand on Breakspear Road on the opposite side to the Crematorium, all in some danger of being swamped by industrial and commercial buildings. St. Catherine's Farm in Howletts Lane is at the centre of a borough housing scheme. Little Manor Farm is in the portion of Howletts Lane renamed Arlington Drive. Woodbine Cottage and Clack Farm in Tile Kiln Lane are probably two of the three tenements which had tile houses in 1587. Two of the other 16th century dwellings were Southcote Manor House itself and Southcote Farm. The remaining six mentioned in the survey can probably be identified with the houses shown on Rocque's map of Middlesex 1754 but have since disappeared.

Ownership 1587-1768

Following Lord Paget's attainder the Queen leased the Westwood woodlands to Sir Christopher Hatton her Lord Chancellor for 21 years. He died in 1591. The exiled Lord Paget died in 1590 and was succeeded by his son William, fourth Lord Paget, who successfully sought favour in circles near the Queen. He was granted Westwood in 1597 for the residue of Hatton's lease at a yearly rent of £16 3s 4d.[21] In October 1603 he sold his Ruislip land to Henry Clarke and Katherine, his wife, for £800 and "divers other good causes and considerations".[22] It was described as *"all that Manor and Lordship called or known by the name of the Manor of Rislippe...with all the rights...thereof situate in the parish of Ruyslippe in the county of Middlesex and all and singular those trees, woods, underwoods and waste ground called or known by the names of Westwood and Lowyshill"*. Lord Paget agreed to pay the annual rent until the 21 years should be expired.

Henry Clarke's daughter, Catherine, married Henry Welsted and appears to have inherited Southcote and St. Catherine's.[23] The Welsted's grave slab lies in the centre aisle of St. Martin's before the chancel arch. Catherine Welsted died in 1634 and her husband Henry in 1651. His will[24] reveals six children living at the time of his death: three sons and three daughters. The eldest daughter Mary, widow of Henry Seymer of Hanford, Dorset, is only mentioned indirectly in connection with a bequest to her five children, but she appears to have inherited her father's property. Her second husband was John Ryves of Rariston[25] who is named as the owner of St. Catherine's in a 1685 survey.[26] Mary died in 1688 and was succeeded in the Ruislip property by her eldest son Robert Seymour who died in 1706.[27] Her son Henry Seymour of Hanford sold the estate to John Child, Banker and citizen of London, in 1719. Christopher Child, son of John, bequeathed it to his four nieces, one of whom Sarah Mico, married John Lewin who purchased the other shares in 1768.[28] John Lewin's daughters Sarah (unmarried) and Susannah (who married William Shepherd of Stiles Hill near Frome) were his co-heirs.

Enclosure 1769

John Lewin, a Merchant of Basinghall Street, wished to enclose the wasteland lying within St. Catherine's, but needed to obtain some agreement with other landowners in the manor before obtaining a private Act of Parliament for this purpose. As lord of the manor he already owned the wooded waste and common still called Westwood or West Coat commons, but as we saw in the 1587 survey the other manorial tenants had grazing and other rights. John Lewin wished to extinguish these rights and fence the common. The tenants were entitled to receive allotments in lieu of their former rights.

In fact there were only 17 manorial tenants who for the most part owned small amounts of property and consequently were due to receive very small and therefore uneconomic allotments of former waste. 15 sold their commoner's rights to John Lewin so that their allotments were added to his; but two, Elizabeth Rogers of Eastcote House and Thomas Bannister, opposed enclosure, refused to sell their rights and were allotted land in lieu.

Table 1 shows the landowners and what they owned in 1769.

Table 1. St. Catherines at Enclosure 1769			
Proprietor	Old Enclosures	Amount	New Allotments
John Lewin	2 messuages and cottages	248a 0r 4p	162a 1r 27p
Elizabeth Rogers	1 messuage	4a	3a
Thomas Bannister	1 messuage	3r 27p	2r 13p
Henry Arnall	5 messuages	8a 2r 26p	
James Weedon	1 cottage	2r 0p	
Wm Bishop	part cottage	15p	
Rachael Ferne	2 cottages	2r 13p	
Samuel Jacques	1 cottage	2a 1r 36p	
Wm Blackstaff	1 cottage	1a 1r 3p	
Rebecca Blount	1 cottage	3r 3p	
James Gladman	1 cottage	36p	
James and Mary Ewer	1 cottage	3r 20p	
Matthew Seach	1 cottage	34p	
Wm Crosier		10a 0r 16p	
Peter Stiles		14a 3r 34p	
Joseph Moss		1a 2r 26p	
Hannah Ewer		3a 2r 19p	
		298a 3r 35p	166a 0r 0p

The Commissioners were George John Cooke of Belhammonds (later known as Harefield Park and now Harefield Hospital), M.P. for Middlesex; Rev. Thomas Clarke of Swakeleys and Henry Deane of Reading (a relative of Elizabeth Rogers). Henry Augustus Bierdemann of Uxbridge was the surveyor, but unfortunately made no map, or if he did it has not survived.

Rocque's map of Middlesex 1754, though small-scale shows St. Catherine's before Enclosure.

St Catherine's Manor and Southcote

Youngwood Farm, in the north-east corner of St Catherine's Manor

Two isolated houses and enclosures are shown; Youngwood Farm and a house near the junction with Breakspear Road North and Fine Bush Lane, which seems to have been known as Fine Bush. Three houses are shown at Tile Kilns, where a Brick-Kiln is marked. All the land south-east of the stream running across from Northwood (nowadays through the reservoir) is enclosed and the houses are served by two roads, Ladygate Lane and Howletts Lane, which both stop at the stream. To the north-west of the stream three houses (Breakspear Garage, Brill Cottage, Rose Cottage) and four other cottages, one called the Six Bells, nestle on the edge of the common. They are clear encroachments on the waste and although 16th century in date, possibly later than St. Catherine's Farm, Little Manor Farm, Southcote Manor House and Southcote Farm, which are set amid hedged fields. Three tracks radiate from the point where Ladygate Lane crosses the stream, one continuing the line of the lane to the enclosures of Fine Bush; one leading to Oak Cottage, which now stands behind the Woodman and the other leading towards Tile Kiln. A faint track is shown leading from Cannon Bridge to Breakspear Road North coming out opposite Willow Farm. The wooded portion of the common is shown to the north and is more or less the same area as the present Mad Bess Wood. The woodland was divided by a track which continued west of Youngwood Farm and eventually joined Jacketts Lane.

The common to be enclosed amounted to 174a 1r 34p (about 10 acres more common than in 1587). Some land was set aside for roads and cartways. The only track shown on Rocque's map which was unaltered and defined by the Enclosure Commissioners, and is to be seen to this day, is the green lane "leading out of Harefield Parish between two of the woods of the said John Lewin and turning along the south side of this wood called North Ridings Wood into Harefield Lane (Breakspear Road North)". In other words the track through

81

The Goodliest Place in Middlesex

Mad Bess Wood. It was laid out as a private road or cartway 30 feet wide. Its drainage ditches have been maintained and may still be seen today.

Breakspear Road was laid out as a 60 feet wide public road "from the south-west end of the said common...leading across to Cannon Bridge, passing by the Six Bells and the other cottages on the south-east part of the said Common". The Six Bells seems to have stood on the west side of Rose Cottage. The present Six Bells was not built until after 1806.

Fine Bush Lane was made as a private roadway 30 feet wide from *"a lane called Howletts Lane across the said common to Harefield Lane passing by the...Six Bells..."*

One other private road from Clack Bridge to Harefield Lane leading to Uxbridge must be Tile Kiln Lane. 150 acres of woodland were mentioned called North Riding Wood, Sanson's Hill Wood, Standale Wood, Westcoat Wood Close and Mad Bess or Censor's Wood (the earliest reference to the name Mad Bess).

The Act[29] laid down that "all ditches of the said new enclosures between the respective allotments of the several proprietors which shall be planted with quick shall be made 4 feet wide and well quicked and hedged and that such of the hedges and ditches as are not already made shall be finished before the 1st day of June 1770". This provision means that nearly all the hedges around the sadly diminishing fields of St. Catherine's are 215 years old and are useful comparative examples for naturalists and historians who try to date hedges by counting the number of species growing in them.

The costs of the Enclosure, £427.9s, was divided between the owners of the new enclosures:
John Lewin Esq.   £418 4s 6d
Mrs Elizabeth Rogers £   7 14s 6d (her main objection to enclosure had been that she feared the cost!)
Thomas Bannister   £   1 10s 0d

Money was to be paid to Jabez Goldar of Uxbridge, the appointed receiver, by 18 January 1770. Jabez Goldar acted as Steward for the manors of Ickenham and Swakeleys and land agent for many local estates. He was an Uxbridge solicitor like his father before him. The Act was signed at the Crown, Uxbridge, 18 December 1769.

The effect of the 1769 Enclosure is best seen by comparing Rocque's Map 1754 with the Enclosure Map of the great manor drawn in 1806. John Lewin owned four farms – Southcote Farm, Clack Farm, Little Manor Farm and Youngwood Farm – the Manor House of Southcote, three other cottages and 462 acres of land. At the same time as the Enclosure he allowed the owners of cottages in the manor who were his copyhold tenants to purchase their Deeds of Enfranchisement for five shillings[30] each. The cottages enfranchised were: Brill Cottage, owned by William Blackstaff, Poulterer of Christ Church, Middlesex; Rose Cottage, owned by Mary Ewer, formerly Mary Anderson, wife of James Ewer; the Cottage next to Rose Cottage which seems to have been the Public House called the Six Bells, belonging to James Gladman; a cottage belonging to Rebecca Blount; and three cottages belonging to Henry Arnall, one possibly on the corner of Breakspear Road and Howletts Lane and two at Tile Kiln, one having a Tile Kiln attached (probably Woodbine Cottage).

Rocque's map 1754 – St Catherine's Manor

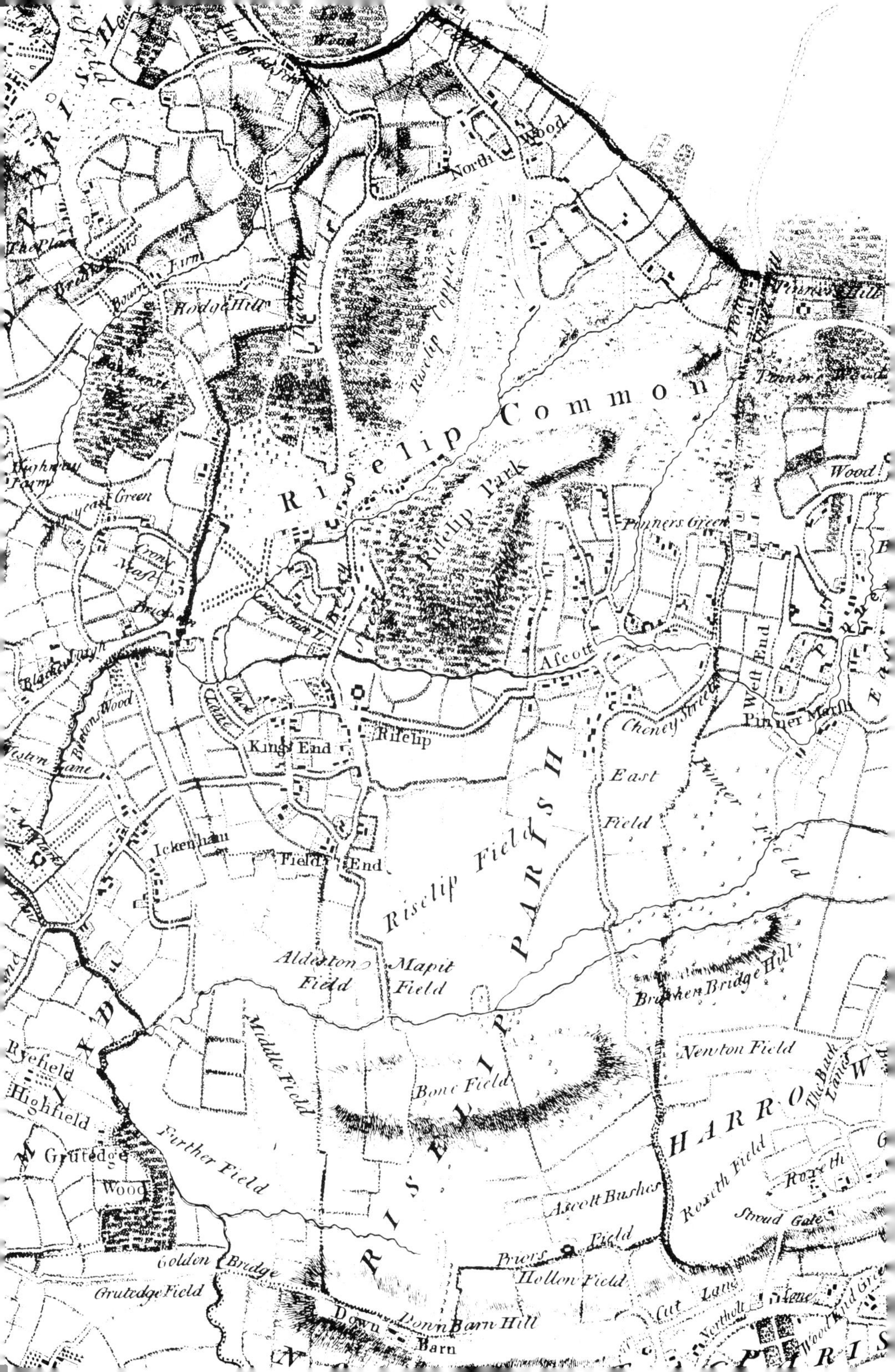

Riselip Common
Riselip Park
Riselip Coppice
North Wood
Rodge Hill
The Place
Bourn Farm
Highway Farm
Green
Crow Wast
Brick
Blackwatch
Breton's Wood
Weston Lane
Pinners Green
Ascott
Riselip
Kings End
Cheney Street
West End
Pinner Marsh
East Field
Pinner Field
Ickenham
Field End
Riselip Field
RISELIP PARISH
Alderston Field
Mapit Field
Brakhen Bridge Hill
Middle Field
Bone Field
Newton Field
The Back Lanes
HARROW
Ryefield
Highfield
Grutedge Wood
Further Field
Roxeth Field
Roxeth
Ascott Bushes
Stroud Gate
Priors Field
Hollow Field
Golden Bridge
Grutedge Field
Down Barn Hill
Down Barn
Cut Lane
Northolt
Wood End Green
Wood

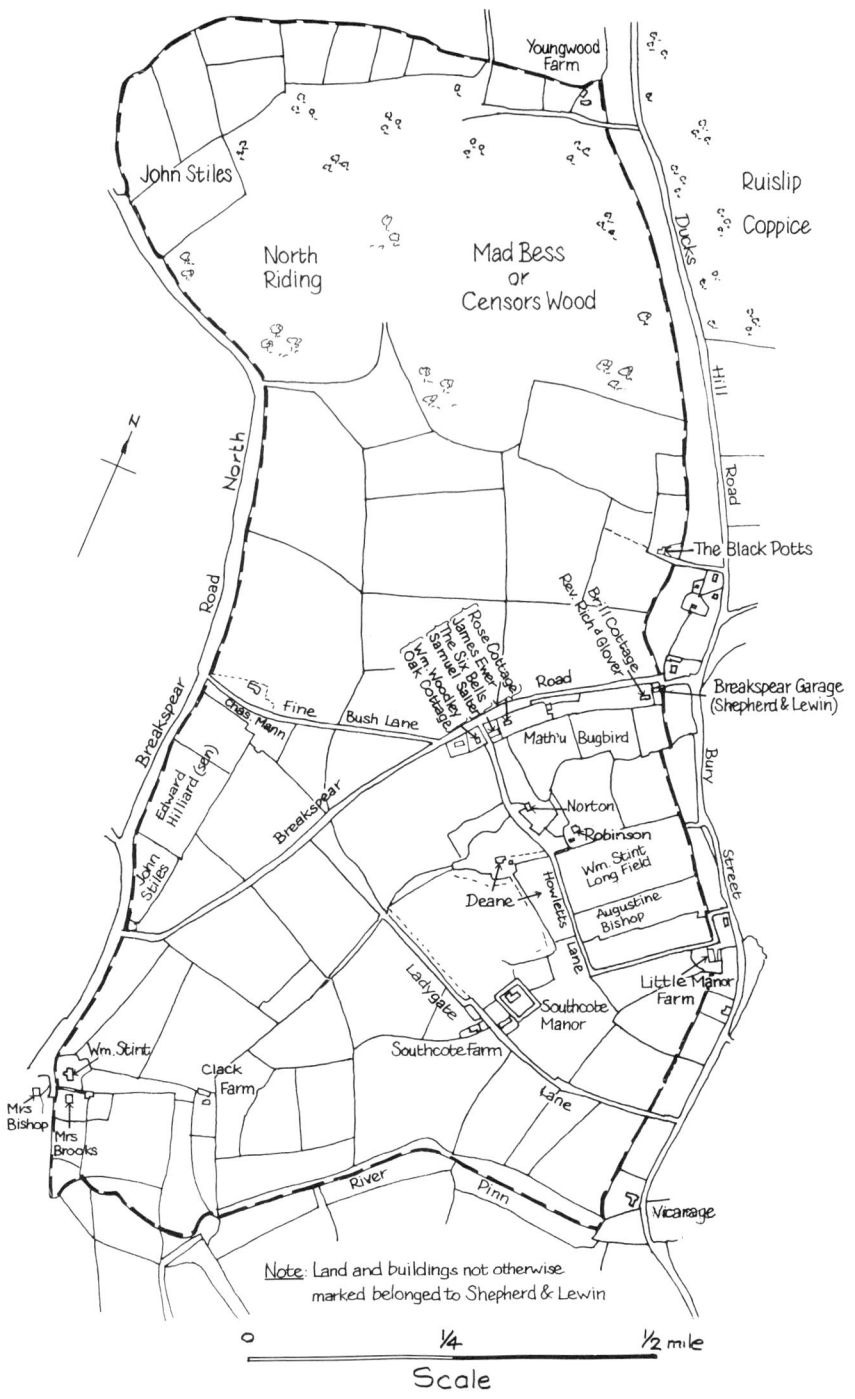

From Ruislip Enclosure map 1806

One of the cottages owned by John Lewin was another public house, the Black Pots. It appears in the earliest Licensed Victuallers' lists of 1748[31] when William Bugbeard was the licensee. The latest reference is in an 1807 Valuation.[32] It stood in the field behind the present Six Bells between the stile and the Crematorium fence. The 1789 workhouse map shows and names it.[33] Mr "Curly" Woodman says that the field was called Black Spots field when he was a boy, about the time of the First World War – a slightly corrupted memory of the old pub. Ann Clayton was licensee from about 1775 to 1806/7. The Six Bells on Breakspear Road owned by James Gladman in 1769 had been acquired by Samuel Salter, the Rickmansworth brewer, before 1807 at which date James Gladman was still resident.[34] Salter obtained 1¼ acres of land between Ducks Hill and the boundary of St. Catherine's Manor in 1806.[35] The present Six Bells was built upon it and the licence and sign transferred from James Gladman's pub some time later. A transaction registered in the Middlesex Land Registry in 1809 (Book 5/576) shows that Samuel Salter sold a messuage "heretofore divided into tenements" known by the sign of the Six Bells to William Woodley. By the time a Terrier was made in 1837, the present Six Bells was erected, but William Woodley was still running a beer shop on the old premises. The 1866 O.S. map shows the present Six Bells, but no sign of the old one, nor of the Black Pots.

Shepherd and Lewin's Estate

John and Sarah Lewin both died young, he in 1770 aged 37 and his wife two years later when she was 35.[36] Their daughter Susanna, wife of William Shepherd,[37] appears to have died before 1800 leaving her interest in the estate to her husband. William Shepherd and his sister-in-law Miss Sarah Lewin were left as co-owners. There was a plan to sell the estate in 1803, which seems to have come to nothing.

Sale Particulars 1803

Particulars advertising the sale for 19 April 1803[38] at Garraway's Coffee House, Change Alley give the total acreage as 434a 1r 5p. Southcote Manor House with its walled garden and 27 acres of grassland was let to John Lulham on a seven year tenancy due to expire on Lady Day 1805. The Manor House is depicted for the last time on the 1806 Enclosure Map. The land seems to have been redistributed among the other farms and the house allowed to decay. Neither Miss Lewin nor Mr Shepherd appear in the Rate Books as residents in the parish and may have had more interest in their rent and particularly in the sales of wood from the woodlands, which they did not let but retained in hand, than in an old moated house. Sarah Lewin died in 1837, aged 69, at Lowestoft and was buried at Herringfleet Church.[39] Her nephew William Hulbert Shepherd of Keyford House. Frome continued to own St. Catherine's until 1873. He owned the largest woollen manufacturers in Frome in 1851, employing a workforce of 1079. He died in 1878.[40]

The 1873 Sale of St. Catherine's

The local paper, the Buckinghamshire Advertiser, carried the following advertisement on 31 May 1873, offering for sale at *"Ruislip, Middlesex: The valuable and important Freehold Estate (with possession): comprising about 466 acres of principally rich Pasture and Woodland, farmhouses and buildings situate in a most picturesque part of the country, finely undulating and beautifully wooded,*

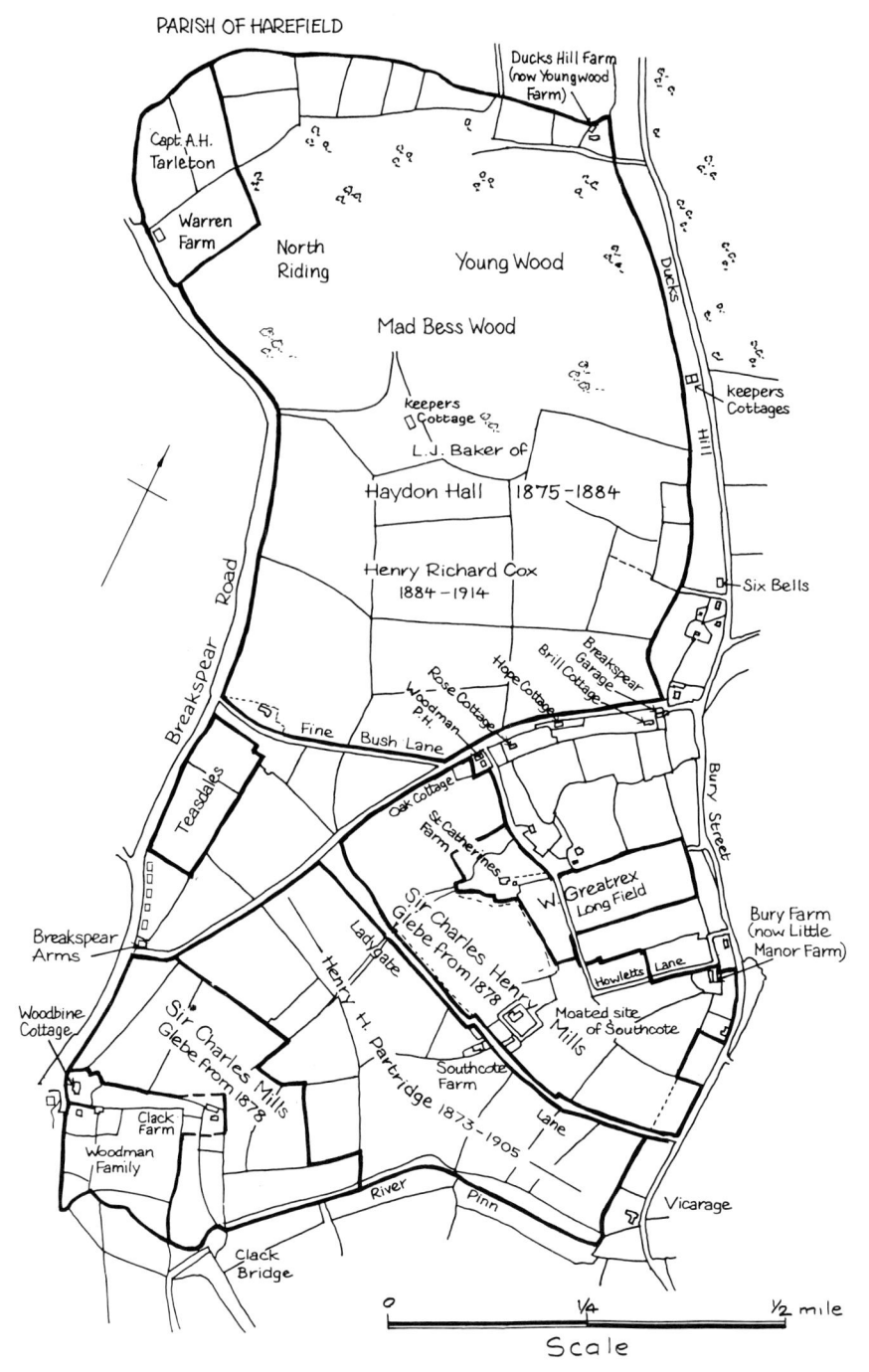

Ownership of St Catherine's Manor after the sale of 1873 showing the Glebe exchange of 1877

St Catherine's Manor and Southcote

bounded and intersected by capital roads and offering most eligible sites for gentlemen's residences, pleasure farms and as accommodation land, 130 acres of which form part of the well known Ruislip Woods offering good shooting, and there is excellent fishing in the neighbourhood. The estate is within 20 miles of the Metropolis four miles of the town of Uxbridge etc., etc., Mr Murrell is instructed to sell by auction at the Mart Tokenhouse Yard, City on Tuesday 10 June. The above valuable Freehold Estate in 14 lots affording the public an opportunity of purchasing large and small pleasure farms some with the necessary houses. The estate has been in the possession of the present family for upwards of a century and is now in a high state of cultivation".

The Woodland After 1873

The auction took place and Youngwood Farm (then called Ducks Hill Farm), the Woodlands (Youngwood, Mad Bess and North Riding) and land running south to Fine Bush Lane and Breakspear Road, amounting to 267 acres, was purchased for £12,000 by L. J. Baker of Hayden Hall.[41] He built three ornamental Gamekeepers' Cottages which are still standing, a semi-detached pair in Ducks Hill opposite the entrance to Battle of Britain House (burnt down 1984) and one in what is now the camping ground at the bottom of Mad Bess Wood. He ran the area as a sporting estate until 1883[42] when at another auction it was bought by Henry Richard Cox of Harefield Place and Hillingdon House who continued to manage the woods to produce timber and underwood and as game preserves for his shooting parties. Shooting rights had become important in the 19th century and are always mentioned in advertisements as an inducement to buy property and were rateable commodities.

L. J. Baker's land had included a thin strip on the south side of Breakspear Road, just east of Rose Cottage, an old encroachment upon the road. It was sold as a separate lot in 1883. The cottages which stand on part of this strip today bear a stone slab giving their name Hope Cottages and the date 1885.

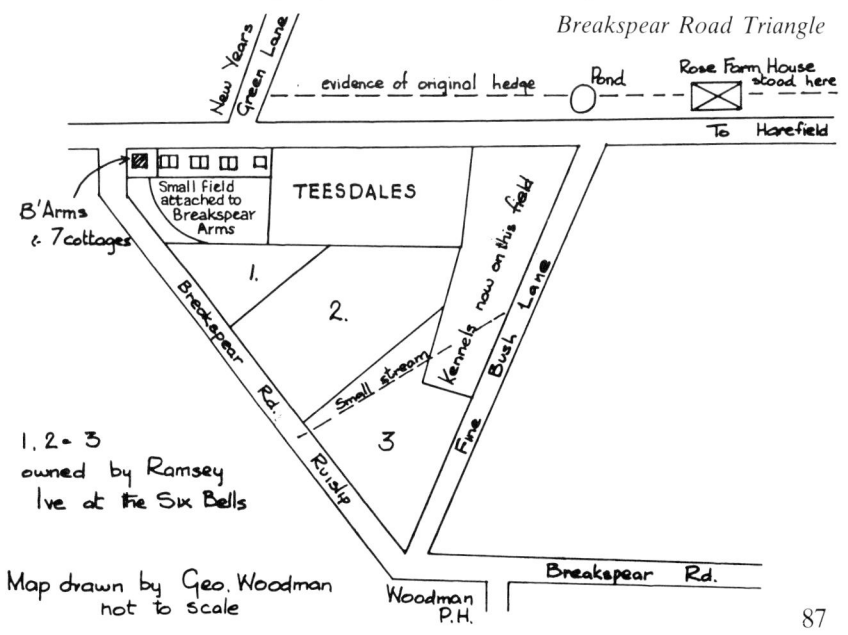

The Fine Bush Lane – Breakspeare Road Triangle

After the death of Col. Cox in 1914, the Harefield House/Hillingdon House estate was auctioned by Knight, Frank and Rutley. Mad Bess Wood, Youngwood Farm and the fields south of the wood, 274.65 acres in all, were not sold, however, until 1918 when the Cavendish Land Company purchased them from R. H. Cox.[43] The whole lot was then sold to H. S. Button (Howard Roberts the Grocer) in 1922, in two sections.[44] He lived for a time at Battle of Britain (then called Franklin House) and used the woodland for shooting. He sold Youngwood Farm and woodland and three fields (about 217 acres) to the Middlesex County Council in May 1936, and 140 acres of woodland was leased to R.N.U.D.C. for 999 years in June.[45] His executors sold the fields south of the wood to R.N.U.D.C. in 1949 for a crematorium.[46] The crematorium built in 1957 so far occupies only about one third of its land.

Three fields in the triangle formed by Fine Bush Lane, Breakspear Road and Breakspear Road North came to be owned by Ramsey Ive of the Six Bells by 1914. The land fronting Breakspear Road in the same triangle came to be known as Teasdales.[47] The field at the corner had a row of eight cottages built in it, the one on the corner becoming the Breakspear Arms. The cottages were built partly on, but mostly over, the parish boundary and therefore fell in Harefield parish. They were built after 1866 and demolished in the 1930s, with the exception of the pub which was replaced in 1975. One cottage was a small school run by a Mrs Willis, "Old Bett Willis," about whom some scurrilous tales are told.

Little Manor Farm

Little Manor Farm (called Bury Farm at the time) and the lands of Clack Farm, though not the farm house, were purchased at the 1873 sale by Sir Charles Henry Mills (later Lord Hillingdon) of Hillingdon Court. Here was another large landowner, with lands stretching south from Hillingdon Court into Hayes and east into Ruislip, who had major sporting interests. He already owned Down Barnes Farm on the southern border of Ruislip and Hundred Acres Farm in West End Road and wished to unite the two. The vicar's glebeland protruded like a tongue between them. An application by his father Sir Charles Mills (died 1873) to buy the glebeland for £7000 in 1870 had been rejected by the patrons of the living, the Dean and Canons of Windsor.[48] An increased offer of £8000 in 1872 had been acceptable to the vicar, the elderly Christopher Packe, who had lost interest in landowning since the death of his eldest son and was happy to invest the money in the three per cents, but the Dean and Chapter, concerned to preserve the value of the living, considered (wisely) that land was the safest investment and still refused to sell, but held out some hope of consenting to an exchange rather than a sale of land.

In June 1873 Sir Charles seized his opportunity at the sale of Mr Shepherd's Estate and bought Little Manor Farm, and land near Clack Farm "highly valuable and improving land very eligibly situated in close proximity to the vicarage", which he intended to give in exchange for the glebe in South Ruislip. Five more years of wrangling were to elapse before the exchange was effected. A surveyor's report in 1874 described the 80 acres of pasture land *"known as Clack Farm and Bury Farm"* as having a considerable quantity of timber giving an ornamental appearance, but alas it had not been well managed.

The farm house (Little Manor) was old but substantial requiring some repair.* There was a newly-built brick and tile cart lodge and a range of old timber and tile buildings *"which are worn out and should be removed and a brick and tile stable for 3 horses and a cowhouse for 6 cows erected in their stead."* All trees containing less than 15 cubic feet timber and some larger trees of ornamental character were recommended to be preserved. The survey concluded with the observation that the farm presented *"several admirable sites for residences"*. With railway schemes proliferating on all sides, all landowners viewed the prospect of their broad acres being built over with equanimity, thinking only of the increased value such a possibility added to their property.

Sir Charles Mills carried out and completed repairs to the farm buildings at a cost of £300 by May 1876. By this time the churchwardens and Vestry had discovered that landowners in the Little Manor were liable for the repair of public roads under the terms of the 1769 Enclosure Award, a fact concealed from them by Sir Charles. The liability would be to maintain 1 chain (22 yards) of Breakspear Road west from Howletts Lane, where a field included in the farm fronted it. Upon Sir Charles agreeing to put the road in good repair and give an extra 1½ acres the exchange was concluded and confirmed on 3 May 1877.

The land which now belonged to the vicar included the old moated site of Southcote.

Augustus Woodman, a member of the far-flung Woodman clan, had been farmer at Clack Farm in 1871 but moved to Little Manor Farm[49] soon afterwards and remained there as tenant through the glebe exchange, although he was dissatisfied with his rent of £3 per acre. The Dean and Canons were advised that if he decided to leave there were many Cowkeepers and Jobmasters in London who would readily take the land at that rent.[50] R. A. Foxlee moved there about 1885.[51] During his tenancy the name changed from Bury or Bury Street Farm to Little Manor Farm. Francis J. Small was tenant in 1902[52] and Mr R. Cross in 1922.[53]

Some of the glebeland in St. Catherine's Manor was sold for development while Mr Cornwall-Jones was Vicar (1923-38).[54] Little Manor Farmhouse with 27 acres was sold to English Houses Ltd in 1935, but the house still stands and is now a private residence. Marlborough Avenue, the northern portion of St. Margaret's Road, Coppice Close and Stanford Close were built on the former glebe before the Second World War. Houses on the south side of Arlington Drive (formerly Howletts Lane) were built in 1952.

18 acres west of Howletts Lane were sold to the owner of St. Catherine's Farm in 1924, who was then Sir Harry Trelawney-Eve.[55] Thomas Champress Parker of the Acton Bolt Company, owner of St. Catherine's Farm about 1945, established the Bees Club on the former glebeland, which later became the Sports and Social Club of Glacier Metals.

Early in the 1970s the site was threatened by a Compulsory Purchase Order. An inquiry was held after a great deal of local opposition had been expressed to council schemes. Eventually Glacier was offered a new site north of Breakspear Road and the old glebeland was developed by Y. J. Lovell between 1982-4. The new roads have been named after the Thames and its tributaries.

---

*The Royal Commission on Ancient Buildings considers Little Manor Farmhouse which has wall paintings in some rooms, to incorporate a medieval hall.

The Goodliest Place in Middlesex

The Rev. Derek Barnsley (vicar 1938-43) leased the strip of glebeland lying between the stream and the Canal Feeder to the Ruislip-Northwood Co-operative Smallholding and Allotments Society Ltd in 1939.[56] Their extended lease had three years to run when Mr Grange-Bennett, (vicar 1952-62) sold the land to J. M. Johnson Esq. of Chalfont St. Peter in March 1956.[57] The following month it was sold again to Mr Clarke and the Model Pig Farm was established there. The Council bought the land in 1972.

Wimpeys acquired the glebeland north of the Canal Feeder and built Whyteleaf Close and Stowe Crescent. They sold some of their land to the Council in 1972 and Leaholme Way and Wallington Crescent were later built as a Council development.

The glebeland surrounding Clack Farm miraculously is still fields and still belongs to the Church. For how long, one wonders!

Clack Farm

The Woodmans were tenants of Clack Farm from about 1806.[58] Augustus Woodman bought the farmhouse and 9 acres from Sir C. M. Mills in 1883. Alfred Woodman was living there in 1881. The 1881 census gives his age as 60 and his occupation as farm servant. One of his sons, Spencer, was also a farm servant and two others Alfred and George, were agricultural labourers. His wife Mary was a domestic farm servant. The son Alfred owned Clack Farm in 1902[59] and the Woodman family stayed there until 1919.[60]

Mr and Mrs Furst moved into Clack Farm after the Woodmans left and restored it. Captain A. Morris Davies followed the Fursts and began collecting timber, old doors, bannisters, fire backs and other materials from old buildings which were being demolished in various parts of the country. He incorporated these items in houses which he built around the field which had always gone with Clack Farm, creating Tile Kiln Hamlet. Lantern House was the first to be erected in 1937-8 and contains much material from Erith Castle in Kent.[61] Tile Kiln Lane is now a much sought-after area, the residents of which no longer depend upon the digging of clay and loam or the making of tiles for their livelihood.

A cottage on the site of the present Cavendish appears to have been part of Clack Farm at the beginning of the 19th century. William Scaffold was running it as a beer shop in 1851 called the Prince Albert. Later it was known as Ebeneezer Cottage. It was destroyed by fire and Cavendish was built in 1921.[62]

Southcote Farm

Southcote Farm was confined between St. Catherine's boundary behind the Vicarage, Breakspear Road, Ladygate Lane, the Pinn and the glebeland. Henry H. Partridge became the new owner after 1873 and kept it until 1905.[63] A Charles Martin had been tenant of Southcote in 1803 and by an odd coincidence another Charles Martin was the farmer a century later. Martins occupied the farm until 1854;[64] then Samuel Ives until the late 1870s. During his tenancy it was called Circuits Farm for a time. Henry James Ewer followed Samuel Ives for a few years before moving to Manor Farm in 1886. He was succeeded by Charles Martin. The Martins, the last farmers, are strongly associated with the area. Some elderly residents refer to Ladygate Lane as Martin's Lane (and occasionally as St.

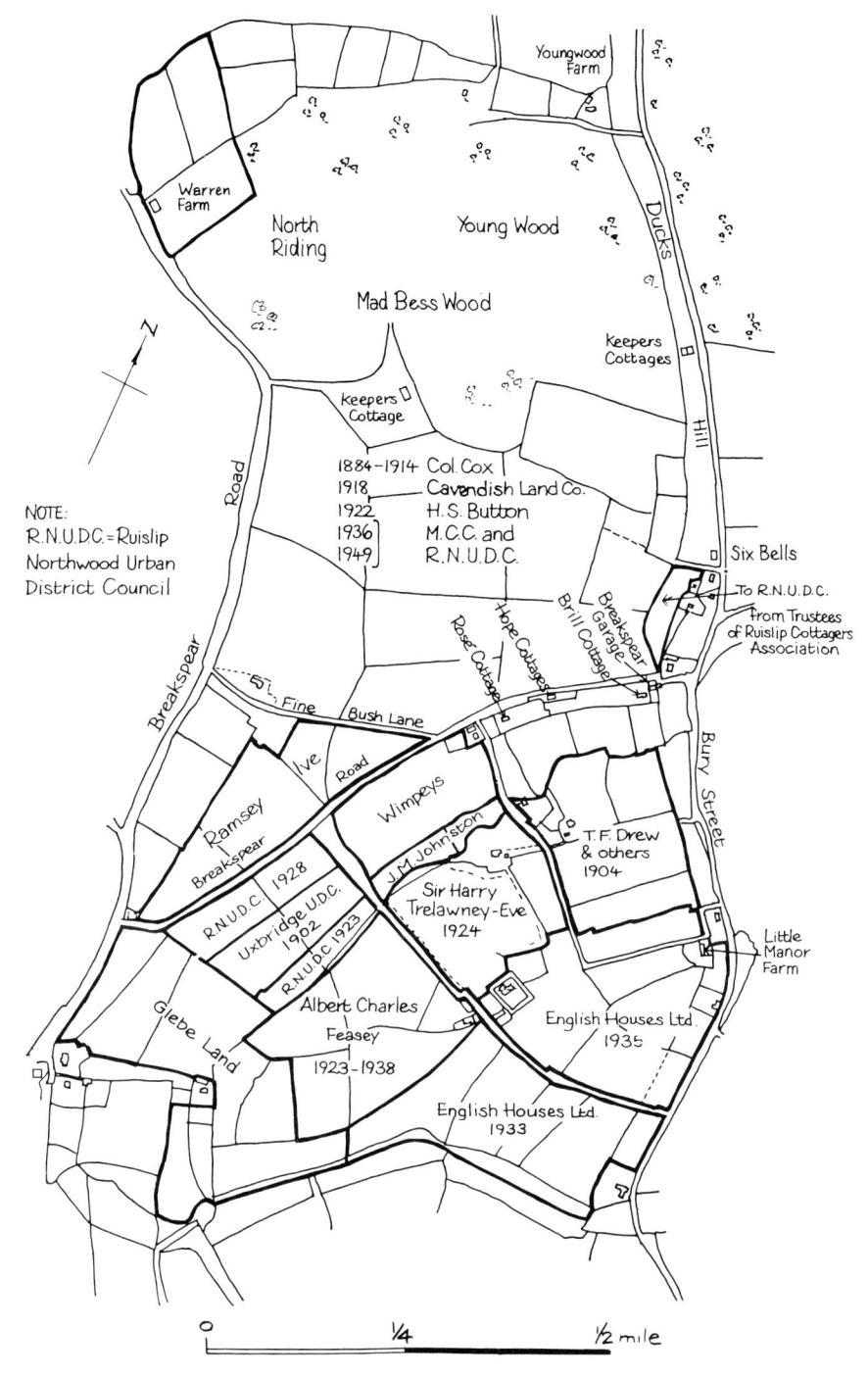

St. Catherine's – 20th Century ownership

The Goodliest Place in Middlesex

Martin's Lane). The farmhouse stood immediately south of the moat. Some farm buildings near the moat north of Ladygate Lane belonged to Southcote Farm, the only piece of land north of the lane to do so, after the St. Catherine's Sale of 1873.

Henry Haines Partridge sold 8 acres near the Canal Feeder to become a sewage farm for the parish of Ruislip in 1902.[65] Three years later he sold all the rest of the farm land and the house (56a 2r 37p) to Thomas F. Drew, a Paddington bootmaker; Arthur W. Nash, J.P. of Dunstable and George Hipwell Green, an architect, for £4,000. Mr Drew was buying other land north of Howletts Lane at the same time and appears to have been speculating in land suitable for building.

A further 8 acres east of the Sewage Works were sold to R.N.U.D.C. in 1923 and 10 acres on the west side in 1928, to extend the Sewage Farm. It was no longer needed in 1936 when the Middlesex Scheme came into operation and Ruislip sewage was taken by gravitation and pumping to Mogden near Isleworth. The site was used as the Ruislip Depot and Nursery until 1984. In 1985 150 houses were being built there.

The farmhouse and 14½ acres were sold to Albert Charles Feasey in 1923. Whiteheath Avenue and School now occupy some of the land.

The remainder of the land bought by Drew, Nash and Green in 1905, was purchased by English Houses Ltd of Wembley in 1933 who developed the southern section of St. Margaret's Road, Glenfield Crescent and Fairfield Avenue. This was the same company that bought Little Manor Farm in 1935.

Breakspear Garage

Another 16th century cottage which belonged to Shepherd and Lewin has become the Breakspear Garage. Henry Tobutt owned it by 1886 and William Buckingham in 1902 when it was called The Ferns. Land behind, as far as the Brook, went with the cottage. Mr Fountain, owner of both the Garage and Brill Cottage next door, sold the land which is crossed by the Canal Feeder to the Council in 1972. At the moment it is largely public open space.[66]

St. Catherine's Farm

St. Catherine's Farm in Howletts Lane is thought to date from the 16th century. From 1686-1700 it was owned by John Kirton of Pinner at which time it included the Long Field on the east side of Howletts Lane.

Thomas Powell succeeded him from 1700-25. James Rogers then bought it and it was part of the Eastcote House Estate for a century.[67] (See Chapter 7). In 1725 it was described as a messuage or tenement called Coats Hawe abutting onto Westcote Common. The lands were 2½ acres meadow by the lane from Bury Street to Katherine End (obviously Howletts Lane but called Holders Lane at that time) and 6 closes of meadow, arable and pasture called Lowys. There were a further 22 acres and 5 acres former wood ground in Harefield parish, between New Years Green Lane and Breakspeare Road North, also called Lowys.

By her will, dated 1803 Elizabeth Rogers left the property to her cousin Susanna Hope, spinster, for life with reversion to Ralph Deane. He sold it for £2,500 in 1825 to George Robinson of Richmond, Surrey, a builder.[68] Mr Robinson who seems to have bought up nearly every farm that came on the market in Ruislip, Ickenham and Northolt from 1818 to about 1840, purchased more property in St. Catherine's in 1837, Woodbine Cottage and the Long Field from the Stent family.[69] George Robinson died in 1852 leaving a considerable estate which became the subject of a Chancery hearing. His property was ordered to be sold in a series of sales between 1857-64. St. Catherine's Farm with 13 acres and 30 acres in Harefield was sold in 1864.[70] John Ashley and Thomas and James Godliman were tenants over this long period.

Walter Greatrex, a commission meat salesman at the Central Meat Market in the City of London (i.e. Smithfield) bought it and appears from Rate Books and Street Directories to have lived there until his death in 1898. The land between Long Field and the stream was added to the small estate and known locally as the Cow Field. Whether he used the land for grazing cattle in connection with his trade is not known. Florence L. Greatrex Emmet sold the whole property to Thomas F. Drew, A. Russan and H. Crawford in 1904.[71]

The land east of Howletts Lane became part of the St. Catherine's Estate (St. Catherine's Road and the south side of Bury Avenue) developed by Thomas Drew Associates from 1910 and later by H.T.H. Syndicates Ltd.[72] A house in Bury Avenue is called Long Field. Building plots between Bury Avenue and the stream were not developed and were purchased by the M.C.C. in 1937.[73] R.N.U.D.C. leased the land from M.C.C. in 1938. A Council development, Standale Grove, was built in 1976 despite the fact that it was green belt land by that time and had been intended as public open space.

The farmhouse and 6 acres surrounding it were owned by William Kirk, a veterinary surgeon from Tottenham, from 1912-21.[74] The Dog Sanatorium which he ran there was advertised in local papers as *"A country home for your dog in sickness or in health"*. A sign attached to the pump outside The George pub pointed the direction to it. Sceptical residents believed that Mr Kirk's treatment simply consisted of exercising overfed dogs in the healthy air of rural Ruislip while feeding them on a meagre diet. Some died and a dogs' cemetery was established at the further end of St. Catherine's Farm gardens.

The next owner Sir Henry Trelawney Eve, a judge (1921-7), also used the cemetery and reserved the right to visit it after he sold the estate to A. S. Priest of Greyhound and Breeding Kennels Ltd.[75] The remaining dogs' gravestones were rescued and repaired by Mrs Elsa Glover c. 1983 and are now fixed to the wall just inside the Bury Street entrance to Manor Farm Library.

Mr Wicks, a bank manager from Wembley, was the last pre-war owner. The farmhouse was used by the Home Guard during the Second World War and purchased by T. C. Parker of the Acton Bolt Company shortly afterwards. Two more private owners followed Mr Parker, one of whom ran a stables there.

Council plans to develop the Model Pig Farm and St. Catherine's Farm together in 1967, brought threats of a C.P.O. and caused local controversy. The Department of the Environment considered that the land made no material contribution to the green belt and allowed housing development in principle.

The owners sold to the London Borough of Hillingdon and municipal housing was begun in the late 1970s; the farmhouse being incorporated in the scheme. The house had never been listed. A letter from the Department of the Environment written in April 1975 explains *"Although we appreciate that it has Tudor origins we understand that it has been so altered that it could not now be regarded as having special interest."* Did anyone actually come and look at it, one wonders?

Woodbine Cottage

Woodbine Cottage in Tile Kiln Lane is a listed building which was evidently built in three stages; a 16th century timber-framed cottage, a later timber-framed addition and a taller 18th century section. It was the cottage and tile-house which belonged to Henry Arnall in 1769 and to William Stent before 1806. Thirty-one years later George Robinson paid £515 to William Stent, butcher of Charles Street, Westminster, for the cottage, Kiln and Long Field.[76] John Stent then occupied the house and John Weedon rented the field.

Francis Woodman was in occupation by 1845. He was a hay dealer and bought the cottage at some stage. Martha Woodman, aged 68, was the head of the household in 1881, which included two boarders: a 19-year old girl classed as an imbecile and a 13-year-old scholar. The cottage has been restored since the Second World War and is still a private house with its land intact. Pieces of the tiles once made there are often dug from the garden.

The Woodman

The Woodman, built on the corner of Howletts Lane and Breakspear Road, beside Oak Cottage, is referred to for the first time in the 1847 Rate Book when George Harman (later Harman's Brewery) owned it and Joseph Hill was the tenant. The Hill family remained into the 1860s. T. Andrews was landlord from the 1880s to this century.[77] The building has been so modernised that it is barely recognisable as a 19th century building.

Brill Cottage

A 16th century timber-framed building it was owned by William Blackstaff poulterer of Christ Church, Middlesex, in 1769 and by the Rev. Richard Glover in 1806.[78] It was rated as a shop in the 1840s when John Weedon owned it, but Thomas Collins lived there. In 1902 it was the home of J. H. Wallis and owned by Austin Carley.[79] The name seems to have been applied to it when "Shorty" Brill, woodward, lived there about the time of the First World War. Today it is a private residence and stands in a secluded position behind the forecourt of the Breakspear Garage.

Rose Cottage

This is an old building with a timber frame hidden behind a brick facade, often overlooked by passers-by as it lies well back from Breakspear Road, a little east of Howletts Lane. It belonged to Mary Anderson in 1769 and to her husband James Ewer in 1806.[80] By 1901 its land extended to the Canal Feeder along the backs of the houses in Breakspear Road. This was purchased by the Council in 1973 and Brickett Close was built a few years later. The council development has been built onto the Canal Feeder itself, which has had its water diverted, presumably into the Cannon Brook, and has been all but obliterated in the Howletts Lane area.

Warren Farm

Warren Farm on Breakspear Road North was not built until after 1866 as it is not shown on the 25 inch Ordnance Survey Map of that year. The three fields between the wood and the old parish boundary were a small estate without buildings which belonged to Mr Peter Stiles in 1789 and to John Stiles in 1806. Later it became part

St Catherine's Manor and Southcote

of the Breakspear Estate. The late 19th century owner probably had the farmhouse built. It was unfortunately hit by a flying bomb during the Second World War, which is why the house presents such a modern appearance.

REFERENCES
1. V.C.H. Middlesex Vol. I p. 202.
2. G.L.R.O. Acc. 446 ED. 103.
3. *'Select Documents of the Abbey of Bec'*.
4. G.L.R.O. Acc. 446/L1/14 and 17.
5. King's College: R. 36.
6. V.C.H. Middlesex Vol. IV p. 136.
7. Ibid.
8. Ibid.
9. G.L.R.O. Acc. 249 153.
10. G.L.R.O. Acc. 446 ED. 103.
11. V.C.H. Middlesex Vol. IV p. 136.
12. G.L.R.O. Acc. 446 EM 37.
13. Ruislip Library: Sales Catalogue dated 1803 (photocopy).
14. V.C.H. Middlesex Vol. IV p. 135.
15. Ibid.
16. Ibid.
17. G.L.R.O. Acc. 446 EM 37.
18. P.R.O. 128/1430.
19. Ruislip Library: Copy of St. Catherine's Enclosure Act.
20. Uxbridge Library: Kiddle – Historical Geography of North-West Middlesex.
21. V.C.H. Middlesex Vol. IV p. 7.
22. G.L.R.O. Acc. 446 ED. 103.
23. Pedigree of Seymer of Hanford, Dorset.
24. P.R.O. Prob 11/221 f. 66 – transcript by J. McBean – Ruislip Library.
25. Pedigree of Seymer of Hanford, Dorset.
26. British Library Add. M.S. 9368.
27. Pedigree of Seymer of Hanford, Dorset.
28. V.C.H. Middlesex, Vol. IV p. 135.
29. Ruislip Library: St. Catherine's Enclosure Act.
30. G.L.R.O. Acc. 865/3.
31. G.L.R.O. L.V. 6/84.
32. G.L.R.O. DRO 19 E3/1.
33. King's College: Workhouse Map Q 48 – photocopy: Ruislip Library.
34. G.L.R.O. DRO 19 E3/1.
35. G.L.R.O. Ruislip Enclosure Award and Map. MR/DE RUI E2/1-2.
36. St. Martin's Church: Mural monument.
37. Letter from County Archivist, Somerset Record Office to J. McBean.
38. Ruislip Library: Photocopy.
39. Gravestone Herringfleet Church – Ex info. Doreen Edwards.
40. Letter from County Archivist, Somerset to J. McBean.
41. Uxbridge Library: Advertiser and Gazette.
42. Ruislip Library: Photocopy Sales Catalogue.
43. Ruislip Library: Copy Conveyance 1918.
44. Ibid: Copy Conveyance 1922.
45. Document penes London Borough of Hillingdon.
46. Ibid.

The Goodliest Place in Middlesex

47. Ex info. George Woodman.
48. St. George's, Windsor: XVII 38 8 Et seq.
49. Census Returns 1871 and G.L.R.O. DRO 19 E2/1-60.
50. St. George's, Windsor: XVII 38 8.
51. Uxbridge Library: Ruislip Parish Rate Books.
52. Ibid.
53. Ibid: Street Directories.
54. G.L.R.O.: Middlesex Deeds Registry.
55. Ruislip Library: Copy Conveyance.
56. Ibid.
57. Ibid.
58. G.L.R.O. DRO 19 E2/1-60.
59. Uxbridge Library: Ruislip Parish Rate Books.
60. Ex info. Mrs Kerr.
61. Ex info. Mr Ethinger.
62. Ex info. J. Sweasey.
63. Deeds of a house in St. Margaret's Road.
64. Et seq. G.L.R.O. DRO 19 E2/1-60; Uxbridge Library; Ruislip Parish Rate Book.
65. Et seq. Deeds of house in St. Margaret's Road and documents penes LBH.
66. Uxbridge Library; Ruislip Parish Rate Book and documents penes LBH.
67. G.L.R.O. Acc. 249/1778.
68. G.L.R.O. Acc. 538/2nd dep./4552 A.
69. Ibid. 4553a.
70. G.L.R.O. Acc. 398/18.
71. Documents penes LBH.
72. Deeds of a house in St. Catherine's Road.
73. Documents penes LBH.
74. Ibid.
75. Ibid.
76. G.L.R.O. Acc. 538/2nd dep./4553a.
77. Uxbridge Library: Street Directories.
78. G.L.R.O. DRO 19 E2/1-60.
79. Uxbridge Library; Ruislip Parish Rate Books.
80. G.L.R.O. Acc. 538/2nd dep./3657.

Chapter Six

The Manor of Ruislip and King's College

Lessees of the Demesne

King's College held the Manor of Ruislip from 1451 until manorial rights were suppressed by the Act of 1925. As absentee Lords of the Manor, the Provost and Scholars chose to administer the estate by farming out the demesne, the woods and other manorial prerogatives, sometimes together and sometimes separately, a process already started by the Abbey of Bec as we have already seen with their 14th century leases of Northwood to Roger Redinge (pre 1384) and to John St. George and his wife (1384) (see Chapter 3). The earliest lease mentioned in the King's College Ledger Books is to Thomas Betts in 1471, who leased both demesne and woods. Demesne leasing continued until 1872 after which the woods were retained in hand and Manor Farm alone was let out.

Table 1. Manorial Leases from King's College – c. 1471-1872[1]

1471	Thomas Betts	Demesne and woods
1472	John Butts	Demesne and woods
1480	James Edlin	Demesne and woods
1505	Robert Drury	Demesne only. Woods to Thos. Bowman
1529	Roger More	Demesne only
1539	John Russell	Demesne only
1549	Thomas Street	
1561	John Smith	
1589	Robert Christmas	Demesne and woods
1602	Sir Robert Cecil	Demesne and woods and right to dig marl
1603	Robert Earl of Salisbury	Demesne and woods and right to dig marl
1618	Wm. Earl of Salisbury	Demesne and woods
	(lease renewed 1625, 1633, 1644, 1650, 1657, 1664)	
1669	Ralph Hawtrey (renewed 1676)	
1683	Richard Hawtrey and Christopher Clitheroe	
1690	Richard Hawtrey	
1697	Ralph Hawtrey (renewed 1705, 1712, 1719)	
1727	James Rogers (renewed 1733)	
1741	Elizabeth Rogers (renewed 1747, 1755, 1761, 1768, 1775, 1782, 1789, 1796)	
1803	Rev. Geo. Deane and Charles James (renewed 1810)	
1817	Ralph Deane (renewed 1824, 1831, 1838, 1845)	
1852-72	Francis Deane, Alfred Caswell, John Walters trustees under will of Ralph Deane	

The Lessees and their Rights

John Smith, one of the 1577 deponents already quoted (Chapter 3) is known to have lived at Ruislip Court (now Manor Farm) and is thereby unusual among the demesne farmers who in the main simply treated the leases as investments and lived elsewhere, sub-leasing the farm.[2]

Roger More's lease of 1529 describes him as the King's baker.[3] The Provost and Scholars let to him their Manor or Priory of Ruislip with all lands, tenements, meadows, feedings, pastures and rents appertaining to it. They reserved to themselves: fines (payments made when property changed hands); amercements (fine, in a manorial court); View of Frankpledge (inspection of the tithings – groups of manorial tenants – usually at the manor court); leets (manor courts with special powers); wards (right to administer the estates of orphaned minors); marriages (right to sell marriage licences); homages (pledges of loyalty by tenants to their lord); scutages ("shield money" a tax paid by the Lord of the Manor to free him from the obligation to provide an armed force – usually recovered from his tenants); reliefs (fines payable by incoming tenants when inheriting land); heriots (death-duties – the best beast of the deceased); escheats (reversion to the lord of the estates of tenants who died without heirs); strays; waifs; franchises; warrens; swarms of bees and palfrey silver (payment made to a new lord in lieu of the palfrey i.e. riding-horse presented to him in earlier times).

Most of the above were customary manorial rights and privileges. Although set out at length most had almost certainly been commuted for money payments and absorbed into the annual rents paid by the copyhold tenants of the manor long before the 16th century. The Provost and Scholars also reserved the woods and underwoods. In fact they were let under a separate lease to Thomas Bowman. Even so Roger More was granted heybote, housebote, ploughbote and firebote, that is the right to have timber and wood allocated to him to repair hedges, his house and ploughs and for fuel. Each year he was to have a gown "like the gentlemen of the College wore" or ten shillings instead.

Roger for his part must pay £68.13s.4d a year, maintain the buildings in good repair and receive into the stable, called the College stable, the horses of the Provost with their horse-keepers whensoever and as often as the Provost should wish to send them, not exceeding 12 horses. Roger was to provide hay, oats, straw and litter, being allowed 4d a week per horse for the hay, straw and litter and 2s.8d for a quarter of oats. Whether College officials made much use of this clause is not known, but as John Smith obtained an agreement in 1568 freeing himself from the obligation in return for paying an extra £7 per annum, it may have inconvenienced the demesne farmers.[4]

The mid 16th Century was a period of high inflation which found King's College, an institution with a largely fixed income, short of ready cash, so it may have been to raise money that four leases were sold to Robert Christmas of Lavenham in 1565-6.[5] Two of them were leases in reversion as existing leases to third parties were not due to expire until 1579 and 1589 respectively. Robert Christmas no doubt had to pay a fine for each lease which helped to swell the College's coffers. He leased the Common Wood for 99 years from 1565; the Courts and Profits of Courts for 20 years from 1566; Woods growing in the Park for 30 years from 1579; Manor or Priory of Ruislip for 20 years from 1589. This meant that Robert Christmas eventually leased all the rights, privileges and profits arising out of the Manor of Ruislip.

His leases were due to expire in 1586: the Profits of Courts; 1609: the Manor and Park; 1664: the Common Wood.

It is not known when Robert Christmas, who has proved an elusive character to trace, died, but before any of these periods had elapsed other men had taken over the leases. A decree in chancery dated 1580-1[6] granted fines, profits of court etc., as previously leased to Mr Christmas, to Robert Ashby of Breakspears, Harefield, following a dispute between Mr Christmas and the tenants (see below). Mr Ashby also acquired the remainder of the Common Wood lease and sold it in February 1605 to Robert Cecil, first Earl of Salisbury for £1750 and one basin and ewer of gilt weighing 100 ounces.[7]

A Mr Smith, whether or not the same John Smith as 1565 is not known, was in possession of the demesne in 1596 and Mr Hawtrey of Eastcote House (Chapter 7) held the Park.[8] Robert Cecil obtained both these leases in 1602, as a result of influence exerted on his behalf by a Mr Tredway, *"one of the ancient Seniors of the College"*. Cecil already Chancellor of Cambridge University first compounded with the existing tenants, Mr Smith and Mr Hawtrey then wrote to the Provost and Scholars seeking their acquiescence in January 1602.[9] The business was completed in December 1602 when Dr Goade, Provost wrote to tell Cecil that it had passed with *"good and general consent which he was glad to see especially in a time and state of a young multitude of some distemper"*. Apparently a faction among the younger fellows was opposed to Cecil.[10]

Although the Cecils, Earls of Salisbury continued as principal lessees of the manor and woods until 1669, it is evident that they sub-leased the Park to the Hawtreys, for Ralph Hawtrey who died in 1638 mentions such a lease in his will, leaving it to his son John.[11] The first Earl of Salisbury has left his mark upon Ruislip to this day. To him we owe the open spaces between Park and Copse Woods (Poors Field, Haste Hill Golf Course, Northwood Golf Course), for he stripped the timber trees from 568 acres of the Common Wood in 1608 which brought him £4000 and no doubt helped build the new Hatfield House.[12] James I had given him Hatfield in exchange for Theobalds in 1606. The Hawtreys obtained leases of both woods and demesne in 1669. They and their descendants the Rogers and Deanes remained in peaceful possession of Ruislip Demesne until 1872.[13] Although not resident at Ruislip Court, (Manor Farm) where they put in a tenant farmer, they lived only a mile away at Eastcote House and were closely involved in parish affairs, which may account for the apparent lack of tension between Demesne Farmer and the copyhold tenants during the next two hundred years.

The Tenants and their Rights

The ordinary tenants of the manor owned their messuages or cottages, farmed the sellions belonging to them in the common fields and tended the small crofts by their houses, for all of which they paid small copyhold rents to the manorial lessee. Tenants who owned land in the common fields also had grazing rights over them, after harvest and on the fallow fields, even over those which were within the demesne, Church Field, Windmill Field (Gt and Lt), Marlpit Field and Bourne Field.

When a tenant wished to sell a house or land he arranged the transaction privately but had to surrender the property publicly to the new owner in the manor courts. A fine was paid. Similarly if a tenant died, his heir had to come to court to take seisin of his property and pay a fine. These fines swelled the profit of courts enormously.

Both these matters caused disputes between the tenants and the manorial lessees during the 16th century. One was settled (1519-21).[14] Sixteen persons testified on oath that the tenants had enjoyed pasture rights for cattle, geese or pigs over Windmill Field, Bourne Field and Bourne Wyck until about 18 years previously when they had been disturbed in their rights by James Edlyn, Demesne Farmer who had fenced the fields and converted them from arable to enclosed pasture. More hedging, ditching and erecting of gates had taken place about three years ago. The inquisition was heard at Uxbridge before the King's Escheator for Middlesex and was considered again at Westminster a month later. According to the complainants the carriage roads and footpaths across these fields, including the roads to London, Harrow, Northall (Northolt) and Southall had been obstructed. More seriously they declared that thirty persons had been deprived of work and fifteen cottages had become desolate, their inhabitants vagrant. (Ten dwellings were still ruinous in 1565). Commissioners appointed to act as arbitrators upheld the tenants' rights to common pasture and free access to these fields.

The problem must have continued as in 1544 Ruislip tenants headed by John Smith and Ralph Hawtrey brought a Bill in Chancery complaining that Guy Wade (Thomas Street's sub lessee perhaps) *"keepeth the said common fields wholly to his own use and will not suffer the said orators to...enjoy their said ways and common of pasture and whereby the said inhabitants are not able to mention and keep their cattall (i.e. plough animals probably oxen) for the tillage and maintaining of their land and ground belonging to their said holdings to their great loss and utter undoing".*[15]

Whether the loss of grazing on two large and one small field (Bourne Wyck) when at least eight other common fields could provide pasture, really led to a serious loss of plough animals seems open to question. The tenants were probably overstating their case. The final outcome is not known, but Bourn Wyck (Torcross Road area) remained enclosed and appears as an Old Enclosure on the 1806 Enclosure Map. Bourne Field and Gt and Lt Windmill Field are not described as Common in 1565 either.[16]

Grazing on the *"freshe and fallow"* fields continued until the Parliamentary Enclosure at the beginning of the 19th century. It was regulated by the manor court in the 16th century to ensure a fair division of rights and to prevent overgrazing. By the middle of the next century manor courts were less influential than they had once been and this may have been why the principal tenants drew up *"an agreement mead betweene Nayebors for the renewing and maintaining of ouer orders of ouer fields of Ruyslipp"* in 1651.[17]

The document mentions cattle, hogs and pigs as the animals normally put to graze in Ruislip's fields, but is unfortunately slightly damaged just where the number of animals each man was allowed to graze, is stated. Enough remains to make it clear that a man's stint (share) depended upon the quantity of common field land which he held. Cottagers with no strips in the fields were dependent upon their enclosed crofts, the Common Wood (a vast expanse of waste after the timber was cleared in 1608) and pieces of roadside waste for their animals.

Fines were imposed on the owners of straying animals which were driven to the pounds by the hayward, who had a general oversight of the common fields as well as the care of the fences. Doharty's Map of 1750 shows the pound

The Manor of Ruislip and King's College

where the War Memorial now stands, but later it was moved to the greensward in front of Numbers 58-60 Bury Street, where it remained within living memory.

Other rules concerned gleaning after harvest. Anyone putting animals into the Wheat Field *"before the pore people hath gathered up what they will"* was to be fined one shilling. Gleaning of wheat only was to be permitted, not peas, beans, barley or oats. This last clause shows that the crops grown in 17th century Ruislip differed very little from those of four hundred years earlier.

The tenants were more successful in their dispute concerning fines. 134 Ruislip tenants complained to King's College in 1579 that they *"the said copyholders find themselves greatlie grieved by excessive fines taken of them"* by Robert Christmas at the Manor Courts at any change of tenant.[18] The Provost and Scholars heard their appeal and agreed that after the expiration of Mr Christmas' lease (1586) fines would be fixed at the equivalent of one years' rent for the space of forty years and the profits of the Courts would no longer be farmed out. Rents, however, were doubled. The hundred per cent increase in rents was quite reasonable in view of recent inflation and the fact that the rates being paid were virutally unaltered from those mentioned in the 1245 Customal.

A note on the payment of rents may be appropriate here. It was agreed that they should be paid at the Mansion House of the Provost and Scholars called "The Provost's Lodging" situate in the parish of St. Andrew near Baynards Castle (close to the modern Mermaid Theatre). The rents had to be paid in two equal portions at Lady Day (25 March) and Michaelmas (29 September). One wonders if all Ruislip decamped to London on these days regarding them as general holidays or whether one or two representatives only travelled with all the money in their saddlebags perhaps with an armed guard.

Within a year of this settlement Robert Ashby had been granted use of all profits of court, as previously leased to Mr Christmas.[19] The Courts were to be held in the manor house (now Manor Farm) "where they have been usually kept" and a new steward, Henry Clarke was appointed, replacing John Newdegate of Harefield Place, who was alleged to have kept some of the court rolls in his custody. Incidentally John Newdegate was married to a daughter of John Smith probably the previous demesne farmer.

No more is heard of the fines until 1616 toward the end of the 40 years period when Ruislip Copyholders again sought a Bill of Chancery seeking further assurances about their rent from the College. An Act of Parliament was obtained ratifying the earlier agreement on the part of the College.[20]

The Demesne

Two major surveys were undertaken on behalf of King's College, in 1565[21] and 1750.[22] The 1565 Terrier (Terrarius = Land roll) covered the whole manor and provides us for the first time with a full description of the demesne lands, including the names of the various meadows with their abbuttals which make it possible to work out their positions. 185 years later John Doharty of Worcester was commissioned to survey and map (how sensible!) the demesne lands only. He constantly referred back to the 1565 Terrier – and interleaved his own survey with transcripts of the relevant pages, which suggests that he considered the Terrier the most reliable previous survey, even though a more recent terrier of the leasehold lands of the Earl of Salisbury had been made in 1643.

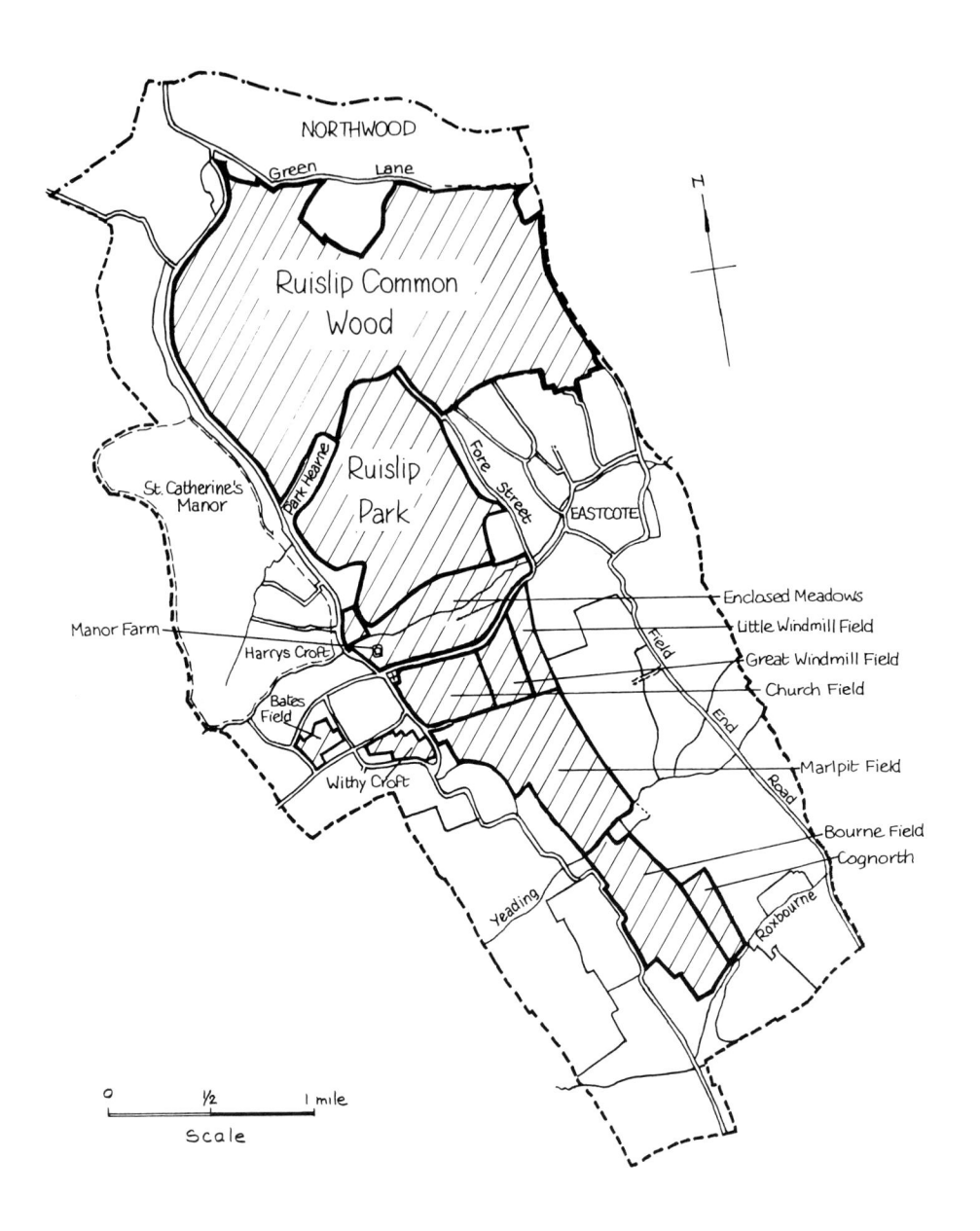

The Demesne 1565

The Manor of Ruislip and King's College

The demesne covered nearly a third of the total area and was concentrated in a central band of the manor, both north and south of the manor house, now Manor Farm. It is shown in Table 2:

Table 2. DEMESNE		1565	1750	
		Wood acres	Statute acres	Wood acres
Woodland	Ruislip Common Wood	860 acres	335 0 0	280 2 10
	Ruislip Park	357 acres	407 3 7	341 2 4
Enclosed Meadowland	along the Pinn and around Manor Farm	170 acres	160 2 7	134 0 34
Arable Land	Church Field	73 acres	66 1 24	55 2 17
	Great Windmill Field	42 acres	40 0 4	33 2 2
	Marlpit Field	236 acres	209 0 2	174 3 26
	Bourne Field	168 acres	149 0 7	124 3 12
	Little Windmill Field	7 acres	7 2 0	6 1 5
	Cognorth	24 acres	31 1 0	26 0 30
Enclosed Pasture	Harry's Croft	12 acres	13 3 0	11 2 3
	Withy Crofts	19 acres	21 1 15	17 3 19
	Bates Field	15 acres	16 0 22	13 2 39

The standard unit of measurement in Ruislip until the Enclosure was the wood acre based upon an 18 foot pole, instead of the statute acre based on the 16½ foot pole, a fact noted by Doharty and commented upon by Lysons. Doharty's survey gives both measures. It will be noticed that neither the wood nor statute acres of 1750 match the 1565 figures exactly. The largest discrepancy, in the size of the Common Wood, is accounted for by Robert Cecil's clearance of 1608 which left only the Coppice (Copse Wood) and the rest of the former woodland as waste. Otherwise Doharty's measurements are probably the most reliable. He probably came to Ruislip himself to make the survey (and charged the College 6d an acre),[23] whereas the area was not physically surveyed in 1565. Information was given on oath at a special court presumably from ancient measurements written down in leases and court rolls. Measurements in the Terrier, therefore, are never exact, and are given to the nearest half acre, never in acres, roods and perches. Furthermore, measurements given in the Terrier fail to tally (sometimes to an alarming degree) with those given for the same pieces of land in a Rental, (see below) which forms part of the same document.

In 1565, the enclosed meadow was mainly around Manor Farm and along the Pinn. The entry in the Terrier runs *"The Demesne Farmer holds the Mansion House of the Manor of Ruislip with barns, stables, dovecots, gardens, orchards, with the courtyard and with one close called the Ortyearde, with a meadow called Copwell Mede and with the Hither Moor and the Further Moor and with the meadow called Twenty Acres and with the meadow called Seven Acres, with Roberts Mead and Reeves Mead and Le Hither Horse Close, Middle Horse Close and Further Horse Close containing in all 170 acres."* Doharty's Map which has a key shows exactly where these fields were, though some sub-divisions had taken place by 1750. The Moors had become Batts Moor, Osier Moor, Alder Moor, the Grazing Moor and Flag Moor for example and there were six Horse

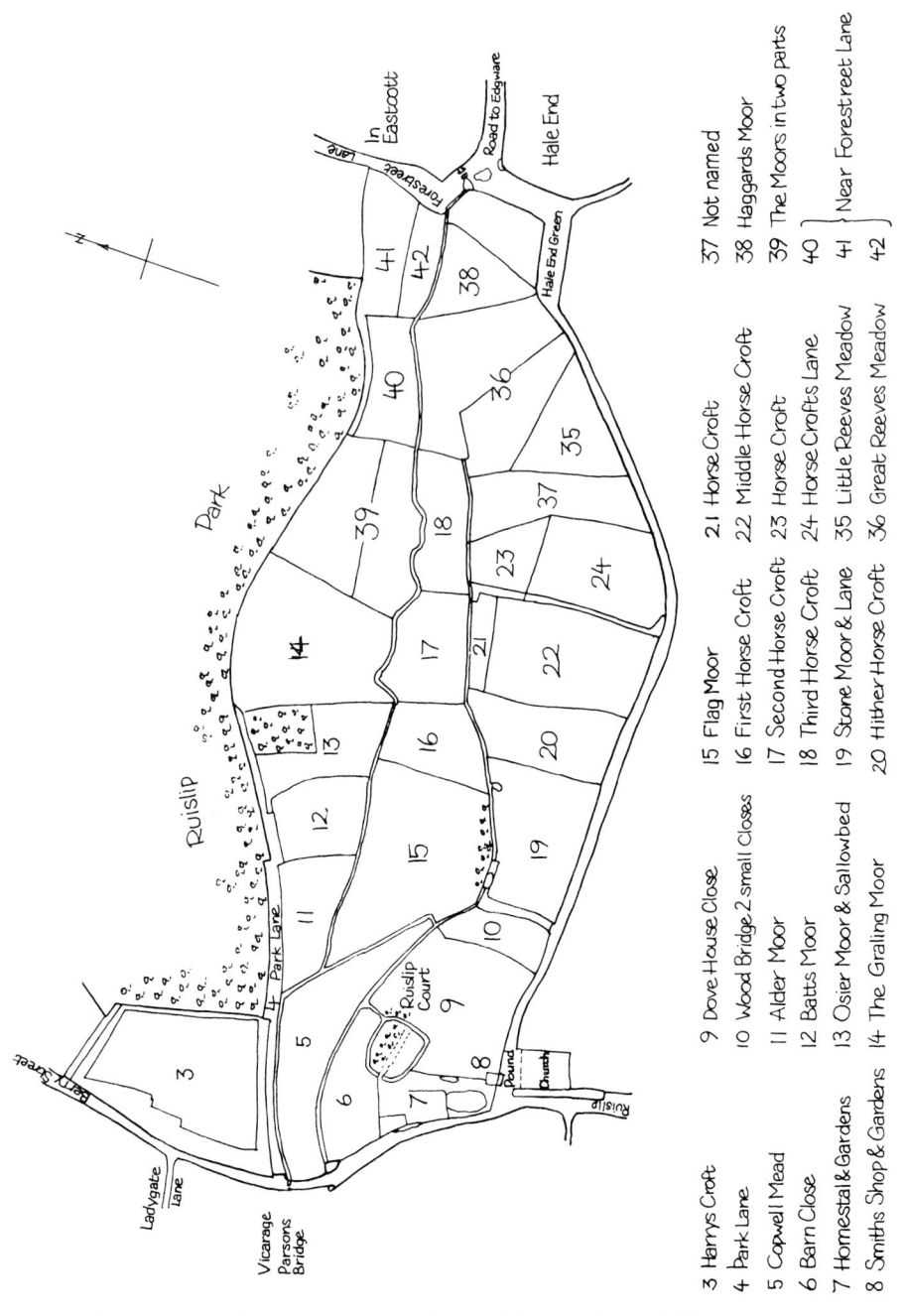

Doharty's map of the enclosed meadows of Manor Farm 1750

104

The Manor of Ruislip and King's College

Crofts. The Moors, a name signifying a wet place, lay north of the Pinn and formed a large part of what are now known as the Pinn Fields. The Horse Crofts south of the river are still partly open space, but Evelyn Avenue, Blaydon Close, Brook Drive, Brook Close, Meadow Close, King's College Road (south of the Pinn) and houses on the north side of Eastcote Road roughly from Pinn Way to a point opposite the Ridgeway, have all been built in them. Elmbridge Drive cuts through Reeves Mead. The exact position of Roberts Mead, the Twenty Acres and Seven Acres are not known as they are not mentioned by Doharty. Three meadows where the old Coteford School now stands and the open space west of Elmbridge Drive, vaguely described by Doharty as *"Near Fore Street"* are probably the Seven Acres. The other two fields had probably been incorporated in the Moors and Horse Crofts by 1750.

The above meadows all lie within the boundary of the Park mentioned in Domesday Book. Copwell Mead, mentioned in[24] 1435/6 is the meadow between Bury Street and Pinn Way, now divided into two by the roadway to Winston Churchill Hall. Harris Croft mentioned in the 14th century, is one of the enclosed pasture fields now occupied by Mead Way, allotment gardens and the east side of Bury Street from the Pinn to Park Avenue. The other enclosed pastures, Bates Field, now part of Ruislip Golf Course and Withy Crofts between Wood Lane, Ickenham Road and High Street/West End Road, are also early enclosures and mentioned in 14th century documents.

Demesne arable in 1565 lay in Church Field (Eastcote Road – Brickwall Lane), Great and Little Windmill Fields, Marlpit Field (Brickwall Lane – Yeading Brook), and Bourne Field (south of the Yeading Brook), forming a consolidated central band between the other common fields of Westcote; Tybber Field, Hill Field, Whittingrove Field and Roxbourne; and those of Eastcote; Steane Field, Well Field, East Field and Roxbourne above Roxbourne. Gt and Lt Windmill Fields were entirely demesne land, but a few copyholders had sellions intermixed with demesne land in the other fields, which perhaps illustrates how land had gradually been gathered into the demesne, probably by a process of purchase and exchange which had not been completed.

The intermixed copyhold formed only a small percentage of the fields in question. It is shown in Table 3.

Table 3. Copyhold land in Demesne Fields.

	1565 wood acres Copyhold	Demesne	1750 wood acres Copyhold	Demesne
Church Field	7 acres	73 acres	6a:	55 acres
Bourne Field	13 acres	168 acres	11a:	124 acres
Marlpit Field	31 acres	236 acres	30a:	174 acres
Total	51 acres	477 acres	47a:	353 acres

Between West End Road and the main part of Marlpit Field were several shots; Rush Shot, Pinfold Shot, White Butts Shot, Kings Wythy Shot, Rythe Shot, Goose Acre Shot and New Field Shot, composed entirely of copyhold land amounting to roughly 75 acres. Rush Shot and Rythe Shot were divided from the main field by the Rivee Brook which ran between the present

The Goodliest Place in Middlesex

Cornwall Road, Willow Gardens and Denbigh Close and accounts for the curve in Cornwall Road. New Pond Playing Fields are on New Field Shot and White Butts Shot, which became New Pond Farm in the 19th century. (See Chapter 11).
    If Doharty excluded these areas from Marlpit Field it would account for the difference in size between 1565 and 1750.
    A note in the margin of the Terrier in Doharty's handwriting says that Bourne Field seems to have been formed out of Roxbourne Field. He was probably right. It looks as though Roxbourne was originally a very large common field crossing the manor from east to west, south of the Yeading and that Bourne Field was enclosed out of it, probably by James Edlyn, in the late 15th century.
    John Redding of Field End (later Field End House Farm) held 39 of the 51 intermixed copyhold acres in 1565. The Reddings had been in Ruislip since at least 1232 when Robert de Reding had granted 13½ acres to the Abbey of Bec and were well established landowners.[25] The 39 acres may have been an ancient half hyde holding of the Reddings who were powerful enough to prevent it being taken over by the lord of the manor.
    A later John Redinge was under-tenant of Manor Farm and much of the enclosed pasture and meadow around it in 1685[26] but the family had disappeared from Ruislip by 1750, by which time the intermixed copyhold land had been divided between many more people.
    John Doharty showed by his cross-reference with the Terrier that the demesne was substantially the same in 1750 as in 1565 except for the clearance of the Common Wood, but some minor changes in land use had occurred. Harris Croft, part of Bates Field and some of the Horse Crofts (all former pasture) had become arable; most of the moors had been turned into pasture and Withycrofts into meadow. Perhaps the difference between meadow and pasture should be explained here. A meadow is land covered with grass which is mown for hay; pasture is grassland, grazed by animals.

Manor Farm House

Manor Farm lies at the centre of the demesne. It is spoken of as Ruislip Court in the 16th century[27] and so labelled on Doharty's Map and is described as the Mansion House in the Terrier. It stands north-east of the mound or motte (kitchen garden 1985) and immediately east of the foundations of the Priory, but within the 11th century moated enclosure, squeezed between the Priory and the moat. The date of the house is uncertain. It is listed as 16th century and 18th century. The last major restoration took place in 1958. While work was being carried out by Walker-Symondson Limited, Harold J. Wood, Engineer and Surveyor to R.N.U.D.C. examined the building and noted that the west wing seemed to have extended further west formerly and that the first floor of the north wall and of the east gable appeared to have been jettied out at one time. The close studding and brick nogging suggest an early 16th century date. Windows and doors seem to have been replaced in the 18th century and the off-shot kitchen was largely rebuilt in 1958.
    It was probably built by King's College to replace the Priory buildings as a more modern Manor House. The Priory itself was still standing in 1613 when the Provost and Earl of Salisbury gave leave to take down "the old ruinated fryer's hall", which was probably spoiling the view![28]

The 1565 Terrier

The Terrier throws a great deal of light upon the layout of the whole of Ruislip, not just the demesne. It is a document of 51 folios written in Latin. It is headed....

"*An extent and terrier of all cottages, tenements and other buildings of both free and customary tenants....together with gardens, orchards and other enclosures situated within the vill of Ruislip with boundaries, roads and lanes as hereafter set down.*"

The manor is divided into three sections: Westcote stretching from the northern boundary of what is now Copse Wood to Down Barnes; Ascotte, the modern Eastcote covering the area running south from the top of Wiltshire Lane to Northolt; Norwood, lying north of the woods, the present Northwood. Each section is treated separately and is dealt with street by street. First the tenant's name is set out, then the type of dwelling and the size of croft, followed by an exact description of its position and usually by the date of the tenant's lease. The following typical entry relates to Mill House in Bury Street:

"*John Sanders, gentleman, holds by copyhold a messuage with an orchard and three closes of meadow and pasture adjacent, containing 8 acres and lying between the Vicarage to the north and James Osmond's Cottage and New Street Lane to the south; as appears by a lease dated 1 May, 4 Edward VI (1550).*"

The abbuttals have made it possible to identify many of the houses with reasonable certainty, but in some cases no more than an educated guess can be made.

Westcote and Eastcote both had common fields listed in their respective sections, and the tenant of each strip is named.

At the end of the Terrier is a Rental, divided into the same three sections, in which the various holdings of each tenant are grouped together, along with the total rent paid to King's College each year.

Settlement Pattern

Roughly, there were woodlands and wastelands to the north, meadows along the three streams, the Pinn, the Yeading and the Roxbourne, and open fields running south from Eastcote Road to Northolt and Down Barnes. There were 135 dwellings (10 ruined) scattered across this area of about 6,500 acres. They were clustered in small hamlets often around greens in the northern upland part of the manor. The streets upon which several of these hamlets are situated lead in parallel lines up the hill between the open fields and the Common Wood and waste; Bury Street; Fore Street; Wylcher (Wiltshire) Street; Gowle (Joel) Street; Giddy Street and Popes End Lane (Catlins Lane). Most of these streets remain today with some of the cottages mentioned in the Terrier still standing among the modern housing developments. Giddy Street has been lost. It ran parallel to Joel Street from the north east corner of Southill Lane. A similar settlement pattern is discernible on Rocque's map of 1754, stretching across north west Middlesex, from Ruislip to Stanmore. King's End Street, New Street (southern section Sharps Lane) Sharps Lane and High Street in Westcote and Clay Street (northern section Field End Road) and Cheney Street in Eastcote surrounded dwellings and crofts in the centre of the two original settlements.

The greens were often at the junction of two lanes. Field End Green, Westcote was at the junction of Wood Lane and the road to London (modern

The Goodliest Place in Middlesex

West End Road) and Field End Green, Eastcote was near the junction of Field End Road and Cheney Street. Both these greens are at the northern ends of their respective common fields. Well Green alias Long Marsh lay at the bottom of Joel Street along Eastcote High Road and was probably marshy because of its proximity to the Pinn.

Silver Street Green in the middle of Bury Street is of particular interest as it is situated just outside the ancient embankment surrounding the Park. The closes attached to the houses form a bite into the present Park Wood (now St. Edmund's Avenue and Keswick Gardens), which suggests that the settlement predated the extension of Park Wood (in late medieval times) north from the old boundary to Park Hearne. Potsherds of Hertfordshire/Middlesex grayware c. 1300, thrown up during building operations in the garden of Woodman's Farm in 1984, support this view.

King's End and Hale End both commemorate family names as does Cannons Bridge, though Hale was the only family with representatives mentioned in the Terrier. The others appear in the 13th century Customal. (Chapter 3). Park Hearne took its name from its position on the corner of Park Wood (O.E. 'hyrne' corner, angle) and was largely submerged when the reservoir now known as the Lido was created in 1811, to supply the Grand Junction canal.

Whereas the word "street" seems to indicate a road with dwellings along it, the appellation "lane" is usually given to roads which led from points within the manor to places elsewhere. Wood Lane and Cleares Lane (Ickenham Road) led to Ickenham and Clack Lane led across the Pinn to the hamlet of Tile Kilns in St. Catherine's and thence to Harefield. In the 13th century there was a mill pond called Sitteclack in that area from which Clack Lane probably derived its name.[29] Clack Lane was clearly more important then. It is now a wide muddy track running through Ruislip Golf Course, degenerating into a footpath. As a further insult the name board at the Ickenham Road end now proclaims "Hills Lane" though some street maps retain the old name. Spratts Lane (now Jacketts Lane) in Northwood led to Harefield and has lost its earlier status to become a footpath, but Green Lane a track to Gate Hill in 1565 is now Northwood's main shopping centre. Popes End Lane in Eastcote (now Catlins Lane) had a house, St. Catherine's Farm at the bottom, and led to Raisons Hill.

Distribution of Dwellings – 1565

Location – Modern name in brackets	Dwellings	Houses still standing in 1985
Park Hearne (Reservoir Road area)	6 Cottages	The Mushroom Farm was re-erected at Turville 1964
N.W. of Cannons Bridge (Withy Lane)	4 Cottages	
Cannons Bridge and Silver Street Green (Bury Street – East Side)	8 Cottages 2 Messuages	Cannons Bridge Farm The Plough Woodmans Farm The Berries
Bury Street – West Side	5 Cottages 1 Messuage The Vicarage	Bury Farm (Rebuilt *c* 1600) Mill House The Old House

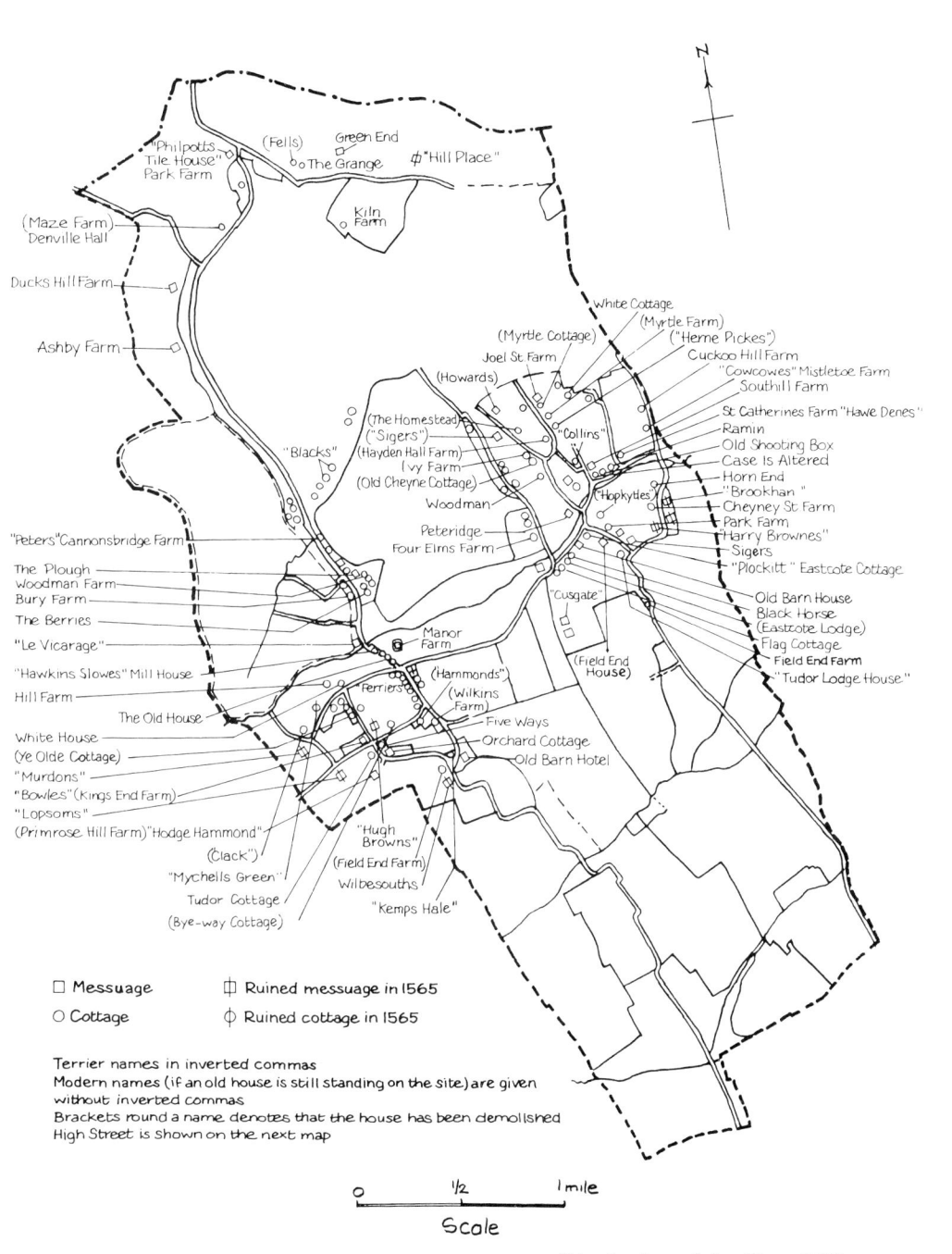

Distribution of dwellings 1565

The Goodliest Place in Middlesex

Lt. Kings End (Corner Sharps Lane/Hills Lane)	2 Cottages 1 ruined cottage	White House (78 Sharps Lane) Hill Farm (Orchard Close)
Clack Lane (track through Ruislip Golf Course)	1 ruined messuage	
Primrose Hill	1 Messuage 1 Cottage 1 ruined messuage	Tudor Cottage
Gt Kings End	1 Messuage	Orchard Cottage
Kings End Street (Sharps Lane, west side)	1 Messuage 4 Cottages	
East side	1 Cottage 1 ruined messuage	

High Street – West Side
  – East Side
  – North End
	8 Cottages
	1 Messuage
	2 Cottages
	1 Shop
	1 Mansion House
	1 Cottage
		B.S. Hall's
		The Swan
		1-15 High Street
		
		Manor Farm
		Village Tea Shop

Clears Lane (Ickenham Road)
  North Side
  South Side
	
	1 Cottage
	2 Cottages	

Field End	3 Cottages 1 ruined messuage	The Old Barn Hotel
TOTAL	63 (inc 5 ruined)	18 still standing

EASTCOTE

Fore Street – West Side – East Side	2 Messuages 8 Cottages 2 Cottages	Four Elms Farm
Wiltshire Street – West Side (including bottom of Joel Street) – East Side (Hayden Hall Site)	 2 Messuages 3 Cottages 1 freehold tenement 1 Messuage 1 Cottage	 Ivy Farm The Woodman
Joel Street – West Side – East Side	2 Cottages 1 Messuage 4 Cottages	 Joel Street Farm (rebuilt)
Gyddye Street – East Side	1 Cottage 1 Messuage	
Raisons Hill	2 Cottages	White Cottage
Long Marsh (High Road) North Side	3 Cottages	Case is Altered (rebuilt) Old Shooting Box Ramin

Popes End Lane (Catlins Lane)	1 Cottage	St. Catherine's Farm
Cheney Street – West Side (including Cuckoo Hill) – East Side	4 Cottages 1 ruined messuage 3 ruined messuages	Cuckoo Hill Farm Mistletoe Farm Horn End Cheney Street Farm
Clay Street (Field End Road – North End)	2 Messuages 3 Cottages	Park Farm
High Road – South Side	2 Messuages 1 Cottage	
Well Green alias Long Marsh (Eastcote Road)	2 Messuages 4 Cottages	Eastcote Cottage Old Barn House Flag Cottage
Hale End (Highgrove)	2 Messuages	
Field End	2 Messuages 1 Cottage	Field End Farm Tudor Lodge Hotel
TOTAL	62 (inc 4 ruined)	19 still standing (2 rebuilt)
NORTHWOOD		
Ducks Hill	3 Messuages 2 Cottages	Ashby Farm (rebuilt) Ducks Hill Farm (rebuilt) Park Farm
Rickmansworth Road	3 Cottages	The Grange/Green Close Kiln Farm
Green Lane	1 Messuage 1 ruined messuage	Green End (now in Dene Road)
TOTAL	10 (inc 1 ruined)	6 still standing (2 rebuilt)
GRAND TOTAL	135 (inc 10 ruined)	43 still standing

N.B. The Terrier does not cover St. Catherine's Manor and Gate Hill which belonged to the Manor of the More.

We are fortunate indeed to have retained nearly one third of our 16th century buildings even though some of them have been nearly swamped by modern housing in recent years. The recent development at Woodman's Farm is a blatant example of an unsympathetic planning authority allowing new houses to overshadow the ancient house, despite remonstrances from local bodies early in the planning stages. It should be an object to preserve the environment of a listed building as well as the fabric.

Several more of the buildings mentioned in the Terrier have been demolished within living memory:
    Cottage in Bury Street
    Cottage in Bury Street next to the Berries
    The George, High Street
    Mrs Gooderson's Shop – Corner of The Oaks and High Street
    Wilkins Farm, High Street

The Mill House, Bury Street, Ruislip. John Sander's messuage in 1565

Bye-Way Cottage, Ickenham Road
Field End Cottage, West End Road
Ye Old Cottage, Sharps Lane
Fore Street Farm, Fore Street
The Homestead, Wiltshire Lane
Old Cheyne Cottage, Joel Street
Laurel Cottage, Joel Street
Hayden Hall Farm, Joel Street
Eastcote House, Eastcote High Road/Field End Road
Sigers, Field End Road
The Barns, Field End Road

It would not be fair, however, to blame only the 20th century inhabitants of Ruislip for the destruction of old buildings. Southill Farm in Southill Lane seems to have been built in the 18th century to replace the messuage which John Ferne the miller owned in 1565. Similarly 18th century Joel Street Farm is on the site of William Kirton's messuage and the Black Horse, probably rebuilt in the 19th century was the cottage of John Robins, junior. Ducks Hill Farm and Ashby Farm on Ducks Hill and Bury Farm in Bury Street have been remodelled and most of the other 16th century houses still standing have been extended and altered.

The houses so far examined have proved to be timber-framed structures with Queen–post trusses. They have lath and plaster interior walls, but appear to have had a brick-nogging infill between the timbers from the time they were built. Poorer structures, perhaps with wattle and daub infill, have not survived. In many cases an outshot scullery with a cat-slide roof was added in the 17th century. Woodmans Farm, Orchard Cottage, Bury Farm are among houses with examples of this type of extension.

Typically when they were modernised these houses had a brick skin added which hid the timber frame. The brick front at Bury Farm was probably added in 1776, if a date and initials (J.S. and a name Jo. Spicer) scratched on can be taken as a safe guide. Ramin on Eastcote High Road has "Pritchard" and 1816 marked on bricks by the door.

A messuage means a dwelling house with its outbuildings and the land assigned to its use. A cottage is simply a small dwelling. However, in Ruislip the only difference between the two types of dwelling in 1565 is that the messuages were heriotable (i.e. had to pay death duty) and the cottages were not. Four of the Westcote messuages had common field land attached to them, but so had nine of the cottages. In Eastcote thirteen messuages and sixteen cottages had common field land.

Every dwelling had some type of enclosure around it, ranging from a pightle (unspecified but small) to several closes of 20 acres or more, usually pasture. There were ten gardens and ten orchards in Westcote and two gardens and seven orchards in Eastcote. Northwood had no gardens but seven orchards. The mean size of enclosure in Westcote (range 0.5a-14a) was 4.5 acres; in Eastcote (range 1a-2a) 5.5 acres; in Northcote (range 0.5a-108.5a) 22.6 acres.

Ramin, Eastcote High Road, a cottage at Long Marsh belonging to James Ferne in 1565

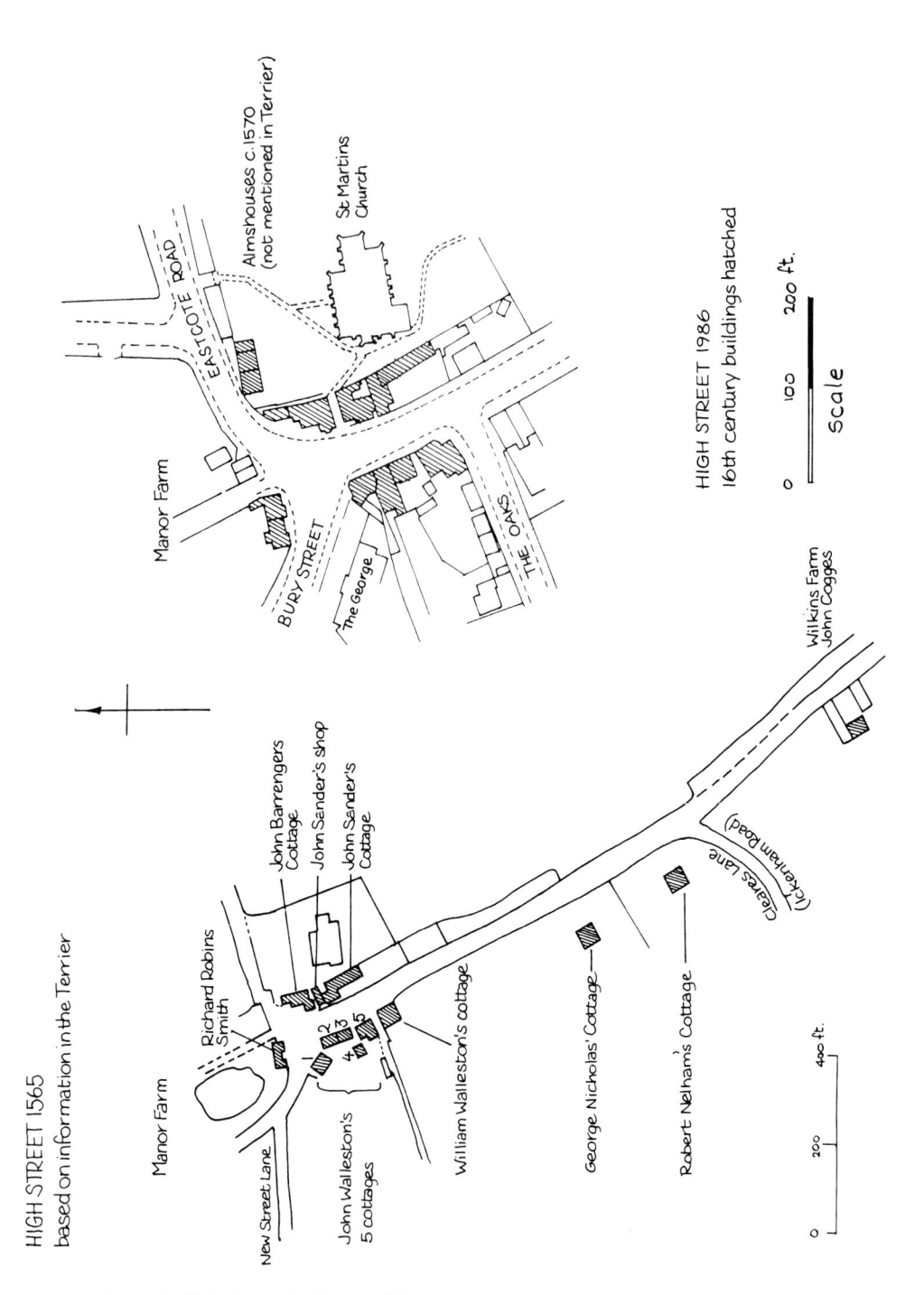

Plans of High Street 1565 and 1986

The Manor of Ruislip and King's College

Northwood in 1565 was quite different from the other portions of the manor having no common fields. There was a great deal of meadow and pasture land there. 68 acres held as six enclosures were called Poor's Field. There were 21 acres of underwood. The nine houses were scattered across the whole area and had been built between the 14th and 16th centuries on land assarted from wooded waste which still extended north to Green Lane and at one point south of Park Farm, across Ducks Hill which must originally have been a woodland track. 95 acres within Northwood were unaccounted for in the Terrier. These were outlying lands of the Manor of the More (Moor Park), and included two more houses, Kewferry Farm and Gate Hill which were not mentioned in the Terrier as they did not belong to King's College.

High Street

The main settlement of the manor was in the High Street leading south from the Manor Farm and St. Martin's parish church. It had 12 houses and a shop. Richard Robins, smith held a cottage standing by the gate to Manor Farm, perhaps the Village Tea Rooms, near where a building is marked "Smith's Shop" on John Doharty's map of 1750. It was the long established site for a smithy. A rental of 1420/1 speaks of a smithy near the Manor House gate.[30]

John Sanders held a cottage and a shop by the church gate. The same 1420/1 rental mentions a shop by the churchyard. There is no reference to any type of shop or Ale House anywhere else in the Terrier.

There was one other cottage on the east side of High Street belonging to John Barringer lying against the churchyard. On the east side of High Street today Nos. 1-15 are dated 16th century. Perhaps Nos. 7-15 were originally a single building of the hall and solar type and was John Sander's cottage and shop. Nos. 1 to 5 which later became the Old Bell might have been John Barrenger's cottage. Numbers 5 and 7 have Victorian additions tacked on to the 16th century building.

West of the High Street John Walleston held five cottages "in one of which he lives" and William Walleston held a cottage there too. These were probably the row of cottages starting at the Old George and ending with Gooderson's shop which stood on the corner of The Oaks and was demolished in the 1930's. The Old George was demolished in 1939. A cottage behind the Swan has also gone, but three cottages, now The Swan and Nos. 4 and 6 still stand. John Walleston was the most considerable landowner in the parish at the time. It is interesting that he chose to live in the High Street, at the centre of things.

Two more cottages belonging to George Nicholas and Robert Nelham lay between The Oaks and Ickenham Road and another where Woolworth's is now. The latter came to be known as Wilkins Farm this century and was owned by John Cogges in 1565. The enclosed crofts belonging to the cottages north of Ickenham Road seem to have been long, narrow tofts typical of a medieval village layout.

The Open Fields

Common Fields "Communes campi"

Fields described as "common" on the Westcote side of the manor were: Tybber Field, Hill Field, Whittingrove Field, Roxbourne Field and Marlpit Field. Those in Eastcote were East Field, Well Field and Stene (Stone) Field. In addition there

The Goodliest Place in Middlesex

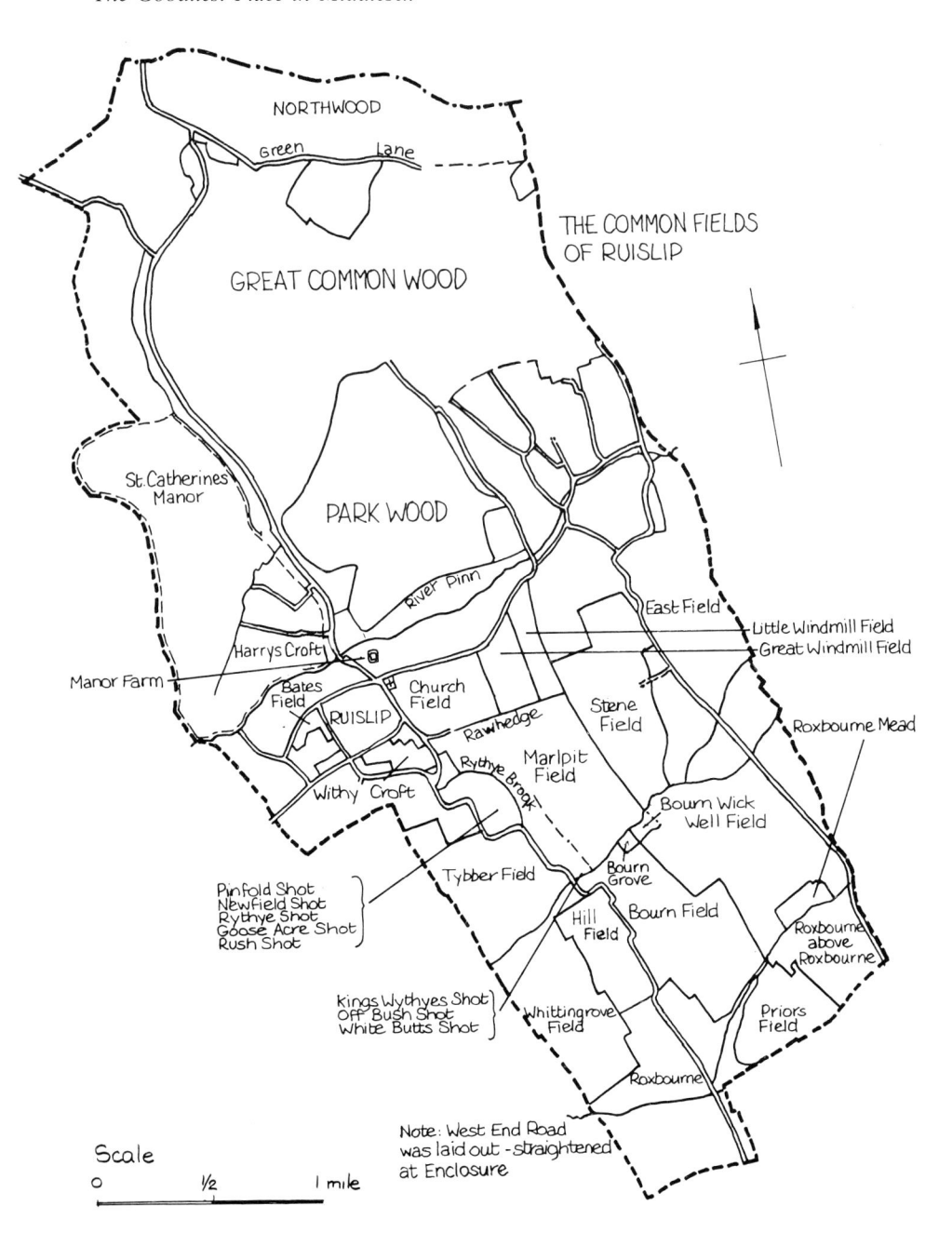

The Common Fields and Wood of Ruislip 16th century

The Manor of Ruislip and King's College

were the demesne lands, Church Field, Gt and Lt Windmill Field and Bourne Field. A glance at the relief map of the area shows the common fields to be situated in the southern lowland part of the Manor of Ruislip marked on the geological map as mainly London clay. Marlpit Field, Stene Field and a portion of East Field are on Reading clay and a band of Reading sand runs across the north east corner of Marlpit Field.

These twelve fields were the arable lands of the manor. Sand, loam and chalk spread on the heavy clay to make it workable were commonly called "marl" in Ruislip records. Marlward appears as a surname in the 13th century Customal and Marlpit Field was already so named in the 1436 Minister's Accounts. The Terrier names Brian Atkinson as tenant of the 3½ acre Marlpit. It may well have been the old, extensive sand pit revealed in 1957 when foundations were being dug for Woolworth's and other new shops by Ruislip Manor Station.[31]

The three Eastcote fields with their simple names are probably the original fields of the vill. The Westcote field names have less obvious meanings. Tybber may be a personal name. That field is called 'Alderton' on 18th century farm maps and on the 1806 Enclosure map and later Anderson Field, which is certainly a personal name. "Hill" and "Whittingrove" Fields lying side by side on the slight hill which rises from the Yeading Brook towards the south could have been a single field divided at an earlier period, as Hill Field is very small and appears to be a "bite" from a larger field. "Roxbourne", "Bourne" and "Roxbourne Above Roxbourne" along the southern edge of the manor are all crossed by the Roxbourne Brook. Ekwall's *Oxford Dictionary of English Place Names* suggests that Roxeth which adjoins the Manor of Ruislip on the south east means "Hroc's pit, well or lake". Presumably Roxbourne is "Hroc's stream".

"Marlpit Field" is named from its marl pit and Church Field from its proximity to the church. Great and Little Windmill Fields retain memory of the Windmill mentioned in the Extent of the Manor taken in 1294.

Hedges
Certain names, Snake Hedges, Rawedge and Fullers Hedge suggest that the fields were hedged. The northern hedge of Marlpit Field (Rawedge) of layered hawthorn is still detectable in the gardens of houses and bungalows built in Brickwall Lane (formerly Hook Lane) in the 1920's.

Shots – "Stadia"
The very large fields were subdivided into shots separated from each other by trackways. Hill Field had the least number of shots, only four and East Field had the greatest, 32. 109 shots are named, some after natural features such as water courses (Waterfurrows, Brook Mead), others referring to the type of soil (Light Acre, Small Stone Acres and Redland). Some shots are named after trees and plants, probably reflecting those growing in them (Elm Mead, Aldershearne, Rush Shot and King Withy Shot). A few shots bear the name of families who appear in earlier Ruislip records, but had disappeared by 1565 (Hammonds, Hodgekins Horse Pool Shot). Fox Holes, Goose Acre and Rooke Acres name animals and birds.

The shots were divided into pieces ("peciae"). The largest, Down Barnes Shot in Roxbourne had 66 pieces and the smallest, in Whittingrove Field, unimaginatively called Small Shot had only three.

A typical entry in the Terrier referring to the common fields runs as follows:

The Goodliest Place in Middlesex

"*There is another shotte called Brook Mead Shot containing 26 pieces whose heads lie South upon the brook and West to East by the parish of Ickenham. Richard Cogges holds the 1st and 2nd pieces containing 2 half sellions. The Vicar holds the 3rd piece containing 1 sellion. John Nelham holds the 4th piece containing 1 sellion...."*
 The expression "containing 1 sellion" suggests that a sellion was a measure of land of standard size, but the one thing that clearly emerges about measurements given in the Terrier is that the sellion was variable in size. In some cases the land which is given as sellions in the main portion of the Terrier is given as acres in the Rental, making it possible for a comparison to be made and an average size given to the sellions. For example John Hale in the Rental has a messuage at Hale End (near Highgrove) with 30 acres in the common fields of Eastcote and a further 6 sellions in Eastcote fields. In the main part of the Terrier he is credited with 36 pieces in the fields, 28 sellions and eight half sellions. From this it appears that 32 sellions = 30 acres. Therefore the mean sellion area is 1.1 acres. However, John Nelham in Westcote has 38½ sellions which are referred to in the Rental as 18 acres. Working from the Terrier, comparing sellions in the fields with acreage in the rental, wherever this was possible (22 times) the average size of sellion was 0.81 acres (Range 0.63-1.27).
 The skeleton of the system whereby arable land in the common fields had been allocated to a particular dwelling in medieval times can still be perceived

White Cottage, Harlyn Drive – Raysons Hill area in 1565

The Manor of Ruislip and King's College

in the Terrier. If we assume that the Ruislip hyde had 80 acres, Epsoms at King's End and Petridge (later Laurel Cottage, Joel Street) in Eastcote, appear to be tenements with hyde holdings attached to them. The lands of the other houses approximate to half-hydes, virgates or half-virgates.

16th century court rolls show a constant redistribution of sellions and most householders had acquired additional ones to those attached to their dwellings by 1565.

For example John Coggs held a messuage in the lower end of the High Street, which later became Wilkins Farm (now Woolworth's) with 31 sellions in three fields of Westcote. He also had a quite separate parcel of sellions in Tybberfield.

41 people (23 in Westcote and 18 in Eastcote) had small amounts of common field land (½-20 acres) although no house of any kind is attributed to them. These are no doubt accounted for by the custom whereby men often split their land among their children in unequal shares, the largest portion normally going with the house to make a viable economic unit for the eldest son and the smaller to provide dowries for daughters and supplementary incomes for younger sons.

43 tenants (29 Westcote and 14 Eastcote) had houses with crofts only and no stake in the common field arable.

A comparison is made between the distribution of land in 1086, 1245, 1565 in Table 4:

Table 4. Land holdings in Common Fields attached to houses

Date	Hyde	½ Hyde	Virgate	½ Virgate	Croft	Total houses
1086	2	1	17	10	15	45
1245	2	12	33	5	51	103
1565	2	11	16	11	76	116

The sellions of each house were spread across all the common fields of the vill in which the house was situated and distributed among several shots in each field as well. For example, John Nicholas with his messuage at Field End (Field End Farm) has:
24 sellions in 12 out of 17 shots in Well Field
13½ sellions in 7 out of 14 shots in Stene Field
21 sellions in 12 out of 22 shots in East Field

John Lyon with his cottage in Joel Street, Hayden Hall Farm held sellions as:
6 sellions in 5 shots of Stene Field
5 sellions in 2 shots of Well Field
9 sellions in 7 shots of East Field

The sellions are nearly always held singly. It is exceptional to find one man with two or more adjacent strips, unless they are two half sellions. Why sellions should have been divided in two, presumably lengthways is not clear unless the practice originated in the division of one holding between two heirs.

The Goodliest Place in Middlesex

John Sanders who had 87½ sellions in Westcote Fields (attached to a ruined messuage – "Epsoms" in Kings End) had more consolidated groups of sellions than anyone else: one group of three sellions in Tybberfield, one group of three sellions in Whittingrove Field, one group of three sellions in Roxbourne, one group of five sellions in Roxbourne. Matthew Harte and Richard Nelham also had groups of five sellions in Roxbourne. John Walleston had a group of six sellions in Stene Field.

These findings show little evidence of serious attempts at consolidation of sellions by individual tenants other than demesne farmers. The lands of each tenant even of the large and presumably more powerful land owners are scattered across the fields of their respective vills.

Open Field Meadowlands
There was a certain amount of meadow interspersed among the arable in the common fields, along the watercourses. Meadow pieces are let out in acres rather than sellions. Whether it refers to a fixed measure of land is uncertain. There were 11¼ acres of meadow in the fields of Westcote and 56½ acres in Eastcote. One rood lying in "Well Mead alias Well Hooke" in "Well Field" was called "Lot Mead" suggesting that it had been let out by lot to various tenants at one time. It belonged to the lord of the manor. "Well Field" was crossed by several watercourses and consequently had a larger amount of meadow than the other fields, 30 acres.

There were seven other separate meadows, "Prior's Field", Westcote, 36 acres, "Prior's Field", Eastcote, 31 acres, "Bourn Wyck", 3 acres, "Bourne Grove", 5 acres, "Dickett's Mead", 11 acres, "Roxbourne Mead", 12 acres and "Fuller's Hedge, 8½ acres, all lying at the southern edge of the manor along the Roxbourne Brook and its tributaries.

The Tenants
The Terrier tells us a lot about the tenants of the manor, their names and their property. What we cannot find out is how many of them lived in the houses they owned. Four men at least almost certainly lived in other places for they are called John Ferne of Rickmansworth, William Nicholas of Perivale, John Redinge of Stanwell and John Vincent of Northolt. Probably most houses were occupied by their owners.

67 tenants possessed only one house, while 22 had another 66 houses between them, but not usually in any quantity (13 had two). Only James Ferne with seven houses and John Walleston with 12 were in a position to derive a substantial income from property letting. However, the extra houses must have been inhabited by Ruislip people whose names are lost to us.

The 129 tenants named represent 72 families, the most prolific being Fernes and Nicholases (nine each), Winchester (seven) and Redinge (six). Four of the Fernes were called John and were differentiated as: John Ferne, Miller; John Ferne, Minor; John Ferne of Rickmansworth and John Ferne of Wylchers. Incidentally there were thirty men called John followed in order of popularity by 19 Williams, 15 Richards and eight Thomases.

Redinges, Nicholases and Fernes appear in the 1547 Terrier of Harrow, Pinner section. Seven other names, Birde, Edlyn, Gate, Marshe, Prest, Smith and Winter are also common to both Terriers.

The Manor of Ruislip and King's College

Comparison with the names listed in the c. 1245 Customal shows that only six surnames were still current in Ruislip in 1565; Flye, Milwarde, Parker, Prest, Robins and White. The population appears to have been slightly smaller in 1565 as there were probably 150 tenants in the Customal and 129 in the Terrier. If we assume five people to each household we arrive at an estimated population of about 750 in c. 1245 and 620 in 1565. We have no knowledge of events in Ruislip during the time of the Black Death but it is possible that an expanding population (assumed from the number of augmented holdings mentioned in the Customal) was struck by the scourge and had taken 200 years to recover.

Seventeen women appear holding property in 1565. Most of them are described as widows. Whereas the men are said to hold their property to themselves and their heirs, the women are mostly said to hold property to themselves during their lifetime and then to a named son and his heirs.

"*Elena Childe holds one cottage with an orchard and close called Sinbotes....to herself during her lifetime and then to Henry Childe her son....*"

It appears that when a widow remarried her second husband acquired rights over any property she had inherited from her first husband during her lifetime.

"*John Stockden holds a cottage and orchard....at Cannons Bridge ....during the lifetime of his wife Joanna, formerly the wife of Richard Redinge, then to rest with Henry Redinge her son and his heirs....*"

Property was left to women. Agnes Winchester alias Mower held 6 acres of land in Westcote Fields "during the minority of her daughter Isabel Winchester" and two cottages, orchards and meadows "during the minority of her daughter Joanna".

John Walleston, John Sanders, Ralph Hawtrey, George Ashby, James Parker and Roger Arnolde are described as gentlemen. George Ashby of Breakspears had a Tile House called Philpots in Northwood at or on the site of Park Farm, Northwood and James Parker held 4 acres of the Common Wood. The others were substantial landowners.

The only tradesmen named as such are a smith and a miller. Again the description is to distinguish between men of the same surnames. John Ferne was the miller but no mill appears in the Terrier. His messuage was in Gyddy Street in Eastcote, possibly on the site of Southill Farm. It is possible that he worked a mill outside the Manor of Ruislip.

The Wallestons – Free Tenants

John Walleston held freely one tenement "Petridge" with three closes, 20½ acres of meadow and pasture adjacent and 80 sellions in three fields of Eastcote, for which he paid 15s 4d per annum by a lease dated 1540. He also held freely "by services unknown" a ruined messuage in Cheney Street, opposite Horn End and five sellions in East Field, for which he paid 8d per annum by a lease dated 1500. William Walleston held only four sellions in Westcote Fields freely, for which he paid 4d per annum by a lease of 1467. Both held copyhold land as well.

Petridge became Laurel Cottage, next door to Sunnyside in Joel Street. It was demolished when Kaduna Close was built.
John held as follows:
1. Cottage "Forrers" High Street. Meadow "Foster's Mead" 4 acres (– later The George).

The Goodliest Place in Middlesex

2. Cottage, garden and close, King's End, 6 acres. (Old Orchard/White House, Sharps Lane).
3. Ruined cottage and close "Barrengers" King's End, 6 acres. (Land between Orchard Close and Southcote Rise).
4. Meadow "The Neat" King's End, 5 acres. (Strip of land along the Pinn now north side of Woodville Gardens).
5. Ruined messuage 20 acres King's End. Murdons in Clack Lane (now part of Ruislip Golf Course).
6. 4 cottages "in one of which he lives" 2 closes and orchards. 8 acres, High Street. (From the George to the Swan).
7. Cottage "Hawe Denes" Popes End, 20 acres closes, 23 acres Eastcote Fields, 12 acres Windmill Field, 4 acres Buttes Mead. (St. Catherine's Farm, Catlins Lane).
8. ½ acre Cheney Street by Field End, 24 acres Eastcote Fields.
9. Messuage 40 acres and 15 acres Northwood. (Ducks Hill Farm).

    Since the Rental makes clear that John Walleston's sellions are equivalent to acres it is possible to total his land at 287 acres, making him the largest landowner in the manor.

Tiles and Bricks

Two cottages and one messuage in Northwood: one lying south of Park Farm, Park Farm itself and Kiln Farm, had tile yards attached to them. The Reading clay was suitable for making tiles, but three tile houses in so small a community appears excessive unless a ready market could be found beyond its borders. Tiles were made at Northwood in the early 15th century and were being sent to Brentford in 1442/3. London must always have provided an outlet. Probably the best route for the transport of goods to London was via the Thames at Brentford.

    Thomas Wetherlye had a Brick Place in Eastcote probably at the house now called Park Farm in Field End Road.

Rents

The smallest rent was ½d per annum paid by Ralph Barnett for a cottage at Park Hearne and the highest was 46s owed by Roger Arnold for a cottage in Northwood called North House and 109½ acres of land in 15 closes and another cottage close by, one of which is now The Grange, Northwood. (See Chapter 11). Rents are roughly related to size of holdings, though with several exceptions. Cottages with an acre or less cost from ½d to 5d per annum.

    In Northwood a messuage with 30 acres cost 9s per annum and one with 40 acres was only 8s. 6d per annum. The cheaper messuage was held by a lease dated 1509, while the lease of the dearer messuage was dated 1554, which is probably an indication that rents rose during the course of the 16th century. The following table shows all the Northwood rents, the various holdings and rents of each tenant having been added together. It will be noted that William Winchester had to pay 2000 tiles a year as part of his rent, although the other two owners of tile yards only paid money. James Parker's rent for four acres of Ruislip Wood was 4s or 4 capons.

The Manor of Ruislip and King's College

Table 5. Northwood Rents

Tenants	Holding	Rent	Date of Lease
Roger Arnolde The Grange Cottage	2 Cottages 108½a. 1a.	46s. 4d.	1541 and 1539
William Winchester Kiln Farm	Cottage Kiln 66a	31s. and 2000 tiles	1563
Elena Childe South of Park Farm	Cottage Orchard 26½a. 20a. Tile Yard	13s. 6d. 6s.	1558 and 1565
Robert Nicholas Green End	Messuage 36a	10s. 8d.	1548
George Ashby Park Farm	Messuage Kiln 22a.	9s. 8d.	1558
John Living Ashby Farm	Messuage 30a.	9s.	1554
John Walleston Ducks Hill Farm	Messuage 40a. 15a.	8s. 6d. 14d.	} 1509 and 1564
William Kirton	18a.	8s.	1562
William Nicholas	20a.	7s. 4d.	1562
James Haydon	18a. and 1 ruined messuage	6s. 4d.	1557
James Parker	4a. Ruislip Wood	4s. or 4 capons	1565
John Winchester	5a.	2s. 4d.	1563
William Wheler	8a.	2s.	1561
Edmund Birde	5a.	18d.	1559
John Ferne	5a.	18d.	1558
Thomas Osborne	3½a.	13d.	1558
Hugo Fisher Nr. Denville Hall	Cottage Pightel	5d.	1559

Westcote had the highest percentage of tenants paying low rents. Northwood had the highest percentage paying very high rents. The various percentages may be seen in Table 6.

Table 6. Percentage distribution of rents.

	<12d	1s→	6s→	11s→	16s→	21s→	>25s
Westcote	37.7%	31.9%	15.9%	8.7%	2.9 %	1.4%	1.4%
Eastcote	17.5%	46.0%	17.5%	12.7%	—	3.2%	3.2%
Northwood	6.5%	37.5%	37.5%	—	6.2 %	—	12.5%

The high number of rents under 12d in Westcote is accounted for by a number of cottages with only a garden or very small close attached.

Assessed on the total amount of rent they paid the chief tenants in each section were: John Walleston in Westcote paying 39s 1d; John Redinge of Field End in Eastcote paying 28s 4d; Roger Arnold in Northwood paying 46s 4d. When the lands of individuals in the three districts is totalled, John Walleston with land in all three paid the most, 75s 9d, followed by Roger Arnolde with 46s 4d in Northwood only and William Winchester with 31s also in Northwood only. John Sanders who held the most common field land, 87 acres in Westcote, lies fifth in the overall rents table. Ralph Hawtrey whose descendants played so important a part in Ruislip affairs, as will be seen in the next Chapter, paid 16s 6d annually and lay in tenth place.

The Terrier shows that in the early years of Elizabeth 1's reign the demesne occupied about one third of the total area of the parish and a further 23% of the land was held by the 5.4% of people who paid more than 20 shillings per annum rent. Those who had common field land also had larger enclosures around their houses (5 acres-20 acres). The 35% of people with no common field land had small enclosures (less than 5 acres) and held less than 5% of the total area. However, as just under 60% of the tenants had almost 40% of the land between them, Ruislip still at that date had a substantial number of small independent landholders.

REFERENCES
1. King's College: Ledger Books.
2. King's College: Q.23.
3. Ibid: 13.
4. Ibid: 20.
5. King's College: Ledger Book Vol II fol. 109, 119, 120, 121.
6. G.L.R.O. Acc 249/107.
7. King's College: Q.42/38.
8. Hist. Ms Commission Series 9 VI Salisbury Cecil MS pt VI.
9. Druett: *"Ruislip – Northwood through the ages"* 1957 pp. 104-5.
10. Ibid: pp. 105-6.
11. Florence Hawtrey: *"The Hawtrey Family"* pp.87-9.
12. King's College: R.36.
13. King's College: Ledger Books.
14. G.L.R.O. Acc 249/39.
15. Ibid: 21.
16. King's College: R.36.
17. G.L.R.O. Acc. 241/4113.
18. King's College: Q.25.
19. G.L.R.O. Acc. 249/107.
20. Nat. Register of Archives – R.N.U.D.C. – 1953.
21. King's College: R.36.
22. King's College: Doharty's Survey.
23. King's College: Q.42/34.
24. P.R.O. SC 6/917/27 Transcript L.E. Morris Collection Ruislip Library.
25. King's College: Q.3.
26. British Library: Add Ms 9368.
27. King's College: Q.23.
28. Ibid: 41.
29. *Select Document of the Abbey of Bec.* Camden Third Series, Vol LXIII Royal Historical Society, 1951.
30. King's College: R.39.
31. Uxbridge Library: Kiddle, Historical Geography of N.W. Middlesex.

Chapter Seven

The Hawtreys, Rogers and Deanes, of Eastcote House

The Hawtrey Family
Ralph Hawtrey, fourth son of Thomas Hawtrey of Chequers, Bucks, married Winifred Walleston of Ruislip before 1527 and with his wife became owner of a cottage at Well Green, Eastcote, called "Hopkyttes", which had been in the possession of the Walleston family since 1507.[1] The cottage became the Hawtrey's principle residence, known as Eastcote House. Ralph (1494-1574) and Winifred (1502-1573) founded the Ruislip branch of the Hawtrey family, which retained Eastcote House until 1930 when Ralph Hawtrey Deane sold the house and surrounding land to Wembley (Comben and Wakeling) Land Company for building development.[2]

During the intervening 400 years the Hawtreys created a large estate in the parish in three ways: by leasing the rectory of Ruislip from the Dean and Canons of Windsor (from 1532-1867), by leasing the demesne lands of the manor of Ruislip, from King's College, Cambridge (1667-1872); and by acquiring lands and farms in Eastcote. Their position as justices enabled them to supervise law and order in the area, influence the election of parish officers and view parish accounts. The absence of a lord of the manor enabled the Hawtreys and their descendants the Deanes to become the most influential gentry family in the parish and to act as local squires. In the 19th century, Ralph Deane and his son Francis were known as Squire Deane. There is even an allusion to them in a poem called *Christmas Morn on the Open Road* by a minor Victorian poet, Julius E. Day:
"*Over the holding of Squire Deane,*
"*By Cuckoo Hill up to Pinner Green*"
Most of the males who lived to maturity embraced the legal profession, becoming Barristers of Grays Inn, Lincolns Inn and Middle Temple.

The family tree overleaf shows the descent of the Ruislip estates through five generations of Hawtreys, two of Rogers, and four of Deanes.

Monuments
Many of the people in the preceding table are buried at St. Martin's, in a vault or in the churchyard. The chancel is paved with their grave slabs and there are several more imposing monuments on the walls; that of Ralph (d. 1638) probably having most artistic merit. It was sculpted by John and Mathias Christmas. The first Ralph and his son John have commemorative brasses, Ralph's on the south

The Goodliest Place in Middlesex

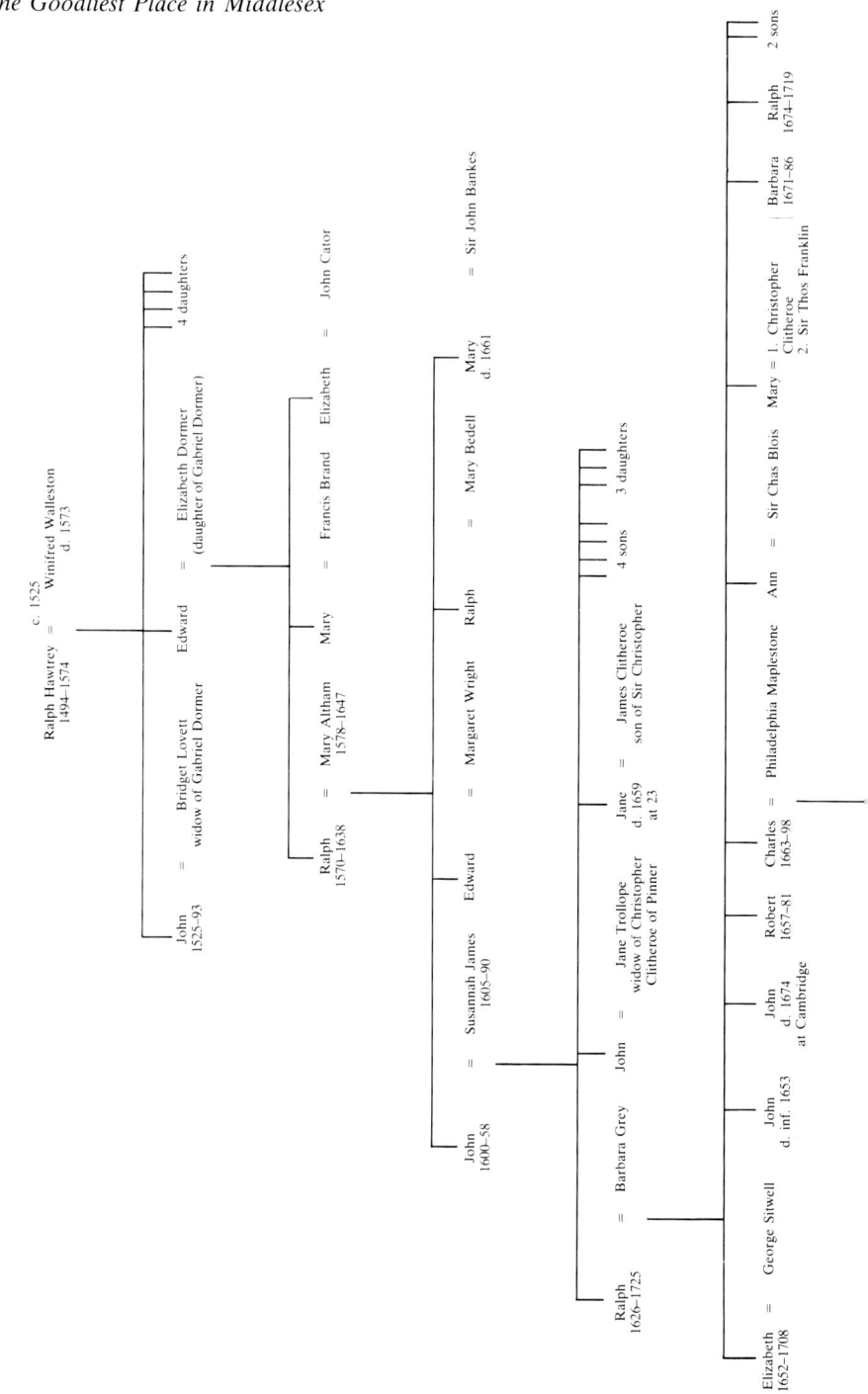

Ralph Hawtrey c. 1525 = Winifred Walleston
1494–1574   d. 1573

John 1525–93

Edward = Bridget Lovett, widow of Gabriel Dormer
      = Elizabeth Dormer (daughter of Gabriel Dormer)
      4 daughters

Ralph 1570–1638 = Mary Altham 1578–1647

Mary = Francis Brand
Elizabeth = John Cator

John 1600–58 = Susannah James 1605–90
Edward
Margaret Wright
Ralph = Mary Bedell
Mary d. 1661 = Sir John Bankes

Ralph 1626–1725 = Barbara Grey
John d. inf. 1653
John = Jane Trollope, widow of Christopher Clitheroe of Pinner
Jane d. 1659 at 23 = James Clitheroe son of Sir Christopher
4 sons
3 daughters
Ann = Sir Chas Blois
Mary = 1. Christopher Clitheroe 2. Sir Thos Franklin
Barbara 1671–86
Ralph 1674–1719
2 sons

John d. 1674 at Cambridge
Robert 1657–81
Charles 1663–98 = Philadelphia Maplestone

Elizabeth 1652–1708 = George Sitwell

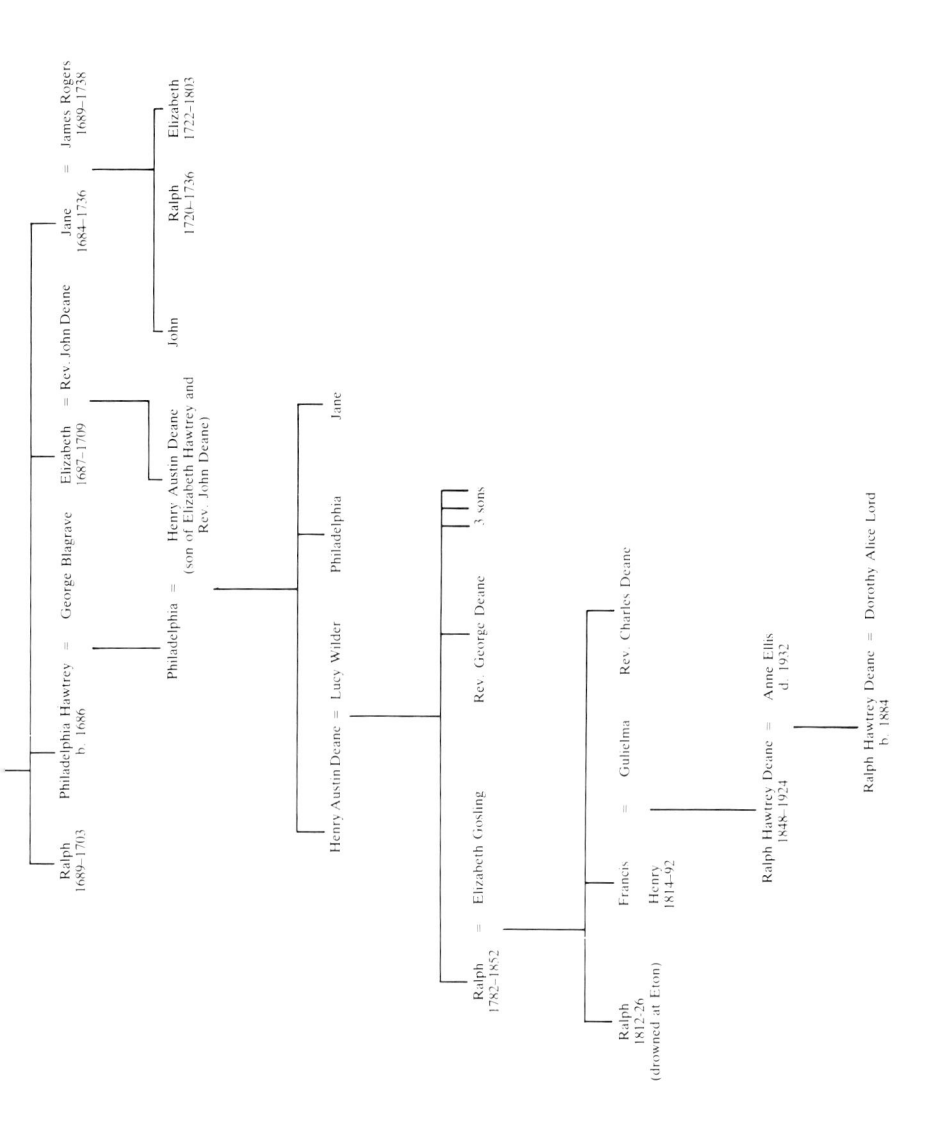

The Hawtreys, Rogers and Deanes, of Eastcote House

Family Tree showing connection between the Hawtreys, Rogers and Deanes.

wall of the chancel and John's more difficult of access within the altar rails, but replicas of both brasses are to be found in the Lady Chapel. The ledger stones on the floor mention thirty-two members of the family and more stones are obscured by the choir benches. Several of the black stones, with incised letters and the Hawtrey or Rogers coat of arms in white, look as if they have been turned over at some time, and reused, as they have a kind of carved label giving the names of people interred let into them. Until the early 19th century the Hawtreys and Rogers were buried intramurally in the family vault, but Elizabeth Rogers (d. 1803) seems to have been the last so interred and the Deanes' graves are in the north-east section of the old graveyard near the boundary with Churchfield Gardens.

Wallestons and Ralph Hawtrey 1494-1574
(Bachelor in Civil Law) Oxon. 1521

The Walaxtons, Wallisons or Wallestons first appear in Ruislip documents in the 15th century when John Walaxton leased Ruislip rectory from the Dean and Canons of Windsor from 1476 for twenty years at a rent of £18.[3] By 1565 two Wallestons, John and William, were the only free tenants of the Manor of Ruislip, John being the principal landowner.[4] One of William's leases was dated 1467. Winifred's place in the family is not known, but her father was probably the John Walleston, gentleman, who in June 1527 surrendered a cottage called Hopkyttes to the use of Ralph Hawtrey and Wenefride his wife and their heirs legitimately begotten between them, together with a 4 acre close adjoining and 13 acres in three fields of Eastcote.[5] Ralph and his wife settled at Hopkyttes although Ralph appears to have had lands in Bucks and Oxon as well.

Ralph was the first Hawtrey to lease the rectory, which he did in 1532 for twenty years at £18 rent, the same terms as offered to John Walaxton in 1476, to John Walaxton in 1497 and John Walleston Esq in 1517.[6] The Dean and Canons of Windsor retained the right to appoint vicars to Ruislip church but Ralph Hawtrey as lay-rector was permitted to collect the Great Tithes (corn and hay). The Small Tithes (milk, eggs, wool, etc) went to the vicar. The 1565 Terrier shows that the rector of Ruislip had a barn in Bury Street, on the corner of Ladygate Lane, presumably to store the tithe corn. (The Scout Hut now stands on the site). The lay-rector had a duty to maintain the chancel in good repair.

Eastcote House within living memory was a stucco-fronted brick building, but this facade seems to have hidden the original Hopkyttes, which is first recorded in 1494 when John Amery, lying "in extremis," surrendered it to his wife Joan for nine years and then to his son Edmund,[7] who in his turn surrendered it to John Walleston in 1507. Ralph Hawtrey is believed to have enlarged Hopkyttes. The 1922 Report of the Royal Commission on Historical Buildings said that the house was built in the 16th century or early 17th century with a central block and north and south cross wings; the roof of the original main block had braced tie-beams and moulded purlins. Much research has gone into timber-framed buildings since 1922 and the report could now be modified. A beam taken from Eastcote House during its demolition in 1964 was incorporated in the Great Barn during repairs. Cecil Hewett, an expert on medieval carpentry, saw it there in 1980 and positively identified it as a beam carved before 1510. His evidence points to the original Hopkyttes building remaining at the heart of the later house. Possibly it formed the central block with Ralph adding one or both of the cross wings.

The 1565 Terrier shows Ralph's personal estate to have been relatively small when compared with that of the Wallestons; only three houses and 39½ acres, against eight houses and 287 acres. He was tenth largest landowner in the area. However he had greater wealth in goods than other Ruislip men. The 1557 subsidy[8] levy valued his lands at £6 which was tenth in order of magnitude, but valued his goods at £30, a figure equalled by only one other, John Smith (presumably the demesne farmer referred to in Chapter 6).

Table 1. Ralph Hawtrey's Estate 1565 from the King's College Terrier

Copyhold Property	Date of lease
1. Cottage "Hopkyttes" 4a. close adjacent.	
13a in Common Fields of Eastcote	Lease 1527
2. Messuage and 7a in Wylchers Street (now Wiltshire Lane)	
5a in Common Fields of Eastcote	
1½a. meadow in Roxbourne	Lease 1547
3. Cottage and garden, Bury Street – "The Old House"	
bought from George Est and Agnes his wife	Lease 1557
4. 1a. meadow in Roxbourne	Lease 1546
5. 3a. meadow "Salters Mede" Well Green	Lease 1546
6. 3a. close "Steven Elmes" with a new built Sheep house	Lease 1548
7. 2a. close at top of Cuckoo Hill	not given
8. The Rectory barn in Bury Street.	

Ralph and Winifred are known to have had six children, but their brass on the south wall of the chancel of St. Martin's shows twelve: six sons and six daughters, and some people have assumed that the brass may not show the Hawtreys, particularly as it has no inscription, except for the ages 79 and 74 above the heads of the two figures.

However the brass is known to have been sold by the churchwardens in 1806 and returned to St. Martin's in 1913 by Miss Eleanor Warrender who found it in a London Sale Room (as recorded on a plaque beneath it) and the late L. E. Morris decided that, in spite of this chequered history, it was indeed the Hawtrey brass when he found a description of it in the Rawlinson M.S. in the Bodleian Library complete with its original inscription which had been intact when Rawlinson saw it in the south aisle of the church in the 18th century.

"*Ralphe Hawtrey Gent and Wenyfryde his wief*
Whose bodies here in the earth lyeth
And heav'n their souls, for aye hath won
God bring us thither when we are gone."

Perhaps the extra children died in early infancy. The estates passed from Ralph to his eldest son John in 1574. John and his wife Bridget were admitted jointly to Ralph's property at a Manor Court held on 17 January 1575.[9]

John Hawtrey d. 1593

John married Bridget Lovett the widow of Gabriel Dormer but had no legitimate issue. Rather oddly his younger brother Edward married Gabriel Dormer's daughter Elizabeth who was probably Bridget's step-daughter. John does not appear to have increased the size of the Hawtrey's Ruislip estate until late in life.[10] A 1589 survey giving gross acreages and rents shows him as holding only 30

Ralph Hawtrey, 1570-1638

Mary Hawtrey, d.1647

acres, but a year later he acquired land near Mill House, Bury Street called Hawkins Long; pasture at Field End, Westcote called Willbesouthes; and two shops and a cottage by the Churchyard Gate, all from the Sanders family.[11] He also built, without licence, a dovecot in the grounds of Eastcote House.[12]

At his death in 1593, Ralph, son of his younger brother Edward, inherited the Ruislip property.

Ralph Hawtrey 1570-1638

This Ralph was the first Hawtrey to lease part of the demesne being Ruislip Park (Park Wood). He specifically mentions this lease in his will, leaving it to his son John.[13] He renewed the lease of the rectory on several occasions.[14] The 1625 lease had a rent of £20 plus £4 for two fat boars for the hospitality of the Dean and Canons of Windsor at Christmas.[15]

The Dovecot which now delights our eyes in Eastcote House gardens was probably built in the 18th century to replace the one built by John Hawtrey, "against the custom of the manor" for which Ralph Hawtrey received a licence in 1601;[16] the right to keep doves and pigeons being a manorial prerogative. Pigeon pie was a useful adjunct to the winter diet in the days before cattle could be fed and kept alive all year. The dovecot which already stood near Manor Farm, on what is now St. Martin's Approach car park, must have been used by the demesne farmer and the granting of a licence shows Ralph Hawtrey's high standing with King's College. Incidentally an amusing legend relating to the dovecot still has currency in some circles. Mr Hawtrey was said to have a gallows in his dovecot and to hang people there. This story no doubt arises from the fact that a revolving pole with projecting bracket called a potence, which is the French word for gallows, stands in the dovecot. A ladder attached to the arm simplified the collection of squabs from the shelves around the walls on which the birds roosted. In their position as local magistrates the Hawtreys frequently had miscreants hauled before them by the constables. If any of the wretches disappeared, it was surely to gaol, not into the dovecot! A further tale that the earthern floor covers a quick lime pit and that bits of human bone have been dug from it should *not* be given any credence.

A further licence was granted to Ralph Hawtrey by King's College in 1617 to build a coach house outside St. Martin's on waste at the side of Eastcote Road.[17] This building and another similar one probably built for the inhabitants of Hayden Hall are depicted on Doharty's map (1750) standing on either side of the Eastcote Road gate into the churchyard. They were probably used as school rooms in the early 19th century.

There is no known survey of Ralph's lands, but he expanded the estate in Eastcote by acquiring Plocketts (now Eastcote Cottage) from John Redinge in 1609[18] and was admitted as tenant to two copyhold estates of the manor of the More in 1601.[19] These were Gyett Hills (now Gate Hill Farm) with 90 acres in Northwood and Hampton Hall with 75 acres at Batchworth (near the Batchworth Roundabout and Hampton Hall Farm, Rickmansworth).

Mr Hawtrey in his capacity as Justice of the Peace seems to have been instrumental in providing Ruislip with its first Poor House. In accordance with the provision of the 1601 Poor Law which empowered Overseers of the Poor working under the guidance of local justices to provide either workhouses, or places of asylum. He laid out £12.13s. on the partitioning of Harker's House, to divide it into ten small cottages (known collectively as the Church House) to shelter people in need.[20] These cottages, more recently known as the Almshouses stand in Eastcote Road backing onto the churchyard and were restored in 1980 (see Chapter 9).

Ralph's marriage to Mary Altham produced three sons and a daughter Mary, who grew up to be the only member of the family to achieve fame outside the parish and who has an aura of romance surrounding her name. She married Sir John Bankes, owner of Corfe Castle, Dorset, which she twice held against beseiging Roundheads while her husband was away supporting Charles I. She was unhappily betrayed by a servant and the castle was ruined.[21] The family built Kingston Lacy as their new home in 1663 and lived there until 1981 when a descendant, Henry Bankes left the house and contents to the National Trust. Portraits of Ralph and Mary and a statue of Lady Bankes can be seen in the house. She is commemmorated in her native parish by Lady Bankes' Primary School in Ruislip Manor and in St. Martin's where a mural monument says that she had the honour "to have borne with a constancy and courage above her sex a noble proporcon of the Late Calamities" and a slab behind the altar proclaims "The Lady Mary Bankes. The best of mothers and the best of wives." At his death in 1638 Ralph left his Park lease and the rest of his estate to his eldest son John, but made suitable provision for his wife, as follows:

"I give and bequeath to Mary, my most loving wife, the use of the moiety of my plate, bedding and household stuff within the doors during the term of her natural life if she shall think good to live in the house with my son John Hawtrey; if not then my will and meaning is that she shall make choice of the furniture of two chambers of the best and two furnitures of the chambers for servants with as much plate as shall be to the value of fifty pounds, such as she please to choose as fittest for her own use, and so much linen both for her bed and board as she shall think convenient for her during her natural life.

My will is that my executor shall pay unto Mary, my wife, the sum of fifty pounds that I owe unto her within one year after my decease, and fifty pounds more unto her within one year after her leaving this my house, if she shall not think good to live with my son John.

I give unto Mary, my wife, my best coach and two of my coach horses, such as she shall please to choose with the harness to them belonging."[22]

She probably did continue at Eastcote House with John, for she made him executor of her own will referring to him as her "loving son" and left him her plate and her wedding ring and to his wife a box of china plate and a border of diamonds.[23]

John Hawtrey 1600–1658
Oriel College, Oxford; Matric 1615, Student at Grays Inn 1617

John Hawtrey owned the family lands throughout the Civil War and for most of the Commonwealth period.

Florence Hawtrey in her history of the Hawtrey Family (published 1903) relates a tradition that he was friendly towards Oliver Cromwell and actually entertained him so well at Eastcote House that he received a gift of a watch from him. Parliamentary influence was strong around London and most local gentry did perforce support Cromwell.

John Hawtrey certainly served King's College, a Royalist institution, as Bailiff of the Manor. His name headed the list of fifteen men who signed an

The Goodliest Place in Middlesex

"agreement mead between Nayebors for the renewing and maintaining of ouer (our) orders of ouer (our) fields of Ruyslipp", laying down rules for regulating the common fields in 1651.[24] Two years later King's College granted him the right to fell 200 elms planted on manorial waste near his mansion in consideration of his fidelity and good service.[25]

John married Susannah James, had four daughters and six sons, and died in 1658. His will written in 1657 was not proved until 1663 which may account for the fact that a survey of lands dated 1660 still gives him as the owner[26] of the Hawtrey property (see Table 2). It shows a tremendous increase in land since 1589.

Table 2. John Hawtrey's Estate at the time of his death 1658 from a Court Book

Copyhold Houses	Amount of land	Position if known
His dwelling house and ground	8 acres	Eastcote House
House and ground at Segars	6 acres	at Field End
House and ground at Popes End	18 acres	Cuckoo Hill Farm
House and ground at The Hill	8 acres	
House and ground at Plucketts	4 acres	Eastcote Cottage
Tanner's house and ground	4 acres	
Harrington's house and ground	1 acre	
Skippe's house and ground	2 rood	
Hooper's house and ground	2 acres	
Potter's house and ground	18 acres	
Cottage at Orchard End	—	
Cottage at Plucketts	1 rood	pt. Eastcote Cottage
Stanley's Cottage	1 rood	by the Church gate
House at Town	1 rood	
3 Cottages	—	
	Total 70 acres	
Grounds		
Harry Smiths	5 acres	
Alders Close	6 acres	
Fore Field	63 acres	
Furletts	5 acres	
Batts	2 acres	
Peterwich Ground	13 acres	Between Joel St and
Roundcross	6 acres	Fore St
Harry Browns	2 acres	Corner Field End Rd
Every Years Mead	13 lands	Cheney St
Close at Green Lane	17 acres	In Northwood
Close at Potter Street	19 acres	
Cooke Closes	18 acres	
Coopers Plowgers Ground	4 acres	
Plowgers Ground in Common Fields		
	Total 160 acres	

Leasehold
Rectory Lease (The Great Tithes) from Dean and Canons of Windsor.
Ruislip Park leased from King's College.

The Hawtreys, Rogers and Deanes, of Eastcote House

Ralph Hawtrey his son at the same time had a House on Raisins Hill (probably White Cottage): 2 Cottages and approximately 90 acres.

He made the following provision for his wife in his will:
"I give unto my most dear and most truly loving wife £200 to be paid her out of my estate within one year after my decease. And my best coach and two of my best store horses belonging to them for that service. And the best of my saddle horses with the furniture for them. I do declare that my will is she shall have the use of one moiety of all my plate, pewter, brass, linen of all sorts both for bed and board bedding and all other household stuff and utensils for the house whatsoever being within the doors or in brewhouse, dairy, cellars and any other the outhouses she shall have occasion to use and belonging to my mansion house in Ruislip during her life without any attempt to be made or given by her for what is worn out broken or lost to my son Ralph Hawtrey to whom I give them after her decease.

"Item my will is that she shall have allowed out of my estate corn sufficient to maintain her housekeeping both bread corn and malt and corn for her horses and hay and straw for them with convenient fuel for her expense. And 40 shillings by the week to buy her other sorts of provisions for six months after my decease....".[27]

She died in 1690 aged 85.
John's eldest son Ralph succeeded him.

Ralph Hawtrey 1626–1725

Ralph Hawtrey was the last male Hawtrey to live at Eastcote House. In 1669 he leased the entire manorial demesne from King's College: the Common Wood, the Park and Manor Farm with its enclosed pasture and arable land in the open fields; leases which remained with his descendants until 1872.[28] Occasionally these may have been given to members of his family. Two of his sons, who predeceased him, Charles (died 1698) and Ralph (died 1713) mention them in their wills.[29]

He took a close interest in the care of the poor of this parish. As soon as he succeeded his father he caused a new book to be kept by the Overseers of the Poor. On the title page is written *"Ralph Hawtrey Esq. His Book of Accounts. Being a true accompt of all them that have served Overseers of the Poor of the Parish of Ruislipp. From the year 1659"* (see Chapter 9).[30] His signature frequently appears on the accounts. Payments were made to him from time to time as he sold firewood from Park Wood to the Overseers to distribute among the poor, for example "1722-3 to Esquire Hawtrey for the Poors' Wood £10.12s". Although he lived to be nearly 100 the book was not filled during his lifetime and continued in use until 1745.

A valuation of Mr Hawtrey's Estate taken 20 October 1718 shows that he paid £196.6s rent for his College leasehold of which £52 was in lieu of an earlier malt rent. The profit of the lease was £343.14s. He paid the Dean and Canons of Windsor £25 per annum for the rectory lease plus a fine of £130 every four years. The tithes brought in £250, a yearly profit of £192.10s per annum.[31]

During his long reign some changes were made in the estate. In 1695 Gy^tts Hill was sold to Sir Bartholomew Shower of the Middle Temple and Pinner Hill, for £2000.[32] A farm at Field End, presumably Field End Farm, Eastcote where 178 sheep were kept, was acquired and appears in Ralph's Farm Accounts for 1723.[33]

Photographs of Eastcote House suggest that it was remodelled

The Goodliest Place in Middlesex

Eastcote House, originally "Hopkyttes", but much altered by succeeding generations

during his ownership. The early 19th century stucco covering the brickwork cannot disguise the plat bands at first floor and parapet level so indicative of the first part of the 18th century. The parapet itself is a feature first introduced into English houses in the late 17th century as a fire precaution as it covered woodwork at the eaves, and persisted as a fashion into the 19th century. The main staircase of the house with its barley-stick balusters, wide and ramped hand rail and cut string course can certainly be dated between 1700-25. Probably Ralph in his old age covered the old timber-framed building with a brick skin and made interior alterations.

Ralph married Barbara Grey by whom he had apparently seven sons and four daughters. Three of the sons died young and nothing at all is known of two others except that they must have existed, for the grave slab of Ralph, who died unmarried in 1719 aged 45, describes him as the seventh son of Ralph and Barbara. In his will he left to *"John Owen my huntsman my pack of dogges and also my horse with all the accountrements belonging to him which he usually rides a-hunting on"*. Robert's monument (third son 1657-81) refers also to two of his brothers both called John Hawtrey. *"His eldest brother dying infant was hereabout interred. And another of riper years so named made the Royal Oratory in Cambridge both his grave and monument in the year 1674"*. The Royal Oratory means King's College Chapel.

Charles (1663-1698) alone among the sons married. His wife was Philadelphia Maplestone of Marden, Kent. They had one son, Ralph, who died in 1703 aged 14 and three daughters Philadelphia, Elizabeth and Jane. The latter married Mr James Rogers as his second wife. As the death of young Ralph in 1703 had ended the Hawtrey male line in Ruislip, old Ralph left his property to his granddaughter Jane Rogers.

Jane Rogers 1689–1736

Jane enjoyed the estate for only eleven years as she died in February 1736 only three weeks before the death of her sixteen-year-old son Ralph. Her husband James bought St. Catherine's Farm (still standing, but greatly altered) in Howletts Lane from the executors of Thomas Powell in 1725.[34]

James' and Jane's daughter Elizabeth inherited the estates at the age of 14. She enjoyed her father's guidance for only two years as his death occurred in July 1738.

Elizabeth Rogers 1722–1803

Mrs Elizabeth Rogers continued to lease the entire demesne from King's College. The College authorities engaged John Doharty of Worcester to survey the College lands in 1750. A letter of John Doharty's shows that he prepared three maps, one for the College, one for the Church and one for Mrs Rogers.[35] Only the College map has survived, which is unfortunate as Doharty surveyed Mrs Roger's freehold and copyhold land as well as the demesne, and marked them all on her map. He prepared a Terrier (land survey) for her as well which is extant.[36] A summary of her lands in 1750 taken from it appears below.

Table 3. Mrs Roger's Land, 1750 from the Doharty Survey

Copyhold	acres	roods	poles
Eastcote House	14	2	12
Eastcote Fields	30	2	19
Field End Farm	95	3	10
13a in Eastcote Fields			
Seymour's Homestall	4	3	28
Hy. Platts Homestall	3	0	22
Jas. Tilliard's Homestall		1	17
John West's Homestall	5	0	30
Jos. Philip's Homestall	10	1	12
Richard Weatherleys's	22	3	39
Widow Ambridge land	21	0	27
William Gladman land	10	3	9
George Barringer land	2	2	23
John Lott land	17	1	32
	240	0	11
Freehold			
Sarah King land	3	3	10
Samuel Page land	11	1	30
John Lott land	4	3	32
George Woods land (Catherine End)	32	0	8
	52	1	0
Leasehold from King's College			
Demesne including Copse Wood	335	0	0
Park Wood	407	3	7
Manor Farm } Enclosed Pastures }	212	2	11
Common Field Land	716	2	12
	1671	3	30

The Old House in Bury Street is missing from the estate. It had been sold to the Rev. Charles Jacques of Hillingdon in 1739.

Elizabeth Rogers lived unmarried at Eastcote House becoming infirm and deaf a few years before her death in 1803.[37] The prefix "Mrs" which like "Miss" is short for "Mistress" was often given to unmarried women in the 18th century. In the earlier years she seems to have been a vigorous and formidable, if somewhat conservative landowner. She strenuously opposed enclosure when it was proposed for the St. Catherine's area of the parish in 1769 because she feared the cost;[38] objected to tithes of wood being granted to the vicar in case her income from her rectorial lease should thereby be reduced;[39] and refused to answer the questionnaire devised by the Rev. Daniel Lysons when he was preparing his histories of Middlesex Parishes, as she considered the inquiries impertinent.[40]

Elizabeth leased the rectory, paying £60 per annum and a substantial fine on renewal every seven years. Wood tithes became a contentious issue again in 1796 after lying in abeyance for the last two centuries, because the Dean and Canons of Windsor were persuaded to grant tithes of underwood (coppiced hornbeam) to Mr Gibbons, (vicar 1794-7) and to his successors. Mrs Rogers refused to renew her lease when it fell due in 1798 unless she could be indemnified against the vicar's right. *"I cannot help complaining that the Dean and Canons have used me very unhandsomely by making a Deed to deprive me of my property in the tythe of underwood".*[41] At the same time she mentioned the very *"heavy fine set upon a very old tenant (near fifty years)"* which she declared was set a full two years value instead of 1½ years. She was *"determined to abide the event of a suit".* The Dean and Canons replied that the increase in fine was solely due to the fact that the Chapter now set the fine on 1½ years value not 1¼ and that the tithe of coppice had always been vicarial. Finding Mrs Rogers intransigent and wishing to renew her lease with them the Dean and Canons informed the new vicar, Daniel Carter Lewis (Mr Gibbons died in 1797) that their 1796 grant had been intended *"solely to establish and strengthen the Vicar of Ruislip in the tythe of Coppice Wood if that right could be shown either by endowment or usage and as neither he nor his predecessors had been able to find the endowment nor show by usage his right thereto they were of opinion he ought to surrender the confirmation that they may be enabled to treat with their lessee for a renewal of lease".*[42] The lease, however, was not renewed in 1798 and there the dispute rested until after Elizabeth Roger's death in 1803.

Ralph Deane 1782–1852
Trinity College, Oxford: Matric 1796: BA 1800: MA 1803, Vinerian Fellow, Magdalen Coll. Oxon 1800-12. Barrister at Law Middle Temple 1811.
Her will appointed Rev. George Deane (second son of Henry Deane of Reading) and Charles James Esq. of New Inn as Trustees of most of her property.[43] Certain annuities were to be paid from the profits and the residue was to go to Philadelphia and Jane Deane (Henry Deane's sisters) then to Ralph Deane (fifth son of Henry Deane). Philadelphia, Jane and Henry were grandchildren of Philadelphia Hawtrey, aunt of Elizabeth Rogers. Ralph, residuary legatee seems to have been in possession by 1810.[44]

The change in ownership precipitated Enclosure in Ruislip (see Chapter 10). The wood tithes dispute was ended as tithes both rectorial and vicarial were extinguished and land given in lieu; 391 acres to the rectors and 120 acres to the vicar with an additional 25 acres of Park Wood and 50 acres on Haste Hill taken out of the Manorial allotment to compensate for the vicar's firewood and illusionary wood tithes.

Philadelphia and Jane Deane renewed the rectory lease in 1803 but were asked to pay an unusually large fine of £4,697.19s.2d because of the lapse of 12 years since the previous renewal. They pleaded that Mrs Rogers had been very old and infirm "....*not fully competent to do business*", a statement belied by her 1797-8 correspondence.[45] They pointed out the cost of Enclosure about to take place and the necessity of building a barn, house and stable on the newly acquired rectory land. They thought (as many do when faced with extortionate official demands) that a mistake had been made. A later appendix to their memorandum shows the accounts of the Ruislip tithes for 1803-6, (Table 4) the last years for which they were collected. Tithes were not collected in kind but had been commuted to a money payment long since.

Table 4. Ruislip Tithes 1803–6

	1803 £ : s : d	1804 £ : s : d	1805 £ : s : d	1806 £ : s : d
Tithes	368 : 4 : 4	411 : 19 : 76½	535 : 12 : 2½	556 : 9 : 8½
Deductions				
Poor Rate	38 : 6 : 5	38 : 6 : 5	48 : 0 : 0	48 : 0 : 0
Rent	58 : 19 : 2	60 : 17 : 0	60 : 1 : 1	57 : 12 : 11
Statute Duty	9 : 15 : 7	19 : 15 : 7	9 : 15 : 7	9 : 15 : 7
Dinner on Tithe Day	17 : 5 : 5	19 : 6 : 6	19 : 10 : 0	19 : 17 : 0
Property Tax	16 : 0 : 0	16 : 0 : 0	18 : 0 : 0	32 : 0 : 0
Total deductions	142 : 4 : 7	144 : 5 : 6	155 : 6 : 8	167 : 5 : 6
Profit	225 : 19 : 9	267 : 14 : 1	380 : 5 : 6¼	402 : 1 : 0¼

The price of corn was increasing during this period as the Napoleonic wars progressed, which accounts for the increased value of the tithes. Provision of dinner on Tithe Day for those paying their tithes was a universal custom. Tithe payers were usually farmers and the dinner was a carnival occasion, one of the customary social gatherings of the agricultural year, considered an untoward expense by many rectors. Parson Woodforde of Weston Langeville, Norfolk describes his 1776 Tithe Day in his published diary as "*My frolic for my People to pay Tithe to me this day. I gave them a good dinner, surloin of Beef rosted, a Leg of Mutton boiled and plumb Pudding in plenty.... They had to drink Wine, Punch and Ale as much as they pleased; they drank of wine 6 Bottles, of Rum 1 gallon and half, and I know not what ale*".

Other expenses not appearing in the accounts fell upon the rectorial lessees. The Church Bridge (presumably the bridge across the Pinn in Bury Street by the vicarage and sometimes called Parsons Bridge) was repaired in 1805 and work was begun on repairing the chancel in 1807.[46]

Before Enclosure the rectorial lessees had only needed to collect their tithes to make their profit. After Enclosure a corn rent was imposed upon the old enclosures (and adjusted every 21 years), based on the prevailing price of corn in Cambridge market. The allotment of 391 acres made the rector a major land owner with the opportunity to increase the value of the rectory by intelligent farming. 100 acres of the land at that time was uncultivated wasteland in Northwood, considered unproductive. The other 291 acres were part of the

BOURNE FARM
South Ruislip

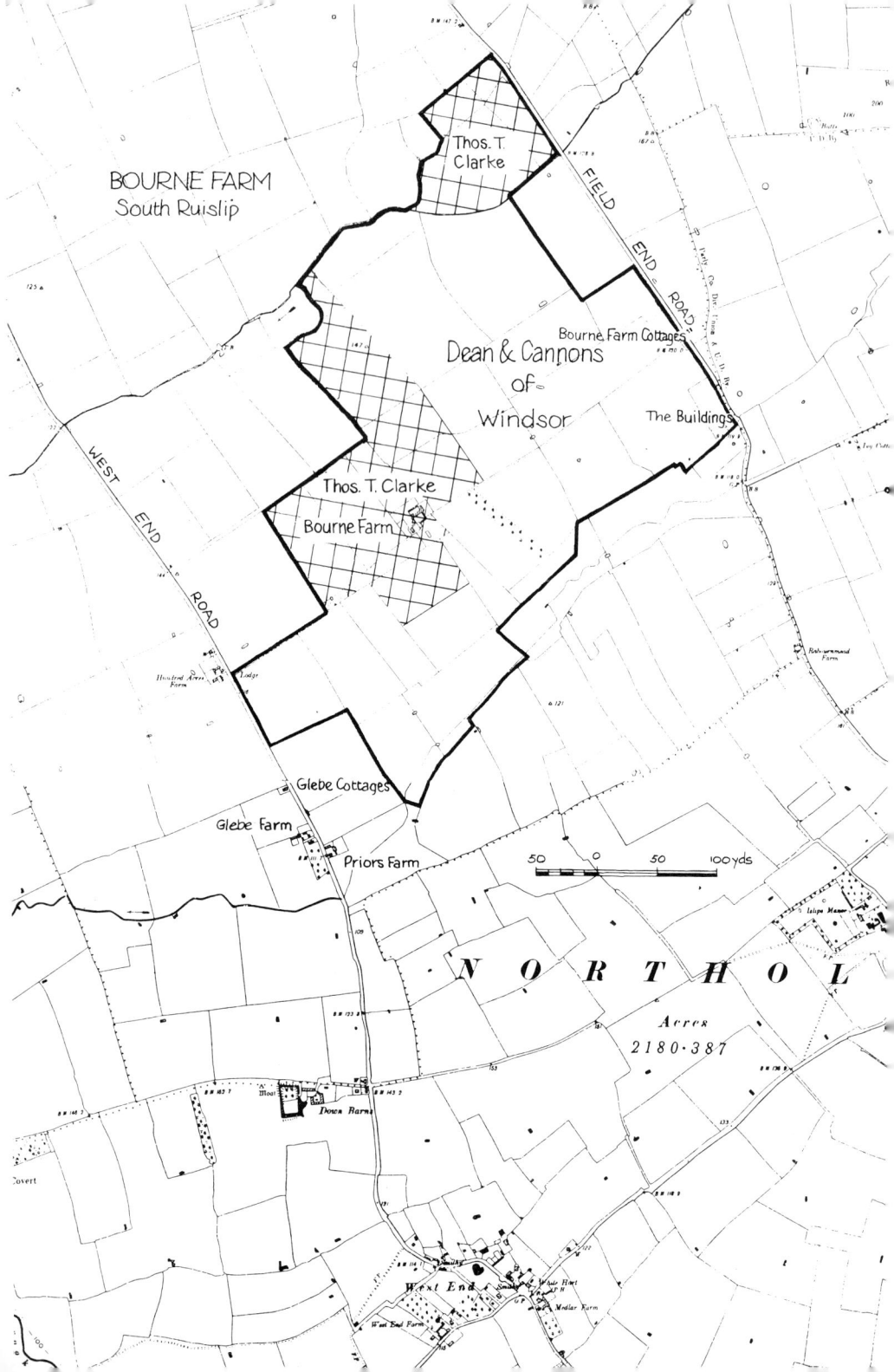

Thos. T. Clarke

Bourne Farm Cottages

Dean & Cannons of Windsor

The Buildings

Thos. T. Clarke
Bourne Farm

WEST END ROAD

FIELD END ROAD

Glebe Cottages
Glebe Farm
Priors Farm

50 0 50 100 yds

NORTHOL
Acres
2180·387

former Bourne Field. Suitable tenants, farm buildings and time were needed to make it profitable.

The rectory, which formed a substantial part of his income, continued to exercise Ralph Deane as it had his aunts. Each time the lease came up for renewal he wrote plaintive letters to Windsor about his "peculiar hardship" and pleading his case for a less extortionate fine. That demanded in 1810 was £1230. The 1817 renewal occurred in the aftermath of the enclosure upheaval. On 12 April 1817 he wrote *"the expense of the subdivision fences is not altogether, I apprehend, less than £1000. You should also consider that the distance of one allotment from the other is not less than three miles. I have had the land in hand three times and at present I am under the necessity of farming at a great loss"*. The corn rents were apparently taking some time to establish. Due to the unsettled state of affairs many parishioners refused to pay them until they were fixed. "The loss I sustained amounted to many hundreds of pounds". He mentions the expense of collecting the corn rents, (about 250) numerous small payments. *"All these things considered tend to reduce much of the value of the tithes. It is also necessary to give them a dinner, which to so large a number makes it very expensive. I also give Mr Shalford who collects them a commission of 5 per cent, for exclusive of receiving the tithes it is necessary to look closely at the occupations for in the case of changes we are without remedy"*.[47] A landlord's lot was not a happy one!

By 1831 farming in general was in decline and the poor rate was rapidly increasing because of the prevailing distress. Once again Mr Deane complained that the rectory lands had no buildings and being for the most part poor agricultural land at the extremes of the parish were difficult to let to suitable tenants. He was considering erecting farm buildings himself, provided that the Dean and Canons would allow the next renewal in 1838 to pass without raising the fine and would vote him a sum of money. The 1831 fine was £1371:11s:11d. The money was not forthcoming and no buildings were erected, but the 1838 fine was only £1341:11s and that of 1845 was £1342:12s.[48]

The Dean and Canons of Windsor never did build farm houses on the rectory allotments but Ralph Deane himself made some provision in the cause of more efficient farming. Before 1812[49] he purchased an allotment from T. T. Clarke (of Swakeleys) immediately adjoining the rectory land in South Ruislip and built a house there soon afterwards. It appears on the one inch Ordnance Survey map surveyed in 1820 as "New House" and was later called Bourne Farm. Having failed to persuade the Dean and Canons to erect anything, he installed a bailiff and used Bourne Farm for his private lands and rectory lands combined. Bourne Farm by mid-century comprised:
297 acres belonging to the Dean and Canons
<u>152</u> acres plus buildings belonging to Mr Deane
449 acres TOTAL[50]

It was occupied by Mr Deane's Farm Bailiffs: Joseph Mann in 1851, John Abbott 1861 and Joseph Moore in 1871.

Similarly the Northwood allotment was farmed from Northwood Farm (still standing on Northwood Golf Course), built on the neighbouring King's College land by 1827. It was composed of:
91 acres belonging to the Dean and Canons
<u>90</u> acres plus buildings belonging to King's College
181 acres TOTAL

Bourne Farm, South Ruislip

The Goodliest Place in Middlesex

Mr Deane's Farm Bailiff, Joseph Herridge, lived there in 1841 and 1851. It is understandable that King's College leasehold, the Rectory leasehold and the private lands, should have been amalgamated for efficient farming, but surveyors from Windsor became confused and assessed the value too highly with a view to increasing the Deanes' fines, producing a spate of anxious letters from Eastcote to Windsor.[51]

At enclosure King's College demesne was increased by 90 acres of former waste around Park Wood, on which Northwood Farm was built. The main part of the demesne as always was Manor Farm with its meadow and pasture along the Pinn and arable land in Church Field, Marlpit Field and Bourne Field running south from the house (700 acres). Although the Hawtreys had leased Manor Farm from King's College, none of them had ever lived there or worked the land themselves. They had always sub-leased it. At the turn of the 19th century Jason Wilshin (1759-1823) was tenant at Manor Farm. Rather amusingly just at the time the Deanes were questioning Windsor about the terms of the rectory lease, Mr Wilshin was querying the valuation set upon Manor Farm by the Deanes and threatening not to renew his lease with them. He submitted to the Deanes' terms after being warned that several other people were interested in Manor Farm.[52] His son Daniel (1783-1864) succeeded him after his removal to the Old House, Bury Street in 1810. Daniel Wilshin stayed at Manor Farm until 1823, the year of his father's death and subsequently moved to Hayes.[53]

The lease made between Daniel Wilshin and Ralph Deane in 1817 has survived.[54] It describes the property as the Mansion House of the Manor or late Priory of Ruislip and a cottage and garden called "Smith's Shop". The latter was probably the forerunner of the lodge which stands at the entrance to Manor Farm, now used as a public convenience. It is shown as a Smith's Shop on

Northwood Farm

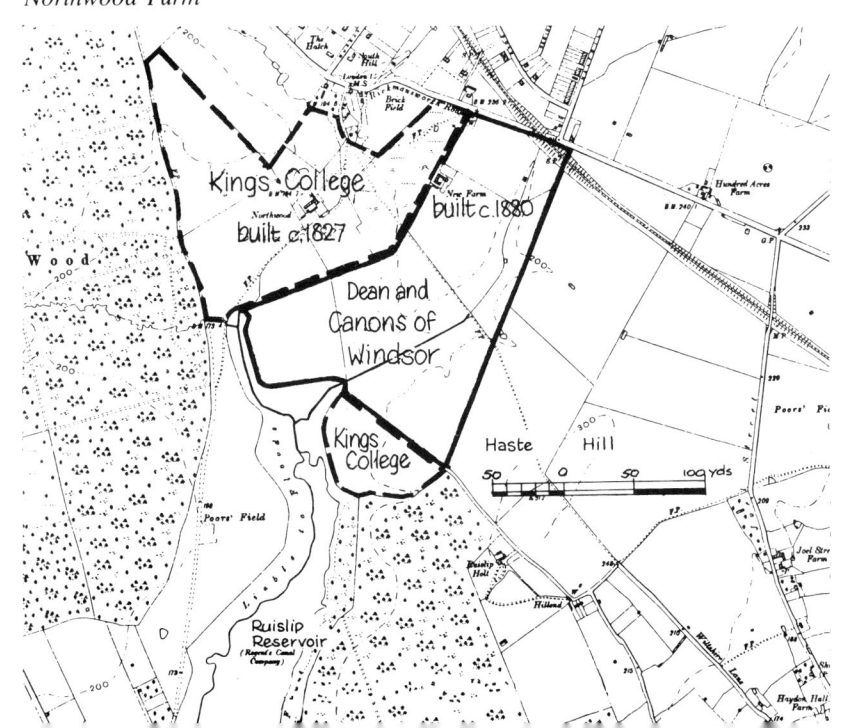

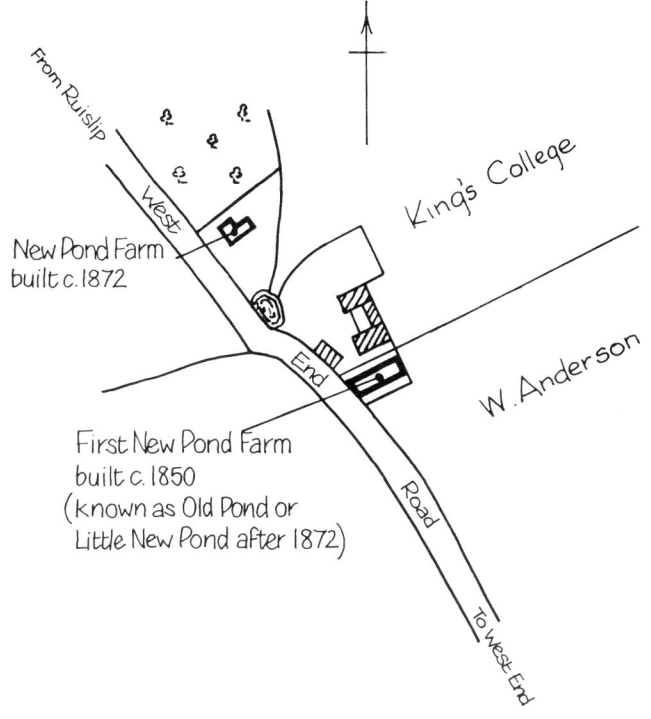

New Pond Farm

Doharty's map, 1750. Manor Farm House had a hall with a long table, benches and a form; a little parlour with shelves in the closet; a kitchen with shelves, jack and chimney box; a copper wash tub; a dairy; best room; yellow room; green room; servants' room and a cellar.

With its yellow and green rooms it sounds to be the home of a gentleman-farmer rather than a yeoman, as befitted the administrative centre of the manor. Courts were held there until 1925.

Daniel Wilshin paid £484:2s:6d p.a. plus £20 for any meadow ground he might plough or break up, and 16 qr. wheat and 28 qr. 6 bushels malt or barley or its monetary value in the Cambridge Market. He was obliged to put dung or London ashes on the land to keep it in good heart (house refuse carried back by returning hay carts).

By 1850 Ralph Deane had built some farm buildings in West End Road just within a piece of land (22 acres) allotted to W. Anderson at Enclosure, later purchased by him.[55] This was probably a cottage suitable for a farm labourer. During the next few years barns and outbuildings seem to have been built on the demesne land immediately adjoining, the whole becoming known as New Pond Farm. From that time onwards the southern portion of the demesne was farmed from New Pond. A labourer Thomas Clayton lived there in 1851, but ten years later Thomas Sanson was farming the 22 acres and 87 acres of the college land from there. After the Deanes had ceased to lease the demesne in 1872 the College built a new farm house a little further north on its own land and transferred the name. That house still stands near Cornwall Road (now a nursing home). Thereafter, the original New Pond Farm was known as Little New Pond or Old Pond Farm.

143

The Goodliest Place in Middlesex

Because of the Enclosure Ralph Deane administered a potentially more valuable demesne than his predecessors. Not surprisingly the rent of the demesne lease was raised in 1810 to £86 per annum.[56]

Mr Deane appears to have been aiming at owning all the land around the rectory lands in South Ruislip. He acquired Priors Farm from Lord Jersey of Osterley on the southern boundary of the parish, probably on the site of the 13th century grange mentioned in Chapter 3. This farm had actually belonged to the Hawtreys a century earlier and had been sold to the Earl of Carnarvon in 1717 for £1300.[57] It was owned by Robert Child of Osterley Park by 1774, grandfather of Lord Jersey.

Ralph Deane, who was evidently a great builder, built a new farmhouse more conveniently placed near West End Road before 1835[58] and had the old one demolished.

When Ruislip parish vestry offered the Workhouse on Ducks Hill for sale by auction in 1838, Ralph Deane bought it and converted it into six tenements.[59]

Eastcote House was improved. *The Beauties of England and Wales* by J. Norris Brewer published in 1816 refers to "the residence of Ralph Deane, Esq." and says "Mr Deane has much altered and modernised this ancient dwelling". Presumably he gave the brick facing and parapet, the plaster facade and long windows depicted in photographs and remembered by many.

Although he was living at Eastcote House at the time of the 1851 Census, Ralph had leased the house and a portion of the estate on at least one occasion before that to John Pearce and Edward Stone, gentlemen.[60] A 12 year lease dated 7th October 1840 lets them Eastcote House, coach-house, stables, barns, yards, pleasure grounds and orchard, plus 30 acres on Ducks Hill (recently grubbed up woodland), other small pieces of land on Ducks Hill (probably the former Workhouse), and shooting rights over all the Deane lands, at a rent of £280 per annum.

Ralph Deane was active in local affairs. His name usually heads subscription lists, as in 1840 when a new National School was being built in Ruislip and he gave £21, the next highest donation being £15 from King's College.[61] He was present at vestry meetings and served on the local bench of Magistrates.

Ralph married Elizabeth Gosling. Their son Ralph was drowned at Eton in 1826. Another son Francis succeeded his father in 1852.

A comparison between the estate in 1806 as shown on the Enclosure Map and in 1847 towards the end of his life graphically shows the expansion and improvement undertaken by Ralph Deane. He is an example of a landowner who took full advantage of the enclosures.

Francis Henry Deane 1814–1892
Wadham College, Oxford: Matric 1832; BA 1836; MA 1840. Barrister at Law: Lincolns Inn 1846

Francis owned Eastcote House and other land and property at the period when industrial Britain was expanding her overseas Empire; when the country's population (and that of the parish) was steadily increasing; when a modern outlook in Parliament, legal circles and society in general was sweeping away the remnants of medieval laws and forms of tenure (copyhold for example) and when large land owners were beginning to find more profit in selling land to railway companies and building developers than letting to tenant farmers. Francis Deane was the last of the family to live at Eastcote House, the last to lease the demesne from King's College and the last to lease the rectory from the Dean and Canons of Windsor, but he did not sell land for development.

He lived at Eastcote House until 1878 and then at East View, Uxbridge Common until his death in 1892.[62] Eastcote House was let to tenants. He and two other trustees of his father's will, Alfred Caswell of Inner Temple and John Eldred Walters of Lincoln's Inn, leased the demesne in 1852 for 20 years. This was the last demesne lease. The Governing Body of King's College decided in May 1872 to retain the woods in hand and let Manor Farm direct to tenant farmers.[63]

The connection with Windsor ended in 1867 when all Windsor's rectorial estates passed to the Ecclesiastical Commissioners.[64] Before 1867 his communications with Windsor were very like his father's, questioning the fines and reiterating the old arguments. In 1866 he complained that the land had no buildings "except a small cottage I have erected for a labourer" (Bourne Farm Cottages) and that the land was distant from a canal or railway. He was prepared to bargain. *"In case of renewal being arranged on fair terms it is my intention to expend a considerable sum on the restoration of the Church".*[65] A major restoration took place in 1869-70 under the direction of Gilbert Scott. *"I believe that at the last renewal the fine paid was too high and I fear that my consent at that time may have misled you in setting the present one".* He paid £1675 for the renewal in June. His future dealings were with the Ecclesiastical Commissioners.

A survey made in 1871 by the Commissioners' Agents showed the Northwood holding of 91 acres 3r 17p occupied by Daniel Hill and the Ruislip holding of 296 acres 2 roods 17 perches occupied by Joseph Moore.[66]

By a deed dated 12th December 1872 the Commissioners conveyed the reversion in the 338 acres 1r 19p of land to the lessee in consideration of the surrender to them of the leasehold interest in the corn rents and a sum of £6,500.[67] Sometime following this transaction New Farm was built in Northwood at the end of New Farm Lane and two cottages called New Farm Cottages on Pinner Road. The cottages still stand, but the farm house and buildings were demolished and the garden developed in 1985/6.

Several cottages, plain but well built, were erected on pieces of former road side waste by Francis Deane: The Rosery and Deane Cottage on Forge Green, Eastcote among them.

Ralph Hawtrey Deane 1848–1924

Ed. Brighton College and Trinity College Oxford; BA 1873. Called to Bar at Lincoln's Inn 1880. Marr. Anne Cordelia Ellis of Chudleigh, Devon 1881-1932

Ralph Hawtrey Deane never lived in Eastcote but is sometimes referred to in reminscences as Squire Deane because of the large estates which he owned. Walford's County Families gives his address in 1920 as 5 Lincolns Inn and his seat as Eastcote House.

The building of railway stations at Ruislip 1904, Eastcote 1906 and Northolt Junction (South Ruislip) 1908, accelerated the demand for land by building speculators. Ralph Deane was one of the land owners who supplied it. Taking advantage of rising land values he sold fields next to Northolt Junction Station which had been part of Bourne Farm to Robert Masson-Smith et al. (later British Freehold Investment Syndicate) in 1910, 1911 and 1921.[68]

The Goodliest Place in Middlesex

Table 5. Ralph Hawtrey Deane's Estate from the 1902 Rate Book	
Frog Lane	2 Cottages and gardens
Field End	2 Cottages and gardens
Bourne Farm	4 Cottages
Raisins Hill	2 Cottages and gardens
Bury Street	1 Cottage and garden
Hill Corner	1 Cottage and garden
Eastcote Roadside	1 Cottage and garden
Agricultural land – Bourne Farm	100 acres
Northolt Road	34 acres
Field End	7 acres
Field End House and garden	
Field End Farm	207 acres
Priors Farm	152 acres
Park Farm	53 acres
Agricultural Land – Cheney Street	23 acres
Raisons Hill	3 acres
Henry Gallops house	
Fore Street Farm	
Field End Lodge	3 acres
Eastcote House	9 acres
New Farm Northwood	89 acres
Cuckoo Hill Farm	65 acres
Bourne Farm	168 acres
6 Cottages at the Old Workhouse	
Agricultural Land – Common	22 acres
Frog Lane	54 acres

Apart from these transactions he mainly sold off small pieces of land around Eastcote and Ruislip, as listed below:[69]

1920 Part of New Farm – land east of The Drive to Universal Housing Company Ltd.
1920 10 acres north of the railway line on the east side of Field End Road to the Metropolitan Railway Company.
1920 The Old Shooting Box alias Southill House to Charles Percy Duncan.
1921 The Old Workhouse to William Page, Builder of May Lodge Northwood.
1923 Land east of The Old Workhouse to Rev. Ralph Potts Guy.
1924 Land on Ducks Hill – near Horsens (later Battle of Britain) to Josef Conn.

His best memorial in Eastcote is perhaps St. Lawrence's Church. An acre was purchased from him in 1913 and he gave an additional acre in 1924, the year in which he died, for the church and grounds.

Ralph Hawtrey Deane b. 1884
Lt. Commander R.N. Marr. Dorothy Alice Lord 1915

Ralph Hawtrey Deane succeeded his father in 1924 and between then and the outbreak of the Second World War sold off the rest of the estate.

1925 Land south of Cuckoo Hill Farm to C. H. R. Grant.
1925 Ivy Farm, Wiltshire Lane to Edward Thomas William Van Baerle.

The Hawtreys, Rogers and Deanes, of Eastcote House

1925 Land by Griffinhurst at Field End to Florence Mertens.
1925 Field End Lodge to B. S. Hall.
1925 Bury Street Farm to Florence Collins.
1925 Cottage, Eastcote Road (formerly used as a forge) to Agnes Tapping.
1926 Ashtree Cottage (The Old Barn House) to Dorothy Benson.
1927 Much of New Farm lands to R.N.U.D.C.
1927 Land which became Morford Way to R.N.U.D.C. (subsequently bought by Telling).
1930 Eastcote House and land to Wembley Estates (C and W) Ltd
1930 Cuckoo Hill Farm to Standard Estates Ltd.
1930 Land at bottom of Fore St. (now Coteford School) to Standard Estates Ltd.
1931 New Farm House and garden to Alfred Ernest Marks.
1931 Bourne Farm and 195 acres to A. J. A. Taylor & Co.
1932 Field End Cottages to Walter Tapping.
1933 New Farm Cottages to Alice Lawford and George Whitehead.
1933 Fore St. Farm to Standard Estates.
1933 Pair of Cottages, Eastcote Road to Agnes Tapping.
1935 The rest of Bourne Farm and Priors Farm to A. J. A. Taylor & Co.
1935 Land east of Field End Road to Helen Silvestra Miller.
1936 Bourne Farm Cottages to London Diocesan Fund.
1936 Land east of Field End Road to Davis Estate Co. Ltd.

With these sales, Commander Deane severed his family's 400 year old connection with the parish of Ruislip.

Eastcote House (1935) The Cromwell Room

The Goodliest Place in Middlesex

Public outcry against the proposed demolition of Eastcote House caused R.N.U.D.C. to purchase it along with 9.1 acres of its grounds in 1931 for £10,500. For nearly thirty years thereafter the house provided accommodation for Scouts, Guides, Women's Institute, Welfare Clinics and other organisations, but received inadequate care from its new owners. It was declared unsafe for public use in 1962 and was demolished in 1964. Today the former coach house (listed as 17th century and used as a billiards room by the Men's Institute), the charming Dovecot and walled garden remain for public enjoyment. These remnants of past glories at least now receive proper maintenance from the Council, who advised and assisted by Eastcote Conservation Panel have imaginatively created a herb garden within the walls of the old kitchen garden and have drawn attention to the ha ha and other interesting features.

Tenants of Eastcote House

During the last sixty years of its existence as a private house, Eastcote House was occupied by tenants. Some had great impact on the neighbourhood, taking an active part in local affairs and providing entertainment. Such a one was Sir Samuel Morton Peto (1809-89), building contractor and engineer, tenant from 1877-86. Perhaps Eastcote was regarded by him as a rural retreat in which to retire after a vigorous public life as MP. He had been responsible for world-wide railway construction; had built the Lyceum (1834), St. James Theatre (1835), the Reform Club (1836), Nelson's Column (1843) and with his partner Thomas Grisell, the Houses of Parliament to Charles Barry's design in 1841. He built Somerleyton Hall and village, Suffolk in 1844. He served as MP for Norwich (1847-54), Finsbury (1859-65) and Bristol (1863-8).[70] His firm Peto and Betts went bankrupt in 1867. While in Eastcote he assisted at Penny Readings in the school room (1877) giving a, no doubt, instructive talk on coal and its various uses. His daughters sang in the choir at the same entertainment.[71] Five of his children were living at Eastcote House at the time of the 1881 Census. He was served by a butler, cook, lady's maid, two housemaids, a kitchenmaid and a footman. Two daughters were married at St. Martin's, in 1883 and 1885, on which occasions triumphal arches were erected outside the house and crowds gathered outside the church, a sign of popularity.[72] The younger daughter, Helen Agnes, married Lawrence Ingham Baker, son of Lawrence James Baker of Hayden Hall, the last in a line of marriages between the two houses. The young couple settled at Eastcote Lodge keeping a Peto base in the area after Sir Samuel left for the Isle of Wight in 1886. One of his sons, Harrison Ainsworth Peto, was an architect and, in partnership with Ernest George, made a great and lasting impression on the neighbourhood. He designed a new Eastcote Lodge in 1886 for his sister and brother-in-law and several cottages which still stand on the Hayden Hall Estate.[73]

Other tenants were Lt. Col. Inglis, (1888-94), J. Boyle (1895-1904), Mr and Mrs Campbell-Mcleod (1907-c.1920), H. J. E. Scott-McDougall (c.1920-1931).[74]

Influence of the Hawtreys, Rogers and Deanes

The family is remarkable for having owned and inhabited one house for a considerable period – 400 years. Their entry into the parish through marriage into the Walleston family began in a period when the parish was divided between a large number of relatively small land owners (60% of the tenants in 1565), saw the build up of much larger estates and ended only when all those estates, even the demesne were finally broken up for building development this century.

Their influence was vastly increased by their leasehold possessions, but even without those, their personal estate had grown to be the largest in the parish by 1814. Perhaps their legal training helped them in their business dealings. Few of the other major land owners actually lived in Ruislip and none for such a length of time.

REFERENCES

1. G.L.R.O.: Acc 249/7 and Acc 249/6.
2. Ruislip Library: Copy Land Certificate Title No. P.59761.
3. St. George's Windsor: XV 31.65.
4. King's College: R36.
5. G.L.R.O.: Acc 249/7.
6. St. George's, Windsor: XV 31.65; 70, 71, 73.
7. G.L.R.O.: Acc 249/5.
8. G.L.R.O.: Acc 247/17.
9. G.L.R.O.: Acc 249/64.
10. Brit. Library Add: MS 9369.
11. Ibid.
12. G.L.R.O.: Acc 249/183.
13. Florence Hawtrey: *The Hawtrey Family* p.89 1903.
14. St. George's, Windsor: XVI. 1. 58-61.
15. Ibid: 1.60.
16. G.L.R.O.: Acc 249/183.
17. Ibid: 236.
18. Ibid:
19. Herts R.O. D/EB 513 T73-76, G.L.R.O. Acc 249/184.
20. G.L.R.O.: Acc 249/234, 235.
21. Florence Hawtrey: op cit.
22. Ibid: p. 87-9.
23. Transcript of Will by James McBean: Ruislip Library.
24. G.L.R.O.: Acc 249/4113.
25. King's College: Q.36.
26. Brit. Library Add: MS 9368.
27. Ruislip Library: Transcript of Will by James McBean.
28. King's College: Ledger Books.
29. Florence Hawtrey: op cit.
30. G.L.R.O.: Acc 249/1574.
31. Ibid 2280.
32. Nat. Reg. of Archives Catalogue p.27 1953.
33. G.L.R.O.: Acc 249/3010.
34. Ibid 1778.
35. King's College: Q.42/34.
36. Ruislip Library: Typescript.
37. St. George's Windsor: XVII.38.8.
38. G.L.R.O.: Acc 249/2708.
39. St. George's Windsor: XVII.4.39.
40. Ruislip Library: L. E. Morris Collection.
41. St. George's Windsor: XVII.4.39.
42. Ibid.
43. Will: Transcript by James McBean.

44. G.L.R.O.: DRO 19 E2/22 – Rate Book.
45. St. George's, Windsor: XVII.38.8.
46. Ibid.
47. Ibid.
48. Ibid.
49. G.L.R.O.: DRO 19 E2/22 Rate Book.
50. St. George's Windsor: 22(a) XVII.21.3.
51. Ibid.
52. G.L.R.O.: Acc 538/2nd dep/3666/2.
53. G.L.R.O.: DRO 19 E2/23 Rate Book and Wilshin Family Tree.
54. G.L.R.O.: Acc 249/3800.
55. G.L.R.O.: DRO 19 E2/33 Rate Book.
56. King's College: Ledger Book.
57. G.L.R.O.: Acc 249/2262.
58. G.L.R.O.: DRO 19 E2/24 Rate Book.
59. G.L.R.O. Middlesex Deeds Registry.
60. G.L.R.O.: Acc 249/3807.
61. St. George's, Windsor: XVII.38.8.
62. Uxbridge Library: Street Directories and Census Returns.
63. King's College: Ledger Book.
64. Letter from Church Commissioners.
65. St. George's, Windsor: 22(a) XVII.21.3.
66. Ibid.
67. Information from Church Commissioners.
68. G.L.R.O. – Middlesex Deeds Registry
69. Ibid.
70. Biographical details researched by James McBean.
71. W. A. G. Kemp: History of Eastcote.
72. Uxbridge Library: Local paper.
73. James McBean: J Ruislip, N'wd and E'cote Loc. Hist. Soc. 1979.
74. Uxbridge Library: Street Directories.

Chapter Eight
Life in 17th century and 18th century Ruislip

General Trends
Documents dating from 11th-16th century give a great deal of information about land ownership and relations between the lords of the manor and tenants. During the next 200 years different types of records were kept, parish registers and vestry minute books for example, relating to the parish rather than the manor; the labouring classes as well as the landowners; and full of information about the more intimate aspects of everyday life.

Parish Registers
The keeping of parish registers was made compulsory in 1538, by Thomas Cromwell, Henry VIII's chief minister. Each Sunday every parson, vicar or curate was to enter in a book the name of every person wedded, christened or buried during the preceding week, in the presence of a churchwarden. A coffer with two locks was to be provided to store the register. The vicar and churchwarden were to keep a key each for security. Failure to comply warranted a fine of 3s:4d which went towards church repairs. The injunction was only sketchily obeyed. Many registers were kept in paper books or on loose sheets. Ruislip's early registers have completely failed to survive, though those of Ickenham and Harefield are extant.
  The order was repeated in 1547 by Edward VI; appropriating the fine to the church instead of church repairs; and again by Elizabeth in 1559. More stringent regulations introduced by Convocation in 1597 ordained that henceforth more durable parchment should be used for registers and that entries in the old paper books must be copied in to the new ones, especially from the first year of Elizabeth's reign. The parish chest in which they were kept was to have three locks. St. Martin's is fortunate in possessing two chests, both iron-bound, probably installed to comply with these injunctions. The one in the north aisle is made of elm and had two locks, that on the south side of the nave is oak and had three locks originally. Entries of the preceding week were to be read out in church on Sundays and once a year about Easter transcripts were to be sent to the Diocesan Registry. In theory at least a safe system of registration was established by 1603 when these regulations were confirmed; with the public reading as a check upon accuracy and the Bishop's Transcripts a safeguard against loss of the originals. In practice Bishop's Transcripts are often incomplete because churchwardens were not paid for sending the transcripts nor diocesan registrars for preserving them. The only Ruislip transcripts in the Bishop of London's Registry are for 1629 and 1630. The keeping of registers often suffered during the Civil Wars and Commonwealth.

The Goodliest Place in Middlesex

For whatever reason, Ruislip's Registers have only been preserved as follows:
Baptisms   1689 – the present
Marriages 1694 – 1717 : 1744 – the present
Burials   1695 – 1705 : 1709 – the present

Apart from the most recent books they are kept in the Greater London Record Office.

The 17th century and early 18th century registers give only the bare facts: date of baptism, name of child, name of parents; date of marriage, names of bride and groom; date of burial, name of deceased, parents or husband of deceased as appropriate.

After Hardwicke's Marriage Act was passed in 1754 marriage entries were kept in a separate book. This led to a great improvement in Ruislip as marriages had only been sporadically recorded in the early registers.

Registers became much more informative from 1812 onwards when Rose's Act required separate books to be kept for baptisms and burials as well as marriages, and printed books were provided by the King's Printers, which led to uniformity. Christenings were to include the name, abodes and occupations of parents and burial registers the name, abode and age of the deceased. Ruislip's marriage registers give the name and occupation of bride's father from 1838.

No Ruislip clergyman felt it incumbent upon himself to write biographies of the deceased in the burial registers, but occasionally one slipped in an interesting comment, as in 1700 when Timothy Green of Eastcote "an old rebellious taylor" was buried.

During the 18th century the average number of baptisms was 26 per year. The trend was downward until 1740 (28-21) then upwards to about 35 per annum before the end of the century.

Accustomed as we are to the bells of St. Martin's joyfully proclaiming weddings, Saturday after Saturday throughout the year, it surprises us to find that a marriage was a rare event in 18th century Ruislip, occurring 5-6 times a year on average, although there were 14 in 1792.

The reason for the high number of marriages in that year is not known, but 1794 had 44 baptisms, the highest number for the 18th century, which is more easily understood.

Few people in Ruislip looked further than their own village to find a spouse. Out of a total of 315 marriages only 51 grooms and 15 brides came from elsewhere, most from neighbouring parishes like Ickenham, Harefield, Hillingdon, Uxbridge, Pinner and Harrow. The groom who travelled furthest from home was Angel Bedford who came from Ampney, Glos. in 1771 and married Mary Gibbs by licence from the Bishop of London. 68 of the 315 marriages were by licence, the rest by banns; many though by no means all of the licences, being where one of the parties was a stranger.

Widowers and widows sometimes remarried forming 5.5 and 5.6% of grooms and brides respectively.

Marriage registers throw some light on literacy levels in 18th century Ruislip as the contracting parties had to sign their names. 48% of the men and 57% of the women were unable to do so and merely made their mark. Both groom and bride were illiterate in 36% of marriages.

Burials took a downward trend towards the end of the 18th century, despite bad harvests and high prices, with accompanying poverty and malnutrition in the 1790s.

Monthly totals of burials from 1701-1750 show a peak in the spring (March-April) and a minor peak in September with a trough in July. The neighbouring areas, Ickenham, Harefield, Stanmore and Rickmansworth have a similar pattern of mortality, but Uxbridge, a market town on the London-Oxford road, differs considerably, probably because of the constant movement of travellers. The spring peak may be accounted for by failing food supplies at the end of the winter, and that in September by infectious diseases associated with hot weather.

There were 23.3 burials per year in Ruislip on average 1701-1750, but certain years had exceptionally high mortality. Crisis years when burials were nearly twice the mean occurred in 1733 and 1741. The high figure in 1733 is accounted for by 18 out of the 42 burials taking place in February. Perhaps there was an influenza outbreak as the epidemic was over within a short space of time. Some families suffered more than one loss. For instance Mathew Bodimead's son Mathew was buried on the 3rd February and his wife Mary on the 5th. James Howard's funeral on the 14th (a day on which three people were buried) was followed by that of Awdria Howard, widow, on the 15th. Whether she was John's widow or perhaps his mother is not clear. William Wright and his daughter Sarah were buried together on the 21st, but the Henry Wright of Haste Hill buried on the 15th seems to be from a different branch of the family. 1741 was in fact a year when smallpox, typhus and measles were sweeping the country and even though no disease is specifically mentioned in Ruislip, 48 burials took place at St. Martin's, the numbers increasing throughout the summer months, reaching a peak in October and declining by the end of a year which had brought personal tragedy to many families. Presumably the weaker members of the community had been taken, as very low numbers of burials are recorded for the next four years.

Villages around were not effected by any epidemic in 1733, but 1741 shows crisis mortality in Ickenham, Harefield, Stanmore and Uxbridge as well.

Only three suicides were recorded, Samuel Edlyn and Armos Tame, buried in May and June 1789, respectively and a pauper, John, who cut his throat in 1791.

As ages are rarely given except in cases of exceptional longevity, it is impossible to comment on life spans in 18th century Ruislip. 12 people are recorded as living into their 80s and 90s and there were two centenarians.

Sometimes the register refers to a still-born child, an infant, a beggar child or a nurse child. For example:
1701 – February 20th. A child of Moses Barnard, Vagabond.
1702 – September 15th. Will Rook a nurse child at Widow Walters.
1703 – George a bastard child of Jane Laurance.
1718 – Samuel Bowler a beggar child buried.
1750 – Elman an infant.

Otherwise a child burial can only be assumed when the wording of the entry runs "son of" or "daughter of". In these circumstances it is not possible to compare child with adult mortality with any degree of accuracy.

Nurse Children

Nurse children were young children, often babies, who were being fostered with Ruislip families. They divided into two categories: offspring of London tradesmen being nursed in the country to preserve them from the exceedingly unhealthy atmosphere of London where nearly 75% of all children christened died under the age of five; and poor parish children either orphaned or abandoned. Many of the latter also came from inner London parishes and had been placed out at Nurse by Overseers of the Poor. Sadly, Ruislip's nurse children are mentioned only in the Burial Registers. Between 1709-22 they formed 3% of total burials.

Strangers

About 7% of all burials were of strangers, the vast majority of whom originated from within a twenty mile radius of Ruislip. Some were "travellers", "beggar-men" or "vagrants", with no fixed abode, who just happened to die while passing through Ruislip. Travellers also had their babies baptised here; about one every three years throughout the 18th century on average. Joseph and Mary "infants of unknown parents left in a basket at Eastcote" in 1724 were probably twins who proved too great a burden for some travelling couple. They were baptised on 7th December and perhaps called Joseph and Mary in memory of the Holy Family who were also homeless in December. Alas, they were buried together in 1727.

About half the strangers were from London. Some, like the six young children of Jeremiah Bright of St. Andrew's, Holborn, named on a fine monument in the chancel of St. Martin's, had local connections. Their grandfather, Thomas Bright, was vicar of Ruislip. London graveyards became overcrowded and insanitary as the medieval practice of removing the bones of old burials to a charnel house died out and many Londoners buried their dead in the airier churchyards of rural Middlesex.

Bastardy

The baptisms of 12 illegitimate children were recorded between 1699 and 1760 and 37 between 1761-1800. For the latter period illegitimate children formed 3% of the total number baptised. The actual rate was probably higher as girls "in trouble" sometimes left home to have their babies and others hoping to hide their offspring would not seek baptism in the local church. The low number before 1761 is more likely to be due to incomplete registers than to a higher moral tone in the village.

Sometimes the parish clerk simply entered a discreet *"father unknown"* in the registers or *"a base born child"*. At others he was more expansive; the entry for the child of Elizabeth Orton, widow, in 1706 says *"Father unknown, unless it be John Farmer one time farmer of Pinner"!* Another child is baptised Hannah and described as the bastard of Samuel Paine by the Widow Bugbeard.

Several of these births seem to have taken place at the Church House indicating that the mothers were homeless and dependent on parish charity. Some may have been girls from other parishes, perhaps shamed into leaving their homes, like Ann Monticue of Bushey, spinster, *"who did stroll into the parish of Ruislip and there was delivered with a child"*[1] in 1797. The Overseers of the Poor had a Bastardy bond made out against Michael William Bellis in respect of her child.

Life in 17th Century and 18th Century Ruislip

Jane Laurance appears in frequent residence at the Church House at the turn of the 17th/18th century. Her daughter Elizabeth with the discreet *"father unknown"* beside her name was baptised in 1699. Four years later the mother appears as Jane Laurance alias Cockman, when *"a second bastard child"* is recorded. An alias usually signifies a common law marriage, but if so the relationship was only short lived, for in 1705 she had reverted to plain Jane Laurance when she had a *"third bastard child"* unaccountably called William Smith.

Population

The 1801 census gives the first definite information about the population of Ruislip parish. 1012 people; 209 families; 201 inhabited houses; two uninhabited houses. Five people on average dwelt in each house. The number of houses in the parish and a population figure based on an assumed average of 5 per house at earlier periods is shown below and compared with the Census.

Table 1 Population 16th–19th century			
Date	Source	No. of Houses	Population
1565	Terrier	124 + 16 in St Catherines + 2 in Manor of More	710 (estimate)
1672	Hearth Tax	139	695 (estimate)
1801	Census	201	1012 (actual figures)

The upward trend in population seems to begin about 1750 as deduced from the greater number of baptisms and lower number of burials shown in the registers. This growth reflects what was happening all over the country and is not peculiar to Ruislip or caused by local conditions. The reasons why people were living longer and producing more children in the late 18th century are complex. Agricultural improvements increased food supply, though these were offset by failed harvests and war in the 1790s. General hygiene standards were better, as soap came into general use and cheap calico produced in Lancashire provided more easily washed clothes. The medical profession took an interest in the relationship between environment and disease and dispensaries were opened to provide ever better treatment for the poor.

Slightly rosier economic conditions encouraged earlier and therefore more fertile marriages.

The age at which Ruislip men and women married cannot be ascertained as insufficient information is given in the marriage registers, but there were 130 marriages and 547 baptisms between 1750-74 and 171 marriages and 862 baptisms between 1775-99, which shows that the ratio of baptisms to marriages went up from 4.2:1 to 5.1:1 and that Ruislip was participating in the general increase in fertility.

Family size cannot be determined without a full-scale family reconstruction which has not yet been attempted, but a few examples are given below of families taken from the baptismal register, picked from various classes of society.

Matthew Bodimead variously described as "poor" and "labourer" had nine children christened between 1691-1707 at an average spacing of 21 months, of whom at least four died young.

The Goodliest Place in Middlesex

Table 2. Ruislip Families – 17th-18th Century.

Matthew Bodimead Poor Labourer	John Wilshin and Mary Yeoman	William Weedon and Elizabeth Publican–"*True Lovers' Knot*"
September 1691: Mary February 1693: Elizabeth and Anne March 1695: Sarah December 1697: Thomas June 1700: Anne June 1701: Thomas October 1702: Susannah June 1707: Jane	October 1695: George April 1697: James January 1700: Mary April 1702: John August 1704: Daniel August 1709: Anne February 1712: Hannah September 1716: Elizabeth	February 1743: William March 1747: James 1750: Elizabeth October 1752: William November 1754: John July 1756: Sarah January 1762: Mary February 1764: Ann

John Wilshin and his wife Mary, from the yeoman class, had eight children, baptised from 1695-1716. The youngest child died at one year and the penultimate also probably died young, but the first six all grew up and married. At least two lived into their seventies.[2]

William Weedon, probably the Publican at the True Lovers' Knot, Northwood (the present pub was built in 1903 in front of the old one) produced eight children between 1743 and 1764. At least one died young.

The most obvious differences between 18th century and modern patterns of fertility are the larger numbers of children born and the longer period over which women bore children. The reasonably wide spacing of the births in the lower and middle class families perhaps indicates that the mothers breast fed their babies for a longer time than is now considered normal, which would suppress ovulation.

Social Class in 17th Century Ruislip

17th century society was more structured than our own, with well-defined social classes. The nobility had only the barest acquaintance with the parish of Ruislip in the shape of the Earls of Salisbury, lessees of the demesne; Lady Alice, Dowager Countess of Derby who built Hayden Hall in 1630 and Lord William Chandos who owned it after her.

None of these resided in the parish, but were simply property owners. Occasionally a Baronet appears in the area; Sir Bartholomew Shower of Pinner Hill who bought Gate Hill from Ralph Hawtrey in 1695 and Sir Thomas Franklin of Willesden, brother-in-law of Ralph Hawtrey, another owner of Hayden Hall.

The other classes are better represented. James McBean who has studied all 17th century Ruislip wills proved in the Prerogative Court of Canterbury and the Bishop of London's Prerogative Court and has transcribed most of them, listed the will-makers according to social class in an article in the 1985 Journal of the Ruislip, Northwood and Eastcote Local History Society.

During the century roughly 3,500 people died in Ruislip, of whom about half are likely to have been children, and one sixth married women who did not make wills. In fact only 212 wills survive out of a potential 1,166 will-makers. The inference must be, after setting aside those who died intestate through lack of forethought, that a large proportion of Ruislip people really had nothing of value to leave to their descendants. These would be the labourers of whom only four made wills.

Life in 17th Century and 18th Century Ruislip

Table 3. Ruislip Will-makers – 17th Century Social Class.

Gentry	8	3.7%
Yeomen	73	34.9%
Tradesmen	18	8.0%
Husbandmen	34	16.1%
Widows	41	19.0%
Spinsters	2	less than 1%
Labourers	4	1.9%
Not Designated	32	15.0% (probably husbandmen from contents of will)
	212	

Note: All quotations from wills in the following chapters are from transcripts made by James McBean and lodged in Ruislip Library.

Labourers

One of these will-making labourers, William Saunders (d. 1647), belonged to a family which had owned a substantial amount of property including Mill House, Bury Street, and a shop by the Churchyard gate, eighty years earlier and whose members had been designated "gentlemen".[3] People did not necessarily stay in the class into which they were born and the Saunders seem to be an instance of downward social mobility, for Mill House had been sold to Richard Ewer in 1589 and the shop to John Hawtrey soon afterwards.[4] William was an unusual labourer for he had a servant, Susan Herman, to whom he left 5 shillings. His bequests totalled £5:10s. All his other goods of unspecified value were left to his wife Amy. He may have been the William Saunders who was a servant to John Hawtrey in 1641[5] and Mr. Hawtrey, a lawyer, may have suggested the will.

Only a very rough estimate of the status of the population can be made on the evidence of wills, but it looks as though poor labourers made up about 27% of the people of Ruislip.

Gentry

At the top of Ruislip's social ladder sat the gentry, only 9 of whom made wills between 1600 and 1700. They were:

Table 4. Gentry will-makers.

Date of Will	Name	Monetary Bequests	Property in land	Dwelling
1616	Thomas Marsh	£ 717	Hendon	
1619	John Smith			
1638	Ralph Hawtrey	£ 212	142a & Leases of Park and Rectory	Eastcote House
1651	Henry Welsted	£ 552	144a	Southcote Manor House
1658	John Hawtrey	£4350	183a & Leases of Woods, Demesne, Rectory & House	Eastcote House
1659	Henry Harriot	£ 32		
1664	Augustine Wingfield	£ 2	At London	In St Catherine's
1671	John Redinge	£1012	70a	Field End House Farm
1698	Charles Hawtrey	£2045	257a & Leases of Woods and Demesne & Rectory	Eastcote House

157

The Goodliest Place in Middlesex

The table shows that a gentleman's position did not necessarily depend upon his wealth or land, since John Smith at the time of his death, at any rate, was endowed with very few of this world's goods. His will was not written down. A memorandum reveals a rather bleak death-bed and says *"....upon the 19th March 1618 Mr John Smith late of Rislippe in the County of Middlesex since deceased laying sick but being of perfect mind and memory and being asked of Mr Henry Welsted of the same place what he would do with such goods as he had. He said he had little and then being told of some money which was owing him upon a bond he said that his sister Mrs Sibill Banister (who was then present)....should have it for he had nobody else to give it to. And then being told that he must give it her or that he must express his will and mind so that if he died she might have it by his gift he presently answered and said that if he died she should have it all. There being then present Mr Henry Welsted aforesaid and the said Mrs Banister"*.

Men called John Smith are not very easy to trace and this one can hardly be the demesne farmer of that name who was 67 in 1577,[6] unless he was a great age at the time of his death, but could be his son.

With this exception the gentlemen left substantial amounts of money and land. Thomas Marsh must have lived in Ruislip in 1616, but his house cannot be identified and the property mentioned in his will lay in Hendon. Nothing is known of Henry Harriot except that his interest lay in St. Sepulchre's, London, where his first wife was buried, and an unusual bequest to his servant of two Books of Entries and *"all other books which do concern the Common or Statute Laws of England"* suggests a connection with the legal profession. Augustine Wingfield was married to Henry Welsted's daughter, Katherine. The £2 bequest to the Poor of Ruislip was only the tip of the iceberg so far as his actual worth was concerned. His property was in London in Shoe Lane and Eagle and Child Court in the parish of St. Andrew's, Holborn.

The other gentlemen had their main interests and property in Ruislip. John Redinge of Field End seems to have lived at Field End House Farm where St. Thomas More's Church and Farthings Close now stand.[7] The six branches of the Redinge family who held land in Ruislip in the 16th century had dwindled to two by the end of the 17th century. In 1685 one John Redinge was at Manor Farm, presumably as under-tenant of the Hawtreys, and the other (son of the man who died in 1671) was at Field End.[8]

Henry Welsted's position as owner of Southcote Manor House and the lordship of St. Catherine's Manor was held by right of his wife, Katherine, the heiress of Henry Clarke, the former owner. (see Chapter 5).

The Hawtreys of Eastcote House were the clear leaders in wealth, land and influence in the parish, even without their leases of the demesne lands and rectory.

Various 17th century lists which give the names of Ruislip people: Protestation Oath 1641, Hearth Tax Returns 1672 and 1676 and Land Tax Assessment, confirm the impression conveyed by the wills that no more than four gentry families lived in Ruislip at any one time during the 17th century and that these families lived at Eastcote House (always the Hawtreys); Field End House Farm (Redinges throughout the 17th century); Southcote Manor (Clarke, Welsted, Ryves, Seymer by descent); and Hayden Hall.

Life in 17th Century and 18th Century Ruislip

Tradesmen and Yeomen
So far as disposable wealth is concerned the better-off tradesmen overlap with the poorer gentry. For example:

John Biddle, Baker	d. 1694	left £425
James Finch, Maltman	d. 1653	left £65
John Priest, Cordwainer	d. 1671	left £101.2s.6d
John Duck, Tilemaker	d. 1679	left £112 and had a house and tilekiln

in St. Catherine's and a house in Harefield Parish

John Hudson, a bricklayer who died in 1696, apparently took over John Duck's tilekiln from his nephew, Robert Duck. Hudson tried to make provision for five dependent children when he made his will. He left *"the tenement I live in called Tilekill"* to his eldest son John, *"the rent and income thereof"* to pay for his maintenance and education. His second son Nathaniel was to have £100 at the age of 21 and the income for his maintenance in the meantime, but the executors could spend such portion of that as they thought fit in putting him forth apprentice for some trade or profession. A similar provision was made for Richard, but with a capital sum of £80 not £100. The two daughters, Martha and Hannah, had £50 each, and were *"to be put forth as apprentice for some trade or employment to get a livelihood"*. He left £60 and household goods and chattels to his wife Mary. Perhaps the business premises were to be rented to produce an income for the eldest boy, but not the house as the letting of that would have made the family homeless. His wife and two of his brothers-in-law were constituted his executors and charged to make use of the residue of his goods and chattels for the benefit of his five children.

John Hudson made his will on 25th March 1694 *"being indisposed in my health but of sound and perfect memory"*. Thirteen months later he was obliged to add a codicil, reducing the legacies to £40 each for John and Nathaniel and £30 each for Martha and Hannah (Richard is not mentioned) saying *"....I have been very sick and often ill since making my will which hath been very chargeable to me and fearing and much doubting my personal estate will not hold out to pay my younger children the said several portions to them given in my will"*. He bequeathed *"the Tilekill"* to his executors to be sold to raise his children's portions.

The Hudsons disappear from Ruislip records. Let us hope they were all apprenticed and found a livelihood elsewhere.

Far more tradesmen lived in Ruislip than made wills. 27 different trades appear in the Baptismal Register 1695-1705 as follows:

Craftsmen	*Service Trades*		*Building Trades*
Blacksmith	Baker	Cordwinder	Brickmaker
Carpenter	Butcher	Victualler	Brickworker
Wheelwright	Cornchandler	Cheesemonger	Bricklayer
Joyner	Mealman	Brooman	Tileman
	Maltman	Shovelmaker	Sandman
	Maltster	Chimney Sweep	
	Taylor	Ashman	
	Cobbler	Carrier	
	Cordwainer	Gardener	

159

The Goodliest Place in Middlesex

Ruislip did not actually sport a cheesemonger's shop at the time. John Weedon of Brentford, the cheesemonger, no doubt related to the Ruislip Weedons, was one of several non-parishoners whose babies were baptised in Ruislip. James Porter, butcher of St. James, Westminster and William Hilder, shopkeeper of All Saints, Stayning, London were others. Often the child's mother is found to be from Ruislip, as in the case of William Hilder who had married Elizabeth Bonnett of Ruislip at St. Martin's in 1701.

However, most of the trades listed above were being pursued in Ruislip and show an absence of any industry save brick and tilemaking.

It is impossible to decide how many members of each trade were working in the parish at any one time from wills and references in the registers, but workers in bricks and tile occur rather more frequently than those in individual service trades, and commonest of all were agricultural workers, farmers, yeomen, husbandmen and agricultural labourers. In a typical year, 1700, the baptismal registers show father's occupations as follows:

Labourer	13	Brickmaker	3	Wheelwright	2
Farmer	5			Carpenter	2
Yeoman	1			Blacksmith	1
				Cordwinder	1
				Cobbler	1
				Victualler	1

Hill Farm, now in Orchard Close. Ezekiel Timberlake owned it in the 17th century

Life in 17th Century and 18th Century Ruislip

The technical definition of a yeoman, is a man who farmed his own land, a definition which probably holds good in Ruislip. By the end of the 17th century "Farmer" seems to have replaced the term. For an eleven year period 1695-1705 the baptismal registers state the occupation of the babies' fathers and only two yeoman are mentioned but eight farmers. The yeomen and tradesmen together formed the middling class of people, so many of whose well-built timber-framed houses still stand.

Yeomen with substantial amounts of money to leave in their wills include:

Edmund Edlin:	1658	£300
Ralph Timberlake:	1663	£400
Edward Brooks:	1682	£400

John Fulmer expressly desired that the annuities for his wife and son were to be paid at the Feasts of the Annunciation (Lady Day – 25 March) and Michaelmas (29 September) *"in the Church porch of Ruislip"*.

Ralph Timberlake had Hill Farm at Little King's End, which still stands in Orchard Close. He seems to have stood high in the opinion of his neighbours as many of them chose him to witness their own wills. No wife or children were mentioned by him, so presumably he was either a bachelor or a childless widower, (Martha, wife of a Ralph Timberlake, was buried in 1630) but many legacies were made to kinsmen, servants and workmen. Hill Farm was bequeathed to his cousin, George Timberlake of Iver, and another messuage belonging to Ralph Timberlake in Ickenham was left to John Hampton of Denham, also a kinsman.

Servants

A number of servants are remembered in wills. Most of the gentry and several yeomen and tradesmen mention them, but William Saunders was the only labourer to do so. The designation "servant" at this period need not imply a particularly servile status, but simply a member of the household. Some so described were clearly relatives of the testator. Servants' legacies varied in value and type. Sums of £1, £5 and £10 were left to them by Ralph Timberlake, but he seems to have been particularly generous. John Hawtrey left those of more than four years standing 40s. each and less than four years, 20s. each. One of Thomas Marsh's servants received 20s. and a black coat. Feather beds, bolsters, bedsteads and other furniture were other gifts and in one case Edward Edlin, yeoman left his servant Sara Taylor a house, one that was rented out, not the one in which he lived.

As an indication of the numbers of households with servants in the parish, only 12 out of the 246 men who signed the 1641 Protestation Oath employed them. (Signatories who were servants give the names of their masters).

Husbandmen

Husbandmen appear from their wills to have had less cash than yeomen. They frequently left animals as bequests. Arable farming was more profitable and widespread in Ruislip than animal rearing before the Enclosures.

The Goodliest Place in Middlesex

Laurel Cottage, c.1860 (left), Primrose Cottage 18th century (centre) Tudor Cottage 16th century – Wood Lane

Bury Farm showing 18th century brick skin

Life in 17th Century and 18th Century Ruislip

Old House, Bury Street. A timber framed building remodelled in the 18th century. Green cottage (right) probably added in the 1820's

Ducks Hill Farm. An old site rebuilt in the 18th century

The Goodliest Place in Middlesex

17th and 18th Century Houses

Comparison of late 17th century Hearth Tax Returns and 16th century surveys suggests that very few houses were built during that period. Ruislip people then were content to repair and extend the houses of their forefathers. Space for such domestic offices as sculleries and dairies was provided in outshots built at the rear of buildings. Many of our "listed" buildings have these outshots with their catslide roofs. It is not always easy to tell whether the outshot is part of the original house or a later addition, but at Woodman's Farm and Bury Farm in Bury Street the framework of windows which look into the outshot remain, showing that they were additions. Much modernisation and sometimes rebuilding took place in the 18th century.

     A number of timber-framed buildings standing in the parish have their frames hidden beneath a brick skin; the brickwork seems to have been added in the late 18th century or occasionally early in the 19th century. "Jo Spicer"; "MS 1776"; "WC 1776" are scratched in bricks on the front of Bury Farm and perhaps indicate the date at which the work was done. The initials could be those of the workmen and John Spicer was probably the owner. The back of the house was left with its woodwork exposed, a phenomenon often found, which seems to show that the new fronts were intended to modernise the appearance of old houses and not to repair them. Recent work has revealed a medieval wall at the north end of this house, surviving from a building of hall and solar type. The hall seems to have been demolished and the present house built on the site early in the 17th century. The central hearth of the original hall was found beneath the floor boards and samples have been sent for archaeomagnetic dating. An extension put up in Victorian times now occupies the position of the solar.

     The Old House in Bury Street was not only given a facade with new windows and a very handsome doorway, but a completely remodelled interior as well in the 18th century. The room divisions no longer correspond with the original four bays of the timber frame and the house was extended northwards about three feet. Still later, probably about 1825-30, Green Cottage was built on, perhaps to serve as a baker's shop.

     St. Catherine's Farm, Howletts Lane; St. Catherine's Farm, Catlins Lane; Park Farm, Field End Road; Eastcote Cottage; Ramin; The Grange and Gate Hill Farm are further examples of houses with partially concealed timber frames.

     A few houses like that at Primrose Hill seem to have had cottages built onto them in the 18th century, while other houses were rebuilt, as is the case with Joel Street Farm, Southill Farm and Ducks Hill Farm.

Hayden Hall

Lady Alice, Dowager Countess of Derby, Lady of the Manor of Colham, (which included Uxbridge) and owner of Harefield Place, built a mansion in Eastcote in 1630 which remained a gentleman's residence until it fell into the hands of the R.N.U.D.C. in 1936. The house was Hayden Hall. The 17th century and 18th century owners are shown below:[9]

    Owners of Hayden Hall
    1630-36   Lady Alice, Dowager Countess of Derby
    1636-62   Lady Chandos
    1662-74   William, Lord Chandos

1674–   Daughters of Lord Chandos
1675–98   George Sitwell
1698–1728 Sir Thomas Franklin
1728–36   Lady Mary Franklin
1736–57   Joseph Musgrave, Senior
1757–63   Joseph Musgrave, Junior
1763   Rev. Thomas Clarke of Swakeleys
1770–76   Gervase Scrope
1777–80   Frederick James Scrope
1781   Thomas Scrope
1786–89   Thomas Watson
1799–1822 George Woodroffe

Hayden is mentioned as a surname in a court roll of 1394.[10] The name of the house came from former owners of the land on which it was built. Francis, John and Lucy Hayden surrendered the land and a messuage to William Nicholas in 1562[11] and the Terrier shows that in 1565 two houses stood in the area which later became Hayden Hall grounds.

Lady Alice's unusual reason for building in Ruislip parish is given in a letter *"That if it should please God to call for me I might have a place to lay my stuff in out of my Lord Castlehaven's fingering"*.[12] She feared that Lord Castlehaven, a most vicious character, second husband of her eldest daughter, might seize any goods left in Harefield Place in the event of her death. In fact he was executed in 1631 having been tried by his peers, while Lady Alice lived on for another five years. Lady Castlehaven reverted to the name of her first husband, Lord

Hayden Hall. The portion shown was rebuilt by Sir Thomas Franklin c.1720

The Goodliest Place in Middlesex

Chandos, after the disgrace and she, her son and granddaughters all owned Hayden Hall in succession.

The daughters of William, Lord Chandos sold Hayden Hall to George Sitwell an Ironmaster from Eckington, Derbyshire who had married one of Ralph Hawtrey's daughters, Elizabeth, in 1668 and was a member of the Mercers Company.[13] His ironworks seem to have been losing money and he was declared bankrupt in 1693 despite assistance from members of his wife's family.[14] Ralph Hawtrey, whether father-in-law or brother-in-law is not clear, had loaned him £1,025 on security of Hayden Hall in 1692, but he failed to repay it and Sir Thomas Franklin, second husband of his sister-in-law, Mary Hawtrey finally bought the house for £2,500 in 1698 and completely rebuilt it about 1720.[15]

No picture of any kind has survived to show us the type of house that was built in 1630 and replaced by Sir Thomas' mansion.

Sir Thomas died in 1728 leaving *"my new erected mansion (which I would have to be called Deanes)"* to his wife and after her death *"to my next kinsman Joseph Musgrave and then to J. Musgrave's son and his descendants"*.[16] The elder Musgrave was his first cousin, being the son of Elizabeth Franklin and her husband Sir Christopher Musgrave of Eden Hall, Cumberland.[17]

The Rev. Thomas Clarke the next owner had been living at Swakeleys since 1750. He and his son Thomas Truesdale Clarke purchased several houses in Eastcote. The Old Barn House, Field End House Farm, Cheney Street Farm, The Case is Altered, (not then a pub), The Grange and a house which stood opposite the bottom of Catlins Lane were still Clarke property in 1806, when the Enclosure Map was drawn, but Hayden Hall remained in their hands for only a short time, being owned by Gervase Scrope by 1770.

The three Scropes were the sons of George Scrope, Esq. of Cockerington, Thomas being half brother to the other two. Gervase may have changed the name of Hayden Hall for a time, for *Burke's Dormant and Extinct Baronetcies* describes him as "of Eastcote Park, Middlesex" at the time of his death in 1776, a more genteel sounding name.

George Woodroffe Esq., of Chiswick, Chief Protonotary of the Court of Common Pleas, lived at Hayden Hall from 1799-1822 and played his expected role in local affairs.[18] He was a Justice for Middlesex and sat on the local bench at Uxbridge. It is uncertain how many of the earlier owners actually lived in Eastcote. Almost certainly Lady Alice and the Chandos family did not. They probably let the Hall. The Sitwells, Franklins and Musgraves probably did, as the Sitwells and the younger Musgrave were buried in St. Martin's where memorials can be found. A ledger stone in the chancel floor commemorating George and Elizabeth Sitwell who died within three months of each other in 1708 can just be seen protruding from beneath the choir benches and Joseph Musgrave has a hatchment hanging in the south aisle above the door to the vestry.

Highgrove

Another gentleman's residence which became one of the more important buildings in the district was erected in Eastcote, in the middle of the 18th century. It was called Highgrove and was situated at Hale End.

Hale End took its name from the Hale family which was first mentioned in the Customal. (see Chapter 3). Early in the 18th century the Hale's messuage seems to have been divided between two female descendants, Martha Hale and Elizabeth Kelly (formerly Hale).[19] Elizabeth's portion included the messuage. It descended to her daughter Elizabeth and son-in-law George Wilchin in 1736.

Elizabeth Wilchin sold a meadow near her house to the Rev. John Lidgould of Harmondsworth in 1747, who built a house, later called Highgrove upon it. Mr Robert Turner, a maltster, from Woodhole, Pinner purchased the new house from Mr Lidgould in 1758.

Meanwhile the Hale's old house was inherited by John Wilchin in 1764 and sold by him to Joseph Cook an Uxbridge draper. The house had been demolished by 1767 when Robert Turner bought the site or plot of ground at Hale End, "whereon formerly stood a messuage and orchard late of John Wilchin," from Mr Cook.

Robert Turner's son, also Robert, sold the property to Rev. William Blencowe, Canon of Wells Cathedral in 1787, who remained as owner until his death in 1810.

The Blencowe estate was sold to John Humphrey Babb for £3,150 in 1813 by Robert Willis Blencowe of Hayes. Mr Babb, Deliverer of the Vote at the House of Commons, appears from the Rate Books to have been occupying Highgrove from at least 1802 perhaps as Mr Blencowe's tenant. He died in 1823 and is buried beneath a heavy body-stone in St. Martin's churchyard near to the north door. One of his executors was James Mitchell who succeeded him in his House of Commons post and was the owner of Highgrove by 1825.[20]

After Mr Mitchell's death in 1833 his widow put the house up for sale. The Sale Catalogue June 1834 shows the earliest picture of Highgrove. The house depicted has a central hall with flanking wings and a high tiled roof rising to a peak above a balustrade at eaves level.[21] It had a stucco front which may have been added during Babb's ownership. It was undoubtedly a building to be classed with Eastcote House and Hayden Hall and of superior status to the timber-framed cottages in the area. The 18th century Highgrove was destroyed by fire in 1879.[22]

A Note on the Civil War

The chief cause of political and social upheaval in the 17th century, the Civil War, seems to have left the inhabitants of Ruislip relatively undisturbed. Like everyone else they suffered heavier taxation and some presumably served in the Army, but the nearest clash of arms was at Brentford in November 1642, after which the tide of battle skirted Middlesex.

Ruislip people going to market in Uxbridge must frequently have seen Parliamentary soldiers, for Essex had 15,000 troops stationed there in 1643 prior to his march to relieve Gloucester; the town was the Army H.Q. for a time in 1647 and in January-February 1645 discussions between the two sides were held at what is now the Old Treaty House to try for a negotiated peace.[23]

John Hawtrey at Eastcote House is said to have supported Cromwell. A family tradition says that he had straw strewn in the hall of Eastcote House for the reception of Cromwell and his troops, and that two watches, a Lady's and a Gentleman's were given him by Cromwell as an acknowledgement for his accommodation. Letters in the Hawtrey Papers discuss the story and relate how the watches were displayed at a Loan Exhibition held in Southampton in 1866.[24]

REFERENCES
1. G.L.R.O. DRO 19 E6/9.
2. Wilshin Family Tree – Michael Wilshin.
3. King's College: R.36.
4. British Library: Add MS 9367.
5. House of Lords: Protestation Returns.
6. King's College: Q.23.
7. British Library: Add MS 9367.
8. Ibid.
9. Compiled by L. E. Morris and J. McBean from G.L.R.O.: Acc: 249 (Hawtrey Papers) G.L.R.O.: Acc: 85; G.L.R.O. DRO 19 E2 (Rate Books); Various genealogical tables.
10. King's College: Q.48.
11. G.L.R.O.: Acc: 85/70.
12. Ruislip Library: L. E. Morris: "Three Houses of Eastcote".
13. G.L.R.O.: Acc: 85/1/70.
14. G.L.R.O.: Acc: 249/779-782.
15. J. McBean: J Ruislip, Northwood & Eastcote Local History Society 1981.
16. Ruislip Library: Will – Transcript by L. E. Morris.
17. Lysons: "Environs of London" – Vol III p. 213 and Burke's Peerage.
18. J. McBean: ut supra.
19. Information re: ownership down to 1824 from the catalogue of Acc: 394 at G.L.R.O. The documents have been withdrawn.
20. J. McBean: J.R.N.E.L.H.S. 1980.
21. Ruislip Library: Photocopy.
22. J. McBean: J R.N.E.L.H.S. 1977.
23. C. Hearmon: *Uxbridge a Concise History*.
24. G.L.R.O.: Acc: 249/2372 – Transcribed by L. E. Morris.

Chapter Nine
The care of the poor

The Poor Law
The poor have always been with us and we have it on good authority will always remain so, but we know very little about their fate in Ruislip before the 17th century. A court case of 1331 suggests that the Monks of Bec had generally made a daily dole to poor mendicants of bread, and on Fridays cooked beans as well.[1] 15th and 16th century wills sometimes included small bequests to "the Poor Men's Chest", showing that a fund for the relief of poverty existed, but not how it was distributed.

       Care of the poor (mainly the aged, infirm or orphans), regarded as a Christian work of mercy, was long left to private charity, which was sufficient to contain it until changed social conditions in the 16th century flooded the country with bands of wandering able-bodied poor, who posed a threat to society and whose needs could not be met by the charitable resources available. Tudor enclosures left some men landless. Ruislip men in their case of 1519-21 (Chapter 6) claimed that the inhabitants of 15 cottages had been made vagrant. The dissolution of the monasteries removed one source of poor relief, but had no direct effect on Ruislip where the Priory had gone out of existence in the early 15th century. At the end of periods of warfare soldiers and seamen often disbanded at ports were left to find their own way home with insufficient means and perforce degenerated into beggars.

       Governments, obliged to consider the problems of poverty, aimed at settling the poor in their own parishes to prevent potentially riotous groups from forming and tried to raise the amount of money available for poor relief by encouraging more charitable donations. Gradually it was realised that the problem was too great to be resolved by voluntary means and a compulsory poor rate was introduced. The Elizabethan Poor Law was enacted in 1601 and placed the burden of the care of the poor upon each parish. Its aims were to provide asylum and relief for the aged and infirm; give work to the able-bodied poor and apprentice poor children to a trade to enable them to become financially independent adults. The scheme was to be financed by a rate levied on all property valued at £10 per annum or more, and administered by officers known as Overseers of the Poor, working within the framework of the vestry. The concept of the civil parish was thus established.

The Church House
The earliest evidence of the new Poor Law at work in Ruislip was the provision of accommodation for the impotent poor in 1616-17. The house chosen for their reception still stands on the corner of Eastcote Road and High Street, and is known today as the Almshouses.

       The term 'Almshouses' is a misnomer, for properly speaking such houses should carry an endowment for the maintenance of the inmates which was

RUISLIP COPSE

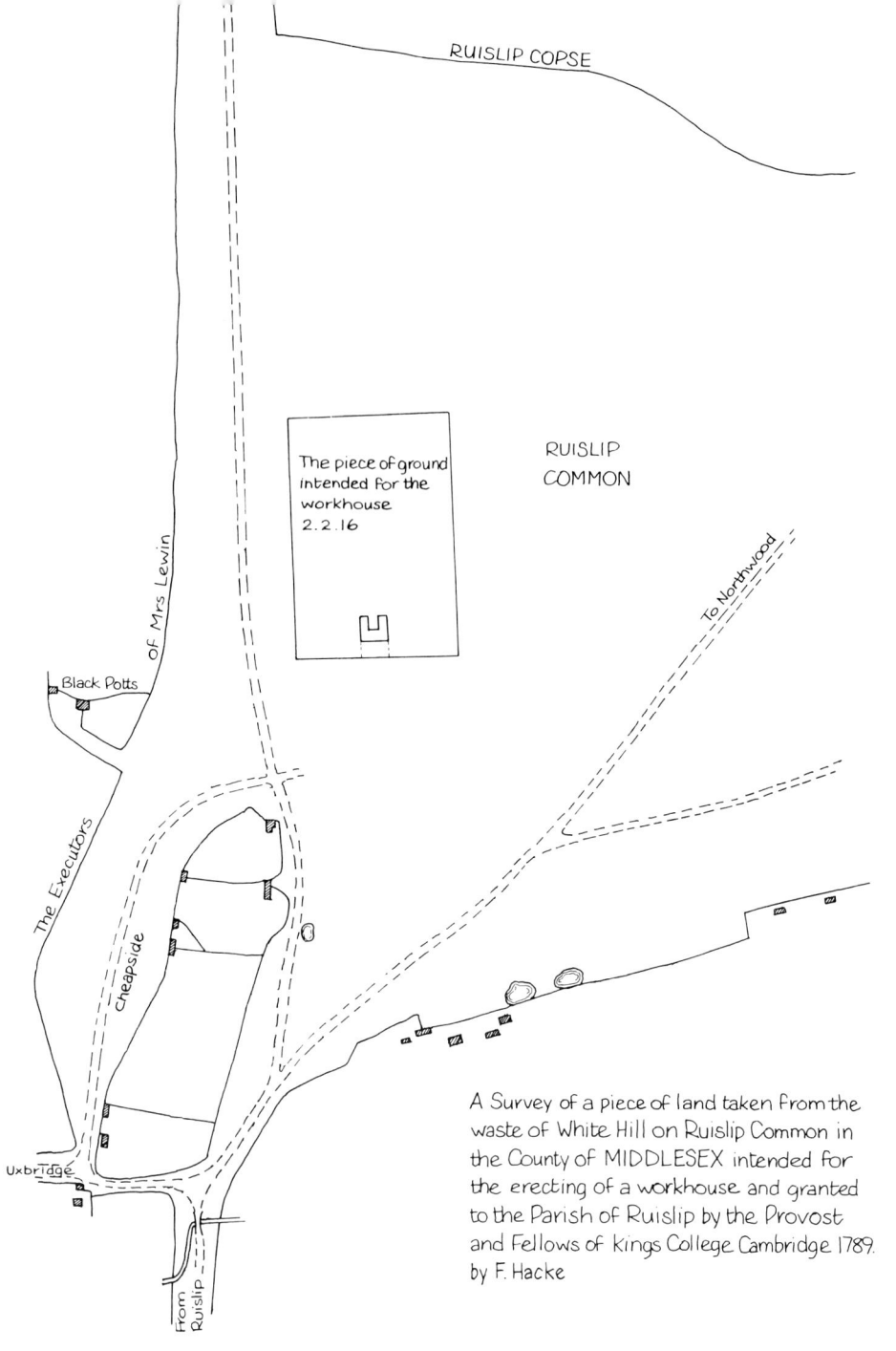

The piece of ground
intended for the
workhouse
2.2.16

RUISLIP
COMMON

Of Mrs Lewin

Black Potts

To Northwood

The Executors

Cheapside

Uxbridge

From Ruislip

A Survey of a piece of land taken from the waste of White Hill on Ruislip Common in the County of MIDDLESEX intended for the erecting of a workhouse and granted to the Parish of Ruislip by the Provost and Fellows of Kings College Cambridge 1789. by F. Hacke

Ruislip Workhouse

The care of the poor

never the case in Ruislip. The building has had many names since 1616, being called variously the Parish House, the Church House or Church Houses and St. Martin's Churchyard Cottages. Use of these names tended to overlap but Almshouses came into favour in the mid-19th century and has superseded all the others in recent years.

Examination of the building construction during the last restoration proved beyond all reasonable doubt that a single five-bayed timber-framed house, with a jetty on the churchyard side and a single internal chimney between the two westernmost bays, was built c.1570. It was known as Harker's House in 1589[2] when Mr Saunders surrendered it to Mr Hawtrey (John Hawtrey d.1593) and in 1617[3] when it was being converted to house the poor by Ralph Hawtrey (d.1638).

Little is known about the Harkers. A Henry Harker had a close of land called Hawkins Long (which later became part of Hill Farm and is now Orchard Close and Heathfield Rise) in the 1580s.[4] Two more Harkers appear in the Middlesex Sessions Records in 1617, when Richard Harker the Younger of Hayes was indicted for receiving stolen cattle and was respited without bail at the request of Ralph Hawtrey. The prosecutors included Richard Harker the elder, a butcher of Ruislip.

It is possible that Ralph Hawtrey paid for alterations to the house out of his own pocket as the accounts are among the Hawtrey Papers and end with *"Mr Hawtrey hath layde out on the Parish House £XII : XIIIs"* (£12.13s).[5]

The money was spent on dividing the house longitudinally and building partitions between the central bays. The house as built had a large

Harker's House was converted into cottages for the poor in 1616-7

The Goodliest Place in Middlesex

three-bayed central room and a single-bay room at either end on each floor. The converted building contained ten small back-to-back houses, five facing the road and five facing the churchyard, each with a living room downstairs and a bedroom upstairs. Two new chimneys were built so that each room could be heated and the downstairs south wall was moved out in line with the jettied upper storey to provide more space (much needed) in the living rooms. Staircases were inserted.

Inmates
These small houses were intended to provide an asylum for the aged and infirm, not to be workhouses where able-bodied poor were set to work. Their form as separate dwellings shows this. A workhouse would probably have included a dormitory and a workroom. The earliest Poor Law Accounts extant for Ruislip are in a book entitled *"Ralph Hawtrey, Esq. His Book of Accts. Being a true Accompt of all them that hath served Overseers of the Poor of the Parish of Ruislip from the year 1651"*[6] (Ralph Hawtrey d.1725). It covers the years 1659-1744 and abounds in references to payment made in money or in kind to poor people lodged at the Church House.

"June 1665 — Widow Fearne of the Church House several
times in her sickness. 13s
March 1666 — Paid to John Bates for carrying 50 bavins to
Widow Fearne 1s:9d
(Bavins were bundles of kindling)
1726 — Moving three women to the Church House,
my Cart Horse 15s
Paid the Carpenter taking down the beds and
setting them up. 3s"

It would appear from Overseers' accounts that the Church House most frequently sheltered widows, but a number of births occurred there and there are a few references to families in residence. In 1679 a beggarman's wife was bought to bed there and in 1690 Henry Howard "of the Church House" had a daughter, Anne, baptised. Several unmarried mothers were sheltered there, Jane Lawrence, already alluded to (Chapter 8), among them.

"Given to John Ford in the Church House from November 24th 1671 to May 3rd 1672 he being sick and very poor" £1:3s

"1708 for removing James Norland into the Church House with their (sic) *goods and lumber and wood"*

Occasionally special gifts were made to the inmates. Dame Mary Franklin, Ralph Hawtrey's daughter and widow of Sir Thomas Franklin of Hayden Hall, died in 1732, leaving £100 to buy land, the income from which was to be used to buy clothing for such of the poor of Ruislip as were in the Church Houses and belonged to the Church of England; the clothes to be distributed every St. Thomas Day (21st December). Her executors failed to buy any land and the £100 was eventually invested in Navy Five Per Cents by the vicar and churchwardens in 1810.[7]

The vestry agreed in 1787 (15th April) to give poor families in the Church House, a bed, a bolster, a pair of blankets, a pair of sheets and one rug each.[8]

The care of the poor

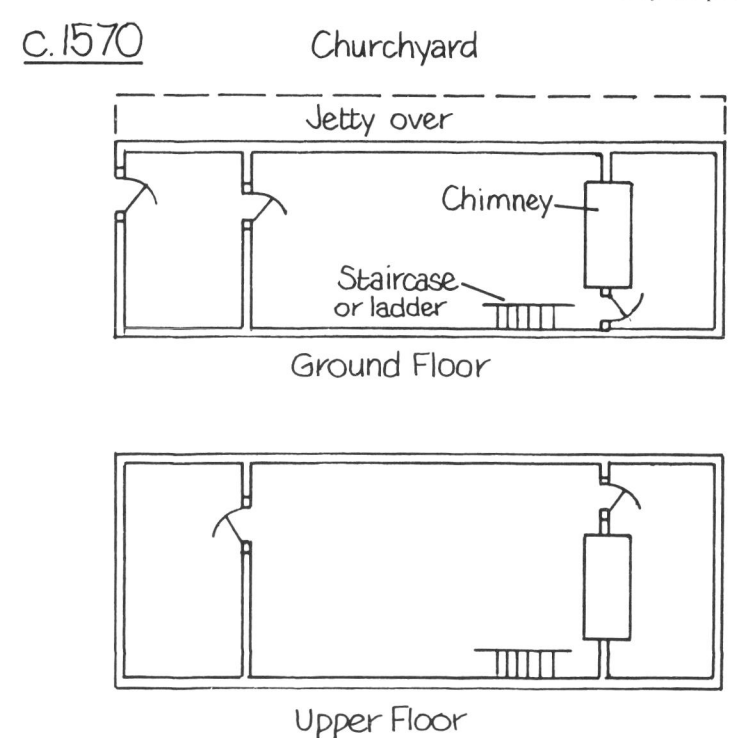

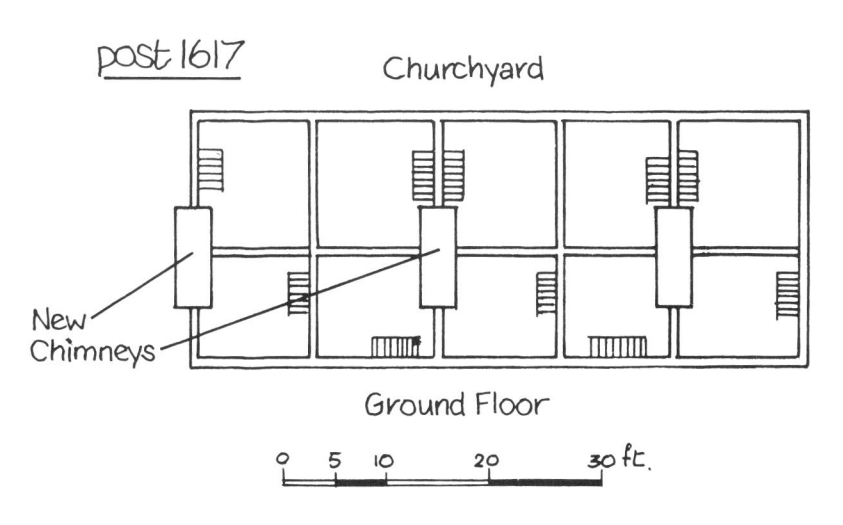

c. 1570 — Churchyard

Jetty over

Chimney

Staircase or ladder

Ground Floor

Upper Floor

post 1617 — Churchyard

New Chimneys

Ground Floor

0 5 10   20   30 ft.

The Almshouses, Ruislip

173

The Goodliest Place in Middlesex

Living space in the little cottages was severely limited. The lower room had a fireplace for cooking and heating. Water may have been available from a shallow well in the early days. The deep well with a pump in front of the George was not sunk until c.1865 and an outside tap was only installed this century, probably soon after Ruislip got a piped water supply in 1899. There was an outside privy. Such accommodation, which should be set against the standards of the early 17th century rather than the late 20th century, was adequate for the widows. When families were resident it must have been greatly overstretched.

The Almshouses continued to give shelter to the elderly after a workhouse was erected in Ducks Hill in 1789. The census returns of the mid-19th century give us our first complete picture of the type and number of inhabitants and some indication of the length of time they stayed. The following table shows the occupants in 1851, 1861, 1871 and 1881.

1851 Census

1.	Mary Moores	Widow	67	Former Agricultural labourer
2.	Sarah C. Woodley	Widow	70	Former Agricultural labourer
3.	Sarah Lawrence	Widow	73	Former Farmer's wife
	John Lawrence	Her Son	41	Agricultural Labourer
	Elizabeth Elliot	Her daughter	39	Agricultural Labourer
	Thomas Elliot	Her grandson	6 weeks	
4.	Uninhabited			
5.	Thomas Franklin		67	Agricultural Labourer
	Ann Franklin	His Wife	49	Agricultural Labourer
6.	Ann Webb	Widow	63	Former agricultural labourer
	John Webb	Her son	25	Agricultural Labourer
7.	Mary Godliman	Widow	71	Former agricultural labourer
8.	Elizabeth Bowden	Widow	65	Former agricultural labourer
9.	John Gomm		73	Agricultural Labourer
	Mary Gomm	His wife	61	Agricultural Labourer

The tenth cottage is simply not mentioned.

1861 Census

1.	Mary Goldliman	Widow	87	Former farm labourer's wife
2.	Sarah Young	Widow	71	Former Dressmaker
3.	Elizabeth Weedon	Widow	69	Former labourer's wife
4.	John Gomm		85	Former farm labourer
	Mary Gomm	His wife	76	
5.	Ann Webb	Widow	73	Former farm labourer's wife
	Sara Webb	Her granddaughter	5	
6.	Ann Franklin	Widow	69	Former farm labourer's wife
7.	Joseph Bowden		48	Farm labourer
	Charlotte Bowden	His wife	47	
	Henry Felions	Step Son	21	Farm labourer
	Mary Bowden	Daughter	16	

174

The care of the poor

	William Bowden	Son	14	
	Joseph Bowden	Son	12	
	John Bowden	Son	9	
	James Bowden	Son	3	
	Eliza Bowden	Daughter	1	
8.	John Bishop		71	Former farm labourer
9.	Martha Martin	Widow	62	
10.	Mary Moores	Widow	77	

1871 Census

1.	Maria Tobutt	Widow	67	Annuitant
2.	Martha Martin	Widow	72	Annuitant and Nurse
3.	Hannah Lavender	Widow	66	Annuitant and Nurse
	Robert Lavender	Son	22	Agricultural labourer
	Daniel Lavender	Son	16	Agriculural labourer
4.	Joseph Bowden		57	Agricultural labourer
	Charlotte Bowden	Wife	54	
	Mary Bowden	Daughter	25	
	Harry Bowden	Son	29	Shepherd
	Joseph Bowden	Son	23	Agricultural labourer
	John Bowden	Son	20	Agricultural labourer
	James Bowden	Son	13	Agricultural labourer
5.	Ann Franklin	Widow	81	Annuitant
6.	John Edmonds		68	Agricultural labourer
	Elizabeth Edmonds	Wife	67	
	Harriet Edmonds	Daughter	25	
	Thomas Edmonds	Grandson	5	Scholar
7.	Ann Mason	Widow	67	Charwoman
8.	Elizabeth Weedon	Widow	80	Annuitant
9.	Thomas Hill		75	Agricultural labourer
	Ann Hill	Wife	76	
	James Hill	Son	46	Agricultural labourer
10.	Uninhabited			

1881 Census

1.	Elizabeth Morten	Widow	75	Formerly Laundress
2.	Charlotte Bowden	Widow	66	Charwoman
	Mary Bowden	Daughter	37	Charwoman
3.	Hannah Lavender	Widow	74	Formerly Nurse
4.	Thomas Clayton		82	Annuitant from Club
	Maria Clayton	Wife	76	
5.	William Lavender		72	Agricultural Labourer
6.	Maria Tobutt		78	Annuity from friends
7.	Charlotte Wingfield		76	Formerly Nurse
	Thomas Wingfield	Son	49	Agricultural Labourer

175

The Goodliest Place in Middlesex

8.	William Brill		66	Agricultural labourer
	Charlotte Brill	Wife	65	Agricultural labourer
9.	Jane Webb		71	Formerly general servant
	Elizabeth Bentley	Daughter	44	
	Walter Bentley	Grandson	6 months	

The vicar and churchwardens chose the people who were to live in their Almshouses. It would appear from the census returns that once in, the majority of occupants stayed for life, at least the older ones. We must hope that the Bowden children eventually made homes of their own.

Most of the males were agricultural labourers or retired from farm work. 75 year-old Thomas Hill was apparently still working, probably intermittently.

Several women inmates are also described as agricultural labourers showing that some women at least did field work in Victorian Ruislip. In 1871 five women, all over 65, are called annuitants, that is in receipt of an annual pension from various sources. Two women were nurses, one a charwoman and one a dressmaker.

Hannah Lavender, one of the nurses was the widow of Henry Lavender of Ruislip Common. She had fifteen children (the youngest when she was fifty if the ages given in the census are correct) and reared twelve of them. At the time of her death in 1899 the Rev. Thomas Marsh-Everett paid tribute to her skill as a nurse, especially during the 1849 cholera epidemic, which badly affected the Ruislip Common area. She ended her long life in the Hillingdon Union Workhouse, although the vicar would have preferred to have kept her in the Almshouses.[9] Incidentally there are a number of age discrepancies in the tables.

Elderly ladies lived in the Almshouses in the 20th century, but residents were not replaced as the cottages fell vacant during the period between the two World Wars, and plans were discussed for a new use for them. Several of the inhabitants were very long lived and the last elderly resident did not die until 1954.

A notable resident in the 1920s and 1930s was Mrs Tobutt, a daughter of Hannah Lavender mentioned above, known to most of the population of Ruislip as "Granny" Tobutt. She celebrated her hundredth birthday in 1937, but by that time was living with her daughter Mrs William Collins at 16 Sharps Lane. One of her granddaughters remembers the interior of her cottage, on the High Street corner of the building, fronting on to Eastcote Road. She had a cupboard beside the fireplace, in which she kept firewood and a bucket of water which she filled from the outside tap. The other furniture was very simple: a table, a dresser and some chairs. On occasions she cooked dinner for her grandchildren who went to school at the National School in Eastcote Road. All the cooking was done on the open fire and she had an oil lamp for lighting.[10]

Threats of Demolition

The Rev. J. J. Roumieu, Curate of St. Martin's published a history of Ruislip in 1875, in which he wrote:

"The Almshouses for ten aged poor stand on a piece of ground adjoining and open to the churchyard. The right of presentation is vested in the Vicar and Church Wardens; unfortunately there is no endowment for their

maintenance and although they have been repaired from time to time and even quite lately by public subscription of the inhabitants they are by no means as comfortable as they should be. It would be a great improvement to the church if a fresh site could be found and the space they occupy thrown into the churchyard."

So much for Victorian notions of conservation.

By 1938 the four cottages at the western end were empty and the Parochial Church Council proposed to convert them into a verger's cottage for Mr

Mr Casemore, Verger at St Martin's Church

A. Casemore and his wife, who were actually living in the vicarage at that time.[11] Mr Casemore was sexton as well as verger and looked after the vicar's cows. Mr F. H. Mansford, a local architect who lived in King's End, drew up plans which converted the four cottages into a pleasant house with a kitchen, dining room and living room downstairs and a bathroom, W.C. and two bedrooms upstairs. Electric light was to be installed as well as modern plumbing. These plans were acceptable to the Ruislip-Northwood Urban District Council and to the Middlesex County Council and the work was put in hand by Battens during the autumn of 1938. A fund was set up to raise the £523 needed for the conversion. The Casemores moved in on the 23rd January 1939 and stayed for the rest of their lives. Mr Casemore died in 1969 and Mrs Casemore in 1972.

During the 1939-45 War all schemes for further conversion were in abeyance as some of the remaining six cottages were still inhabited.

The Goodliest Place in Middlesex

In 1948 Miss Nellie Bray, Mrs C. Lavender and Miss Ellen Collier were still living there in accommodation which failed to reach the standards required by the 1936 Housing Act. Under the terms of this Act, the vicar was served with a formal order of demolition respecting the Almshouses, including the Casemore's cottage, in December 1948. This calamity was averted through the intervention of a Ministry of Works Inspector and an undertaking made by the Parochial Church Council that they should be brought up to standard.[12]

As an interim measure electric light was installed in November 1950, running water was put into a room which could be used communally by all the tenants and the roof was repaired. The plans were drawn up by R. H. A. Jones and £150 was given towards the (£350) costs by the Ruislip Village Trust. The work was undertaken by Prowtings. The Guides were given the use of the front cottage at the eastern end. Meanwhile plans were still being discussed for a major reconstruction when the whole building should finally become vacant. Mr Hooper of the Ruislip Village Trust suggested that the whole of the upper storey should be made into a Council Chamber with modernised living accommodation beneath. This scheme and several others did not come to fruition. When Mrs Lavender died aged nearly 90 in the autumn of 1954, the Rovers were given the use of her cottage as a Rover Den, which came to be known as the Holt and other empty rooms were used for storage.

At the beginning of 1956 a curate, Fr Lingard, indicated that he would be happy to live in the four central cottages next door to the Casemores. He got a gas cooker and a more modern fireplace and lived there happily for two years, before leaving to get married. Once again a great query hung over the future use of the Almshouses. An American gentleman, Mr De Blois, who was teaching in Ruislip for three years, offered to restore the empty cottages at his own expense and live there at a peppercorn rent with his wife and daughter. In order to prepare a lease, proof of the Church's ownership had to be established and as no deeds could be found, no lease was granted and the De Blois were obliged to withdraw their offer.

In September 1959, another curate, Fr Curzon, moved in and had a proper bathroom constructed. He was followed by Fr Grant. When he left, that section remained empty again until March 1972, when Mrs Leek spent the last fifteen months of her life there. Fr Reid next lived there and lastly Fr Goff, who moved into Midcroft in 1975.

By 1973 the dilapidated state of the whole building was causing public concern as well as to members of the PCC. Brick nogging was falling from the timber framework, shaken by the heavy traffic passing along Eastcote Road and wooden supports and hardboard covers were placed against the brickwork to prevent further damage, pending discussion on ways and means of preservation. An architectural report was drawn up by Norman Haines Partnership. The long delays were caused by the old problem of the church having to establish proof of ownership before any leases could be made or grants obtained. It was 1980 before work on converting the Almshouses into four flats and one maisonette was begun.

The restoration work was carried out splendidly by Mr Badovsky and his team. Much pleasure was felt in the neighbourhood when the Almshouses were once again fully inhabited with the new tenants, housed as comfortably as present day standards require. There are now four flats and one maisonette held by the Harding Housing Association on a 75-year-lease. The church authorities have right of nomination to the maisonette.

The care of the poor

Settlement

The Civil War caused as much social disruption as religious strife and warfare had a century earlier. An amendment was made to the Poor Law in 1662 aimed at preventing the poor from moving about the country and becoming vagrant. It empowered Justices to grant warrants to overseers or churchwardens to remove from their parishes poor people who were not legally settled there. Settlement could be established by birth; by 40 days residence after notification to a churchwarden or overseer; by serving as a parish officer; by paying the parish rate; by apprenticeship to a parishioner or if unmarried by one year's service in the parish.

This law hindered the mobility of labour and prevented the unemployed from seeking work, so casual workers, such as hay-makers were permitted to bring certificates of settlement with them from their home parishes, if they lived in property valued at £10 or less per annum.

The poor were an expensive burden on the ratepayers of Ruislip, who had no wish to support beggars or outsiders, a feeling still quite often volubly expressed by their descendants in the pages of the Gazette in relation to homeless immigrants arriving at Heathrow. The expenses involved in removing the poor to their place of settlement were sometimes so great that with hindsight it would have been cheaper to keep them. In 1695 John Edlin and his wife were sent to Ruislip from Harrow. Their child died and Mrs Edlin was sent to Hendon by Ruislip Overseers and back to Ruislip by Hendon Overseers. In 1697 a case was heard in the Court of King's Bench to settle the dispute between Hendon and Ruislip, which cost Ruislip at least £9 in legal costs.[13] Provided that a settlement case was not disputed between parishes the costs were not so great. The following extract from the 1791 accounts is probably more typical.

"*Paid for Warrant against Josiah Hempton*   3s:0d

"*Paid Douglas the Constable for going to Hampstead with Jos Hempton*   5s:6d

"*Paid James Deane for going to Hampstead with Hampton and family*
     10s:0d"[14]

Constables were empowered to whip beggars from the parish, but there is no record of this ever having happened in Ruislip. Travelling paupers were simply given temporary relief and encouraged to remove themselves.

"*1702: for bread and beer for a travelling woman with child lay sick in the Churchyard and at John Kellys a night with little girl.*   1s:0d

Oatmeal sugar and candles one day and night   6d

Given her in money to go from the parish   1s:0d"[15]

Women who were confined in the parish were particularly expensive and efforts were made to remove pregnant women:

1725: Given a great-bellied woman to get her away   4s:0d"[16]

A "*poor woman that lay in at the Black Horse*" Eastcote in February 1732 cost the overseers £2:10s:9d.

Ruislip received paupers removed from other parishes. In 1828, James Tucker was removed from Uxbridge; Philip Jordan and child Thomas aged two from Uxbridge; William Biggs and Ann his wife and three children from

The Goodliest Place in Middlesex

Jeremiah Bright's bread cupboard

The care of the poor

Birmingham and Henry Seymour aged 65 from St. James, Clerkenwell. They were all returned to Ruislip.[17]

Treatment of settled paupers

Settlement and removal cases show the workings of the Poor Law in its harshest light. In their dealings with known parishioners, looked upon as the deserving poor, the overseers showed compassion and provided every aspect of care from the cradle to the grave.

Who were the poor? Gregory King, a 17th century demographer, considered that at least one third of the population of England and Wales was poor when he worked out a table of population for the year 1688. The old and infirm, the chronically sick, widows and their children were numbered in their ranks, from both the middle and lower eschelons of society. Several people helped by the Ruislip overseers are entitled Goodman, Goodwife or Goody, which indicated yeoman status. Members of the widespread and apparently comfortably off Redding and Ferne families crop up in the overseers accounts as recipients of relief. Tradesmen too fell upon evil times. Henry Barringer, a weaver was *"very poor"* in 1679 and was buried at the parish's expense in 1684. His coffin, digging the grave, ringing the bell and registering his burial cost 9s.1d.[18]

Agricultural labourers when working could maintain themselves and their families more or less at subsistence level, but such work being seasonal and dependent upon the weather, they were often in want, particularly in the winter time as the following extract from the accounts shows.

"1691 "To John Whitwell at several times having a great charge of children and being very poor in the Winter".[19]

In old age or illness they had no savings to fall back on. 1688 *"To William Trulove he being an old man and taken with sickness in winter and past his labour, at severall times   16s:0d."*[20]

By 1692 William Trulove had become a pensioner of the parish, receiving 6s. a month.[21] Pensions were given according to need and consequently varied in amounts and type of recipient and could be taken away at the will of the vestry.

Occasionally a note is made that someone (usually a widow) is to have a pension for life.

"At a meeting of parishioners of Ruislip the 30th day of April 1693 it was agreed then that the persons hereunder named being very poor should have their pensiones continued to them till further order and to be paid by the Overseer of the Poor of Westcote side."[22]

Widow Brice	by the month	10s
Widow Harper	,,	6s
Widow Franklyn	,,	6s
Widow Trulove	,,	6s
Widow Long	,,	8s
Widow Lyveing	,,	5s
Goody Grove	for a Nurse child	8s
Widow Kerton	by the month	10s
John Ford	,,	4s
		£3.3s

The Goodliest Place in Middlesex

It will be noted that decisions about the disbursement of parish funds were not taken solely by the overseers but by "a meeting of parishioners" in other words the vestry. One should not, however, imagine several hundred parishioners cramming into the small vicar's vestry attached to the north side of the chancel. "Parishioners" should be read as "Principal Parishioners", for vestry meetings were rarely attended by more than 14 men and sometimes only two or three. The following men were present in April 1693.

Ralph Hawtrey	John Fearne	
Robert Ronswell	Joseph Nelham	Thomas Puddifant
Charles Hawtrey	William Hedger	John Souter
Richard Living	John Biddle	
John Bonnet		
James Robin		

} Overseers

Poor people applied to the vestry for relief and "discretionary" payments were made after discussion of the merits of each case.

The accounts are divided between "Westcott side" and "Eastcott side". Northwood was shared geographically between the two.

Food was given quite frequently and not merely the bare necessities. One Elmes received much help in 1664, having at different times *"bread, milk, grosery ware" "pudding and beef"* and *"a neck of mutton"* as well as candles, and tobacco. Walter Randall had *"cheese, butter, shuger, currants and reasons"* (raisins) in 1681. In 1691 not only oatmeal to make porridge but a nutmeg to flavour it, figures in the accounts.

Clothing including shoes was a constant requirement. The Widow Grissell had a gown and petticoat (£1:6s:8d), a new pair of bodices (8s:6d) an under waistcoat (3s:6d) and a pair of clogs (8d) in 1701.[23]

In 1787 it was agreed to give William Spleen a *"fowl weather"* coat.[24] Hats, breeches, shirts were all regularly given out. Payments were made for making, mending and washing clothes and repairing shoes. The Ruislip vestry certainly seems to have been determined that no one should go badly clad.

That other necessity of life, fuel, was not neglected. Kindle wood made up into bundles called bavins were delivered to the poor. It came out of the woods and therefore the payment went to swell Squire Hawtrey's coffers. On rare occasions coal is given, the first reference being in 1662.[25]

Nor were families allowed to become homeless because of inability to pay rent. The April 1693 vestry decided to pay 20s. towards John Whitwell's rent *"he being very poor and having a wife and six small children"*. The £1 constituted a whole year's rent, but some cottages were even cheaper. Goody Rudd's annual rent was only 12 shillings in 1723. She may have only had a room in a divided house.

The sick were nursed, but the quality of the nursing is unknown and almost certainly left much to be desired, as those paid for "looking to" the sick were often widows, themselves in receipt of parish relief.

"1712 Paid Widow Goame for looking after James Newman Sen and his wife in time of their sickness — 14 weeks at 3s. a week – £2:2s"[26]

Smallpox before the introduction of vaccinaton in 1796 was a common scourge and sufferers were relieved by the parish. In the early 19th century a surgeon was paid to vaccinate the poor. Dr Curtis was paid a retainer of £8 per annum to tend the poor in the late 18th century.[27] The 1694 entry saying

The care of the poor

that Ezekial Timberlake was to have a guinea for the cure of Richard Grove's leg *"when it is cured"* suggests payment by results![28]

Care of the sick often meant in practice care of the dying and several months payments for "looking to" often end with the funeral expenses.

Mental illness caused especial distress to some families. Elisha Horne's wife seems to have suffered intermittently for several years. Thomas Gardiner was paid 7 shillings for seven days looking to her *"when she was in a frenzy fit"*. Other people were paid for *"watching with her"* and for nursing her child while she was sick. By 1684 she was sufficiently bad to be taken to Bedlam in Moorfields for nine weeks. Her expenses were listed.[29]

'For watching Goody Horn before she went to Bedlam	*10s:1d*
For 9 weeks board for her	*£1:0s:0d*
For entering her name there	*18s:0d*
For the Overseers journey to London with her 2 days and a night with his horse	*10s:0d*

Other items relating to Goody Horn include her diet in Bedlam and letting her blood.

George Redding brought her home again, we must hope at least temporarily cured.

Work seems to have been provided for the able-bodied poor, perhaps to be done in their own homes. Flaxen yarn and tow were purchased in 1694, raw material to be transformed into linen cloth and rope.[30] In the same year the overseers paid Jack Trayle for weaving 36 ells and 3 quarters of cloth. Later James Brown had 4s 6d for weaving of "lynning cloth".[31]

Children figure quite prominently in the Overseers Accounts. They were nursed when young and put out as apprentices at about the age of twelve. In the 17th century the standard rate for fostering children was 2s. a week, later rising to 2s:6d. From the burial registers we know that poor children from inner London parishes were put out to nurse in Ruislip where some of them died, but those nurses were paid by the overseers of the London Parishes and such transactions do not appear in the Ruislip accounts. Some London tradesmen like James Porter, butcher of Westminster made private arrangements to have their children nursed in the pure air of rural Middlesex, hoping to preserve them from the smoke-laden air which was thought to be a prime cause of London's exceptionally heavy child mortality (75%). James Porter was unfortunate as three of his children died in Ruislip between 1701-9.

Many children were looked after for short periods only, while their mothers were ill or in prison.

"1684: To Goody Carter's children while their mother was in prison for selling beer without a licence, 5s"[32]

Education of the Poor

We know very little about schools in Ruislip in the 17th century and 18th century, but the overseers paid for the *"schooling"* of a number of children in 1701 at the rate of 2d a week.[33] As the teacher seems to have been Goody Hill one can only surmise that it was a dame school where only basic requirements were taught.

A meeting was held in September 1812 "for consulting on the best mode of educating poor children" and agreed that education based upon the principles of the established religion was to be provided gratis. The following week estimates were required for the expense of repairing and making fit for the reception of a certain number of children *"a Room called the School Room situate in the Churchyard at Ruislip";* which suggests that this was not the first time that a charity school had been attempted.[34]

Thomas Gregory expressed himself willing to receive between 40 and 50 children for £20 per annum and more in proportion. Mrs Seymour and Mrs Goulding were each prepared to teach 15 children reading and plain needlework for £13:10s per annum. Subscriptions were solicited from the principal inhabitants. As writing does not appear to have figured in the curriculum it is hardly surprising that 50% of the brides and grooms married during the next two decades at St. Martin's could not sign their names. This school became a National School in 1835 and probably raised its standards as there was a marked improvement in Marriage Register literacy after 1848, up from 50% to 65%.

Apprenticeship

Many poor girls were fitted out with clothes to go into service. Boys were apprenticed to tradesmen, often away from Ruislip, like one of the Horns who was apprenticed to John Hartwell an Ealing shoemaker in 1690.[35] Being a rural area many boys were apprenticed to husbandmen and yeomen. Charles Long who was baptised in 1705 was bound to Ralph Bugbaird, husbandman in 1717.[36]

Apprentices, usually bound until they were 24 years old, were utterly dependent on their masters, but it should not be assumed that all were ill fed, poorly clad or badly treated. They were protected by the law and cases of brutality to apprentices, like the appalling case in Uxbridge in 1655 when a boy was whipped and scorched over a fire, shocked people then as much as reports of child abuse horrify us today.[37]

Militia

Wives and dependents of men serving in the militia were maintained by the poor rate. Each county had a levy and parishes were obliged to provide a certain number of able-bodied men or pay for substitutes. An Act of Parliament in 1795 called for the raising of men for the Navy. Ruislip and Harefield together had to provide one man. The parishes shared the expenses of paying a bounty of £21 to John Crosby, stay-maker who volunteered.[38] If no one had come forward the press-gang would have visited the area.

Rising Costs

The care of the poor continued on the lines set out in 1601 until the Poor Law Amendment Act of 1834. The numbers relieved varied from year to year reflecting climatic and social conditions and as bad harvests and war in the 1790s, brought inflation, the costs of maintenance and consequent burden upon ratepayers increased alarmingly.

£72:2s:11d was collected in 1665-6 and £60:0:8d was expended. Incidentally this was the year of the Great Plague in London, but no reference to such a visitation occurs in the Ruislip accounts.[39] In 1788 £340:7:2d was collected from five assessments and £288:5s:1¼d paid out.[40] Expenditure had risen astronomically to £868:9s:0¼d by 1801 and continued to rise to a peak of £1,240:19s:3d in 1807, after which it levelled out.[41]

The care of the poor

Enclosure of the common fields and common waste was taking place between 1804 and 1814 (See Chapter 10). A list of occupiers entitled to pasturage of the 60 acres of common land allotted for the benefit of poor cottagers has 49 names, 29 from Westcote and 20 from Eastcote, suggesting that about 25% of the populace was poor. Strips of land up Ducks Hill between the road and St. Catherine's Manor boundary were let to *"industrious, poor labouring men"* in 25 perch allotments *"to raise potatoes or other vegetables for the use of their families"*. Those favoured had large families, were of good character, and were not to erect any buildings on the land, nor trespass in the wood.[42]

Unemployment became a problem in the early 19th century. The "redundant poor" as they were designated were required to go round the parish each day and diligently inquire for work before going to the overseer for employment. If unsuccessful on their own account they were sent by the overseer to farmers who were obliged to take them on and pay a set wage. 14 men had no constant employment in 1820, but by December 1830, 37 redundant poor were set to work by the overseers and Edward Sceney the constable was sent round the parish to make inquiries among the farmers about the numbers of workmen they had and to ensure that those who paid £4 or more to the Poor Rate should employ the redundant poor in proportion to the amount paid.[43] At that time the poor's wages were laid down by the overseers on a scale according to the number of their dependants — single men 5 shillings per week – man, wife and 6 children 13:6d a week. Some were employed cutting and grubbing up furze in the Poor's allotments and planting the young furze to make a mound round part of the Gravel Pits at Northwood. Later in 1832 the rates were raised to 6 shillings for a single man and 7 shillings for a married man to be paid by the employer, the remainder for any children to be made up by the overseers.[44]

During the Napoleonic War, corn prices kept artificially high by the Corn Laws had helped make farmers, who were chief among Ruislip ratepayers, prosperous and able to shoulder the heavy rate burden. By 1830 they too were feeling the pinch of poverty and vestry meetings discussed minor economies. *"Jan. 1833 — that a saving may be effected in Parish expenditure if the aged persons inhabiting the north side of the Almshouses be removed to the south side and families put in ..."*. Were the aged persons expected to double up? Since 1829 the parish had rented three cottages at Tilekilns from Mrs Murphy of Uxbridge to house families who would otherwise be in the workhouse. These were agreed to be given up as a further economy at the same meeting, but wiser counsels seem to have prevailed and the first measure was rescinded. The cottagers were left in peace until November 1834.[45]

Illegitimate births increased between 1821 and 1840 making up 2.9% of all christenings in the 1820's and 4.2% in the 1830's, placing an increased burden on the rates. Unmarried pregnant women were normally taken before a magistrate to name the putative father who was then expected to pay toward the child's upkeep.

Eliza Woodley's daughter was born on 15th January 1831 and noted as *"now chargeable to The Parish"* on the 7th February. William Stent an Ickenham labourer, the reputed father, was ordered to pay 10 shillings to date and, 2 shillings per week in future, but he evaded his responsibilities by enlisting as a soldier.

Eliza was unfortunate in her relationships for Thomas Brill, a Ruislip labourer who fathered her second daughter, born September 1833, failed to provide for her and was imprisoned by the magistrates in default. Eliza's story ended happily (perhaps) when she married George Allday in 1835.[45a] In 1851 the census returns show that she was living at Ruislip Common with her husband, an agricultural labourer and six children, the eldest of whom was Emma, Thomas Brill's bastard, then aged 18.

Mark Clayton, publican at the Six Bells, was churchwarden from 1824-31, but never again after Charlotte Poulter bore his child in September 1831. Probably because he was better off than the labourers he was ordered to pay 2s:6d a week and Charlotte Poulter 6d a week towards the child's maintenance. Payments ceased when Charlotte married James Massey in 1835.

It was in this atmosphere that the new Act was introduced in 1834 aimed not at removing poverty by improving social conditions but by reducing the burden on the rates by making outdoor relief difficult to obtain. Assistance was to be made available only within the walls of a workhouse and conditions within were to be unattractive enough to act as a deterrent to all but the most desperate.

Ruislip had in fact had a workhouse since 1789 but under the new order the parish was incorporated in the new Uxbridge Union and a large workhouse was built at Hillingdon to accommodate paupers from all the parishes in the Union: Uxbridge, Hillingdon, Northolt, Ickenham, Harefield, and Ruislip. The small parish workhouses or poor houses were sold to help cover costs.

Ruislip Workhouse (Now the Old Workhouse, Ducks Hill)

The vestry decided to build a workhouse in 1789. King's College granted a piece of land from the waste at White Hill, just south of Copse Wood.[46] Mr Saich contracted to build the house for £461:4s and began work in April 1789.[47] The churchwardens: James Ewer who lived at Mill House and William Weatherley,

The Workhouse built on a portion of Ruislip Common in 1789

The care of the poor

and the overseers of the poor: John Birch and Benjamin Branch, were empowered by the vestry to borrow £400 at 5% from Daniel Wilshin, a farmer of Pinner (he lived at Pinner Green Lodge and was grandfather of Daniel Wilshin Soames who owned Gate Hill Farm in the mid-19th century.) The principal parishioners stood security for the loans.[48]

Work proceeded quickly as the house was ready for the reception of the poor by the end of October. Total costs for the house and fittings were £760:10s:4d. According to the rather messy accounts kept in James Ewer's diary, the pleasant-coloured red bricks were brought from Cowley. Mr Paig (Page) charged £10:7s:6d for digging the well and providing a new pail for it, but Mr Nash only required a modest 1s.6d for *"digging a whole for the Necessary"*. James Ewer's spelling is always idiosyncratic!

The maintenance of the poor in the workhouse was contracted out to John Burbidge in October 1789 at £353:5s per annum and he became the first governor. Upon his death in 1795 the vestry decided to stick up handbills in the neighbouring villages and market towns to give notice that the maintenance of Ruislip poor was to let. Would-be governors sent in tenders and Ralph Weatherley's low estimate of £286 per annum, was accepted.[49]

From his salary Ralph Weatherley had to feed and clothe the poor, maintain the furnishings of the house and to provide raw materials for the inmates to work. It was up to him to make what profit he could from the sale of their work and from the sale of agricultural produce grown on the workhouse land. The system was clearly open to abuse. In bad years the governors of many workhouses must have been tempted to economise on the quality and quantity of food which they provided for the inmates. Vestries were aware of these dangers and churchwardens and overseers tried to safeguard the paupers' interests in the articles of agreement set out in their contracts with governors. Ruislip set up a committee to inspect the workhouse in December 1795.[50]

Ruislip workhouse was granted an allotment of 10 acres lying between the house and Copse Wood by the enclosure commissioners in 1806 which were to be ploughed and cropped.[51]

Ralph Weatherley overspent by £47:11s at the end of a year, quit his post, then accepted a higher contract and stayed on until 1798. Edward Charles governed the workhouse in 1800 for £343 per annum but in 1804 (the year before Trafalgar) he found £440 insufficient and was granted £550 guineas by the vestry.[52] In an effort to keep down costs later governors were allowed a weekly amount per pauper rather than a lump sum.

The contract[53] made between the churchwardens and overseers and Martin Webber, a yeoman of West Ham, Essex, in 1830 allowed him 3s:9d per week for each inmate. He agreed to provide sufficient wholesome meat and drink, clothing, lodging, firing, employment and all other things necessary for their maintenance and support. The weekly diet was to include at least four *hot* dinners with good butcher's meat and plenty of vegetables. In summer broth could be served only on the day it was made and next morning for breakfast *"unless anybody chose it"*. Good small beer was to be provided every day. Any christenings or burials from the workhouse had to be paid for by Martin Webber. He also had to see that any children there were taught reading and spelling. In return he was to have the benefits of the garden and land of the workhouse and the labour of the paupers. Work at that time included winding silk for a merchant in Hertfordshire.[54]

The Goodliest Place in Middlesex

Workhouse Diet Table – undated – c. 1835 (GLRO DRO 19 Cl/6)

Sunday	Bread and Butter or Cheese	Seven ounces good Mutton or Beef with Vegetables and Beer
Monday	Broth	Rice, Milk or Pea Soup
Tuesday	Milk Porridge	Seven ounces good Mutton or Beef with Vegetables and Beer
Wednesday	Broth	Rice, Milk or Pea Soup
Thursday	Milk Porridge	Seven ounces good Mutton or Beef with Vegetables and Beer
Friday	Broth	Rice, Milk or Pea Soup
Saturday	Milk Porridge	Rice Pudding 14 ounces

Cheese and Butter weekly in the proportions following: Cheese 8oz and Butter 4 oz. If all Cheese – 1lb. If all Butter – ½lb. Bread daily ¾lb. From this allowance the supper must be provided.

Children's diet at the discretion of the Governor

The Parish Officers reserve to themselves power to establish a second table of diet for refractory Poor.

James Ewer ⎫
Thomas White ⎭ Church Wardens   Chris. Kingston Fountain ⎫
William Durbridge ⎭ Overseers

    It is difficult to assess what conditions in Ruislip workhouse were really like. On paper the poor were looked after well, but they were totally dependent upon the goodwill of the governor and vigilance of the vestry.

    An inventory dated 1795 exists.[55] There were seven bedrooms, a governor's room, parlour, kitchen, work-room, store-room, pantry, cellar, scullery, brewhouse, wash-house with a large room over, sickroom and a bedlam. The latter contained a stump bedstead, a flock bed and bolster, four blankets and a coverlet, and a lock and key. It may have been used to confine vagrant lunatics who wandered into the parish, and were taken to the workhouse by the constables.

    The clothing and goods of the paupers were listed. There were 22 inmates, five men, four lads, 12 women and one girl, but no complete families. Two of the lads, James and John Hill, were presumably the sons of Edward Hill, one of the men. Another lad, John Yates, appears to be in the workhouse with his mother, Ann Yates. The girl was called Charlotte Cook and there was a Mary Cook among the women. No adult had the same surname as the remaining lad, Thomas Richardson, but the goods of Eliza Richardson are included among the effects of poor people stored at the workhouse. These lists make pitiful reading. Eliza Richardson's is the longest – Feather bed, bolster, bedstead, two blankets, two tables, pottage pot and cover, copper saucepan, tea kettle, flat iron and a candle stick – presumably all her wordly goods.

    In 1830, a particularly bad year, there were about 40 inmates, but about 20 was the more usual number.

    Ruislip workhouse was used as such for only 49 years as the Union Workhouse was ready by 1838.

    The Guardians of the newly-established Uxbridge Union met for the first time on 30 June 1836; Christopher Packe, the vicar and Orlando Stone of

The care of the poor

Ruislip Park House (now the British Legion) being the Ruislip representatives.[56] The prime task awaiting the new body was to provide funds for the Union House. It was resolved on 3 August 1836 that indoor paupers from Harefield, Ickenham and Northolt should be sent to Ruislip workhouse to join the 20 paupers already resident there so that the other parish workhouses could be sold to raise money.[57] By August 1838 the new house was ready for the reception of paupers and W. H. T. Newman, an Uxbridge auctioneer, sold the Ruislip property to Ralph Deane of Eastcote House, who converted it into six cottages.[58]

In 1921 the then Ralph Deane sold the Old Workhouse to William Page the Northwood builder.[59] Shortly afterwards Waldo Emerson Guy, an architect, restored the Old Workhouse to a single dwelling and a wing near the road was added about 1923.[60] Since then the house has had several owners and still stands in its beautiful grounds south of Copse Wood on the former waste.

Later Overseers' Accounts Books show that many of the former discretionary payments ceased after 1834 but help was still available for the sick and elderly in Ruislip, financial assistance being granted in special circumstances, on application to the relieving officer of the Union. The Union provided £200 per annum to be shared between four medical practitioners who were to attend the poor. Mr Paston was appointed to Ruislip, Ickenham and Cowley in 1836.[61] M.O.s were occasionally tardy in their attendance and incurred the displeasure of the Guardians. Nathaniel Soames of Northwood House (now the Grange), a Guardian in 1841, lodged a complaint against Mr Rayner, he *"having refused with imprecations to attend a lad named Field"*. Mr Rayner satisfied the board with his explanation that the servant who had summoned him had said that another M.O. could be fetched if he were not at liberty to attend.[62]

The Guardians established a workhouse hospital at Hillingdon to which sick paupers could be removed, provided that they had a medical certificate saying that they could be removed without risk or danger. They also contributed to the maintenance of pauper lunatics at Hanwell Lunatic Asylum (now St. Bernard's – opened 1831).

Four Guardians visited the hospital in January 1841 and reported[63] that the building containing three rooms and six beds, was totally inadequate and should be replaced by a new hospital for at least 40 patients with separate male and female wards for infectious disease. (From these small beginnings Hillingdon Hospital eventually emerged). The Guardians had been grieved to see two beds each containing four children! The patients were suffering from itch (8), scald head (2), sore eyes (2), erruptions (6). Many cases of Itch and persons suffering from venereal disease had to be kept elsewhere in the workhouse because of lack of space. The nurses were themselves inmates.

What faced Ruislip people who sought refuge in the Union Workhouse? First, separation. Males, females and children were housed in different quarters. Many considered this the most inhuman aspect of workhouse life and it was hotly debated in the House of Commons, when predictably stories were told of old men begging workhouse governors to free them from the constant companionship of nagging wives!

Children received schooling. All were taught reading, writing and cyphering and were instructed in the principles of Christian religion, but only the boys received lessons in handicraft. A trained schoolmaster was appointed at a

The Goodliest Place in Middlesex

salary of £35 per annum with board and lodging in the house.[64] Older children were sometimes sent out to service.[65]

The work was boring, consisting of picking cocoa-nut fibre and sorting bristles; picking oakum (old tarred rope) and breaking granite (which was sold to the Metropolis Roads Commissioners at 16s. per yard).[66]

Food was just adequate with very rare treats. Roast beef and plum pudding was given on Christmas Day in the early years but in December 1840 the master was instructed to inform the inmates that the Guardians would be willing to give them a feast dinner on Christmas Day as heretofore but were sorry that they were not permitted to do so by law.[67] There were nine different classes of diet based on age, sex and degree of infirmity. The Guardians received so many complaints from the old men in 1838 that they increased their bread allowance to 12oz a day (equivalent to 12 slices of sliced white bread from a Sainsbury's loaf).[68]

Life in the House was not intended to be comfortable, but neither were the inmates cruelly treated as deliberate policy. A certain amount of concern was felt for the elderly, shown by the Guardians' resolution in November 1837 to have back and elbow boards added to the seats in the day rooms for the old men and old women.[69] The Guardians zealously attended meetings, inspected conditions and made improvements, all the time treading the fine line between putting an intolerable burden on the rates and providing adequate care for the poor.

The Admissions and Discharge Book exists for the years 1864-7.[70] It makes interesting reading, showing that most paupers stayed only a short time in the house and left at their own request. Many came during periods of ill health; pregnant women to have their babies; and vagrants for a meal and night's lodging.

Between April 1864 and December 1866, 42 admissions were from Ruislip. 35-year-old Mathilda Wright with her daughters aged two and seven was admitted on 25 June 1863 because she had been *"deserted by her husband"*, but the domestic upheaval was soon over as she was discharged next day being *"taken out by husband"*. George Chamberlain was brought in by the police having suffered an accident. He had fallen off a hayrick. Ann Biggs arrived with her two-year-old son on 26 June 1865 *"out of employ and pregnant"*. Her female infant was born on 8 July and the little family discharged themselves on 16 August. Edward Weatherley stayed in the house for nine weeks in spring 1866 when he had a bad hand. Hezekiah and George Bunce with smallpox and Thomas Collins with a bad leg were let in on the same day just before Christmas 1866. One of the women from Ruislip, only 20 years-old was a prostitute.

The 42 admissions were not 42 people. A Philip Tobutt appeared on seven occasions, never staying longer than five weeks. The reasons for his admission are given as sickness, destitution, out of work and infirmity. On one occasion his condition was *"dirty and lousy"*. It may be that those entries refer to three different men all from Ruislip and with the same name as the year of birth is given variously as 1788, 1800, 1810. John Wilding sought refuge three times and the prostitute on two occasions.

Four Ruislip people died in the house during the two and a half years, one of typhus, one an elderly man and another an illegitimate infant born in the Union eight weeks earlier. Daniel Kirby left after only two days at his own request *"not liking the stone breaking"*.

The workhouse was certainly not a Pauper Palace but it was not a prison either.

REFERENCES

1. L. E. Morris: *History of Ruislip*.
2. British Library: Add MS. 9367
3. G.L.R.O. ACC 249/235
4. British Library: Add MS. 9367
5. G.L.R.O. Acc 249/235
6. Ibid 1574
7. V.C.H. Vol IV p. 147
8. G.L.R.O. DRO 19 C1/1
9. Ruislip Library: Extract from Parish Magazine: Helen Hoare Collection.
10. Ex info Mrs Richardson (grand-daughter of Mrs Tobutt)
11. Information re: conversion from P.C.C. minutes. G.L.R.O. DRO 19 D1/1.
12. Information about the Almshouses, 1945-60. G.L.R.O. DRO 19 D1/2.3.4.
13. G.L.R.O. Acc 249/1574
14. G.L.R.O. DRO 19 E1/1
15. G.L.R.O. Acc 249/1574
16. Ibid
17. G.L.R.O. DRO 19 C1/6
18. G.L.R.O. Acc 249/1574
19. G.L.R.O. DRO 19 E4/1
20. G.L.R.O. Acc 249/1/1574
21. G.L.R.O. DRO 19E4/1
22. Ibid
23. G.L.R.O. Acc 249/1574.
24. G.L.R.O. DRO 19 C1/1
25. G.L.R.O. ACC 249/1574
26. Ibid
27. G.L.R.O. DRO 19 E1/1
28. Ibid E4/1
29. G.L.R.O. Acc 249/1574
30. G.L.R.O. DRO 19 E4/1
31. G.L.R.O. ACC 249/1574
32. Ibid
33. Ibid
34. G.L.R.O. DRO 19 C1/1
35. G.L.R.O. ACC 249/1574
36. G.L.R.O. DRO 19 EG/10
37. C. Hearmon *Uxbridge a Concise History*.
38. National Register of Archives Catalogue 1953.
39. G.L.R.O. ACC 249/1574
40. G.L.R.O. DRO 19 E1/1
41. Ibid
42. Ibid
43. G.L.R.O. DRO 19 C1/1 and C1/6
44. Ibid C1/6
45. Ibid
45a. Ibid
46. King's College: Q48
47. Building costs from James Ewer's Diary G.L.R.O. ACC 538/1st dep/8/11
48. G.L.R.O. DRO 19 C1/1
49. Ibid
50. Ibid
51. Ibid
52. Ibid
53. Ibid C1/6

The Goodliest Place in Middlesex

54. Herts RO D/EB 1157 B11
55. G.L.R.O. DRO 19 E5/1
56. G.L.R.O. B.G. U.1
57. Ibid
58. G.L.R.O. Middlesex Deeds Registry
59. Ibid
60. Information from Mrs. Woodbridge
61. G.L.R.O. B.G. U.1
62. Ibid
63. Ibid
64. Ibid
66. Ibid
67. Ibid
68. Ibid
69. Ibid
70. Ibid

Chapter Ten

Enclosure in Ruislip Parish

The parish of Ruislip at the beginning of the 19th century had changed little in appearance since medieval times. Cottages standing within small areas of enclosed lands (known as Old Enclosures) clustered near the church and Manor Farm and lay along the parallel streets running up the hill from the Pinn to the common waste and in hamlets at the Field Ends. To the south lay the arable in large common fields, subdivided into shots and again into strips (formerly called sellions but usually known as "Lands" by this time). A large tract of woodland and waste separated the hamlet of Northwood from the rest of the parish.

The prosperity of the parish was dependent upon agriculture. 1,012 people inhabited the area in 1801 when the first census was taken, of whom 493 were employed on the land. Most of the other 519 were women and children.

Proprietorship in Ruislip

During the first four years of the century, the Rate Books[1] list about 209 ratepayers as occupiers of property but only 49 of them were owner-occupiers. All the rest were tenants. The property they rented ranged in size from cottages with

The cottages in front of the Old Shooting Box, owned by John Bray in 1806

small gardens to substantial farms. Several of the tenant-farmers were small proprietors as well. For instance John Bray Sen. *rented* a farm from a large proprietor, Edward Hilliard Sen. which was valued at £117 per annum and was almost certainly Primrose Hill Farm, but owned three cottages on Eastcote High Road which used to stand in front of the Old Shooting Box, which had 14 perches of land attached to them, together valued at £5 per annum. John Bray let the cottages to Thomas Balding, George Brill and John Shackell, respectively.

The entire parish of about 6,500 acres was owned by 108 proprietors, 59 being absentees. 3,199 acres constituted the Old Enclosures. The rest was open field (about 2,000 acres) or waste. The division of the common field land about 1800 is uncertain as arable is not specified in the early rate books, but it appears that no more than 35 people had land in them. A third of it in any case was demesne and belonged to King's College.

The Old Enclosures were very unevenly shared among the 108 proprietors shown in the table below:—[2]

Table 1. Proprietorship of Old Enclosures				
Over 50 acres	10a-49 acres	1a-9 acres	under 1 acre	Total
15	22	40	31	108

King's College, lords of the manor, not surprisingly headed the list with 535 acres. The largest private owner was Ralph Deane of Eastcote House with 462a.1r.6p (Eastcote House, St. Catherine's Farm, Cuckoo Hill Farm, a Cottage on Raysons Hill, Old Chene Cottage, Fore Street Farm, Eastcote Cottage and Sigers). His nearest rivals, Shepherd and Lewin, had 462a.0r.39p being joint owners of St. Catherine's Manor and Southcote (see Chapter 5).

Edward Hilliard Sen. came next with 217 acres and his son Edward Hilliard Jun. lay eighth with 82 acres. The Hilliards had acquired lands in Cowley, Hillingdon, Ruislip, Harefield, Ickenham, and Northolt by marriage. Elizabeth Stafford Crosier married Edward Hilliard, a lawyer, in 1779.[a] The Crosier lands settled upon her at marriage, had by 1806 devolved upon her widower, the Edward Hilliard Senior of the Rate Books. He owned Primrose Hill Farm, Sherleys Farm (now The Old Barn Hotel), Field End Farm (Pond Green now on site), the White House (Sharps Lane), Knowles Farm (near the site of the London Bible College) and Kiln Farm, Rickmansworth Road. His second son, Edward Hilliard Junior had Wilkins Farm (Woolworths now on site), Woodman's Farm, Bury Street and South Hill Farm, all inherited from his great uncle John Crosier of Ickenham who had died in 1801.[b] Like Shephard and Lewin the Hilliards were not resident in Ruislip.

Neither was Thomas Truesdale Clarke who lived at Swakeleys but owned 116 acres of Old Enclosures in Ruislip parish: Hill Farm (Orchard Close), the Old Barn House, Eastcote; Field End House Farm; Cheney Street Farm; The Case is Altered; The Grange, Eastcote High Road and a house which had disappeared by 1866 which stood on the south side of Eastcote High Road opposite the bottom of Catlins Lane.

Other landowners with more than 50 acres Old Enclosures were the Trustees of Robert Child of Osterley Park (Priors Farm); Richard Heming of the Manor House, Hillingdon (Ducks Hill Farm); Robert Hucks who had large estates in Hertfordshire (Park Farm, Northwood); Edward Howard of Astin Lodge, Moor Park (Kewferry Farm); Henry Pine Martin (Gate Hill Farm); John Rowe of the New River Company (The Grange, Northwood); J. H. Babb, Deliverer of the Vote in the House of Commons (Joel Street Farm and land near Highgrove). James Forbes (a farm north of Green Lane which disappeared before 1866) and George Woodroffe of Hayden Hall, (Hayden Hall Farm; the Homestead, Wiltshire Lane; a Cottage south of Park Wood and land in Fore Street; White Cottage on Raysons Hill).

It is immediately noticeable from the above list that most of the large compact farms lay in Northwood where the land had been enclosed from the wooded waste before the 16th century. (See Chapter 6).

Ralph Deane, Henry Pine Martin, John Rowe, J. H. Babb and George Woodroffe were the only principal proprietors to live in the parish, but a higher proportion of the smaller proprietors were resident. See Table below.

Table 2. Residence of Proprietors in relation to extent of property

Size of Property	Over 50a	10a-49a	1a-9a	u.1a	Total
Resident	5	8	18	18	49
Non-Resident	10	14	22	13	59
Total	15	22	40	31	108

The general picture is of a parish largely inhabited by tenant-farmers and rent paying cottagers, with a few gentry families in the larger houses.

Agriculture c.1800

The method of agriculture employed in the common fields was under attack from agrarian improvers during the second half of the 18th century. The practice of rotating crops (wheat, peas or beans) including a fallow year, meant that roughly one third of the arable land was constantly unproductive. Experiments with new crops like clover, which smothered weeds, cleansed the land and made a fallow year unnecessary, were difficult to conduct in fields where every man must work in union with his neighbour. Ploughing being possible in only one direction and not athwart because of the danger of trespassing on neighbouring lands could not produce a good, sweet tilth and drainage was inadequate for the same reason. Time was lost in moving from one strip of land to another (See Map).

Reformers believed that the common fields should be enclosed and the land reallocated in consolidated blocks, which could be fenced to enable individual farmers to experiment with crops and new stock-breeding and rearing methods. The expected result of enclosure was increased productivity.

The waste land technically belonged to the lord of the manor, but property owners had rights of commonage on it. The reformers saw it as "wasted land" and thought that it could be cultivated and made profitable.

The Board of Agriculture formed in 1793 to popularise new forms of agriculture caused three reports to be written on Middlesex. That of John Middleton published in 1798[3] said that Middlesex was a very fertile county farmed by conservative people and therefore under productive. Implements were old fashioned. The swing plough was still used in preference to wheeled ploughs which were easier to keep straight. Drills were not to be seen at all and threshing machines were only just coming into general use. Oxen were still the draught animals and were used for ploughing. Horses were bought at fairs as they were not bred in the county. Middleton was particularly scathing about the practice of fallow. *"On the whole I have good reason to think that the idea of giving rest to the land is now exploded in every part of the County, except in Ruislip and Ascot (i.e. Eastcote), and even there I have no doubt but that the superior crops and evidently higher profit of their neighbours will soon convince them that the raising of clean, smothering green crops and feeding stock with them on the land is not only much more profitable but is also the most effectual method of procuring large crops of wheat".*

Middleton recommended enclosures of the common fields and a change to hay production in most parts of the county. The proximity of the London market (hay was the petrol of the 19th century) he thought would double profits within 21 years.

Other land due for enclosure and improvement was the common waste. *"The commons of this county as everywhere else are thinly stocked by poor, half-starved, ragged-coated and wretched-looking sheep. On the commons above Ruislip and Pinner there are many kept, and folded on the arable land".* The author, John Middleton of West Barn Farm, Merton and of Lambeth, Surrey was a land surveyor, member of the London Society for the encouragement of Arts, Science and Commerce and corresponding member of the Board of Agriculture.

Machinery of Enclosure

A number of landholders in Ruislip agreed with Middleton. A private Enclosure Act was introduced in 1804. The promoters were R. W. Humphrey Sumner D.D. Provost of King's College, the Rev. George Deane, Charles James, Esq., the Rev. William Blencowe, John Humphrey Babb, Esq., "and several other persons". George Deane and Charles James had just inherited the lease of the manor and the Eastcote House Estates, being trustees of the will of their elderly cousin Elizabeth Rogers.[4] Ralph Deane mentioned above as the chief landowner in the parish was the residuary legatee. It is from this quarter that pressure for enclosure came.

Preparatory letters were despatched by Charles James of New Inn to all the other 107 proprietors of land (at a cost of 1s:6d a letter!).[5] The one quoted below was addressed to Jason Wilshin who leased Manor Farm at the time, but owned Cannon Bridge Farm and other property at King's End (probably Orchard Cottage). In 1810 he gave up the lease of Manor Farm and moved into the Old House on the other side of Bury Street.

The letter was dated 19 September 1803.[6] *"I take the liberty of applying to you as a Proprietor of land in Ruislip and to request the favour of your attendance at a meeting which is to be held on Tuesday the 27th instant at 12 o'clock at Ruislip to take into consideration the propriety of enclosing the Common Fields and the Common. The late Mrs Rogers devised to Dr Deane and myself her Estates in Ruislip and Eastcote and which including The College Land contain 1517 acres. I felt it my duty to go over and examine the different Estates and I am confident after much consideration that the value of the property may be increased one-half by an enclosure. The trustees (of Mrs Roger's estates) subsequent to my examination*

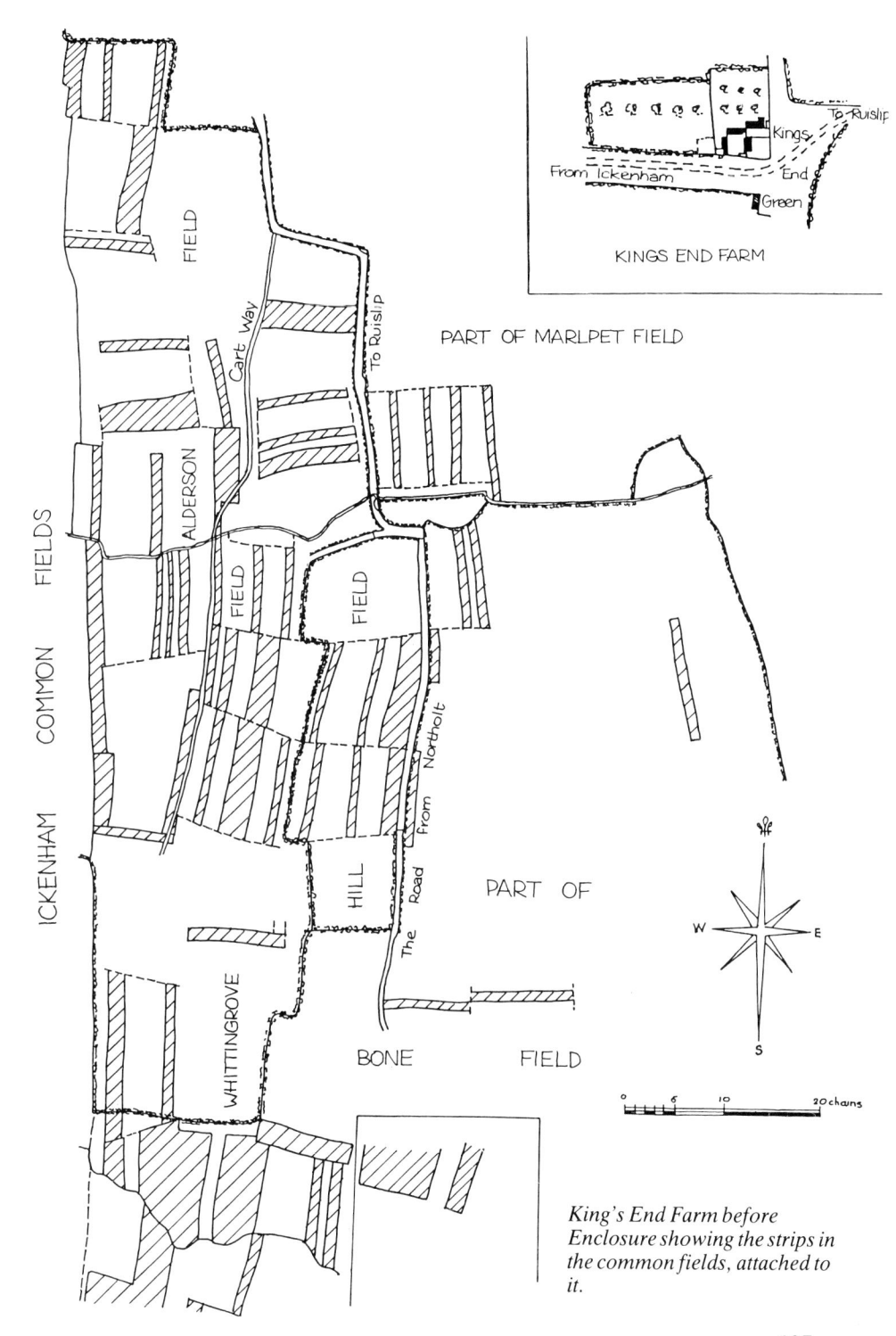

King's End Farm before Enclosure showing the strips in the common fields, attached to it.

employed Mr Wyatt of Maidenhead, a man of great knowledge and experience and after he had surveyed the Common Fields and the Common he was decidedly of opinion that an enclosure would be highly advantageous."

The "very numerous" meeting on the 27 September 1803 decided on Enclosure.[7] A Draft Bill was ready to be shown at The Bell on 21 November 1803 and on 3 March 1804 the work of collecting proprietors' signatures on copies of the Consent Bill began.[8] This was a task which took some considerable time and involved the solicitor in a lot of travelling. The following is an extract from the accounts: 30 April 1804 ... *"journey to Mr Paynes at Chesham, Bucks to procure his signature to the course of the Bill and afterwards attending a considerable number of the proprietors in the neighbourhood to procure their signatures to the Consent Bill. Out three days £9:9s."*[9] Although the Bill received its third reading on 20 June 1804, signatures were still being collected in October. A trip to Bath to see Mrs Hogard owner of Maze Farm, Ducks Hill took four days and cost £12:0s. Other journeys in the same month were to Hammersmith, Twickenham, Bedfont and Staines; to Hemel Hempstead, Aldenham and Stanmore and to Acton, Ealing and Greenford!

Some proprietors declined to sign and could not be persuaded. *"Attending Mr Harvey at White Hart, Holborn and entered into a long explanation. He objected to it alleging that the enclosure would not be beneficial and could not be convinced."* The objectors seem to have been in the minority in Ruislip and there is no evidence of organised opposition like The Association opposing the Harrow Enclosure formed in 1802.[10]

The business of the Enclosure proceeded. Three Commissioners, Thomes Wyatt of Maidenhead, John Trumper of Harefield and William Sedgewick of Rickmansworth, nominated by the promoters, were appointed to allot the respective lands to the different proprietors *"in as convenient a manner in every respect as circumstances will admit of"*[11] Henry Bierdeman of Uxbridge worked as Surveyor under the direction of the Commissioners. Holders of lands and people having common rights (i.e. the 108 proprietors) were invited to attend meetings of the Commissioners, advertised in the County Chronicle and Morning Chronicle and in notices affixed to the *"most public door of the Parish Church of Ruislip"* in order to stake their claims. Proprietors received letters dispatched on the day of the third reading requesting *"the favour of you in case you should wish to have any adjoining piece of land or a desire to make an Exchange or Purchase of Lands to communicate the particulars of such intention as early as you conveniently can in order that the commissioners may make the necessary arrangements."*[12]

Sales of Land

Expenses were naturally incurred in introducing the Bill, surveying the lands, making the roads, writing letters etc. The same letter continued. *"Part of the Common and Wastelands will be sold to defray a proportion of the expenses of the act....if you should wish to purchase any particular spot either of the commons or waste you will be so good as to point it out and favour us with a line upon the subject."*

Sales took place by auction in July and October 1805 at the Bell Inn and in January 1806 at The George.[13] The first lands auctioned were situated in Church Field and Marlpit Field and had frontages to Ruislip High Street and West

End Road. Further lots were in the angle of Joel Street, Pinner Road and Potter Street. All were advertised as being *"in situations peculiarly adapted and extremely desirable for Building upon...."*

Jason Wilshin bought the High Street lands which extended as far as Sherleys Farm (now the Old Barn Hotel) paying £1298:3s for 28a 0r 9p (about £46 per acre). His descendants reaped the benefit when building development eventually began about 120 years later.

At the second sale 100 acres of the common waste was sold to Jeremiah Steel and subsequently became Hundred Acres Farm, Northwood. (Express Dairies Depot). 50 acres on West End Road immediately north of the Yeading were sold at the same time. 46 acres fronting Field End Road and lying south of the Yeading went at the third sale.

Several other small pieces of land (under five acres) appear to have been sold privately and one larger sale was negotiated in the same way. The Grand Junction Canal Company seeking a valley in which to create a reservoir to serve as Canal Feeder, approached the Commissioners and bought two pieces of common waste, 39 acres and 16 acres in size.[14] The asking price was £70 per acre. The Company offered £50 and agreement was reached in March 1805 when £55 per acre was accepted. 35 acres of Park Wood and several cottages at Park Hearne were also purchased from King's College and the respective proprietors, for the reservoir.[15]

About 365 acres were sold altogether; but insufficient money was raised to cover the expense. A special rate was levied to close the deficit. King's College's portion of the rate was £597.10s.7d.[16]

Roads

The Commissioners had about 3,000 acres of open field, roadside waste and common to enclose. Their first step was to lay out the course of public roads across the waste.[17] Previously travellers from Pinner to Rickmansworth and from Eastcote to Watford had made the best way they could across the unfenced common, muddy in winter and dusty and rutted in summer. Now the course of Pinner/Rickmansworth Road was set from the Pinner boundary to join the old road at the corner of Hills Lane which wound round the Old Enclosures of Kiln Farm and up Kewferry Hill to Batchworth Heath. The top end of Joel Street and Potter Street were laid out to link the old winding part of Joel Street with Potter Street Hill. The two new roads crossed each other at what is now Northwood Hills Circus.

The new roads were drawn on the Enclosure Map with a straight edge. This straightness apparent still on modern maps characterises all the new roads across the former waste. The new roads had set widths (40ft – Rickmansworth Road – 30ft Joel Street and Potter Street) and had drainage ditches on either side. The cost of making up had to be met by the Commissioners. The road-makers were Seabrook and Fisher who had begun work by mid 1805.

The Down Barnes Road (West End Road) and the Northolt Road (Field End Road) 30ft wide apiece, replaced and straightened out the tracks which had led between the open fields of Westcote and Eastcote. Bridle Road was marked as a bridle way from Eastcote to Pinner. Twenty private roads giving access across strips of wayside waste, also now enclosed, to cottages or to new allotments were marked on the map and ten public footpaths. The roads swallowed up a further 103 acres. Maintenance of public roads fell upon the parish, except for Down Barnes Road (the highway to London). Two public gravel pits, one on Ducks Hill in the strip beside Young Wood, and a larger one by Rickmansworth Road (now the Gravel Pits Open Space), were set aside to provide road-mending materials. Ducks Hill proved too steep for horses pulling laden gravel carts from Northwood to Ruislip, so a right of way, to what is now Reservoir Road was opened for gravel-carrying each May, to provide a flat route.

Tithe Allotments

Newly enclosed land was to be tithe-free so both rector and vicar had to be compensated. The Dean and Canons of Windsor received 290 acres in South Ruislip and about 100 acres on Haste Hill. The vicar was given about 120 acres in lieu of tithes; 75 acres (25 acres of Park Wood and 50 acres on Haste Hill) because of an ancient and long disputed right to collect tithes of wood and to cut fuel for his fire (see Chapter 1); and 40 acres glebe in South Ruislip. The glebe allotment was equivalent in size to his former sellions. Tithes were extinguished on Old Enclosures at the same time, but a corn-rent (reviewed every twenty-one years and based upon the prevailing price of corn in Cambridge Market) was substituted.

New Allotments

The land sold, made into roads and given in lieu of tithes reduced the amount of land that the Commissioners had to allot to the claimants (by about 1,000 acres) but the enclosing of the formerly uncultivated waste more than made up the discrepancy in acres, though not in fertility.

The new allotments varied in size from 506 acres to King's College to 2 perches to small proprietors like John Bray and Joseph Bedford (who lived at Park Farm, Eastcote). Twenty-one men with very small allotments, (including Bray and Bedford) sold them to Francis Stubbs Esq. The allotments all lay on the west of Wiltshire Street at the top end and adjoined Francis Stubb's house, Eastcote Cottage, which seems to have been built in the late 18th century (see Chapter 11). Fairacres is now built on the site. (This Eastcote Cottage should not be confused with the Eastcote Cottage – formerly Plucketts – which stands on the corner of Eastcote Road and Field End Road).

Where a proprietor's former common field holdings are known, as is the case with King's College and the vicar, or can be estimated on the basis of late 18th century surveys (Clarkes of Swakeleys), it seems that the New Allotments were commensurate with the amount of land formerly held. Whether the very small new allotments made up for loss of grazing rights on the common fields is open to question.

The pattern of land ownership remained much the same after the Enclosure as before. 31 people still owned less than one acre and another 50 less than 10 acres, 23 people had between 10 and 50 acres. Those with more than 50 acres are listed below.

Poors Fields

Did anyone lose by Enclosure? The greatest loss was of the common waste, where free grazing was to be had and possibly some fuel in the form of kindlewood.

Table 3. Landowners with 50 acres or more.

	acres	roods	poles
King's College (leased to R. Deane)	1041	2	25
Deane Ralph	636	0	36
Shepherd and Lewin	436	2	27
Hilliard Edward Senior	461	3	1
Clarke T. T.	451	3	28
Dean and Canons of Windsor	388	3	34
Hilliard Edward Junior	307	2	37
Vicar	215	2	13
Child R. (Trustees)	151	1	16
Wilshin Daniel	130	0	35
Steel Jeremiah	100	0	0
Stiles John	99	0	29
Heming Richard	96	0	13
Howard Edward	92	1	19
Grand Junction Canal Co.	91	2	4
Babb J. H.	82	1	31
Hucks Robert	80	3	15
Rowe John	78	2	37
Martin Henry Pine	74	3	9
Edgell Harry	68	3	36
Anderson William	64	2	25
Woodroffe George	61	3	32
Forbes James	58	1	1
Sellon Sergeant	54	0	22
Harvey & Co.	53	3	18
Miss Phripp	51	3	22
Hill Daniel	51	3	17

These 27 people owned about 5000 of the 6500 acres.

There would have been no free turf-cutting as the soil of the waste belonged to the manorial lessees. It is doubtful whether very poor cottagers in Ruislip used the waste very much for grazing. The tenant farmers, however, did run cattle on the common, as is evident from documents relating to a minor legal battle between the owners of the Little Manor and King's College.[18]

In autumn 1803 Mr Shepherd and Miss Lewin claimed rights on the waste of the Great Manor and consequently expected an allotment from the commissioners in lieu. King's College sought legal advice and statements were taken from Isaac Stebbins, aged 80, who had lived in Ruislip for fifty years and "carried sand about on a jackass"; from Mr Living, formerly at Southcote Farm, Charles Martin aged 40, his successor at Southcote; Mark Clayton aged 42, owner of land near Youngwood Farm; James Gregory, aged 37, Bailiff since 1792; and James Ewer, aged 75, of Mill House.[19] From their evidence it was deduced that before St. Catherine's Enclosure of 1769 cattle put out on West Wood Common in the Little Manor and on the waste of the main manor had wandered freely from one to the other and there had been in legal terms a *"Tolerance of mutual Trespass"*. After 1769 gates had been erected to keep the two commons separate, but fencing around West Wood Common did not seem to have been completed and farmers in the Little Manor continued to turn their cattle onto the Great

The Goodliest Place in Middlesex

Entrance to Poors Field, set aside for Cottagers' grazing at the Enclosure

Manor's waste. James Ewer said that his cattle were all kept in the Little Manor (at Rose Cottage, Breakspear Road, which he owned), but were turned on the main waste in right of his property in the Great Manor (Mill House). He also said that he did not know any person who occupied land in the Little Manor only. Legal opinion was that Mr Shepherd and Miss Lewin had *"not even the shadow of a claim."*

However underused grazing rights might have been by the very poor, the commissioners realised that the enclosure of the commons constituted a loss to them and provided three Poors Fields in reparation. 39 acres of the common, between Park and Copse Woods, two acres behind the present Six Bells known as "the allotment in the Wythys" (Wythy Lane is in the area today) and 18 acres east of Joel Street were vested in the vicar, churchwardens and overseers of the poor to provide grazing for "the real, true occupiers of cottages only; as their share and interest of the common and waste lands in respect to their occupation and residence therein only; whose rents shall not exceed £5 per annum and having no other house or place of residence." 60 acres was a generous Poors Allotment. Twickenham Enclosure commissioners provided only ten acres for a similar purpose in 1818.[20]

Roadside waste between Ducks Hill and Youngwood and near the workhouse were given to the overseers of the poor for letting to poor men of good character as potato grounds.[21]

The main burden imposed upon small proprietors by the Enclosure Act was the cost of fencing the new allotments, which may be why some chose to

202

Enclosure in Ruislip Parish

sell out to larger landowners. Fencing cost 10s:6d per pole.[22] The bill for fencing Copse Wood was £526:5s:6d.[23]

It has often been said that enclosure led to the demise of the sturdy yeomen of England, because they lost the commons, and could not support themselves on their small allotments. This is obviously not the case in Ruislip where the yeomen were already rent-paying tenants long before enclosure. If anyone was totally dependent upon the commons for his livelihood, which seems doubtful, it would have been an occupier of a cottage, for whose benefit the Poors Fields were provided.

Effects of Enclosure

The map was drawn in 1806, but the Enclosure Award was not enrolled until 1814, perhaps because of time taken to adjust the allotments. It was proclaimed during Divine Service on the 18 September 1814 by William Weedon, parish clerk.

(a) Landscape

The immediate effect of the enclosure was upon the landscape as new hedged fields appeared between West End Road and Field End Road; upon Haste Hill; between Rickmansworth Road and Green Lane and across the top of Joel Street to the Pinner boundary. The new fields were large, being 35-50 acres in size and were bounded by straight hedges, not the sinuous lines of the Old Enclosures. All the allotments had to be hedged with quickset (hawthorn) within six months; the bushes to be placed between a double three-railed fence to protect them from browsing livestock until they were established.

Ironically this sylvan landscape thought of as typically English was short lived, mostly disappearing under a rising tide of bricks and mortar in little more than a century.

Hedge-setting and road-making increased labouring work in the parish for a time and the maintenance of the miles of hedges and new roads provided constant employment for roadmen and hedgers and ditchers.

The Grand Junction Canal Company's reservoir has been a feature of the Ruislip landscape ever since it was constructed in 1811. Having purchased common land from the Enclosure Commissioners the General Committee of the Canal Company still had to negotiate with King's College for a piece of Park Wood and with the proprietors of cottages at Park Hearne. The College lessees valued the woodland at £65 an acre; £40 an acre more than the value placed upon it by the Company's man! Two years elapsed before a satisfactory agreement was reached by surveyors named by both parties; but in February 1807 the Company paid £1,068 for 35a.3r. Ten acres were valued at £45 per acre and 25a.3r. at £24 per acre, the difference presumably being the amount of timber growing in the different sections of the wood.[24] The lessees (Deane and James) were allowed £77:5s of the total to compensate them for loss of underwood.

There may have been some opposition to the creation of a reservoir in Ruislip for Henry Golder owner of one of the cottages refused to treat with the Company on any terms.[25] Other proprietors simply hedged until better prices were offered. Both Henry Golder and Robert Lively sold out to John Dean, another owner in the summer of 1807 and in August the Company was able to complete the purchases. They paid £210 to Rev. William Blencowe for a cottage and 1½ acres; £100 to Daniel Hill for a cottage and 21 perches and £250 to John

Ruislip Reservoir, built 1811 as a canal feeder

Dean for three cottages and 5½ acres. The Company Minutes state that these prices *"were collectively more moderate than purchases formerly made for the reservoir in that parish".*

For a few years the land was let, but by 1811 construction work was in progress; John Rennie being the consulting engineer and Hugh Mackintosh the Constructor.

On 5 December 1811 Rennie reported to the General Meeting of the Committee of Management of the Grand Junction Waterworks Company, *"The Reservoir at Ruislip has now been completed and although doubts were entertained with respect to its capability of being filled with water owing to an extensive bed of sand which was found near to its Head, yet this has answered the most sanguine wishes as it is now nearly full of water and from the latest accounts transmitted to me there is no appearance of any leakage in it."*

Hugh Mackintosh was paid £2,780 in April 1812 for excavating and banking the reservoir but there were probably earlier payments which have not been recorded.

The Grand Junction Canal Company was empowered to supply piped water from the canal to the inhabitants of Paddington in 1798. An Act of Parliament of 1811 transferred these powers to the Grand Junction Waterworks Company which undertook the works at Ruislip. In February 1813, having presumably ensured that the water held, the Company resolved to make a feeder to connect the reservoir with the canal. The route chosen was between seven and eight miles long and entered the canal near Hayes Bridge. The land through which it was to pass had to be purchased from many owners, which took time to accomplish and work did not begin until February 1816. The water ran in the feeder for the first time on 4 June 1816, according to James Ewer's diary.[26] It was entirely man made and did not make use of any natural water courses because of objections from millers who did not want water to be deflected from the River Colne which was fed by the streams.

The feeder was not a success as it collected drainage and flood waters from the lands on either side of it and contaminated both the canal and Paddington's water supply. An extension was devised by the engineers from Hayes Bridge to the Brentford Arm to avoid pollution of the Paddington Arm and that was constructed in 1817.

The reservoir itself was not entirely successful either, being rather shallow in comparison with its surface area and was not used by the canal after 1851. The Grand Union Canal, successor to the Grand Junction began to develop it as a lido with boating, swimming and fishing facilities in the late 1930s. After nationalisation of British Waterways it came under the aegis of the British Transport Commission, from whom it was purchased by R.N.U.D.C. in 1951.[27]

(b) Effect of Enclosure on the poor
Expenditure on the poor increased after enclosure, but had already been growing heavier at a fairly steady rate from the 1790s due to the effects of war with France. Dreadful weather conditions which adversely affected crops, pushed up the price of corn and pulled more labourers down below subsistence level. (see Chapter 9).

There was a drop in expenditure in 1802 (probably due to the Treaty of Amiens) but this was short lived and the rise was constant from 1803-7, after which it declined again. In view of the background it would be wrong to blame the increase entirely upon the enclosures, especially in the very years when road-making and hedge-setting was at its height.

Census returns show no sign of depopulation at the time of the Enclosure.

Population 1801-51
1801 – 1012   1831 – 1117
1811 – 1239   1841 – 1413
1821 – 1343   1851 – 1392

However by 1831 a significant drop occurs in the population which may be attributable to nationwide agricultural depression, but could have been caused in part by a long term effect of the enclosure. The changeover to hay production prophesied by Middleton gradually occurred. The less labour-intensive crop provided fewer opportunities for employment than the growing of cereals and legumes and may have led people to leave the area in search of work.

The three Poors' Fields appear to have been little used by the occupiers of cottages for whom they were intended, but overgrazed by others. The trustees of the Poors Ground, (the lessee of the lord of the manor, the churchwardens, overseers and renters of property valued at more than £100 per annum) met in April 1834 to apportion the stints.[28] Each cottager was entitled *"to turn out one cow, horse or ass (which shall be Bona Fide their own property without collusion direct or implied) from Old May Day (11 May) next ensuing until the Christmas following, on the commonable land awarded and set out by the*

Commissioners under the Enclosure Act of this parish and that all persons claiming such rights shall produce a receipt for such rental or agreement for such rental to the Vestry Clerk to be by him entered in a book to be kept for that purpose and presented to the Trustees for their inspection".

On the 16 May some of the trustees: Ralph Deane, Esq.; Thomas White, churchwarden; William Durbridge, overseer; Christopher Kingston Fountain, overseer; Daniel Kirby and Samuel Weedon; accompanied by Thomas Collet, the vestry clerk; and two constables Edward Sceney and Charles Tillet; attended the Poors Field near the workhouse to examine the state of the fences and the cattle. They intended to order the marking of each beast either by clipping or branding with a number, but were prevented from proceeding with the business of the day *"in consequence of a riotous assemblage of Persons"*. Matthew Saich, Christopher Brill and William Hill were taken into custody and subsequently prosecuted. Presumably they were using the ground illegally and resented the prospect of losing the free grazing.

Three days later the Trustees went to the Eastcote Poors Field in Joel Street and found cattle trespassing. Their owners, John Cammack of Harefield, Daniel Matheson and James Pritchard of Eastcote and Hill, Morton, Collins, William Collins, John Page, Henry Webb and Churchill were all fined by the magistrates at Uxbridge Petty Sessions. Efforts were made to maintain the field in better order. Bailiffs were appointed to look after the Poors grounds and in most years the cattle were ticketed or marked in some way. The ponds made in 1809 by William Poulter were cleared out from time to time and a mole-catcher was employed. William Lavender was paid 12s. for catching 96 moles, i.e. 1½d each, in 1851.[29]

The trustees considered ways of making the Poors Fields more profitable for the poor and consulted John Woods, Esq. of the Society for the Improvement of the Labouring Classes in 1844, who recommended letting them as small allotments for vegetable growing etc.[30] This was not considered practicable at the time, though Mr Soames and Mr Deane offered to let small plots of their own land for the same purpose.

When J. J. Roumieu, Curate of Ruislip, wrote *Ruislip, a history of the parish and church* in 1875, few, if any, poor people had cattle and they sold their rights for sums varying from 6 shillings to 10 shillings. In 1882 the Charity Commissioners allowed the trustees to let the Joel Street land and the Wythies as allotment gardens. Pasturage on the main field could be let, or the land made profitable in some other way and the income used for charitable purposes.

The Cottagers' Allotment Charity[31] as it became was reorganised in 1909 when only five or six persons were still exercising grazing rights. R.N.U.D.C. was to elect eight of the 13 trustees. The rental limitations for those allowed to benefit was raised at various times to £8 in 1882, £20 in 1909 and to £27 in 1922.

The Charity had added 5½ acres to its Joel Street land over the course of the years, which it exchanged with Southern Estates Ltd. in 1935 for 9½ acres of Hundred Acres Farm. The new land called the Hogs Back was leased to the R.N.U.D.C. for £50 per annum from 1936-45 and then sold to the Council for £1,750. The original 18 acres has been registered as common land and is still allotments.

The main Poors Field was conveyed to R.N.U.D.C. in July 1939 in fee simple and without charge, to be maintained as open space for recreational

Enclosure in Ruislip Parish

purposes only. Some grazing continued until 1956, when it was ended because of an outbreak of Foot and Mouth Disease. It too is registered as common land.

The Little Poors Field in the Wythies was sold in October 1961 to R.N.U.D.C. with the approval of the Charity Commissioners.[32] It now forms the south eastern portion of the crematorium grounds.

The Ruislip Cottagers' Allotment Charity with an invested income still exists and dispenses charity to a select few at Christmas time, in the form of small cheques.

(c) New Farms

Several new farm houses were built in the parish on the new enclosures, mostly by the principal land-holders: King's College, Ralph Deane and an outsider Charles Mills of Hillingdon Court. None appeared immediately after Enclosure. The College land in Northwood had a barn erected on it by 1816.[33] This is most likely the barn that now stands in a sadly dilapidated state on Northwood Golf Course, next to the farmhouse called Northwood Farm (newly renovated and converted into two cottages – 1984-5) which was built about 1827. Ralph Deane installed his farm bailiff to farm all his leasehold land in Northwood, both College and rectory land from it, (see Chapter 7). This arrangement continued until 1872, when F. H. Deane (son of Ralph) ceased to be the manorial lessee. Thereafter Northwood Farm was let by the College directly to farmers, Stephen Cooper in 1881 and Daniel Matheson in 1886.[34] In 1902 it was leased to T. Fergusson Esq. for use as golf links[35] and was subsequently purchased by Northwood Golf Club.

New Farm

Francis Deane purchased all the former rectory lands from the Ecclesiastical Commissioners in 1872 and built a farm house, New Farm, on the Northwood allotment some time later (see Chapter 7). Job Kempton, farmer and hay dealer, seems to have been living there in 1881. E. Weedon, R. A. Foxlee and Mr Wild were all later tenants of the Deanes at New Farm. Much of the land was sold to R.N.U.D.C. in 1927 and subsequently became Haste Hill Golf Course and the house was empty for a time. Mr A. E. Marks a butcher of the Pavement, Northwood bought New Farm from the Hawtrey Deane estate in 1931. He kept sheep prior to slaughter in the outbuildings and rented grazing land for them on Pinner Hill.[36] He was succeeded by his son. The house and farmbuildings have been demolished in 1985 and houses are being built on the site.

Bourne Farm

Soon after Enclosure Ralph Deane bought land adjoining his leasehold rectory allotment in what is now South Ruislip and built a farmhouse on it from which the rectory lands were farmed by a farm bailiff, (Chapter 7). It is marked New House on the 1 inch O.S. map surveyed in 1820. Later it was called Bourne Farm. After the purchase from the Ecclesiastical Commissioners in 1872, Bourne Farm continued as part of the Hawtrey Deane Estate, the Smith family being the tenants. It was sold to A. J. Taylor for development in 1931 and 1935 and the house ended its days as the A. J. A. Taylor/Deane Estate Office. It stood by the roundabout at the junction of Victoria Road and Long Drive and was demolished after a fire in 1964. A. J. A. Taylor & Co now has its Deane Estate office in Station Approach, South Ruilsip.

The Goodliest Place in Middlesex

New Pond Farm (See Chapter 7)

Ralph Deane realised that the new allotments would be more efficiently farmed from farm houses built on or near them and that neither the Dean and Canons of Windsor, nor King's College, were inclined to provide them. Having established Bourne Farm on his own land to supply the deficiency of buildings for the rectory lands he set to work to make similar provision for the southern section of the College land.

He purchased a 22 acre field in West End Road lying immediately south of the College allotment. The land is now mainly New Pond Playing Fields, though Northdown Close has been built within its curtilage. He built a labourer's cottage and farm buildings on it. More farm buildings were erected on the College land soon after 1850, so close to the boundary that both sets of buildings were known collectively as New Pond Farm and are thus shown on the 1866 6 inch O.S. map.

In 1851 Thomas Clayton, a farm labourer, was in residence. By 1861 Thomas Sanson was farming the 22 acres and 87 acres of the College land from New Pond as tenant of F. H. Deane. In 1872 Mr Deane ceased to be manorial lessee, so the College was obliged to provide a new farmhouse on their own land a few yards north, which still stands today near the north side of Cornwall Road and

New Pond Farm built by King's College c.1872

Enclosure in Ruislip Parish

Little New Pond alias Old Pond Farm, built by Ralph Deane

is called New Pond Farm (now a Nursing Home). The older house which was on the opposite side of Cornwall Road but has been long demolished came to be called Old Pond or Little New Pond Farm. By 1886 Henry Taylor leased the new house and 87 acres from King's College and Henry Powell leased the old house and the 22 acres from Mr Deane.[37]

Richard Ewer was the last farmer to live at New Pond Farm. King's College sold the New Pond Farm to Southern Estates Ltd in 1930[38] but Richard Ewer continued to rent the land from them for a few years until building actually started, although he removed to Manor Farm. He had been farming both farms together in any event since the death of his father, H. J. Ewer in 1916. The Scotts are remembered to have sold milk from Old Pond Farm in the 1920s.

Priors Farm (See Chapter 7)

By 1835 Mr Deane had purchased some old enclosures on the southern boundary of the parish which had probably formed Priors Field in medieval times. A farmhouse which belonged to the Hawtreys had stood there in the 18th century and been sold to James, Earl of Carnarvon, in 1717.[38a] The lands passed to Robert Child of Osterley and were held by his trustees in 1806. Ralph Deane built the new Priors Farm house on a new allotment which joined the old enclosures to West End Road. Joseph Watson was the tenant farmer in 1835. The house built by Ralph Deane was demolished in 1964 and the present premises built. Stanley Thomas Jones leased the farm from the Hawtrey-Deane estate in 1926.[39] In 1935

The Goodliest Place in Middlesex

Priors Farm, built by Ralph Deane on a new enclosure before 1835

it was sold to A. J. A. Taylor & Co along with Bourne Farm, but was bought by R.N.U.D.C. in 1954 to be part of a Country Park. It is now owned by the London Borough of Hillingdon and is farmed by Mr Jones's son.

Hundred Acres Farm

Sir Charles Mills of Hillingdon Court bought land on the west side of West End Road from the Hilliards before 1850 and built Hundred Acres Farm which stood where the builders yard opposite Station Approach is now.[40] His son Charles Henry Mills built a cottage which still stands, embellished with his monogram, CHM and the date 1872. The farm land was mainly taken into Northolt aerodrome in 1915.[41] The house was sold with the rest of the Hillingdon Court Estate in 1925.[42] Mr Ellis was the farmer in the early years of this century. His son-in-law, Mr Platford, put up Hundred Acres House, where for a time Mr Albery bred ponies,[43] which were raced on Northolt racetrack.

Glebe Farm

Sir Charles wished to link Hundred Acres with another of his properties, Down Barnes Farm, by buying the vicarial glebe allotment which protruded between them. The protracted negotiations were completed in 1878, (see Chapter 5). He built the attractive neo-gothic style Glebe Farm in 1882 by which time he had erected a pair of cottages close by. The farm house still stands and is run as a small-holding. Lord Hillingdon's coat of arms, with the date, adorns the gable. Glebe Avenue is on the site of the cottages.

Rose Hall
Rose Hall Cottage had been built in West End Road before 1866 on a small allotment granted to John Deane at enclosure.

Although never more than a small-holding it was sometimes known as Rose Hall Farm. It belonged to Jason Wilshin late in the 19th century and was let to Thomas Boyles at the beginning of this century. It stood where Willow Gardens is now.

Some smaller farms were built on the Eastcote side of the parish.

Rabourne Mead Farm
A small house appeared in the very south-east corner of Ruislip parish before 1850.[44] It belonged to a John McWhinnie. In 1886 it was called Starvall Farm and had 27 acres of land.[45] William Turner Edlin was the tenant. The name changed to Rabourne Mead Farm before 1897. This century it was carried on by Mr Edlin's son and later his nephew who ran it as a small pig farm, though some of the land was let. It came into Council ownership in 1954. Such buildings as remain are in Eastcote Lane just beside the railway bridge and future development of the land is under discussion.

The Buildings
A little group of buildings is actually labelled "The Buildings" on the 1897 O.S. map.[46] Brackenbridge is now on or near the site. The buildings were erected on a very small allotment made to Mr Demembray by the Enclosure Commissioners.

Model Farm
The Model Farm stands near the Clay Pigeon. It was built after 1897, but before 1916 where it first appears on the O.S. map of that date. Mrs Harris and later the Cradocks lived there. A few of the outbuildings have also survived. It was part of the Deane's estate and the land had formed a section of Bourne Farm.

REFERENCES
1. G.L.R.O. DRO 19 E1/21.
2. This and following information compiled from: G.L.R.O. Ruislip Enclosure Award and Map. G.L.R.O. MR/DE RU1 E2 DRO 19 E1/21-22 (Rate Books); G.L.R.O. DRO 19 E3/1 (Valuation).
    a. G.L.R.O.: Acc 289/51.
    b. G.L.R.O.: Acc 289/60: Acc 398/18.
3. Uxbridge Library: Middleton "View of The Agriculture of Middlesex 1798". John Middleton of West Barn Farm, Merton and of Lambeth, Surrey was a Land Surveyor and a member of the London Society for the Encouragement of Arts, Manufacture and Commerce and corresponding member of the Board of Agriculture.
4. Ruislip Library: Will of Elizabeth Rogers transcribed by J. McBean.
5. King's College: R53/26.
6. G.L.R.O.: Acc 538/2nd dep/3666/10.

The Goodliest Place in Middlesex

7. G.L.R.O.: Acc 538/2nd dep/3666/1.
8. Ibid 3666/6.
9. King's College: R53/26.
10. G.L.R.O.: Acc 76/2216.
11. G.L.R.O.: Acc 538/2nd dep/3666/8.
12. Ibid.
13. Ibid 3679, 3650, 3681.
14. Ruislip Library: L. E. Morris Collection.
15. King's College: R53/22.
16. Ibid 25.
17. Et seq. G.L.R.O. Ruislip Enclosure Award and Map. MR/DE RU1 E2 1-2.
18. King's College: R53 1/1.
19. Ibid 14/1.
20. Cashmore: *Twickenham in 1818* 1977.
21. G.L.R.O. DRO 19 C1/6.
22. King's College: R53/3.
23. Ibid 22.
24. Ibid 23.
25. Et seq. Ruislip Library L. E. Morris Collection.
26. G.L.R.O.: Acc 538/1st dep/8/11.
27. Documents penes London Borough of Hillingdon.
28. Et seq. G.L.R.O. DRO 19 C1/1/6.
29. G.L.R.O. DRO 19 E1/4.
30. G.L.R.O. DRO 19 C1/6.
31. Et seq. Ruislip Library L. E. Morris Collection.
32. Documents penes London Borough of Hillingdon.
33. King's College R53/6.
34. Census Returns and Ruislip Parish Rate Book at Uxbridge Library.
35. Ex info the late John Saltmarsh of King's College.
36. Ex info Mr D. Marks.
37. Uxbridge Library: Ruislip Parish Rate Book.
38. Uxbridge Library: Documents relating to Southern Estates.
38a. G.L.R.O.: Acc 249/2262.
39. EX info Val Jones.
40. G.L.R.O. DRO 19 E2/29-34.
41. Norris & Hayward: *History of Northolt Airport.*
42. Uxbridge Library: Sales details Hillingdon Court.
43. Ex info Rene Twitchen.
44. G.L.R.O. DRO 19 E2/29-34.
45. Uxbridge Library: Ruislip Parish Rate Books.
46. 6 inch O.S. map 1897.

Chapter Eleven

Growth of Estates in the 19th century and their eventual break-up

J. Norris Brewer writing in the *Beauties of England and Wales* published in 1816, described Ruislip as "a village of a rural character" whose farm buildings had *"an air of neatness and comfort"* and where there were a few houses *"sufficiently capacious for the accommodation of retired gentility."* The scenery was *"tranquil and pleasing".* The houses he considered worthy of mention were Eastcote House, Hayden Hall and Highgrove, only the latter being mentioned by name, the others simply called *"the residence of Ralph Deane, Esq."* and *"the seat of George Woodroffe, Esq."* Southcote Manor House was probably in a state of decay (see Chapter 5) and that other gentry family, the Readings of Field End, had disappeared from Ruislip records by that time.

The history of the Eastcote House lands is given in Chapter 7; that of the other estates is detailed below under separate headings.

Table 1. Gentry Houses – and their estates			
Changes in size in the 19th century			
Estate	*No. of acres in 1814*	*No. of acres*	*Year*
Eastcote House	637	c. 1000	1886
Hayden Hall	62	387	1883
		(Sale catalogue)	
Highgrove	90	61	1886
The Grange, Northwood	72	279	1864
		(Abstract of title)	
Northwood Park	26	196	1891
		(Sale Catalogue)	
Eastbury	Nothing in parish	450	1887
situated in Herts	265	312	
Eastcote Cottage (Wiltshire Lane)	6	24	1886
Eastcote Lodge	16	part of Hayden Hall estate	1883
Field End House Farm	indeterminate	92	1886
Myrtle Cottage, Joel Street	3½	12	1837
		(Parish Valuation)	
Mistletoe Farm	c. 6	6	1886
Ruislip Park		40	
Bury House	5	5	1886

(1814 acreages are taken from the Enclosure Award, 1886 acreages are taken from the Parish Rate Book)

The Goodliest Place in Middlesex

The population of the parish grew during the 19th century from 1012 people in 209 households in 1801 to 3566 people in 703 households in 1901; and the social balance changed slightly as rather more professional people and wealthy merchants (the gentry) sought rural retirement in this corner of the county.

Houses with "Pleasure Grounds" became a feature of the neighbourhood and whereas there had been only four gentry houses in the 17th century, they numbered 13 in the middle years of the 19th century.

It was the gradual break-up of these estates and their development for housing which completely and drastically changed the appearance, economy and social composition of the old parish of Ruislip between 1887 and the outbreak of the Second World War in 1939.

It will be seen from the above list that the gentry preferred Eastcote, as eight of their houses lay in that part of the parish. Westcote was the least favoured locality with only two. (Incidentally, the division of the parish into Westcote and Eastcote for rateable purposes ceased in 1833 and thereafter Westcote was simply called Ruislip).[1] Had Ruislip had a personal lord of the manor instead of an absentee corporate body like King's College, it is likely that a substantial mansion, somewhat akin to Swakeleys would have been built for him somewhere near the church. As it was, Manor Farm was the administrative centre of the manor and Eastcote House, home of the manorial lessees (the Hawtreys and Deanes), performed the social function of a domestic Manor House.

Ruislip Park House

The small estate called Ruislip Park House actually tried to usurp the position of Manor Farm and at the beginning of this century was known as The Manor House, to the annoyance of Henry James Ewer, farmer at Manor Farm and the Provost of King's College. Solicitors' letters were exchanged in 1906 when the estate was being sold, which brought little satisfaction to the College or to Mr Ewer. *"An owner can call his house any name he selects,"* they were told.

Park House, one of the most easily overlooked historic houses on Ruislip High Street, now belongs to the British Legion. It stands end on to the Street and modern appendages: a florists, a children's clothes shop and an estate agent, prevent passers-by from viewing it properly and realising that an old house lurks in the background. The 40 acre estate bounded by High Street, Ickenham Road and Sharps Lane (but exclusive of The George to The Swan in the north east corner and of The Orchard in the south west corner) was created by Harry Edgell, Esq. who acquired the land piecemeal over the period 1790-1827.[2]

Mr Edgell, a barrister-at-law was related by marriage to Ralph Deane of Eastcote House, their wives being sisters, Caroline and Elizabeth Gosling. He seems to have obtained King's End Farm about 1790 and to have bought a house on the site of Park House about 1806 from a Mr Tudsbury.[3] At enclosure he exchanged new allotments to which he was entitled for old enclosures near the house and purchased other cottages and land at the same time.[4]

Four houses were demolished and the land thrown into the new park.[5] Three stood along the High Street roughly where the Post Office, Barclays Bank and Currys are at present. They were replaced by a lodge (Ickenham Road, High Street corner) a rookery and a carriage drive. The fourth

Growth of Estates in the 19th century and their eventual break-up

Ruislip Park House Estate, early 19th century.

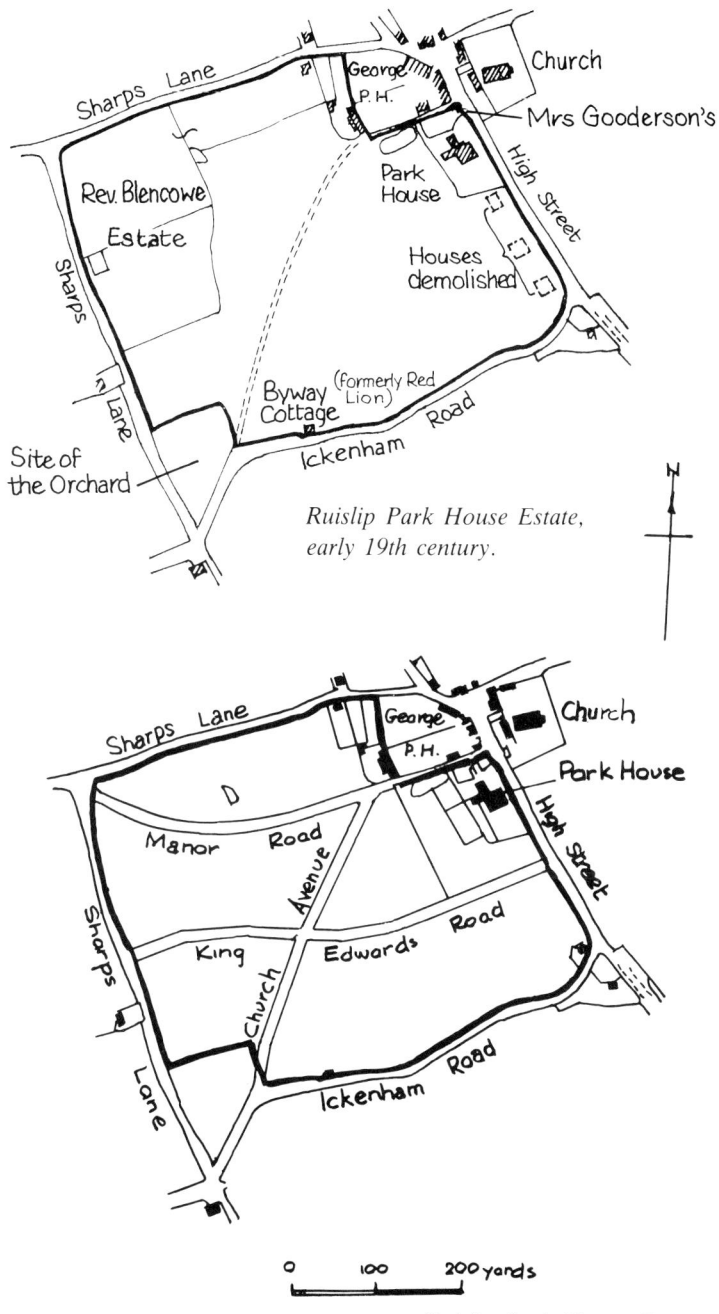

Ruislip Park House Estate 1911.

215

The Goodliest Place in Middlesex

house on Sharps Lane (where King Edwards Road now comes out) was formerly a farmhouse with 12 acres belonging to the Rev. William Blencowe who also owned Highgrove.[6] Byeway Cottage which lay between the present Byeway House and St. Cloud in Ickenham Road was left standing until after the break up of the Park, perhaps because it was sufficiently far from the main house not to detract from the view.[7] It was licensed as the Red Lion from 1748 to about 1810 when Mr Edgell purchased it from S. Salter, the brewer, and became a Mounted Police Station in 1842.[8] The Twitchen family moved there in 1914 and served teas to trippers.[9] A group of cottages on the corner of The Oaks was also left. For some years one of them was Ruislip's Post Office and is best remembered as Mrs Gooderson's shop.

Harry Edgell probably improved and extended the house about 1826 for the Rate Books for 1827 show that the general value of the property had increased by £10 because of *"improvements to the mansion"*. He probably lived there until about 1830, but had removed to Iver by 1832.[10] Later he lived in Chelsea where he died aged 96 in 1863.[11] He and his wife and several other members of the family are buried in St. Martin's where his monument may be found high on the south wall of the Lady Chapel, bearing a shield with the Edgell arms impaling those of Gosling.

Photographs show the house with a white stucco front, a balustrade round the eaves, sash windows and a pretty iron verandah. It has two distinct halves, one with three storeys, the other with only two, as if the original house was built onto and doubled in size. An auction catalogue of 1906[12] lists twelve bedrooms, a spacious square entrance hall, dining room, elegant drawing room, comfortable library and that requisite of a gentleman's house, a billiard room. This imposing mansion stood in equally attractive grounds which had two sheets of ornamental water (one exactly where the police houses stand in The Oaks, the other to the north of Manor Road), a rookery, shrubbery, a walled kitchen garden, greenhouse and a vinery.

Many owners followed Harry Edgell during the 19th century and Mrs Fanny Rosina Thompson bought the estate for £5,000 in 1885. She died in 1900 leaving it to her husband Cornelius Thompson for life, then in trust for her grandson.[13]

After Cornelius Thompson died in July 1905, the estate was put up for sale. The solicitors, Withers, Benson, Withers and Davies, wrote to King's College on 4th May 1906: "Ruislip Park was sold today for £9,500. It was considered a cheap sale. The purchaser is a Mr Morford of Eastcote who has bought it as a speculation either to resell at a profit or else to develop for building purposes".[14]

Walter Morford of Swan & Edgars and one-time resident at The White House in Sharps Lane re-sold the estate immediately to Dickens and Welch of High Wycombe and it was offered for sale as building plots on 7th July 1906.[15] The plan showed Manor Road and Church Avenue laid out along the lines of old footpaths which had led across the Park from the village to Little King's End and Great Kings End respectively. The one which became Church Avenue was called Church Path, being used as a short cut to St. Martin's. It is still a short cut, but now used by motor vehicles wishing to avoid the congested High Street. King Edwards Road was also shown.

At least three sales were held, two in 1906 and one in July 1911. Bidding does not seem to have been brisk as many lots were called in having failed to reach the reserved price. The police wanted land for a new police station and

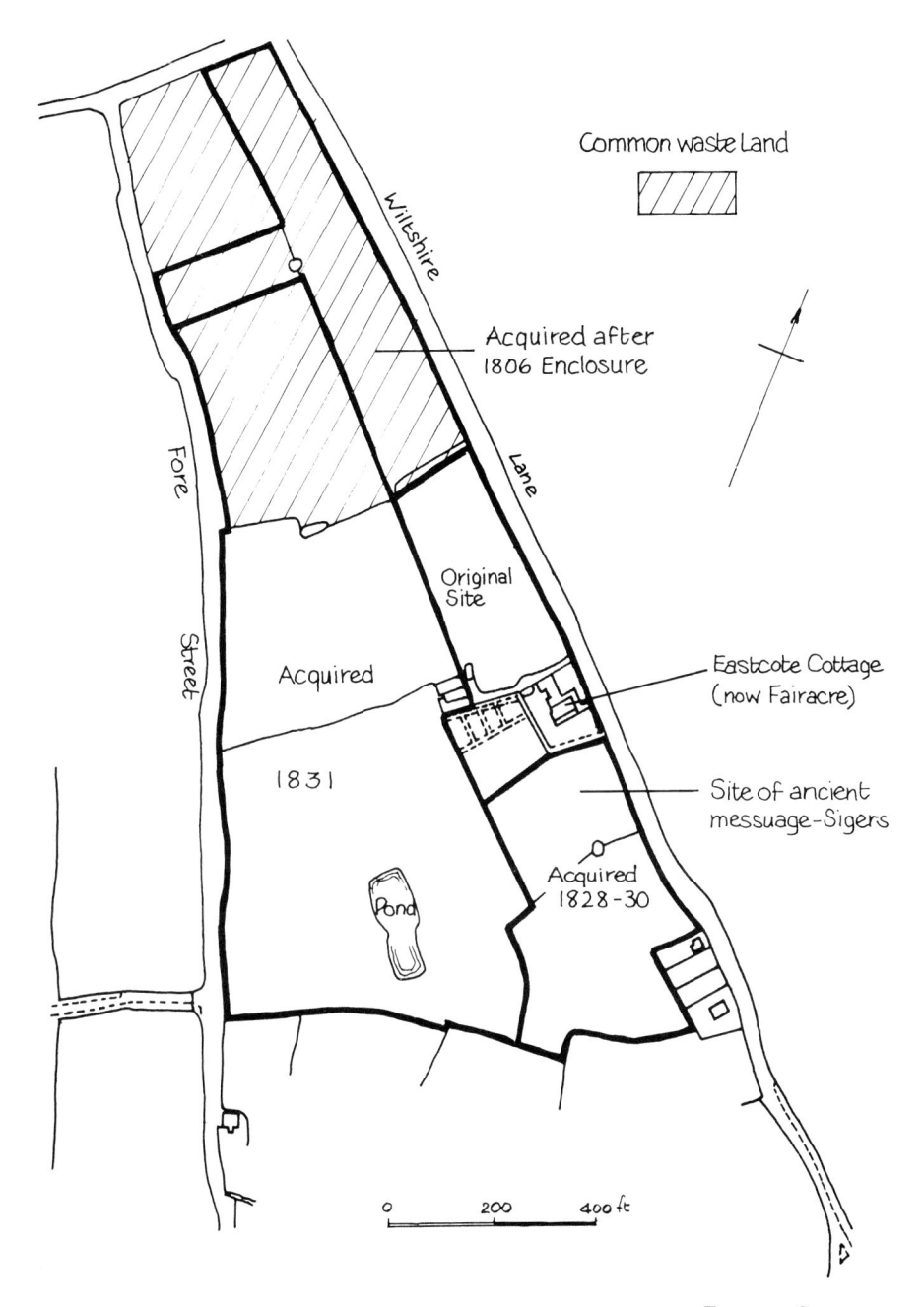

Growth of Estates in the 19th century and their eventual break-up

Eastcote Cottage

The Goodliest Place in Middlesex

bought Mrs Gooderson's shop and land behind for £840. The new police station was built fifty-seven years later! Three bids were made for Park House itself which was being offered for sale with 4 acres of garden. At £1125, the auctioneer said that he was not going to sacrifice this fine old building at this figure and that he had no doubt that it would be sold in the course of a few days.[16] He was probably optimistic as the house seems to have remained empty until 1913. The British Legion rented it in 1930 and bought it for £13,000 in 1946.[17]

A fuller account of the tenants of Ruislip Park House is given in the Journals of R.N.E.L.H.S. 1981 and 1985 and in *Ruislip Around 1900* published by R.N.E.L.H.S. Research Group.

Eastcote Cottage

At about the same time as Harry Edgell was buying up cottages and land along Ruislip High Street for Ruislip Park, Francis Stubbs, Esq. was similarly occupied at the top of Wiltshire Lane, creating pleasure grounds around his house, Eastcote Cottage. It stood at the northern end of the land adjoining the common waste, where Fairacre now stands. Mr Stubbs was a landowner in Kingsbury as well and one document describes him as a coachmaker of Long Acre.[18] At the time "cottages" midway between farmhouses and great houses were fashionable as country retreats. Mr Stubbs' cottage stood immediately north of a 16th century house once called Sigers which is shown on the 1806 Enclosure Map, when it belonged to Richard Hatch. It appears to have stood in what is now the roadway of Salisbury Road. Rather confusingly another 16th century house which stood to the east of Field End Road, Eastcote was called Sigers at the beginning of this century. It was demolished in the 1930s to make way for Eastcote Park, Eastcote.

The Enclosure Commissioners responsible for enclosing the waste, allocated the land lying between Wiltshire Lane and Fore Street (where the council housing estate now stands), to several different people in very small plots. Francis Stubbs received the piece adjoining his garden just over half an acre in size and bought up most of the other small allotments which faced onto Wiltshire Lane to give his house all the frontage to the top of the lane. He seems to have lived in Eastcote from about 1805 to 1820, when his property changed hands, as his name disappears from the Rate Books at that time.

Henry Gardiner Esq. purchased the estate from William Payne in 1823 and proceeded to acquire adjoining lands as they became available.[19] An *"ancient messuage"* next door, the original Sigers, was his first purchase in 1828, followed in 1830 by a field to the south which increased the Wiltshire Lane frontage. Finally the Howard family, owners of Ivy Farm (still standing on the corner of Egerton Close), sold him three fields on the east side of Fore Street, giving Eastcote Cottage a twenty-three acre estate. He remained in possession until 1839. Charles James Jenkins, Esq. of Albany Street, Regent's Park paid £1,700 for the estate in 1839. After his death in 1850 his widow, Martha, sold it to Alexander John Augustus Mann, a civil engineer of Bexley Heath and his sister Jane Mary Mann. Francis Stubbs, Henry Gardiner and Charles Jenkins resided at Eastcote Cottage but the Manns considered it only as an investment. They mortgaged it for £1,356 two days after taking possession and let the property. Alexander Mann died in October 1860 and Jane having repaid the mortgage in 1869, put it on the market. The Sale Catalogue may be seen at Manor Farm Library. John Todd, Esq. of 1 Alderman's Walk, London bought it for £2,950.

Growth of Estates in the 19th century and their eventual break-up

John Todd was described as a retired Australian merchant in the 1871 census. His wife, three children and three female servants made up the household. His was the last family to inhabit Eastcote Cottage. Sometime before 1881 it seems to have been demolished as reference to it is missing from the census of that year. He had probably died. Ann Todd conveyed the estate to J. C. Taylor for £1,800 in 1883 and no mention is made of a house in the description of the property. Nor is any building shown on the accompanying plan. The reason for the demolition is at present a mystery.

Tenants during the Manns' ownership. The tenants were mainly professional people. Thomas Price, a banker was there in 1850 and 1851. He may have interested himself in politics for he was entertaining Feargus O'Connor, the Radical MP, on the night of the census in 1851. O'Connor, a Chartist leader, believed in settling working men on small holdings to give them independence, and formed a land co-operative at Rickmansworth for this purpose. The Prices, both in their early thirties, had three small children and farmed their land. Their household included six servants, all of Irish birth. A man and wife were employed as bailiff and dairymaid while their son was an agricultural labourer and their daughter a nursemaid. A nurse and cook completed the domestic staff.

The next tenant, Mr George Baylis, started a brickfield on one of the fields. His lease dated 15th September 1853 permitted him at his own cost and charges *"to raise dig and get clay brickearth for the making of bricks, tiles, draining and other pipes or tiles upon Stony Field....but upon no other part of the premises and to manufacture the same into draining and other pipes or tiles and to sell....the same when so manufactured"*.

Mr Baylis was to pay £101 per annum rent and in addition rents upon his manufactures as follows: 1s 6d per 1000 bricks of common size, paving, oven tiles and oven bricks; 9d per 1000 draining pipes and tiles above 4 inches in the bore; 6d per 1000 covering tiles; 6d per 1000 draining pipes and tiles; 9d per 1000 pantiles, hiptiles, gutter tiles and ridge tiles above 4 inches in breadth. For the first two years no rents were to be paid on manufactures not exceeding 1½ million bricks and 2½ million pipes and tiles.

Only four months later in January 1854 George Baylis assigned the residue of his lease to Robert Vaughan-Williams, a barrister of Lincoln's Inn. Little is known of the fate of the brickfield, but a pond in Stony Field, presumably the kiln pond, appears on later maps. The present Salisbury Road runs through it.

Thomas Burcham, a barrister lived there in 1861. A bachelor, his household was composed of a cook, a house servant and a groom. Later the Rev. A. A. Harland, curate of St. Martin's lived at Eastcote Cottage paying like George Baylis £101 per annum. He was there in 1869 when Miss Mann sold the property to John Todd, but moved out shortly afterwards upon becoming Vicar of Harefield. His parting gift to St. Martin's was the eagle lectern to be seen on the north side of the nave.

The House: Sale Particulars, 1869,[20] describe a small country estate suitable for a professional gentleman. The house was sheltered by a verandah and had an entrance hall, breakfast room, dining room, drawing room with French windows, five bedrooms, two attics and a WC. The offices included a butler's pantry, larder, kitchen, scullery, wash-house, beer and wine cellar. Outside were a cow-house, piggeries, cart and cattlesheds, a coach-house, stabling for three horses, harness room and a groom's room. Lawns, gardens and an orchard surrounded the house. It was a desirable residence, in a high position, with clear

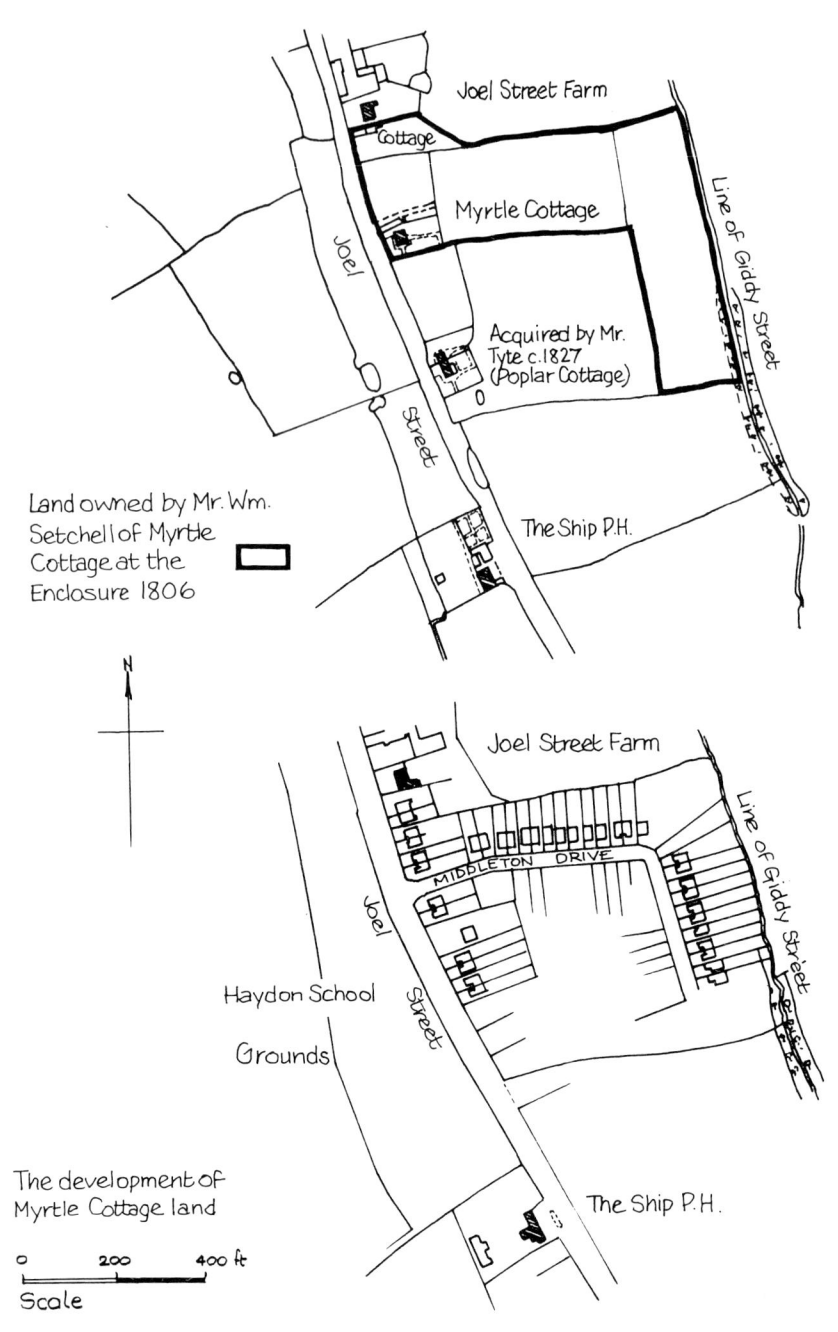

Myrtle Cottage, Joel Street

220

views across fields to Pinner and hills beyond on one side and to Park Wood on the other. The auctioneers, Sedgwicks, pointed out its other attractions; the close proximity to Pinner Station (now Hatch End), only twenty minutes drive away *"from whence the metropolis may be reached in a little over thirty minutes";* the *"picturesque and highly respectable neighbourhood".* Sporting gentlemen were advised that the Old Berkeley Fox Hounds hunted the surrounding country. Most enticing of all, here was an opportunity for investment. The long frontage onto Wiltshire Lane *"might be readily laid out in desirable sites for villa residences".* There was no fear of competition or that the area would become spoiled by development as the writer of the Sale Catalogue assured prospective buyers that the property was surrounded by large estates (King's College, Hawtrey/Deane and Hayden Hall) *"not at all likely to be built upon".*

Fairacre: In 1909 members of the Taylor family sold the field upon which the house used to stand to Lilian Minnie Carmen of Hayden Hall, who seems to have built a cottage there called Joy Cottage. It was sold to Mary Collins in 1919, who may have changed the name to Fairacre. Her widower, Mr Cyril Collins, leased it to R.N.U.D.C. in 1962. Eight old persons' homes were erected in 1963 adjoining Malmesbury Close and a further ten in Salisbury Road in 1974. Fairacre was converted into 4 flats at the same time.[21]

Myrtle Cottage

There was another "cottage" of this superior sort, though possibly on a smaller scale, in Joel Street. It was called Myrtle Cottage and was owned by a Mr H. Setchel in 1789. It was the home of R. W. Tyte Esq., a retired Naval Captain, from 1818 to about 1860 and after his death was sold to A. W. Tooke of Pinner Hill.[22]

At the time of the Enclosure, William Setchell owned a small cottage immediately south of Joel Street Farm and a larger house in the next field, which was Myrtle Cottage. From about 1827 the Rate Books show that Mr Tyte also acquired another cottage further down the hill, which he let.[23]

Myrtle Cottage became Myrtle Farm when it was part of the Pinner Hill estate. Joseph Herridge was the farmer. It was Mr George Golding's house early this century and was demolished when Middleton Drive was built in the 1950s.

According to W. A. G. Kemp in his *History of Eastcote* the cottage further south was either divided or extended to become two, one of which was called Poplar Cottage.

Field End House Farm

Field End House Farm is depicted on the Enclosure Map as a large group of what are presumably farm buildings in an L-shape with what must be the house at the rear and a little to one side. The only part of these buildings left standing today is Retreat Cottage, which was the end barn in 1806, but has been a habitation for many years. Farthings Close has replaced the barns, stables, etc. and St. Thomas More's occupies the rest of the site.

Once owned by the Reading family and later by James Dunton, it had passed to Thomas Truesdale Clarke of Swakeleys by the turn of the 18th/19th century.[24] After Mr Clarke's untimely death in July 1840 (he was drowned in the Pinn between Swakeleys and Hercies) Washington Cornelius Winter bought it.

Field End House Farm

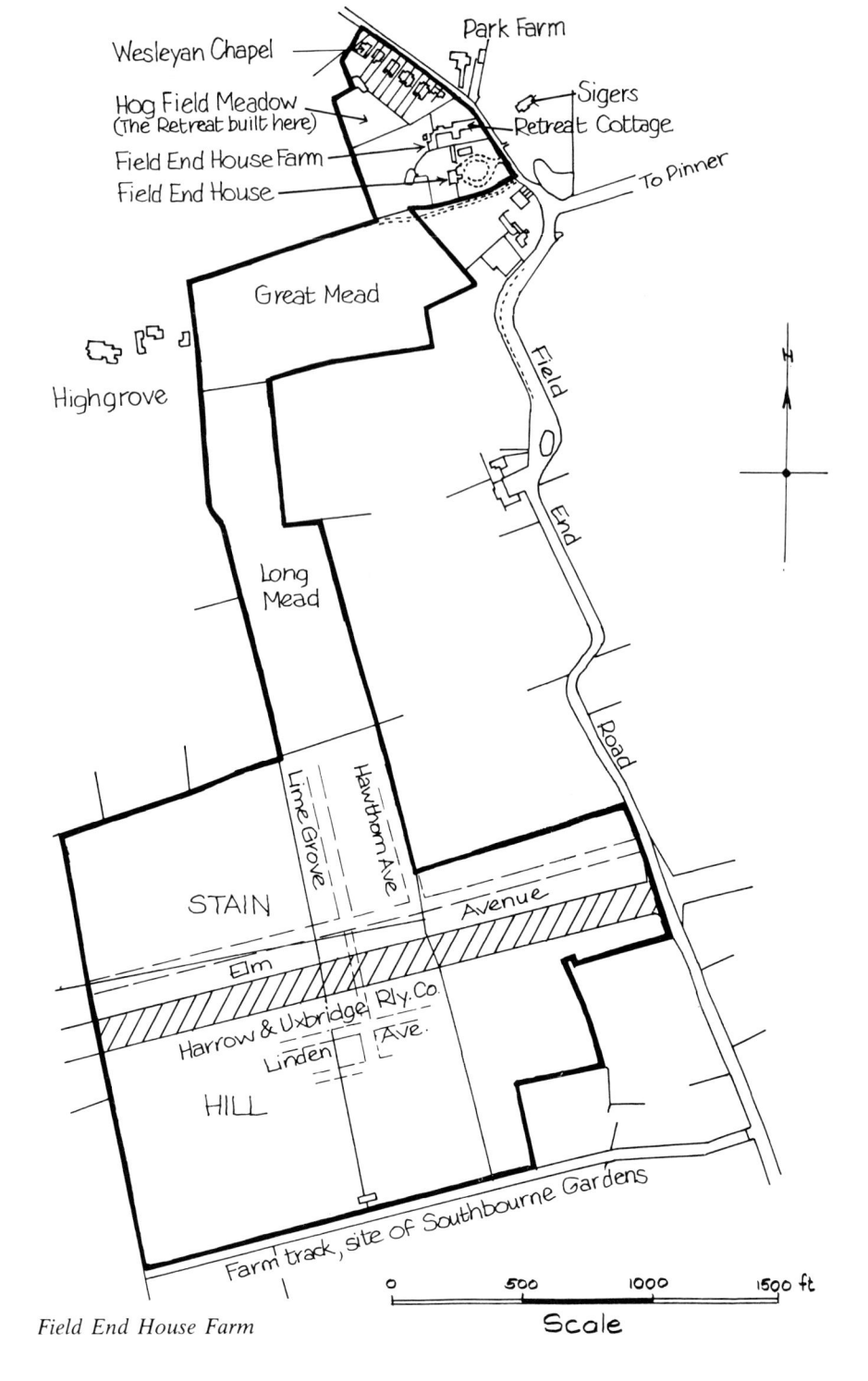

Growth of Estates in the 19th century and their eventual break-up

At least according to an Abstract of Title of Field End House Farm (in the author's possession), Mr W. C. Winter was admitted copyhold tenant at a Manor Court held in October 1841, but rate books from 1841 show Miss Cordelia Winter as owner and occupier. In 1841 the estate was described as a dwelling house with barns, granary, cowhouse, cart sheds, stables and three fields near the house, Hog Field Meadow, Great Mead and Long Mead; 77 acres on Stain Hill and a piece of upland meadow east of Cheney Street. W. C. Winter was also admitted tenant to two cottages (formerly one messuage) which stood on Field End Road in front of the house.

A Wesleyan chapel, opened May 1848 was built upon a small corner of Hog Field Meadow, erected as the handbills advertising the opening said *"by the munificence of a lady on a part of her estate"*.[25] The lady in question must be Miss Winter, but her relationship to Washington Cornelius Winter is not clear. The chapel land was made over to William Bowles and others in 1849.

Washington Cornelius Winter's will, made originally in 1838 but with a codicil written a few days before his death in 1851 left all the Field End property to William Lawrence of Paradise Row, Chelsea, who was the son of a carpenter Edward Lawrence, but was himself a farmer.[26] He was living at Field End House Farm in March 1851. He married his housekeeper Sarah Beard at St. Martin's in 1852, when he was 46 and shortly afterwards began erecting a series of buildings along his road frontage which look more suited to a town street than a country lane. Admittedly Field End Road can no longer be called a country lane, but it was then.

His new Field End House, built south of the barns and outbuildings, was a square symmetrical building of three storeys, the bottom one being a semi-basement. A flight of about twelve steps led up to the front door which was at first-floor level and all the sash windows at the front had shutters. He also built four pairs of villas and a cottage in Hog Field Meadow between the chapel and the farm buildings. Numbers 1 and 2 Field End Villas were ready for occupation in 1857, Numbers 3 and 4 by 1861 and the others by 1862.[27] Each pair is built to a different design, but mainly of brick with slate roofs. They are all pleasing in appearance and were obviously meant to attract professional people, the sort who could afford a general servant as numbers 1 and 2 have back stairs as well as a main staircase. People with private incomes, clergymen, doctors, and retired majors lived there.

William Lawrence was probably encouraged to build these middle-class houses having seen similar developments in Pinner, following the opening of Pinner Station (now Hatch End) in 1838. Building developers in surrounding areas encouraged new settlers in the early 1850s by extolling the pleasures of country life combined with easy daily travel to town by train. Any early Eastcote commuters faced a three mile walk to the station but mainly along footpaths and through fields, a distance more acceptable to the Victorians than to their descendants.

The farmlands of Field End Farm at that time covered 101 acres and stretched south as far as Southbourne Gardens. William Lawrence employed a farm bailiff, a post filled from 1874 to 1902, by John Whiting who lived in part of the original farm barns, converted into a house.[28]

William Lawrence died in November 1880 leaving his property to Mark Coakes, a corn dealer of Hayes and Henry Charles Lawrence, a clothier of

The Goodliest Place in Middlesex

Somers Town, on condition that it was not to be disposed of during the lifetime of his widow.[29]

Sarah Lawrence died in February 1901 and Walter Morford of The Laurels, Ruislip (now called White House, Sharps Lane) purchased the estate for £6,200 in July 1902. This was the same man who bought Ruislip Park House four years later and this purchase like the later one was a speculative venture.

In October 1901 a strip of land was sold to the Harrow and Uxbridge Railway Company which was preparing to extend its line to Uxbridge.[30]

About 1909 the part of Stain Hill lying north of the railway and Long Mead were bought by British Freehold Investments and subsequently developed as Elm Avenue, Acacia Avenue, Myrtle Avenue, Lime Grove and the west side of Hawthorn Avenue. The War Office eventually took over Great Mead and The Retreat was built as a private house, on what remained of Hog Field Meadow sometime before the First World War. After Walter Morford's death in October 1915 Robert Masson Smith, who was associated with British Freehold, bought the part of Stain Hill lying south of the railway, which was subsequently developed as the east end of Linden Avenue, Beech Avenue, Oak Grove and the north side of Southbourne Gardens.[31]

Field End House remained a private house until 1934 when it was acquired by The Grail, a Catholic organisation. When a Catholic parish was formed in Eastcote in 1937 the house became the presbytery and St. Thomas More's church was built in the grounds. A new church was put up in 1978, the old one remaining as a church hall. The house remained standing until *c.* 1967 when a new priest's house was provided and it was demolished. John Whiting's house was preserved as a handsome private dwelling called The Barns until 1967 when

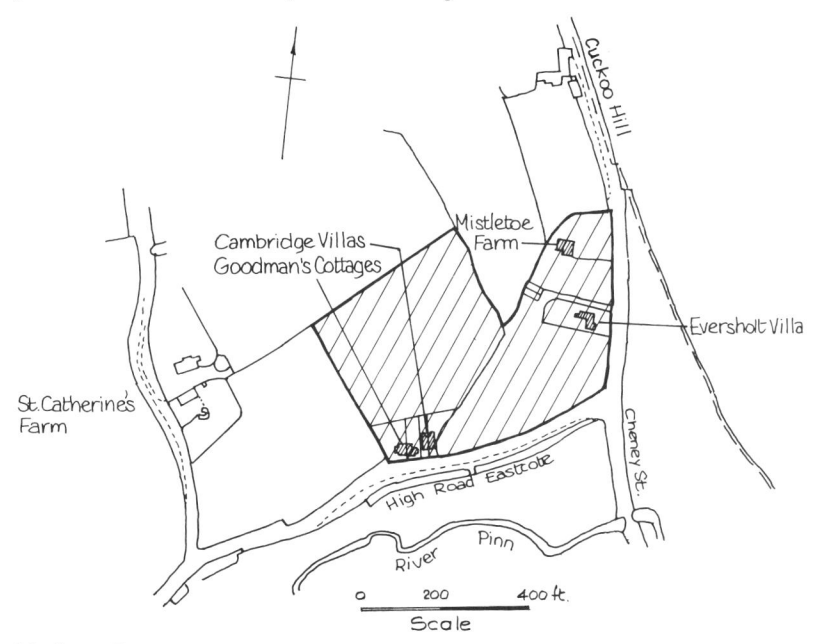

Mistletoe Farm, Eastcote

Growth of Estates in the 19th century and their eventual break-up

Farthings Close was built. For the first year the new close was called White Chapel Close as a reminder of the Methodist Chapel which had recently been demolished, but new residents objected to the name on the grounds that it made them sound like Eastenders! One end of The Barns was left standing at the entrance to Farthings Close called Retreat Cottage.

Mistletoe Farm

Mistletoe Farm at Popes End was called "Cocowes" i.e. "Cuckoos" in 1565.[32] From the beginning of the 19th century until 1840 it was owned by Robert Shepherd Esq. and occupied by the Deacon family.[33] It was only a smallholding with about 6 acres of land. For a few years in the 1840s Edward Powell was both owner and occupier. He was followed by John Goodman in 1847, who was described as a proprietor of houses and lands in the 1851 Census.

He built a house in Cuckoo Hill quite close to Mistletoe Farm and a pair of cottages called Goodman's Cottages in a corner of one of his fields.[34] A little later, another pair, with the upmarket name of Cambridge Villas, was erected beside them. All four houses occupied only 11 perches of land.[35] The house by the farm also ranked as a villa and was given the name Eversholt Villa. (Census Returns show that he was born at Eversholt, Oxon). Perhaps he was inspired by William Lawrence's Field End Villas or vice versa. Certainly the two men were developing land on a small scale at about the same time.

John Goodman, himself married Ann Staples, the widow of Edward Staples of Joel Street Farm, and moved to his wife's house before 1861, letting Mistletoe Farm to a wine merchant.[36]

Mr A. J. Trythall took over all the Mistletoe Farm estate about 1885 and held it until this century.[37] The 16th century farmhouse remains as a private residence but the villas and cottages have made way for modern houses. Treetops and Danemead are on the site of Goodman's Cottages and Cambridge Villas. Eversholt, in which the gardener lived in the 1920s has also gone.

Bury House

The large four-square house called Bury House, standing in Bury Street, was built in 1904,[38] but replaced a much older residence dating from at least 1565 when it seems to have belonged to John Fly.[39] The Rev. Richard Glover owned it at the beginning of the 19th century and sold it to Miss Elizabeth Truesdale during the enclosure upheaval. She was the sister of Rev. Thomas Clarke's second wife, Frances, and actually lived at Ruislip Vicarage for a few years before moving to Bury House.[40] The Vicar, Daniel Carter Lewis, must have been hiring it out while living outside the parish.

Miss Truesdale's income tax assessment for 1815[41] shows that she was taxed for 17 windows, hair powder, armorial bearings and two male servants. Perhaps they were footmen and wore powdered wigs. Bury House with its 17 windows must have been one of the larger houses on the Westcote side of the parish at that time. When she died in 1831 aged 86, her nephew, Thomas Truesdale Clarke of Swakeleys, inherited Bury House. His son, another Thomas Truesdale Clarke, came to live in the house until 1840, when he and his wife returned to Swakeleys after the elder Mr Clarke's death. Caroline Louisa Clarke was left the house by her father and resided there for a period.[42]

The Goodliest Place in Middlesex

Bury House

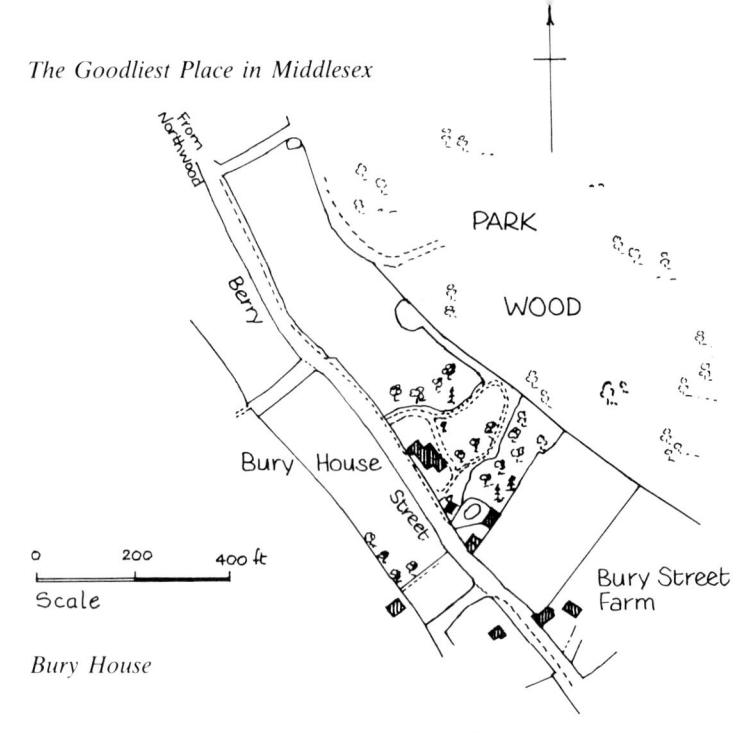

Samuel Danford owned it by 1855. What happened next is not clear, but at some stage the old house was demolished. A 1904 auction catalogue at King's College describes the present house as newly-built but unfinished and has a photograph showing it with scaffolding round it. The wording suggests that a group of houses was intended to be built alongside. Instead, the house and land were sold and no further development took place until after the Second World War. Some of the residents from the 1920s and 30s are still remembered: an aviator who drove a car shaped like a gondola and Mr Green of Green and Vardey Ecclesiastical Carpenters who became something of a lion in Ruislip society, news having percolated through that a Cabinet Minister was coming to live at Bury House. Although he turned out to be a cabinet maker hopes were not altogether disappointed as his major interest was philately and he exchanged stamps with King George V.

Hayden Hall

Dr Adam Clarke, a highly-respected Methodist scholar and preacher, lived at Hayden Hall from 1824-32.[43] He established a place of worship in a cottage near the house, probably Redbournes, opposite the Hall at the bottom of Joel Street, in 1826 and elicited an immediate response from the poor people of Eastcote who filled it to overflowing, and clamoured for a Sunday School where reading might be taught as well. By March 1827, a stable and coach house had been converted into a chapel, which according to Adam Clarke himself, was "completely thronged" for the opening ceremony. More than 70 children promised to attend Sunday School regularly and older people too sought admission. He wrote *"There are some young people coming, 17 and 18 years of age, who cannot read a letter, and yet who desire to learn"*. Such illiteracy is slightly odd in view of the school founded in 1811 which continued to flourish and became a National School. It

Growth of Estates in the 19th century and their eventual break-up

may be that parents of children living in Eastcote felt that the school in Ruislip was too far distant for daily attendance. The reluctance of children from the Fore Street area to go to day school continued, for in 1851 a significantly smaller number from that part of the parish were described as scholars in the Census forms.

Dr Clarke became a personal friend of the Duke of Sussex, brother of George IV, after serving on a Committee to investigate the old Public Record System and the Duke visited Hayden Hall twice.

After Adam Clarke's death from cholera in August 1832, which attacked him while staying in Bayswater, his widow, Mary, remained at Hayden Hall until 1837. Their son John Wesley Clarke succeeded her, but died young in 1840. His will entitled his widow Elizabeth to *"Hayden Hall and a meadow called Redbournes with two cottages thereon one of which is used as a school and chapel"* and £200 in the 3½%. Elizabeth married John Harnett in October 1841 and he became owner of the Hall in his own right when she died in 1848. It is said that John Harnett turned the Wesleyans out of their cottage, an event which led Miss Winter to endow the new chapel on Field End House Farm land. He retained Hayden Hall and its estate until 1864.

John Wesley Clarke and the Harnetts did not live at Hayden Hall. A Miss Maitland, Alfred Price and Dr J. Ross Diamond in turn were tenants. Dr Diamond was a Medical Officer at St. Pancras Royal General Dispensary for ten years, probably during the period that he was resident at Hayden Hall.[44]

The Hayden Hall estate as shown on the 1806 Enclosure Map when it belonged to George Woodruff comprised the Hall and grounds; Hayden Hall Farm, Joel Street; a group of cottages in Wiltshire Lane, later known as the Homestead; another group of cottages in Fore Street where Wood Rise is now; The Ship in Joel Street; White Cottage, Harlyn Drive (then on Raysons Hill); land and small pieces of former waste in the ancient way called Giddy Street which ran north from Southill Lane; the whole being about 63 acres.

Adam Clarke, not surprisingly, never owned The Ship (known at the time as the Sun and Ship) which passed into the ownership of J. Fearnley.[45] About 1820 he bought Peteridge and the meadow Redbournes beside it. Peteridge was probably divided into two cottages at this time, one becoming the chapel. After 1848 the two cottages became separate residences called Laurel Cottage and Sunnyside. John Harnett lived at Laurel Cottage in his widowerhood and was there as late as 1871. In the late 1840s Hayden Hall Farm, farmed by Daniel Matheson, and The Homestead were sold to George Robinson of Richmond (see Chapter 5) and subsequently to A. W. Tooke of Pinner Hill.

The Hall and the rest of the estate were bought by Lawrence James Baker in 1864, a member of the London Stock Exchange, a very wealthy member to judge by his activities in Eastcote. His father John Law Baker, late of the Madras Army, came to live in Eastcote Lodge, lying between the Black Horse and Eastcote Cottage, which became part of the Hayden Hall Estate.[46]

There is no record of any major alterations to the Hall itself between Sir Thomas Franklin's rebuilding (see Chapter 8) and mid-Victorian times. Mr Baker added two wings to the house, greatly enhanced the pleasure grounds and built or rebuilt several cottages for estate workers, often employing Harold Ainsworth Peto, son of Sir Samuel Morton Peto of Eastcote House, and his partner Ernest George, as architects.[47]

A description of the mansion in 1883 runs *"It is very substantially built*

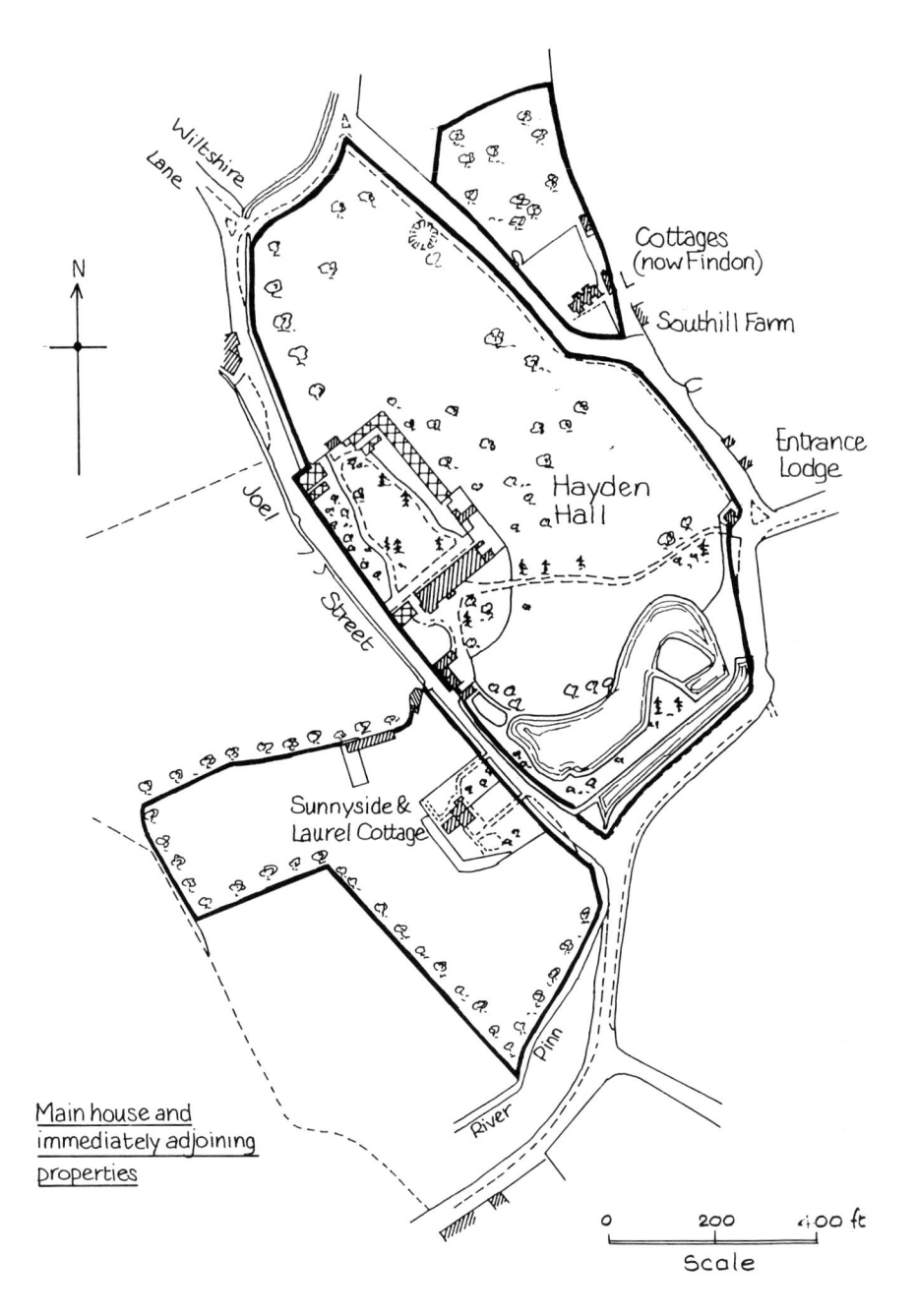

Hayden Hall 1883

228

Hayden Hall prior to demolition in 1967 "nothing worth preserving"

of brick with strong slated roof. The centre of the house is a square structure of the Queen Anne period of two storeys with attics and bold cornice; the wings being modern and the whole in excellent substantial and decorative repair throughout, having recently been artistically re-decorated by Mr Frederick Arthur of Motcomb Street from the designs of Messrs Ernest George & Peto, the eminent architects. The parquet floors being supplied by Messrs Howard & Son of Berners Street. The internal walls of the old part of the House are panelled oak, decorated in the style of the Queen Ann period." The principal drawing room was painted a rich chocolate brown, hung with maize-coloured embossed paper and had a massive statuary marble chimney piece; while the library was salmon colour with embossed paper and a veined marble chimney piece. An organ had been installed there in 1872. One wing contained a billiard room lighted by a dome of ornamental coloured glass. All the main rooms and corridors were heated by hot water and hot air pipes.

The pride of the grounds was an iron and glass conservatory built at a cost of £1500, containing a rockwork fernery. Vineries, a fig house, peach houses, pine pits and melon and cucumber houses stretched for more than a quarter of a mile down the Joel Street edge of the grounds. The park was adorned by an ornamental sheet of water fed by the Pinn.

An elaborate entrance lodge (still standing) built about 1880 at a cost of £1100 supplied the finishing touch to this typical mid-Victorian wealthy (perhaps nouveau riche) gentleman's residence. Several other cottages were built for L. J. Baker: three on Southill Lane, now a single dwelling called Findon; 124 and 126 Fore Street; Homeside in Fore Street; Keepers' Cottages on Coteford Close and at the bottom of Mad Bess Wood; and New Cottages, Eastcote High

Road. 124 Fore Street was used as a laundry and Homeside was the cowman's cottage. The keepers' cottages were necessary because Mr Baker made Hayden Hall the centre of a sporting estate, leasing shooting rights over the demesne lands from King's College and over the glebe land from the vicar. In 1873 he bought Mad Bess Wood and much of St. Catherine's Manor (see Chapter 5) so that eventually he could shoot over 2000 acres which included 735 acres of covert. The annual bag was usually about 1000 pheasants and 30 woodcock. 700 pheasants were reared in 1883 in the hatching pens attached to the keepers' cottages.[48] All the cottages were strongly-built and presented a decorative appearance as lines of multi-coloured bricks and tiles were used in their construction and all had gables. Wood Cottages, 124 and 126 Fore Street were particularly picturesque with Dutch gables, diamond-shaped chimneys and patterned windows. All Mr Baker's workers' cottages still stand, but some are less attractive than they once were, having had the beautiful brickwork covered in paint.

    The vicar of Ruislip, Thomas Marsh Everett, married Edith Baker in October 1882.[49] During the rebuilding of Ruislip Vicarage, 1881-2 (probably in preparation for his marriage), he had been living at Sunnyside, the property of his future father-in-law. An account of the presentation of a wedding gift to the Everetts from the parishioners in the local paper suggests that the Bakers had already left Eastcote by 1882 and certainly the whole estate was put up for sale by auction in September 1883 and again in June 1884. On neither occasion did the main property change hands. For what reason is not known, but the land in St. Catherine's Manor was sold. Lawrence James Baker went to Ottershaw Park, Chertsey, became Liberal M.P. for Frome and later moved to Brambridge Park, Eastleigh, where he died in 1921, aged 94. However, he retained the Eastcote property and the 1902 rate book shows him owning Hayden Hall, Sunnyside, Findon (3 cottages), 2 cottages in Fore Street (presumably 124 and 126), Cheney Street Farm, agricultural land in Northolt Road (Field End Road), Eastcote Lodge and New Cottages. The Eastcote Lodge of 1902 was a different house from that inhabited by John Law Baker. He died in 1886 and was buried at Holy Trinity. His house was demolished and George & Peto created a new one which was built on the site in 1888 for Lawrence Ingham Baker, grandson of John Law Baker and his wife Helen Agnes Peto, sister of the architect.[50] L. I. Baker was Vicar's Warden at St. Martin's and a member of the Ruislip Vestry and later Parish Council. He died at Crewkerne in 1934. The three cottages called New Cottages had already been built in 1879 on land belonging to the old Eastcote Lodge, and still stand opposite the bottom of Fore Street, half-timbered, with incised plaster decoration portraying flowers, foliage and faces.

    Eastcote Lodge stables lying between the house and Flag Cottage had a picturesque and much photographed entrance arch. At one time a small farm functioned from there.[51] Eastcote Lodge itself was demolished in 1963, when Flag Walk was built on the site. The imposing architrave and other quality features, such as elegant door knobs and finger plates, were removed to Flag Cottage.[52]

    Sunnyside was bought by a Commercial Traveller, Mr Lee, who wanted a house large enough to accommodate his billiard table! He laid out the tennis courts which still exist and built St. Michael's School (demolished 1985) as a private school. The house was pulled down to make way for Kaduna Close.[53]

    Hayden Hall with its lodge, stabling and pleasure grounds was let to Captain Bennett-Edwards from 1886. He and his wife stayed at Hayden Hall,

Growth of Estates in the 19th century and their eventual break-up

opening its grounds for flower shows and Sunday School treats and providing and maintaining a cricket ground for the use of Eastcote Cricket Club which is still there.[54] Eventually Mrs Bennett-Edwards became the owner of Hayden Hall. After her death in 1936 the house and 14.7 acres were purchased by R.N.U.D.C. and M.C.C. Plans to form a Civic Centre there were frustrated by the Second World War and the house was demolished in 1967 having been allowed to fall into a state of decay.

Protests about this act of vandalism from the Ruislip, Northwood and Eastcote Local History Society elicited little sympathy. A letter from George Hooper the Town Clerk to Mr R. G. Edwards in the L. E. Morris Collection says that the hall contained nothing at all worthy of preservation, although photographs taken at the time show the original early 18th century panelling intact. The only relic of this house is a carved shield surrounded by scrollwork bearing a dragon's head, preserved at Ruislip Library.

Highgrove

Lt Gen Sir Joseph Fuller bought Highgrove in 1834.[55] His only child Juliana married Sir Hugh Hume-Campbell of Marchmont in October 1841 only a few days before her father's death. Lady Hume-Campbell became the owner after her mother's death in the 1860s and she herself died without issue in 1886 leaving the house to her husband. He had been married before and had a daughter Helen by his first wife. Her six children, the Warrenders, inherited Highgrove in 1894.

All of them seem to have spent time in Eastcote, but only two: Eleanor and her brother Col Hugh Warrender, made their permanent home there after the First World War. Eleanor and Hugh were friendly with Jenny Churchill. Indeed Hugh was said to be in love with her, which may account for the unproved story that Sir Winston Churchill, Jenny Churchill's son, spent part of his honeymoon at Highgrove. The house was also let to the Dowager Queen of

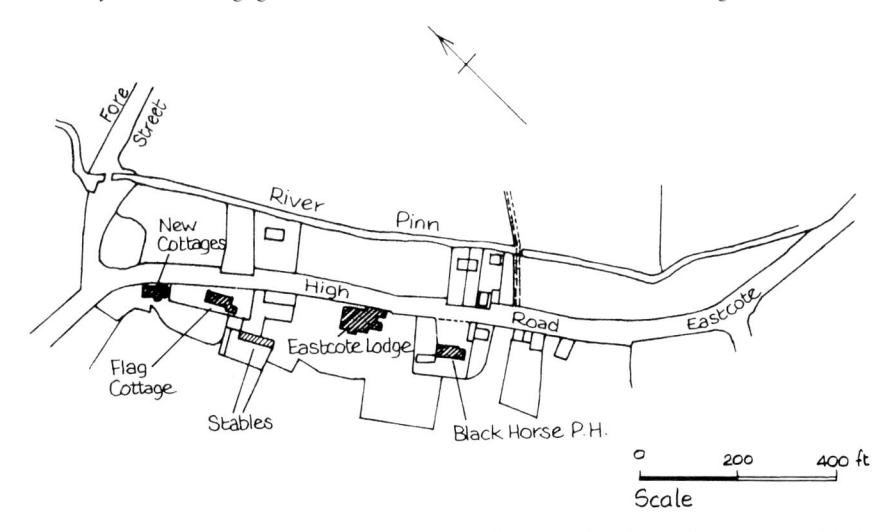

Eastcote Lodge and surrounds 1896

The Goodliest Place in Middlesex

Sweden (who bought her meat from Crookall, the butcher at the end of Ruislip High Street).

Eleanor had been a VAD and served on hospital ships in the South African War. In 1914 she was too old to be accepted as a Nurse in the British Army and worked for the French Red Cross instead, being awarded the Croix de Guerre. Her other legacy from the war was her religion, for she was received into the Roman Catholic Church in France and in 1921 founded the Sacred Heart Church in Ruislip High Street.[56]

She had long been a benefactress to the neighbourhood, providing the Institute opposite St. Martin's in 1907 (demolished 1930) and the Church Rooms in Bury Street in 1911. She founded Eastcote and Pinner Girl Guides, and was District Commissioner for many years. Her generosity was a by-word and the full extent of her gifts is not known.[57]

The 18th century Highgrove was destroyed by fire in 1879 and the present house was built to the designs of Edward Prior in 1881.[58] Miss Warrender offered it to service personnel during the 1939-45 War and it was used by English and American Officers from Northolt. She herself moved into a modern cottage built in the grounds.

She died on 30th September 1949, aged 87, and was buried in St. Martin's graveyard after requiem mass at the Sacred Heart Church. Tributes in the local paper referred to her philanthropy and spoke of her as a *"dignified old lady"* who was *"known as Squire of Ruislip"*. Although she had always been Miss Warrender, for some reason Highgrove was known locally as Lady Warrender's. The only Lady Warrender in the family was Eleanor's sister-in-law, Sir George Warrender's wife, and she lived in London, not Eastcote.

Highgrove was purchased by R.N.U.D.C. and later made over to Middlesex County Council with the intention of converting it into an old people's home and half way house. The London Borough of Hillingdon restored it with great care after another disastrous fire in 1978 and now runs it as temporary accommodation for homeless families.

Miss Warrender sold 10½ acres lying south of the house to the Council in 1935 to provide a children's playground now called Warrender Park.[59] A 13 acre field was bought by Ideal Homes at the same time. Warrender Way, Highgrove Way and Westbury Close were partly built by the company 1935-9 and completed by E. A. Cox after the War. The original Ideal Homes Estate Office still stands at the foot of Highgrove Way, now occupied by Stoneguard. The rest of the Highgrove grounds went to the council along with the house and provided sites for Highgrove Swimming Pool opened 1964, Manor Senior Upper School built 1965 (changing its name to Bishop Ramsey in 1977) and Hale End Close, Hume Way and Campbell Close, 1974.

The Grange, Northwood

During the first half of the 19th century, a large portion of Northwood was gathered into the estate based on the house now called The Grange, and in 1864 that estate was swallowed by the even larger Eastbury Estate. The laying out of the Eastbury lands in building plots brought about, the urban development of Northwood at the end of the century.

The Grange has been mentioned in earlier chapters as the probable site of The Abbey of Bec's grange at Northwood and as "North House", one of two houses belonging to Roger Arnold in 1565. The time has now come to

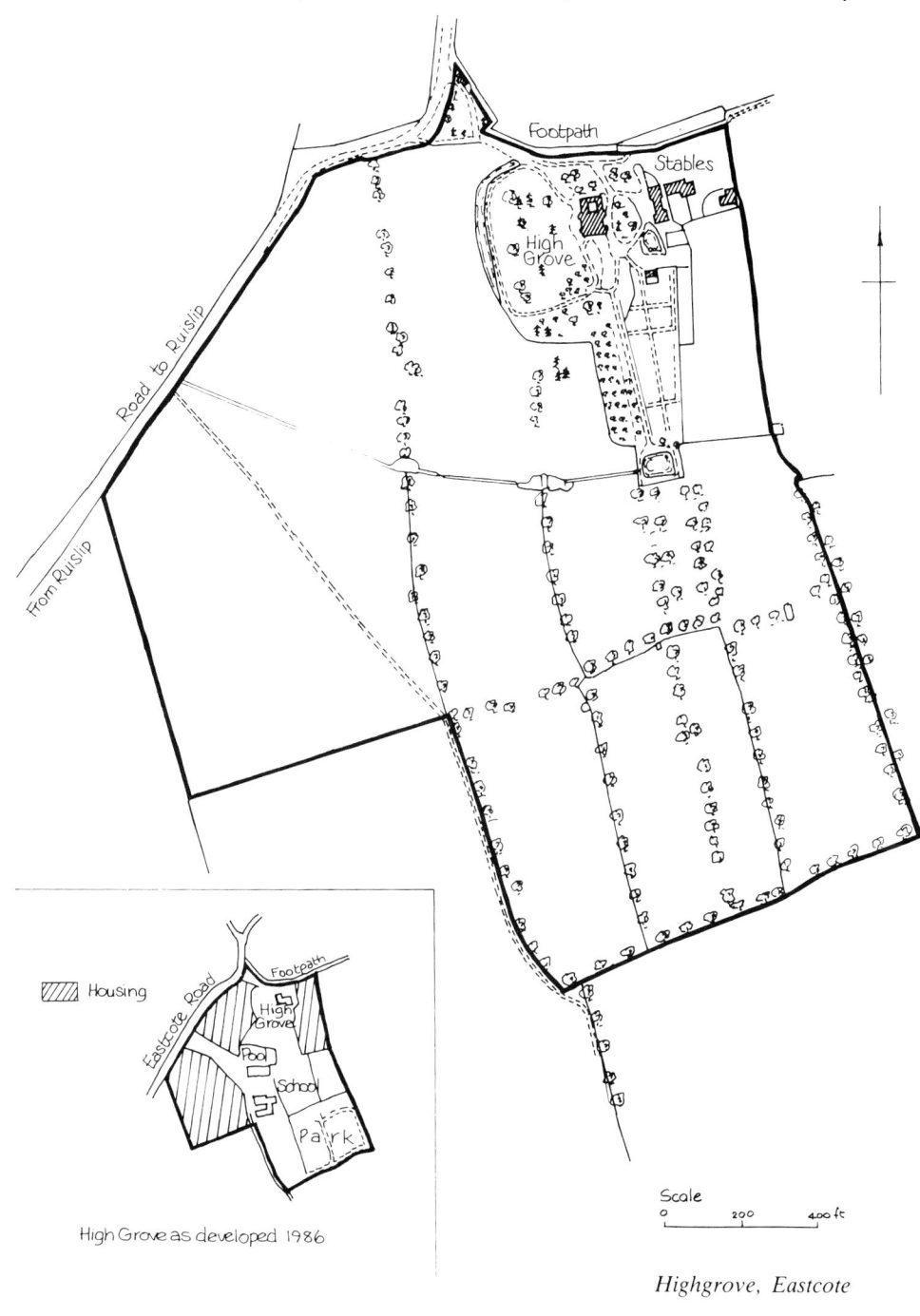

Growth of Estates in the 19th century and their eventual break-up

Highgrove, Eastcote

The Goodliest Place in Middlesex

examine the history of the site in more detail. Immediately prior to Enclosure William Parsons owned and occupied The Grange and rented a cottage a few yards to the north-west from Mrs Eastham. The fields lying north of Mrs Eastham's cottage were called First Fell, Second Fell and Lower Fell and there is some evidence that the cottage itself was known as Fells in the late 18th century, but later as Northwood House.[60] For the sake of clarity I shall refer to the two buildings shown on the Enclosure Map as The Grange and Northwood House respectively.

During the Enclosure upheaval John Rowe, Secretary of The New River Company, purchased both The Grange and Northwood House in 1808-9[61]; 100 acres of newly-enclosed waste along Pinner Road and Joel Street Farm in 1809; small pieces of roadside waste near the junction of Green Lane and Pinner Road in 1811; Green Lane Farm in 1812; Green Hills Farm (now Green End, Dene Road) c. 1815. He was succeeded by his son John Paul Rowe also of the New River Company. Mr Rowe seems to have lived at Northwood House and let The Grange as a farmhouse. About 1825 it was let to John Grace and known as Grace's Farm.

Today The Grange and a private house called Green Close are one long building, but the Enclosure Map of 1806 and a plan accompanying an indenture dated 1864 show two entirely separate buildings. The gap was probably filled and the two joined together in 1865 as the 1866 O.S. map shows a single range. During the Rowe's ownership The Grange appears to have been the farmhouse and what is now Green Close a cottage and barn.

After his father's death John Paul Rowe leased Northwood House. The lessee William Harwood died in 1827 and his executor William Wyatt White sub-let the house. Edward Empy was the sub-tenant in 1831.

Between 1829 and his death in 1835, John Paul Rowe, who was then living in Clapham Park, sold his Northwood land.[62] Most of it was purchased by Nathaniel Soames: The Grange, occupied by John Grace in 1830; Northwood House occupied by Edward Empy 1832; the Hundred Acres along Pinner Road 1834; and Green Lane Farm occupied by John Joel and Green Hills Farm in 1835.[63] Joel Street Farm was sold to George Robinson in 1835, which ended the Rowes' connection with the district.

Nathaniel Soames the Younger of Gravely nr. Stevenage, Herts, as he is described in an 1830 deed, married Rebecca Gainsford Soames (probably his cousin) at Pinner in 1831. She was the grand-daughter of Daniel Wilshin of Pinner Green Lodge and daughter of George Soames. After the marriage they settled at Northwood House and played an active part in local life. Mr Soames increased the estate by buying a good deal of land from the Hilliards in 1839; Kiln Farm occupied by Joseph Stone; a tenement near Kiln Farm, probably a kiln occupied by Daniel Kirby; much of the newly enclosed waste between Kiln Farm and High Street allotted to the Hilliards by the Enclosure Commissioners; and a small farmhouse on Green Lane which was later known as Knowles Farm.[64] He built a farmhouse on the Hundred Acres.

Hundred Acres Farmhouse first appears in the rate books as a cottage in 1845 and seems to have been occupied by a farm labourer. It was built near the 14th milestone on the turnpike road from London. Nathaniel Soames sold the cottage and Hundred Acres of land to A. W. Tooke of Pinner Hill in 1858.[65] Thereafter it was part of the Pinner Hill Estate and Benjamin Golding farmed it into this century. The cottage, much enlarged, still stands near the

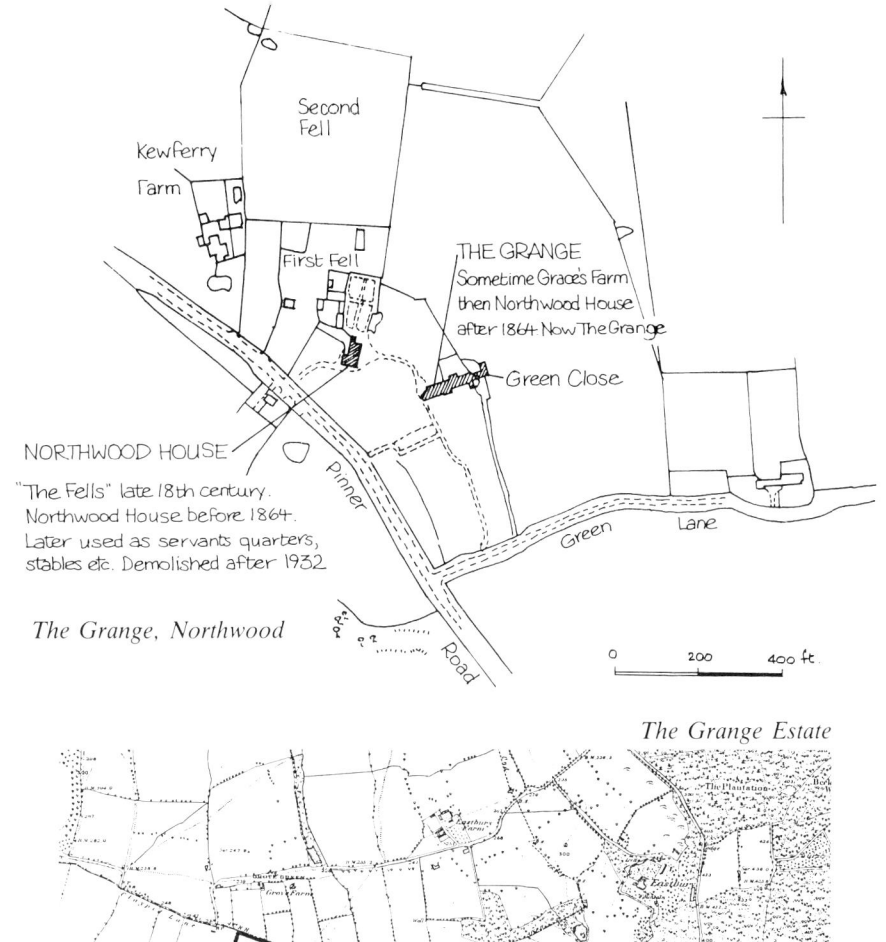

The Grange, Northwood

Second Fell

Kewferry Farm

First Fell

THE GRANGE
Sometime Grace's Farm then Northwood House after 1864 Now The Grange

Green Close

NORTHWOOD HOUSE
"The Fells" late 18th century. Northwood House before 1864. Later used as servants quarters, stables etc. Demolished after 1932.

Pinner Road

Green Lane

0 200 400 ft

The Grange Estate

Northwood House
Grange
Greenhill Farm
Knowles Farm
Green Lane Farm
Green Lane

THE GRANGE ESTATE
1864

Kiln Farm

Hilliard Land

Lodge Farm

Hundred Acre Farm
(part of Grange Estate 1809–1858)

Rickmansworth Road

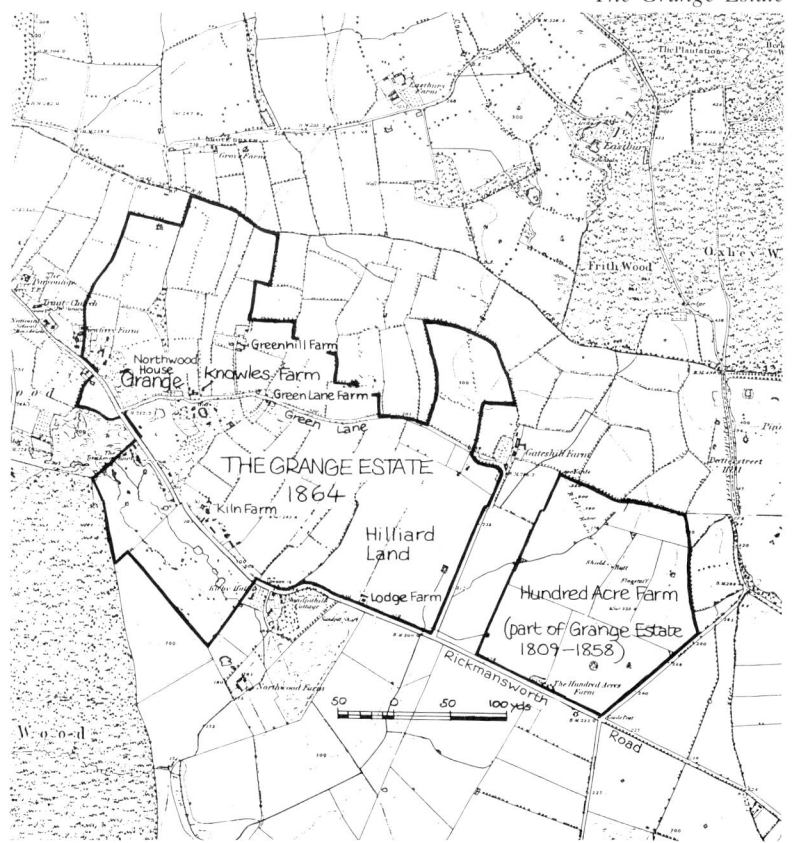

The Goodliest Place in Middlesex

Express Dairy Depot. The Roberts family, founders of Express Dairy, took over Hundred Acres Farm about 1915 and purchased the house in 1927.[66] Since 1955 it has been a private house. Addison Way and Close, Acre Way, Northwood Way, Stanley Road, Hillside Gardens, Crescent Rise and Road and the Hogs Back are all on the original Hundred Acres. Incidentally Hogs Back is *not* an old name appearing only at the time of the building developments in the 1930s; it may be named after Philip Edlin Hogg who bought the land from W. A. Tooke's brother-in-law in 1911.[67]

The Soames' special interests seem to have been in the church. Nathaniel was churchwarden at St. Martin's and generously converted the cottage at The Grange (now Green Close) into a chapel as described in Chapter 1. After the opening of Holy Trinity in 1854, it reverted to its former use. He let his house to Mr Thacker in 1862 and two years later sold the entire estate to David Carnegie of Eastbury.[68]

The Buildings – Northwood House and The Grange after 1864

Mr Carnegie appears to have set about refurbishing The Grange as soon as he became owner. The farmhouse and cottage/chapel were joined together to make one large house. It became the principal residence and the name Northwood House was transferred to it, the original house in which Mr Thacker was living, degenerating into a cottage and servants' quarters and possibly stables. The old Northwood House is shown on maps as late as 1932 and was presumably demolished when Lea Cottage and Redwood were built. They in their turn were re-developed along with 65 Dene Road as Woodlea Grove in 1976 and the garages seem to be on the site of the old Northwood House.

The newly-decorated house was let to Robert Dunlop who was there in 1871; to George Cheetham, son of a cotton mill owner from Stalybridge, Cheshire, from 1878-1882; then to his widow Jane until 1886.[69]

The entire Eastbury estate was sold in 1887[70] and two years later The Grange with the old Northwood House in its grounds was sold to Dr Walter Llewllyn Nash, a Welsh medical practitioner in Hong Kong, who on his retirement took a great interest in Egyptian archaeology. A piece of land adjoining on the east was sold to Mr Thacker in 1891.[71]

Dr Nash built on a library and added several antiquities to The Grange: a medieval screen from a London church, for example. It was probably he who gathered up large pieces of flint and constructed the buttress and archway with a niche which today gives the grounds a slightly ecclesiastical air. His daughters have left their recollection of life at The Grange in letters, kept in Ruislip Library, which show that they had a romantic, rather than a realistic, view of history. The soft tread of monkish footsteps was often heard after dark, for example.

The family was forced to move to a smaller house in Northwood for financial reasons and The Grange was sold to Col Blaythwaite in 1904.[72] The Old Northwood House was included in the grounds.

At some stage the old cottage/chapel at the eastern end of The Grange became a separate residence, Green Close.

After Col Blaythwaite's death in 1929 The Grange was in great danger of being demolished. His son sold The Grange, two cottages (probably Northwood House and Green Close) and pleasure grounds to Frank Pratt of Frith Lodge. He in turn sold it to W. A. Telling in 1932 for building development.[73] At

Growth of Estates in the 19th century and their eventual break-up

this point Mrs Garrett (the former Miss Rowland-Brown, founder of St. Helen's School) stepped in and generously bought the house (excluding the Green Close end) for £2,040 in 1934.[74]

Mrs Garrett converted the ground floor of The Grange into a meeting place for parochial organisations to use and the upper floor into two flats. The ground floor was dedicated by the Bishop of Willesden in October 1934. The house was requisitioned during the War and afterwards made over to R.N.U.D.C. It now belongs to the London Borough of Hillingdon and is used for public purposes.

Green Close became a private house, but the one time barn attached to it on the east was pulled down and a house called Westwood built there (now Camross).[75]

Detached houses were built round the perimeter of the former pleasure grounds by Telling. Mr Thacker's land on the east, referred to as Thackers Common, became the site of the London Bible College, built as the London College of Divinity in 1955.

The later story of the other portions of The Grange lands is told in the section on the Eastbury Estate.

The Eastbury Estate

Eastbury is now Coastal Command and it lies in Hertfordshire. Originally it was in the parish of Watford, but in 1854 was incorporated in Holy Trinity, Northwood.

Eastbury Farm on Batchworth Lane was in Rickmansworth Parish until 1854. During the 13th century Eastbury was a manor belonging to the Abbey of St. Albans. A map by Cushee, dated 1728, shows the main house "Eastbury" in

The Grange. Green Close is beyond the hedge on the right

237

Batchworth Lane on the site of the present Eastbury Farm and a small house on the site of H.M.S. Warrior apparently called Whitwells or Whittleborough Farm.[76]

The Tuach family of Rickmansworth were the owners from before 1758-74. For the next twenty years Humphrey Bache of St. Leonard's, Shoreditch, owned it, but had a mortgage from John Bate, a distiller of Aldersgate Street. He must have run into financial difficulties for an auction of his household furniture, brewing utensils, live and dead farming stock was held in April 1794 *"under an execution"*.[77]

Andrew Knox Esq. of Edinburgh who bought it seems to have made many alterations on the estate. A sale catalogue of 1818 carries a plan showing the Eastbury Farm area completely cleared of buildings and a new stucco-fronted villa standing close to Whittleborough farmhouse.[78]

Sir John Vaughan, Sergeant-at-Law, bought the 265 acre estate in 1820 and made some alterations to the house and lived there until his death in 1839.[79] He was followed by Arthur Cuthbert Marsh, whose widow stayed at Eastbury until 1857. Either Mr Marsh or his predecessor added the woodland called Frithwood and Gate House Farm to the estate and built the present house and barns at Eastbury Farm. When it was auctioned at the Auction Mart by Mr Humbert (later Humbert & Flint) on 10th June 1857,[80] Eastbury Estate was 134 acres, and extended right along the county boundary from the site of the present Bourne End Road to Sandy Lane. The only road crossing the estate was Batchworth Lane (Watford Road did not exist until 1893). The mansion was approached by three drives; one from Batchworth Lane, which still exists as a grassy track; a short one from the bend in Sandy Lane; and the longer main drive from the lower part of Sandy Lane. A lodge is shown on the 1857 plan on the south side of this drive, which by 1866[81] had been replaced by the much more elaborate and highly decorative Frith Lodge, which still stands on the north side of the drive.

The new owner was David Carnegie (1813-90) of Stranraer, Lochernhead, Perthshire. His family was connected with the Earls of Southesk whose coat of arms is a spread eagle, an emblem used to embellish the new mansion which he built in Scottish baronial style soon after becoming owner. He seems to have been an improving landlord as he provided a handsome stable block at Eastbury Farm (demolished 1984-5) and as, already noted, restored and extended The Grange when he bought The Grange Estate in 1864. At the same time he appears to have built a house, Lodge Farm, on the former Hilliard land. Daniel Matheson and his son Samuel farmed there until 1894[82] when W. J. Page, the builder, took it over and lived in the house, eventually replacing it with May Lodge. Page's builders' yard still occupies part of the old farm buildings. Highfield Road and Crescent, Hallowell, Chester, Roy and Reginald Roads and the west side of High Street are built on the land of Lodge Farm.

The Grange was his first purchase in Middlesex, followed in 1866[83] by the acquisition of Gate Hill Farm from Daniel Wilshin Soames (Mrs Nathaniel Soames' brother). This made him owner of 312 acres in Herts and 450 acres in Middlesex, together making a 762 acre estate.

In 1886 he was 73 and probably ready to retire to Scotland. The Harrow-Rickmansworth extension of the Metropolitan Railway required a strip of land which he sold to the Company probably intending to sell Eastbury for building development. Northwood Station was being built and in June 1886 25

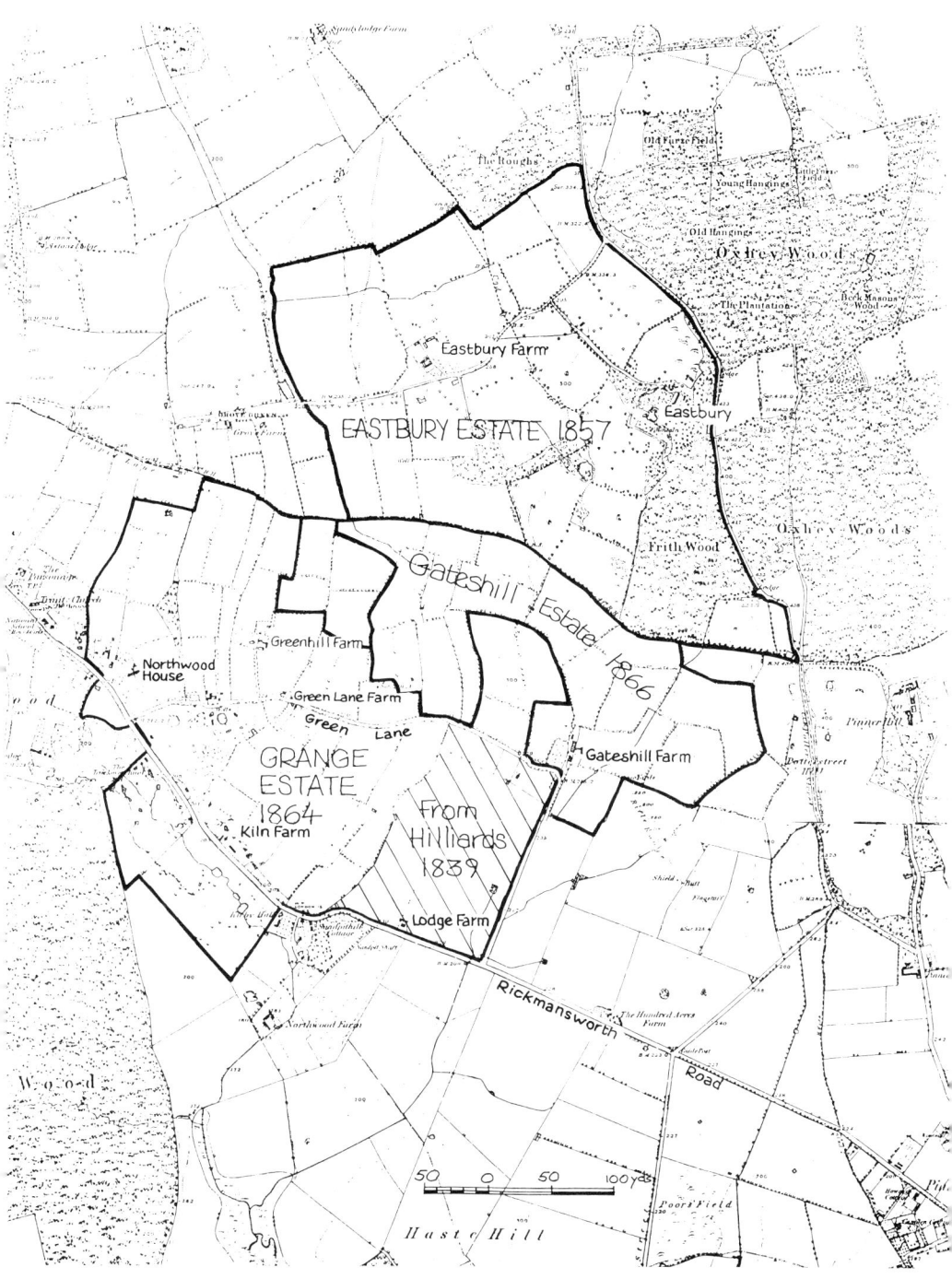

The Eastbury Estate 1857

acres along a new road between the station and Rickmansworth Road were advertised as building plots 200ft-500ft deep, *"with panoramic views over Ruislip Reservoir" "in every way adapted for villas and better class houses"* coming up for auction soon.[84] They were withdrawn in the January following and on 25th March 1887 David Carnegie conveyed the entire estate to Frank Murray Maxwell Hallowell Carew for £59,422.[85]

Frank Murray Maxwell Hallowell Carew, 1866-1943

The man who has so conspicuously left his mark on Northwood was the great-grandson of Admiral Sir Benjamin Hallowell (1760-1834) who had succeeded to the Carew estates at Beddington, Surrey in 1828 after the death of his cousin, Mrs Anne Paston Gell, on condition that he assumed the family name. F. M. M. H. Carew's grandmother was daughter of Capt Sir Murray Maxwell and his father was Benjamin Francis Hallowell Carew. Thus all his names were inherited.[86]

When he bought Eastbury he was only twenty-one, and had married on the day before the Conveyance, Edith Gillibrand, an actress who used Chester as her stage-name.[87] Two sons were born to them, Reginald in 1888 and Roy in February 1889, but in the autumn of 1890 Mrs Carew discovered that her husband was having an illicit relationship with a woman living in a London suburb, and petitioned for divorce on the grounds of cruelty and adultery in February 1892.[88] The Queen's Proctor tried to prove that Mrs Carew had condoned her husband's matrimonial offences, but the plea was dismissed, the divorce granted and Mr Carew remarried in 1894. During the proceedings he was described as *"a man of considerable independent means"* a member of a firm of bill-brokers, Vaile & Carew, and more damagingly as *"a man of loose pursuits, who favoured the company of prize-fighters, frequenters of race-courses and loose ladies who indulged in the midnight amusements of dancing saloons".*[89]

Mr Carew certainly had no intention of settling at Eastbury. During the five years in which he owned it, he lived at Bishops Sutton, Arlesford; Langley House, Slough; 11 Barleston Gardens; Albany Mansions, Shaftesbury Avenue; and the Hotel Victoria, Northumberland Avenue. His death certificate 1943 says he was a retired major in the Tank Corps domiciled in Knightsbridge. What he did seem determined to do was to develop Northwood, purely for profit.

His method was to lay out, but not make up roadways; divide the area into building plots and sell them, having fixed a minimum cost for the houses to be erected on them.

All the roads were named after himself, his sons and his wife. Two roads honoured Mrs Carew, Chester Road (her stage name) and Edith Road. After divorce proceedings were instigated the latter was altered to Dene Road, probably a reference to the dene hole or chalk mine in one of the fields of Green Hills Farm. (The shaft is capped by a manhole cover in the lawn just in front of Melthorne Court). Some conveyances of land sold before 1893 show the old name.

The stipulated prices were £750 for a detached house or £1,300 for a pair of semi-detached houses on Carew, Maxwell and Dene Roads; £400 detached, £700 semi-detached pair on Chester and Murray Roads; £120 for terraced cottages on the west side of High Street. Provision was made for shops in Green Lane, Maxwell Road and High Street, thus setting Northwood's social scene.

Growth of Estates in the 19th century and their eventual break-up

F. M. M. H. Carew waited until Northwood Station was open before trying to sell the land. New railways in the London area did not necessarily lead to surburban development, but where the line ran across the land of an owner eager to realise his capital, and providing that the railway company would run sufficient trains to encourage commuters (a word not then in vogue) to settle in the country, the one usually followed the other.

An inspection train ran along the extension line on 30th August 1887 and Maj-Gen Hutchinson on behalf of the Board of Trade declared the line open to traffic. A half-hourly service from Aldgate to Rickmansworth was soon passing through the new station, providing as a writer in the Watford Observer of 8th October said *"new ground for the rambler"*. The same writer noted that not a house was in view from the station platform and remarked on the propensity of nightingales to sing in the neighbourhood.

The area, that was about to be advertised in such glowing terms as to entice people out from inner London, was rural in the extreme at the time of the 1881 census. Only 409 people inhabited its houses and cottages in that year, most of whom worked on the land. It had had its own church provided by Lord Ebury of Moor Park since 1854 and a school from the same generous source since 1848. A few men were employed in brick and tilemaking and sand mining. Before 1887 Northwood was usually dismissed rather contemptuously in such terms as *"an accidental aggregation of houses"* (1851)[90] or *"a destitute district near Moor Park"* (1871).[91] As soon as sales of building land began, the first on 28th September 1887, the phrases employed to describe Northwood contained words like *"charming"*, *"picturesque"* and *"salubrious"* and much was made of its *"elevated but at the same time sheltered position"*.[92]

Ten sales were held between September 1887 and July 1891, usually in a marquee on the estate and preceded by a free lunch for limited numbers. The plots were sold freehold, not on the building leases which were more usual at the time.

With a building lease, a land-owner sold parcels of plots leasehold to a lessee who, undertook to build houses which would become the landlord's property on the expiry of the lease. This method of development enabled the builder to use the land without tying up too much capital, and to make a profit by letting the houses during the term of the lease. It led to frontages being divided into very many plots and the provision of narrow tunnel-back houses, an evil on the whole avoided in Northwood.

By 1891 Northwood had 115 houses and one shop (later Ripple Tea Rooms, now Bellair Restaurant) and a population of 711. Some of the larger plots, in Green Lane for instance, had been bought by private individuals for their own houses. Other parcels of land were purchased by builders on speculation who built and let the houses. Norfolk Terrace, consisting of eight houses, was the earliest building in Half Mile Lane (later High Street) put up in 1887. It was owned by James Pesley. A number of cottages had been erected in Hallowell Road by Thomas Elkington, owner of the brickfield in Hills Lane. The vast majority of the houses were rented, only about 17% being owner occupied.[93]

Meanwhile, Mr Carew had sold 191 acres of the Hertfordshire side of his estate to T. F. Blackwell of Oxhey in 1889, and had been raising cash on other portions by mortgaging them. Mrs Georgina Hull advanced him £1,700 in June 1888, repaid in June 1889, and the United Estate and Investment Company seems to have tided him over with a loan of £2,500 for a short time in 1890. In December

The Goodliest Place in Middlesex

1892 he ended his association with Northwood when all unsold portions of the Eastbury Estate amounting to 345 acres were conveyed to George Wieland for £28,160.[94]

The estate continued to develop along the same lines and Northwood increased its population at an ever accelerating rate as other landowners joined in the boom. In 1901 it had 2,500 people, 496 houses, 26 shops and 3 public houses. The True Lovers Knot had held a licence since 1750 and The Gate had been a beer-house since 1838. To these older places of refreshment Mr Carew had sought to add a superior establishment at the top of Maxwell Road called The Carew Arms. In spite of a petition[95] against it, signed by 38 of the more influential inhabitants of Northwood, this was opened in 1887, but changed its name to Maxwell House and later became the Northwood Hotel. Bowleys, etc. is now on the site. Northwood's other pub, the Clifton Arms (now the Ironbridge) was licensed after several petitions, a little later in 1903, in the name of Thomas Hillmorton of Hillmorton House, which still stands next door to it.[96] A new True Lover's Knot was built in the same year in front of the old Knot.

One of the other landowners willing to develop his land was Mr Norton of Northwood Hall.

Northwood Hall and The Northwood Park Estate

Northwood Hall in Ducks Hill has been called Denville Hall since 1925. The house took on its present form about 1851, but is on an ancient site. The estate was created by Daniel Norton (1806-88), a timber merchant associated with Uxbridge, where he was Senior Lord in Trust for the Manor and Borough. He bought Maze Farm about 1841 (an old house standing in an area named Symbotes in the 16th century) and rebuilt it leaving only part of one of the old walls standing.

He and his first wife Louisa were living in the farm with their eldest child, two female servants and two agricultural labourers at the time of the 1841 Census. In 1851 the family was absent, presumably because of building operations, but Mary Puddifont, lodge-keeper, was living with her husband James, a gardener, at the very pretty lodge newly built in the style of a *"cottage ornée"*. The Nortons were well established in their Victorian Mansion by 1861 and formed the largest household in the whole parish. Daniel and Louisa then had six sons and three daughters (aged between 6 and 25) and were looked after by five female servants. Louisa died in 1869 and he remarried. About 1880 he retired to the Isle of Wight seeking a warmer climate for his bronchial chest and died there in 1888, being succeeded by his son, also called Daniel Norton.[97]

During his time in Northwood Daniel Norton had formed an estate of 196 acres. He bought Park Farm (called Philpots Tile House in 1565) about 1855 from Miss Noyes.[98] At about the same time he acquired an old house (which had also been a tile house in the 16th century) to the south of Park Farm, demolished it and threw the land into his park and dealt in a similar manner with a house shown on the Enclosure Map just to the north of Maze Farm possibly called Snail Holes. In 1860 he bought the timber-framed cottage which still stands in Jacketts Lane from the Howard family and acquired French Grove.

A piece of land opposite Northwood Hall, on the east side of Ducks Hill, had been part of Maze Farm since the Enclosure, being former waste allotted to Mrs Hogard, then owner, by the Enclosure Commissioners. Daniel Norton built a coach house, stabling and a gardener's cottage there about 1863. These buildings all stand and are now private houses. The rest of the land north of

242

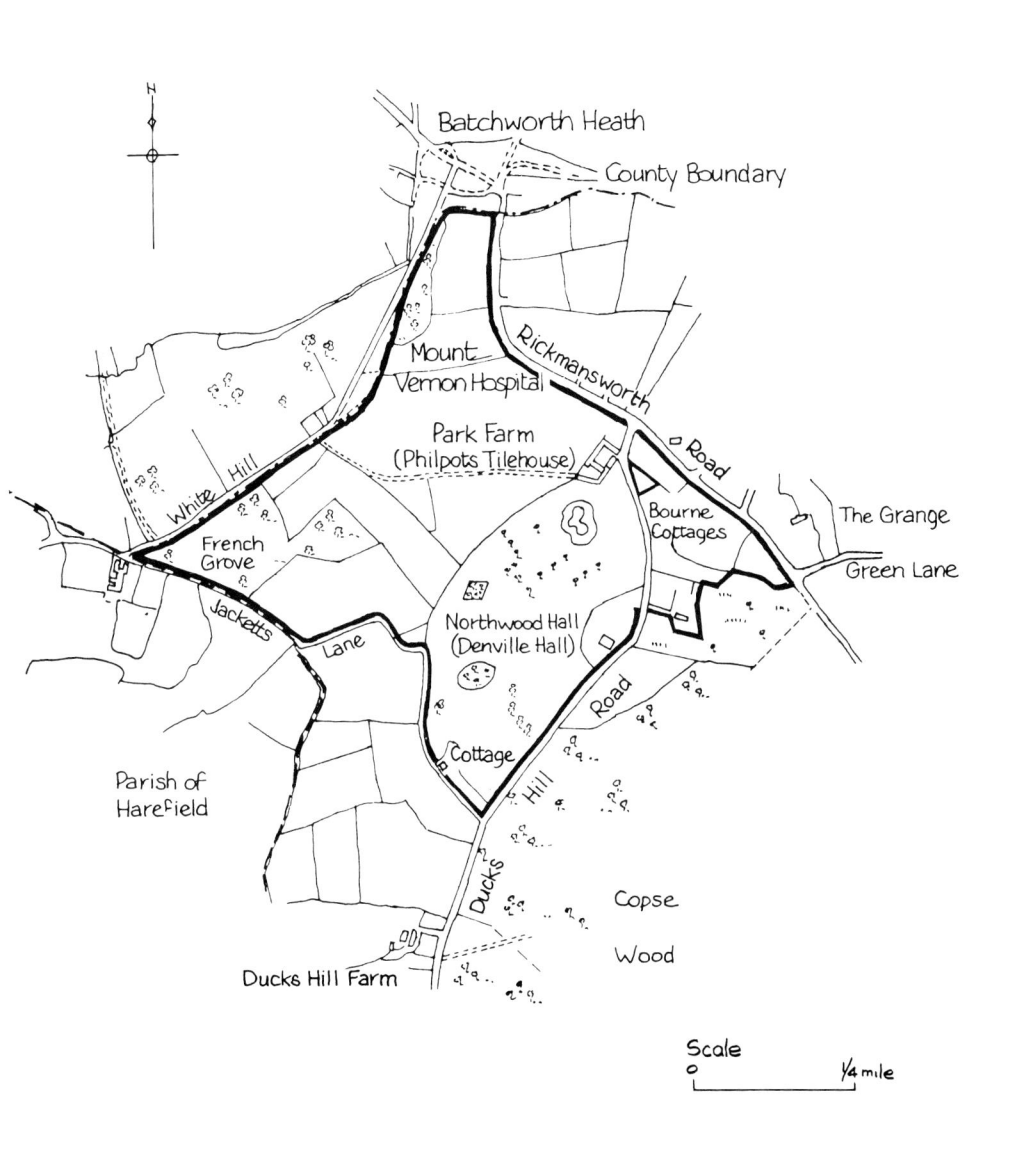

Growth of Estates in the 19th century and their eventual break-up

Northwood Hall and Northwood Park Estate

the coach-house etc., in the triangle bounded by Ducks Hill and Rickmansworth Road/Kewferry Hill, also became part of the Northwood Park estate, with the exception of a triangular-shaped piece on which Bourne Cottage was built by Lord Ebury for Mrs Bourne, formerly of The Gate.

Mr Norton provided model farm buildings at Park Farm (then called Home Farm) and built a pair of cottages in White Hill by a trackway which led across to Park Farm and Ducks Hill about 1860. They still stand close to the back entrance to Mount Vernon Hospital.

In more frivolous vein he had two battlemented towers erected, to serve as summer houses at the bounds of the gardens surrounding his mansion. That on the south still stands.

Daniel Norton jun. leased the house and pleasure-grounds to Mrs Gladstone who came from Manchester; the Farm and Park to Mr Edwin Nichols (21 years from 1882)[99]; and the land between Ducks Hill and Kewferry Hill to Thomas Elkington on a building lease. He offered the estate for sale by auction in 4 lots in August 1891,[100] with £40,000 as the reserve figure. It was described as peculiarly adapted to building purposes and was said to embrace views of great extent and beauty including Crystal Palace, Knockholt Beeches and the grand stand at Epsom! Not a single offer was made, either for the whole or individual lots. A few years later, however, in 1902, 105 acres of the former farm lands, but not the farmhouse, were sold to the Trustees of Mount Vernon Hospital[101] (then at Mount Vernon, Hampstead) and the Hall was leased to H. H. Cunliffe-Pickersgill, Esq. The house, park and farm were again auctioned in 1907.[102] The park and farm are now Park Farm, a riding stables.

The house seems to have been the home of a Boys' School, Tivoli House, during the First World War; the Headmaster being Baron Isidore Berkovitz.

Alfred Denville MP bought the house in 1925 after it had stood empty for a period and turned it into a rest home for retired members of the acting profession. It was opened by the Princess Royal in July 1926 and still fills this function. The house still retains many of the features paid for by Daniel Norton, for example a white marble mantel exhibited by the Coalbrookdale Company at the 1851 Exhibition.

The Ducks Hill Road frontage was gradually developed with large, detached houses, many since redeveloped at a much higher density and Mount Vernon Hospital was opened in 1904. But the lovely undulating parkland with its small copses, lake and island remain and are best viewed from the lower part of Jacketts Lane.

The building of what amounted to urban streets in Northwood from 1887 onwards led to a very strange and unbalanced situation in the parish of Ruislip.

REFERENCES

1. G.L.R.O. DRO 19 C1/6.
2. G.L.R.O. – Ruislip Enclosure Award & DRO 19 E2/19-23.
3. G.L.R.O. Middlesex Deeds Registry 1831/5/349.
4. Et Seq. Ibid.
5. Ruislip Library: Plans of Ruislip Park.
6. G.L.R.O.: Acc. 538/2nd dep/3660.
7. G.L.R.O. Middlesex Deeds Register 1831/5/349.
8. P. C. Jephcote: "The Police in Ruislip" – Ruislip Library.
9. Ex info R. Twitchen.
10. Uxbridge Library: List of Middlesex Electors.
11. Monument in St. Martin's.
12. Uxbridge Library: Auction Catalogue 1906.
13. V. J. E. Cowley: Journal R.N.E.L.H.S. 1985.
14. King's College: Bundle of letters with sales catalogue.
15. V. J. E. Cowley: ut supra.
16. Uxbridge Library: Advertiser and Gazette.
17. V. J. E. Cowley in *Ruislip Around 1900.*
18. G.L.R.O. Henry Sayer Map of Kingsbury.
19. Unless otherwise stated all the following information is taken from conveyances, leases, etc. in Eastcote Cottage file at Ruislip Library.
20. Ruislip Library: Photocopy. Sale Plan 1869.
21. Documents penes London Borough of Hillingdon.
22. Extracts from Rate Books by J. McBean.
23. Ibid.
24. Enclosure Award.G.L.R.O. MR/DE RUI E2/1-2.
25. R.N.E. L.H.S. *Eastcote – a Pictorial History.*
26. Abstract of title.
27. Karen Spink – in *Ruislip around 1900.*
28. Abstract of Title.
29. Ibid.
30. Ibid.
31. Ibid.
32. King's College R.36.
33. Ruislip Library: Rate Books transcribed by J. McBean.
34. Ibid.
35. Ibid.
36. 1861 Census.
37. Uxbridge Library: Ruislip Parish Rate Book.
38. King's College: Sales details 1904.
39. King's College: R.36.
40. Ruislip Library: Rate Books transcribed by J. McBean.
41. G.L.R.O. DRO 19 H1/1.
42. Will of Thomas Truesdale Clarke – transcribed by J. McBean.
43. Et seq. W. A. G. Kemp: "History of Eastcote" pp 75-7 and Rate Book transcribed by J. McBean.
44. Letter from Librarian's Secretary, Royal Coll. of Surgeons.
45. Et seq. Rate Books transcribed by J. McBean.
46. J. McBean: Journal R.N.E.L.H.S. 1979.
47. Ibid.
48. Ruislip Library: Photocopy of Sale Particulars of Hayden Hall 1883.
49. Harrow Gazette Supplement 22 Oct. 1882.
50. J. McBean: Journal R.N.E.L.H.S. 1979.
51. W. A. G. Kemp "History of Eastcote."
52. Ex info owner of Flag Cottage 1978.

53. K. Spink & J. McBean: Journal, R.N.E.L.H.S. 1984.
54. Uxbridge Library: Local newspapers & Ruislip Parish Rate Books 1886-1902.
55. J. McBean: Journal R.N.E.L.H.S. 1978.
56. Ex info Mrs Pym, Miss Warrender's niece.
57. Obituary in Local Paper 1949.
58. J. McBean: Journal R.N.E.L.H.S. 1977.
59. Uxbridge Library; R.N.U.D.C. Minutes 1935.
60. G.L.R.O.: Acc. 538/2nd dep/3658.
61. Et seq. Ruislip Library Abstract of Title 1864: and Rate Books transcribed by J. McBean.
62. Ruislip Library: Extract from John Paul Rowe's Will made by J. McBean.
63. Ruislip Library Abstract of Title 1864.
64. Ibid.
65. G.L.R.O. Middlesex Deeds Registry 1858/4/660.
66. Ruislip Library: Copy of Conveyance 1927.
67. Deeds of a house in Potter Street.
68. G.L.R.O. Middlesex Deeds Registry 1867/2/79.
69. Ruislip Library: Notes by J. McBean.
70. G.L.R.O. Middlesex Deeds Registry 1887/8/867.
71. Ibid 1889; 1891/11/458.
72. Ibid 1904/26/479.
73. Deeds of Green Close.
74. Archives of Holy Trinity Church.
75. Deeds of Green Close.
76. Herts. R.O. 8741/306.
77. Herts. R.O. 25551 and DEL 5623.
78. Herts. R.O. 25678.
79. Herts. R.O. 25683.
80. Herts. R.O. D/E GO P1.
81. 1866 Six inch O.S. map.
82. Uxbridge Library: Street Directories.
83. G.L.R.O. Middlesex Deeds Registry 1866 8/839.
84. Uxbridge Library: Local paper 1886.
85. G.L.R.O. Middlesex Deeds Registry 1887 8/867.
86. W. A. G. Kemp *History of Northwood and Northwood Hills* and Mitchell *The Carew, of Beddington.*
87. Marriage and Birth Certificate passed on by Mrs Pharoah.
88. Times Feb. 9 1892.
89. Times Nov. 30 1893.
90. St. George's, Windsor.
91. R. Bayne *Moor Park.*
92. Uxbridge Library: Local Newspapers 1887-95.
93. Uxbridge Library: Ruislip Parish Rate Books & Street Directories.
94. Deeds of houses in Rickmansworth Road and Hallowell Road.
95. G.L.R.O.: Acc. 1042 128.
96. Uxbridge Library: Local Newspapers 1903.
97. Obituary in Local Newspapers 18 Feb. 1888.
98. Et seq. Rate Books transcribed by J. McBean.
99. Brit. Lib (Maps) 137c 7 (17).
100. Ibid.
101. G.L.R.O. Middlesex Deeds Registry 1901/30/119.
102. Ruislip Library: Plan accompanying sales details.

Chapter Twelve

The present century

Situation c. 1900 – Vestry/Parish Council
At the time when new streets and shops were being built in Northwood, encouraging an influx of people quite different in background, occupation and expectation from the farmworkers who formed the bulk of the resident population, the parish of Ruislip was still governed as it had been since the beginning of the 17th century by the vestry of St. Martin's church. The powers of the vestry in the late 19th century were somewhat limited as responsibility for the poor had been in the hands of the Uxbridge Union since 1835 and any public work such as a major drainage or similar public health scheme could only be undertaken under the aegis of the Rural Sanitary Authority of the same Union, but it still collected the rates, provided fire engines, a parish chest for the archives, managed allotments, repaired footpaths and roads and administered the parochial charities.

In the later years of the 19th century the vestry was composed of farmers and land-owners under the chairmanship of the vicar, Thomas Marsh-Everett, all of whom seem to have been either unaware of the implications of the developments in Northwood, or unwilling to accept them. Their attitude is exemplified by their actions when a scheme for sewage disposal was put forward by the Uxbridge Rural Sanitary Authority in the autumn of 1884.[1] Complaints about the state of the Pinn at Eastcote into which the drains of Eastcote House and Hayden Hall both emptied themselves, had led to an Inspector of the Local Government Board visiting the area and recommending the RSA to prepare a Sewerage and Sewage Disposal Scheme and to provide houses without wholesome water with supplies from the Colne Valley Water Company. Naturally the cost would mainly fall upon the parish.

Mr Marsh-Everett said at a meeting that he did not see that they, as a vestry, could entertain the scheme at all, as the parish had a very small population (under 1200) and was an essentially country one. The cost would be enormous. He was indignant that the Inspector had singled out Ruislip for such a proposal *"because there was a little nuisance existing in two or three different parts of the district", "Surely it is possible for a nuisance of the sort to be abated without going the length of having a main drainage scheme."* A committee composed of Edwin Ewer of Wilkins Farm; W. Long of Cheney Street Farm; Lawrence Ingham Baker of Eastcote Lodge; R. M. Jackson; S. Matheson of Lodge Farm, Northwood; Mr Stilling of King's End and Mr Curzon of Horn End was set up to confer with the Rural Sanitary Authority.

All this was said in November 1889 when five major sales of land on the Eastbury Estate had already taken place and building had begun in Maxwell and Murray Roads and Green Lane. The vicar also underestimated the population of the parish which was 1455 in 1881 and had jumped to 1836 by 1891.

The vestry ceased to serve any civil purpose in 1895 when the Local Government Act of the previous year came into operation and henceforth confined itself to church matters. The new act divided counties into county boroughs and district councils, either rural or urban and permitted the establishment of parish councils in rural areas with a population of more than 300. Ruislip became a parish council within the Uxbridge Rural District and was divided into three wards, the ancient vills of Ruislip, Northwood and Eastcote.

Nine councillors were elected by a show of hands at a parish meeting held in Ruislip Schoolroom:[2] Thomas Marsh-Everett, vicar; Edwin Ewer, Wilkins Farm; Henry James, Ewer, Manor Farm; Daniel Norton (owner of Northwood Hall, but not resident); Samuel Matheson, formerly of Lodge Farm now of the Northwood Hotel; Daniel Sydney Waterlow of The Thorns, Northwood; G. I. Brush of Highgrove Lodge; L. I. Baker of Eastcote Lodge and W. J. Bray of King's End. This was largely the vestry under a new name. Mr Waterlow was the sole representative of the newcomers to Northwood, who were largely professional men; doctors, solicitors, architects or superior tradesmen, who owned high-class establishments in town, many of whom travelled daily to the City.

During the next six years while the population leapt to 3,566, about 2,500 of whom lived in Northwood, a rift appeared in the parish between the agricultural and newly suburban areas. The division was physical, as the woods and reservoir formed a barrier between the two that was not crossed by any direct road suitable for vehicles, but the greatest gap was a social one. Northwood, for example, had an orchestral society and golf club, while the people of Ruislip and Eastcote were still being entertained with talks by the vicar illustrated by lantern slides.

Worst of all from the point of view of the newcomers, their most pressing needs were not being catered for by the parish council. The drainage scheme was still pending and for several years was only discussed as relating to the Eastcote side of the parish. By 1895 Mr Bertram Freeman, Surveyor to the RDC planned a trunk sewer from Goodman's Cottages at the bottom of Cuckoo Hill to a tank 15 feet × 7 feet × 12 feet in a field near Guts Pond (corner of Fore Street and Eastcote Road), where solid matter would be caught in a screen, the liquid filtered through chemicals and discharged into the Pinn.[3] The cost of £500 could be raised by loan if a parish meeting (open to all parishioners) agreed and if the RDC approved. In fact approval was withheld as a wider drainage scheme was deemed necessary.

More than one hundred people turned out to a parish meeting held in Northwood Schools in June 1897 and demanded proper drainage for Northwood. In August, a scheme which would cost £9,500 to drain Northwood and £2,563 for Eastcote gained assent and the RDC applied to the Local Government Board for a £1,300 loan. Months elapsed bringing no reply. Tempers waxed high and Mr Waterlow in an impassioned speech claimed that the Local Government Board was treating the people of Northwood like Outlanders whereas they had a right to be treated like Englishmen!

An inquiry by the Local Government Board in May 1898 resulted in the recommendation by the Inspector that Ruislip should be drained as well as Northwood and Eastcote. Discussion of a suitable outfall site led to further delays. Meanwhile the Council minuted its regret over the outbreak of diptheria in Hills Lane! After more representations and yet another inquiry in July 1899 an outfall site was agreed and a loan of £21,000 approved. The only further delay was caused by the death of Mr John Anstie, the engineer, but a substitute for him was found and the Sewerage Works at Southcote Farm, Ladygate Lane came into operation in 1902.

The concomitant question of a piped water supply for Northwood posed no problems as the Colne Valley Water Company (founded 1873) supplied water from wells near Watford from 1887, and new houses were connected immediately. The old farmhouses in all areas had their own wells though some cottagers had to rely upon ponds. If the wells were sunk deep into the chalk, like the public well and pump outside The George in Ruislip, (1864) the supply was good, but shallower wells were liable to dry up during drought. Eastcote had piped water in 1888 and Ruislip in 1899, the parish council having guaranteed the Colne Valley Water Company £45 per annum. Constant complaints were made about the state of roads and footpaths, particularly the one from Northwood Station to Murray Road.

The struggle and delays over the drains convinced many Northwood people that the area needed urban powers if it were to run its own affairs efficiently and be free of the restrictions imposed by having to apply to the Uxbridge Rural District Council before taking major decisions. By 1901 they were more strongly represented on the parish council. A proposition that the council apply for conversion to an urban district was put before a parish meeting in April 1902 and carried on a show of hands. However, a poll was demanded and held on 3rd May, when the motion was lost by only eight votes: 155/163. The local paper reported: *"The result was declared in the evening amid applause at Ruislip, but it did not appear to cause much acclamation at Northwood"*. The opposition was based on fear of increased costs, as an urban district would need council

Reverend W. A. G. Gray who swayed his parishioners in favour of an Urban District

offices and officers, a surveyor and medical officer, for example, and the farmers and agricultural labourers could not foresee any benefit from such things.

A new report prepared by the Chairman of the Parish Council, Mr Frank Elgood (later Sir) and the Clerk to the Council, Mr Edmond Abbott, both of Northwood, was read on 1st October 1903. By then Northwood had 2,700 people living in 530 houses and was described as residential in character with large houses, villas and cottages. The rest of the parish was agricultural. Therefore it was suggested that Northwood should separate from Ruislip and Eastcote and press for urban powers on its own.

A parish meeting held in Ruislip Schoolroom to discuss this on 28th October 1903 was crowded long before 8 o'clock. The Harrow and Uxbridge Railway was extending its line from Harrow to Uxbridge and everyone present knew that a station would be opening in Ruislip the following year and that King's College, the major landowner, was already considering freeing land for building development. In other words, in a very short time, Ruislip was likely to become as suburban as Northwood and as much in need of an Urban District Council. The vicar, W. A. G. Gray, *"speaking disarmingly"* according to the local paper *"suggested to his audience that they would all quickly admit that the agricultural mind did not travel quite so quickly, and did not come to a conclusion quite so promptly as the city or business mind did; but he did not know that it was not in the end likely to come to a right conclusion"*. He proposed that the whole parish be converted to urban powers, a motion that was carried with only seven dissentient votes.

Ruislip-Northwood Urban District Council

Ruislip-Northwood Urban District Council came into being on 30th September 1904, and held its first meeting at Northwood Schools on 1st October.[4] The members were William Page Edwards, chairman; F. M. Elgood; H. J. Ewer; H. Ewer; William Gregory; S. Matheson; Rev. Harvey Roe (Methodist minister, Northwood); J. Westacott and A. M. Hooper. Mr E. R. Abbot, a solicitor, was appointed clerk at £100 per annum and retained his position until 1931. They set up three committees: Finance and General Purposes; Public Health, Buildings and Sewerage; and Highways; but did not avail themselves of their powers to form an Education Committee to deal with secondary education. In November 1904 Mr Walter Louis Carr, aged 27 of Sandal, Wakefield, was appointed Sanitary Inspector at an annual salary of £130 (£50 as Inspector of Nuisances and £80 as Surveyor) and Dr L. W. Hignett of Northwood as Medical Officer of Health at £20 per annum salary. The first and second floors of 7 Maxwell Road were rented as council offices.

These business matters settled, the main aim of the new council seems to have been to cut costs, evidently at the expense of services. The Highway Committee for example decided to dispense with the services of three of the ten men then employed and that ditches abutting roadways would no longer be cleaned out by the council. The workmen received 18 shillings per week wages (the foreman 25 shillings), and finished early on Saturdays at 4.00pm. In January 1905 it was recommended that they should be permitted to work through without a dinner interval and finish at 2.00pm for a long weekend.

Five men were employed at the Sewerage Works, an engineer (£2 per week), two labourers (£1:3s per week) and two on sewer maintenance at £1:6s and

£1:1s a week respectively. The lowest paid man was considered redundant and workman Collins who lived outside the parish was informed that he could continue to be employed only if he were willing to move into the district and to accept £1:3s a week instead of £1:6s. Unemployment was high and workman Collins expressed himself agreeable. Continuous inspection of manholes was discontinued however and also of interceptors on private property.

Regular refuse collection was another need of the new street dwellers and this was a service which was provided. Mr Wallis of Ruislip agreed to collect from 190 houses in Northwood for £120 a year and 30 houses in Ruislip and Eastcote for £26. He asked for an extra 2 shillings for every additional five houses. A year later E. Lee's tender of £129:12s for 280 houses was accepted.

Despite the availability of piped water, many houses in Ruislip continued to use private wells or the pump outside The George, so the Public Health Committee had the pump water analysed by Professor Kenwood of University College Hospital Laboratory in 1905. It was satisfactory. A notice was fixed on the pump warning persons against pouring any slops or sink water into the trough. In 1908 there were said to be about sixty wells in the district, twelve of which were *"suspicious"*. These too were subjected to analysis. A well supplying two cottages in Sharps Lane had already been closed in 1905.

Patients suffering from enteric fevers (perhaps through over indulgence in well water), smallpox and other infectious diseases were taken to Hendon or Yeading Smallpox Hospital and later to Kingston Lane Hospital (now St. John's) Uxbridge, where new accommodation became available in 1909. Their houses were disinfected at the Council's expense with Formalin lamps and Invicta sprays. The workmen received a shilling an hour extra for this duty.

Gas mains were laid from the Highgrove Estate to Ruislip Village in 1903 by the Pinner Gas Company.

The new MOH recommended that the four cottages, which are now the Ruislip Village Trust property in front of St. Martin's, should have their paper stripped off and their ceilings cleaned and whitewashed. Similar notice was served on the owner of two cottages at the back of The Swan. All were said to be in a very dirty state, which is borne out by contemporary photographs.

Planning

Perhaps the main concern of the Council was to ensure that the new urban district developed along pleasant residential lines.

Since the building of Bedford Park, between 1875-81, much consideration had gone into planning interesting and spacious environments where all the needs of a community were provided in a picturesque setting. Planning for recreational areas and space for shops, pubs and churches, as well as houses, was the order of the day. The Bedford Park houses all had well-planned kitchens and bathrooms and individual gardens and were situated along tree-lined avenues and crescents. The garden city and garden suburb movement gained momentum with the building of Port Sunlight (1888), Bournville (1893), New Earswick and Letchworth (1903) and Hampstead Garden Suburb (1906). Frequently the houses built in these areas had a consciously "olde-worlde" appearance which fitted in with the concept of craftsmanship and design extolled by William Morris and the Pre-Raphaelites. In Ruislip Mr Elgood, Chairman of the Council 1906-8 and

1912-15, who was an architect, and Mr Abbot, Clerk to the Council, were particularly influenced by these ideas. When the movement culminated in the Housing and Town Planning Act, December 1909, they were quick to prompt the R.N.U.D.C. Councillors to adopt a scheme to enable them to control the style and quality of future developments.

The Housing and Town Planning Act was an enabling act which allowed Local Government Boards to make general rules for the layout of streets and buildings and provision of open spaces, and more imaginatively for the preservation of objects of historic interest or places of natural beauty.[5] They also planned such amenities as sewerage, drainage, lighting and water supply. Local authorities, under the Boards, could prepare planning schemes alloting certain areas for domestic, recreational, commercial or industrial use and could decide such matters as the density of the houses, building regulations and the width of roads.

Mr Elgood's peers probably needed little persuading as they thought poorly of *"The badly-arranged and closely-packed working-class area near Northwood station,"* and were appalled at some of the new developments already under way, particularly in Eastcote and South Ruislip.[6]

Early Developments at Eastcote

The new line from Harrow to Uxbridge had come into service on 4th July 1904 and building development had followed in its wake as stations opened one by one. Ruislip station opened on the same day as the line itself, followed by a halt at Eastcote in May 1906. The Great Eastern and Great Central Joint Committee opened a station called Ruislip and Ickenham (now West Ruislip) in 1906 and Northolt Junction (now South Ruislip) in 1908.

The major landowner around Ruislip station was King's College as it was situated in the middle of the demesne. Eastcote Station lay between the property of Walter Morford (Field End House Farm) and Ralph Hawtrey Deane; while Northolt Junction was on Bourne Farm, another of his properties. All three were prepared to make their land available for development, but proceeded in slightly different ways.

The British Freehold Investment Syndicate acquired part of Field End House Farm in 1909 and began developing it by dividing the land into small plots which were sold individually or in groups at public sales. The group registered as a limited company on 21st July 1909, directed by George Augustin Hensley, a financier, and Robert Masson-Smith, a Canadian barrister, and began selling plots on 21st August. Prospective buyers were encouraged to invest in land by booklets embellished with pretty photographs of the "village" of Eastcote and the assurance that only £3 down would secure any plot. The balance could be paid interest free at the rate of 10 shillings a month.[7]

The land: Long Mead and the portion of Stain Hill lying north of the railway (now Lime Grove, the west side of Hawthorne Avenue, Myrtle Avenue, Acacia Avenue and Elm Avenue), was laid out in 100ft × 20ft plots. *"Elaborate improvement"* of Eastcote in the form of *"Park-like roads, Duplex drainage, electric light"* was promised and the entire property was to be ornamented with rose bushes and fruit trees at no cost to the purchaser.

The promotors probably hoped that some buyers would materialise from the provinces (builders perhaps), as they offered to refund rail fares for

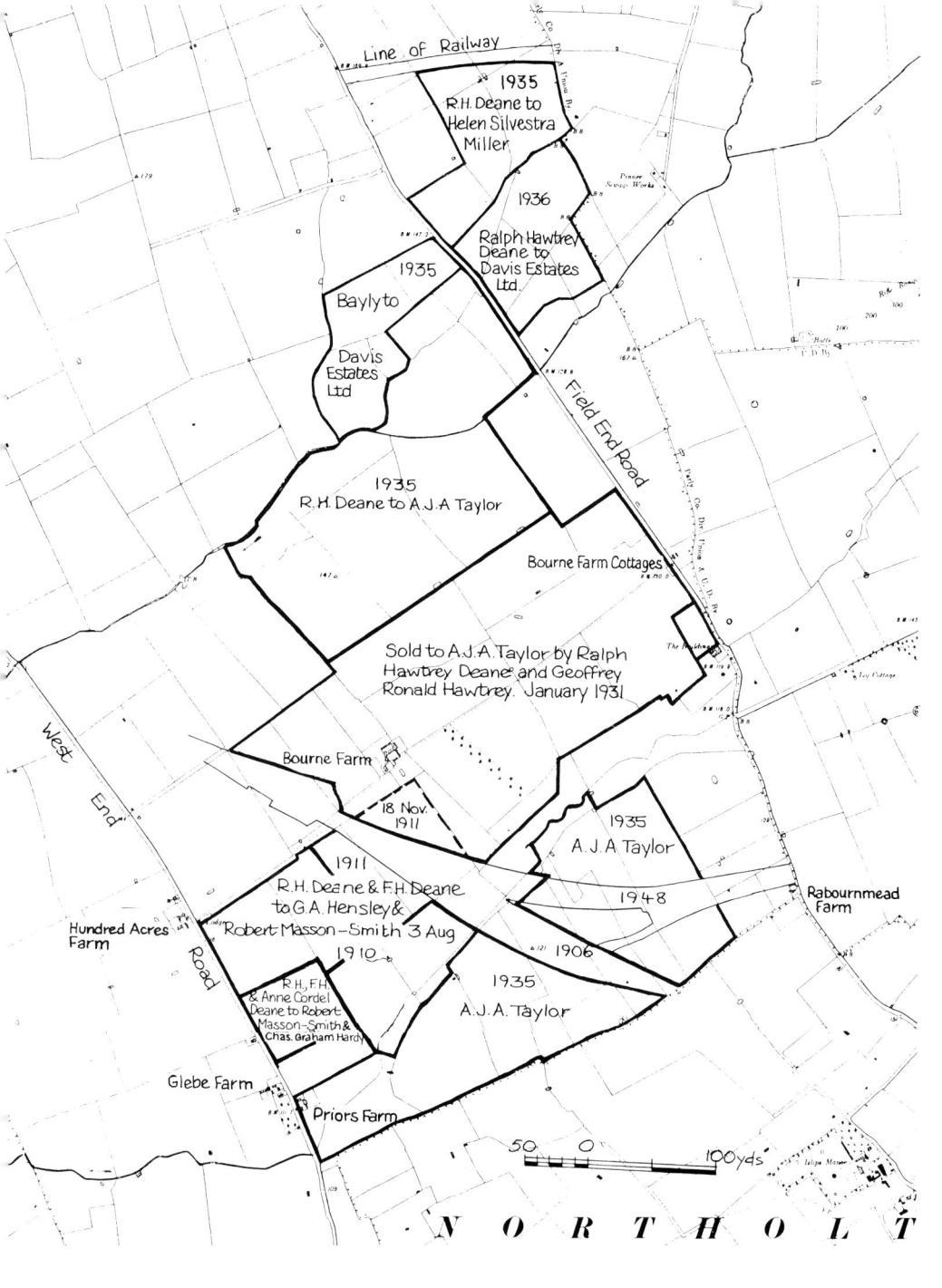

Sales of land for suburban development in the south of the Parish

travellers from more than 50 miles away, but their literature was aimed mainly at people living and working in central London parishes. *"The property adjoins the station.... There are 143 trains running daily between the Metropolis and Eastcote"... "can also be reached from any of the principal City stations"* ran their brochures. The death rate at nearby Pinner (5³⁄10 per 1000) was contrasted favourably with that of Shoreditch (30 per 1000) to show *"the superiority of this locality from a healthful standpoint"*. Eastcote being *"beautifully situated 200 feet above sea-level"* was on *"such a high level"* as to be quite free from the fog and dirt so prevalent in the City.

Eastcote's attractions, to be obtained at so low a cost, proved very popular with the public. Within a period of sixty days, from 21st August, 179 buyers had bought more than 400 plots, paying an average price of £50 per piece and a further 250 had been sold by May 1910.[8] The initiation of so successful a scheme caused more of the land of Field End Farm, south of the railway, to be parcelled out in the same way. It subsequently became the eastern end of Linden Avenue, Beech Avenue and Oak Grove. Ralph Hawtrey Deane, then living at 98 Sinclair Road, Kensington, and the Rev. Francis Henry Deane of Halstead Rectory, Kent, were encouraged by these successes to sell two of the fields of Bourne Farm in South Ruislip to Mr Hensley and Mr Masson-Smith in August 1910 and more land adjoining in November 1911. These fields were also staked out in plots. The earliest building erected there subsequently became South Ruislip Post Office and still stands in Station Approach (now Crittall Windows).

The Council was alarmed. There was no control over the use of the land and rather flimsy bungalows or even mere sheds were being built by owners with little capital. "Shanty Towns" seemed to be in danger of mushrooming in Eastcote and South Ruislip. A walk down Lime Grove today reveals several of these small bungalows. Standing in mature gardens and being well decorated they exude a certain individuality and charm, and no doubt look much better than they did in 1910.

Another point deplored by the authorities was that roads as laid out in 1909-10, surrounded by farm land, were nearly all cul-de-sacs; Myrtle, Acacia and Elm Avenues all ended at the ancient ridgeway between Westcote and Eastcote (marked by a footpath today) and Lime Grove at Great Mead. Myrtle and Acacia Avenue had only one exit each into Lime Grove which in turn had only one exit into Elm Avenue which also had only one exit into Field End Road. The six cul-de-sacs south of the railway had only one narrow bridge approach (now Oak Grove). Councillors thought *"this was just the kind of thing they ought to prevent occurring"*.[9] They felt compelled to take action and in May 1910 decided to adopt a Town Plan.

King's College as Developers

Had all landowners behaved as responsibly as King's College there might have been less anxiety. When the College began to develop the demesne it attempted to control the quality of buildings rather as Mr Carew had done earlier in Northwood.

Until 1904 the nearest part of the demesne land to a station had been Copse Wood and Northwood Farm. The College had considered building in the woodland in 1899[10] and had made plans for a road across the worked out gravel

The present century

pits, but negotiations with the parish council made slow progress and prospects in Ruislip looked brighter. Withycrofts (or Withycuts/Widdicutts) the old enclosed pasture between Wood Lane, Ickenham Road and High Street/West End Road was advertised for letting on building leases in 1903 and a new road called King's End Avenue from the station to Great King's End was begun in 1905. Amenities were not forgotten as the following year an agreement was made with the Council to lay a sewer down the High Street to the bottom of the new road, the College agreeing to repay the principal and interest at a rate of £60 per annum.

Frederick Herbert Mansford, F.R.I.B.A. (1871-1946) built the first two houses, now No. 13 and 15 King's End.[11] To meet the College's requirements for imposing housing, he made the pair look as much like a single large house as possible, adding wings to enhance their appearance. Alterations to No. 15 in the past 25 years have destroyed the original unity. The Mansfords moved into No. 15 in 1907, calling it Walden after the book by the 19th century philosopher, Henry Thoreau, which described a simple life passed in idyllic solitude. The same name had been used for a house in Northwood a few years earlier and reveals the impression of rural Middlesex held by newcomers from the City. Mr Mansford, born in Tottenham and brought up in Finsbury Pavement, was typical of the people who very slowly began to trickle out to Ruislip. They were greeted by friendly mockery, soon being known as "Squatters" and retaliated by dubbing the original inhabitants "Ancients".

The plots sold so slowly (only six went in 1906) that King's College found its capital tied up for too long and considered other means of utilising the land to bring a quicker return. The jolliest-sounding proposal, made in 1906, was when £55,000 was offered by an entrepreneur wishing to convert New Pond Farm into a racecourse. The governing body of the College was tempted and a hot debate ensued. Only the casting vote of the provost prevented Ruislip from becoming another Kempton Park.[12] The entrepreneur went to Northolt for his racecourse, and old members of the College were invited to invest in Ruislip Building Company Limited which was formed in 1907, to acquire blocks of land and build houses and thereby expedite matters at King's End. It functioned until 1910 by which time its property was producing a net income of £180 per annum, and the company assigned its assets and liabilities to a new company called Ruislip Manor Limited.[13]

Meanwhile, members of the College began to consider the desirability of planning the layout of the entire demesne on garden suburb lines and had discussions with Garden Estates Limited, a company associated with Hampstead Garden Suburb Trust 1909-10. When Mr Elgood and Mr Abbot approached major landowners in May 1910 to test their reactions to the idea of a Town Planning Scheme, they were much encouraged by the news that the College was already contemplating such a plan for its own estate which formed the central portion of the Urban District.

Garden Estates Limited entered into an agreement with King's College on 30th June 1910. Provided that the company acquired 133 acres of King's College Estate before 31st July 1911, it would be entitled, but not bound, to take up additional lands at prices averaging under £167 an acre during the next 21 years. Pressure was put upon the railway company to open a new station on the estate, as a further encouragement to development, and Ruislip Manor Halt was ready in 1912.

The Goodliest Place in Middlesex

The company's intention was to plan a suburb worthy of the College and allow it to be built slowly over future decades as the need for new accommodation occurred. Co-operation with R.N.U.D.C. produced an outline plan of the area suggesting main traffic routes and general principles of land use. The Company then proceeded to draft a detailed plan for the College Estate. With a view to securing the best possible layout it instituted a town planning competition which elicited 62 entries, mainly from architects. While the results were being considered, Garden Estates, like Ruislip Building Company, assigned its interest to Ruislip Manor Limited which then proceeded on the same lines.

The Managing Director of Ruislip Manor Limited, Alderman William Thompson, was also Chairman of the National Housing and Town Planning Council and his public work in furthering the improvement of housing conditions and his interest in garden suburbs and town planning was well known.

The Town Plan

At this juncture the results of the town planning competition which had been judged by Sir Aston Webb and Raymond Unwin, designers of Letchworth and Hampstead Garden Suburb were announced. The winners were Messrs. A. and J. Soutar of Wandsworth, who produced a symmetrical plan which owed more to geometry than the levels and contours of the parish of Ruislip.[14] A main axial road ran north-south, right through the woods to South Ruislip with diagonal roads giving direct access to the outlying portions. Some small bands of Copse Wood and Park Wood were to be left as public open space, just enough to form a pleasing backdrop to the houses, and the golf course was to remain as a magnet for the "right type" of resident.

Socially the estate was graded from north to south with large houses at low density to the north (three to the acre in Copse Wood and four and a half to the acre in Park Wood). Medium-sized houses (8 to the acre) and shops were planned between the woods and the railway, while to the south smaller houses could be built (10 to the acre) and some land was made available for industrial purposes. Six shopping areas were envisaged about the north-south axial road, the main one being at the junction of Eastcote Road and the new road at Windmill Hill where public buildings were to adorn the summit. The Reservoir and Pinn were both intended to become recreational areas, with aquatic sports on the one and football, cricket grounds and ornamental gardens alongside the other.

Messrs Soutar envisaged 7,642 houses being built on the estate eventually, with 35,000 residents, by which time the entire Urban District was expected to have a 70,000 population. This formed a reasonably accurate estimate. When R.N.U.D.C. went out of existence in 1964 the population had reached 75,000.

Many features of Soutars' plan were excellent, low density housing (nowhere more than 10 to the acre), good sized gardens, land-scaped streets and space for churches, schools and public amenities were all to be commended. What so horrifies most modern residents is the complete disregard for every ancient feature except St. Martin's Church and their plan for the wholesale destruction of most of the woodland. Manor Farm, with its Great Barn and other farm buildings, was to be torn down to give place to houses and workshops. The 16th century timber-framed buildings at the end of the High Street (admittedly in a poor state

The present century

at that time) were also to be lost. Instead of restoring old houses and incorporating them in the new suburb to form an anchor, a clean sweep was preferred with every building modern. This approach is still too often employed by modern architects and permitted by present-day planners, as seen particularly blatantly in recent developments in Uxbridge.

The R.N.U.D.C. worked to persuade all the other landowners to accept a Town Planning Scheme for the whole area. The Outline Map was shown at a public meeting at Emmanuel Church Hall on 30th November 1910. Only six out of 300 landowners objected and the U.D.C. felt confident enough of success to take the next step: a Local Board Inquiry. This was held on 17th February 1911 and the Council were authorised to prepare a scheme. Two years of delicate negotiations followed, persuading landowners to conform to the Council's views, until eventually the Joint Town Planning Scheme (incorporating an adapted Soutar plan) was completed in February 1913. Final approval was given by the Local Government Board in September 1914. It was a dual scheme, a municipal plan for over 9 square miles, with a detailed owner plan for the King's College demesne lands. Previously developed areas, like the Eastbury Estate in Northwood, Ruislip Park House and British Freehold lands, were omitted from the plan but the Town Planning Scheme was extended in 1930 to cover the areas excluded in 1914. It controlled all development, until it was abrogated by the Town and Country Planning Act of 1947.

One of the main features of the Council's scheme was the improvement of road communications with main roads to London and other villages and with railway stations. It is hard to imagine now, but Ruislip Manor Halt had no roads approaching it at the time it was opened, nor any houses at all in its vicinity. The other important points were the allocation of areas for special uses; the provision of open spaces both public and private; and the limitations of the number of houses. The Soutars' detailed plan fitted into these general provisions.

In his account of the Ruislip Scheme in *Town Planning in Practice* Alderman Thompson stated that architects believed that the indiscriminate intermixing of large and small houses was inadmissable, but that a judicious sprinkling of medium-sized houses among large ones would not depreciate values. He also thought it necessary to provide *"specific areas near large houses for housing the working classes employed in connection therewith"* – charladies, gardeners, etc.

Ruislip Manor Cottage Society Limited

With this provision in mind a subsidiary company called The Ruislip Manor Cottage Society Limited was registered in October 1911.[15] Its purpose was to take up land to build small houses and cottages for either selling or letting. It had the same bankers, auditors and registered office as Ruislip Manor Limited, and the same architects A. and J. Soutar. Most of the Board were local men and women: Miss Lydia Bigwood of King Edwards Road; Dr T. Ashton-Davies; Mrs Alice Edwards, The Barns, Eastcote; Miss Gertrude Hammond, King Edwards Road; Mr H. Rogers-Honchin, The White Cottage, Sharps Lane (called The Laurels when Walter Morford lived there); Mr F. Herbert Mansford, "Walden", Kings End; Councillor G. T. Weedon, "The Poplars". They all had philanthropic leanings and hoped to build well-designed and attractive cottages for *"persons in*

The Goodliest Place in Middlesex

receipt of moderate or small salaries and wages", while encouraging such people to be thrifty and careful tenants by making provision for a profit sharing tenancies scheme. Small houses were to be rented at 6 shillings-15 shillings a week and tenants, who would be obliged to invest a minimum of £5 in the society, would share in the surplus profits. A rent-purchase scheme was also contemplated. For a down payment of between £25-£50 plus annual payment equal to the rental value, ownership could be achieved within 15-20 years.

Land was conveyed freehold to the Cottage Society by Ruislip Manor Limited with roads, sewers and open spaces ready made. The main sphere of operations was between Eastcote Road and the new halt, but two smaller areas were also acquired, one between Fore Street and Park Wood (now Coteford Close) and the other at Northwood (Chestnut Avenue).

Only Manor Way, Windmill Way and Park Way were constructed before the First World War. Posts marked the end of Park Way and Windmill Way terminated in a field gate at the end of Brickwall Lane or "Muddy Lane" as it was then known, a grass road to the High Street. The first two houses erected at the corner of Eastcote Road and Manor Way were designed by architects Bunney and Makins, and are still extremely attractive. They are built of grey and brown Tring bricks, have oak half timbers and soft red hanging tiles. Their jettied upper storey, oak doors with iron strapping and decorative chimneys typify the Elizabethan style favoured in garden suburbs, and seen here at its best, built with quality materials and good workmanship. What is so odd is that the architects who strove to imitate 16th century styles, viewed the proposed destruction of genuine Tudor buildings on the High Street and at Manor Farm with equaninimity.

Some rooms in one of the pair were to be set aside as offices for the Society and indeed still fulfil that purpose. Twelve more houses built in Manor Way in 1911 are grouped around a large green (four pairs and a group of four) and were designed by three different architects, H. A. Welch, A. & J. Soutar and Courtenay M. Crickner. All had bathrooms and inside WCs and three bedrooms. Most had tool sheds to meet the requirements of the tenants who were expected to be artisans who would need such things. They were rented at 11 shillings and 10 shillings a week, which was expensive when Council workmen's wages were 18 shillings to 26 shillings a week, but were good value for the quality of the accommodation.

A similar development was begun in Windmill Way of fourteen houses around a green, designed by Cecil H. Hignett, the Letchworth architect. He specified local multi-coloured bricks, Norfolk pantile roofs and ivory-white woodwork. These slightly simpler houses did not have bathrooms, but had a bath as well as sinks and washing boilers in the sculleries. They were cheaper than the Manor Way houses being rented at 6s:6d-8s:6d per week.

The outbreak of war put an immediate end to building, leaving the trucks of bricks and sand and the light railway laid by the contractor from Ruislip Station sidings as a playground for small boys, as the son of Mr F. H. Mansford remembers. Work was taken up again in 1919 but less was achieved by the Cottage Society than had been envisaged. Only four houses were built in Eastcote, the rest of Coteford Close being sold to the Council for council houses. Eighteen Manor Cottages were built in Chestnut Avenue, Northwood in 1926. Green Walk and Manor Close were built in Ruislip, but the remaining area of Windmill Hill was sold to private developers.

The present century

Plans for a public hall on the corner of Manor Way and Midcroft and a fine shopping centre on Windmill Hill did not materialise, and few houses were purchased from the Cottage Society. In many respects, however, the Society has been and still is highly successful. It built cottages of great charm and placed them in green, spacious areas which still delight the eye and set a high standard for the Council to aspire to when it too started providing accommodation for the working classes.

Pace of Development

Development was fairly slow at first, but speeded up a little in the 1920s, as contractors built whole estates. In Eastcote, Telling Brothers Limited, later W. A. Telling Limited, began a development with houses, shops and a community hall (later the Ideal Cinema) about 1923. They continued until the late 1930s, building lovely houses in Morford Way and Morford Close with unusual decorative features and shops in Field End Road.

Large scale estate development became more commonplace in the 1930s. H. L. Bowers was busy around 1930 building three-bedroom houses south of Ruislip Station on Eversley Crescent to be sold at £695. Bowers Limited at the same time were putting up better class dwellings, with three or four bedrooms on the Church Croft (Croft Gardens, Midcroft, South Drive) to sell from £945-£1,175 freehold. The latter were advertised as having *"the dignity, tone and distinction so much sought after by gentle folk."*[16]

A. J. A. Taylor and Davis Estates Ltd. developed much of the Deanes' lands in South Ruislip. The description of South Ruislip given in an advertisement for houses in The Fairway makes surprising reading today – *"the elevation (standing as it does, at an altitude of about 120 to 140 feet above sea level), with a sub soil of loam, surrounded by a beautiful stretch of country, free from anything suggestive of overcrowding, give to this charming spot an inestimable value for residential purposes, and for those who desire fresh, pure air, bracing climate and rural peace it can be highly recommended"*. The advertiser must have known that the rural peace was soon to be shattered.

Development of the other Deane lands in Eastcote was taking place at the same period.

Part of Hundred Acres Farm, Northwood and land at the top of Joel Street became the modern Northwood Hills, created by Southern Park Estates and Belton Estates after the station was opened there in 1933. Morgan and Edwards was another company at work there.[17] Southern Park were beginning work in Ruislip on land around New Pond Farm (Shenley Avenue) at the same time.

Perhaps the largest estate of all was the Manor Homes built by George Ball between 1933-39, which now forms the area called Ruislip Manor.[18] King's College sold him 186 acres south of the railway and he agreed to erect no more than 2,322 houses at no greater density than fourteen to the acre. In order to have space for a school (later Lady Bankes) George Ball agreed to forgo fifty houses in 1934 and reduced the number of houses by a further 34 in 1935 in return for permission to put up a Church (St. Paul's) and a public house (Black Bull). Land near the Yeading was set aside as public open space in 1937.

The distinctive style of houses built by George Ball made little pretence to "olde worlde" charm. They are small houses built along the functional lines typical of the 1930s. The Crittal windows in particular epitomise

The Goodliest Place in Middlesex

The Manor Homes built by George Ball 1933-9

the period, but these are becoming a rarity as most of them have been replaced in recent years.

The Manor Homes were advertised with much verve by novelties like firework displays and entertainments by such popular figures as Elsie and Doris Waters. The homes sold from £450 and were intended to attract working men. The slump was on and a substantial number of Manor Homes were occupied by men from Tyneside and other parts of the north who had come south to seek work.

Northolt Aerodrome

The land in South Ruislip on which A. J. A. Taylor was busy building in the 1930s had nearly become the Harrow Aerodrome in 1912, but plans for an airfield with thirty hangars plus a complex of sports facilities were dropped. However, as interest in flying grew between 1910-14, many areas around London were viewed as possible airfields. Most of the land in South Ruislip met the requirements, being open, fairly flat and well drained and with rail connections with central London.

The outbreak of war increased the need for new aerodromes where men of the Royal Flying Corps could receive instruction. Major W. S. Brancker, Deputy Director of Military Aeronautics at the War Office, ordered land in South Ruislip to be requisitioned for Northolt aerodrome. There is some doubt as to which land the Major actually wanted as there has long been a story that the official who came to Ruislip held his map upside down and took the land of Glebe Farm, Hundred Acres and part of Down Barnes Farm by mistake.[19]

The aerodrome opened on 3rd March 1915 with No. 4 Reserve Aeroplane Squadron. Throughout the War there were many accidents during training, some fatal. Sixteen men were killed during 1917. Military funerals, the coffins draped with a flag, winding their way up West End Road to St. Martin's were a thrilling sight for Ruislip's children who stood by the Station bridge to watch.[20]

Some of the young women found that a stroll down the road through the fields and a chat with officers at White Butts Bridge (where the road crosses the Yeading) was a pleasant way to pass a summer's evening.[21]

The full story of Northolt, its part in the Second World War and later aviation history can be read in *The History of Northolt Aerodrome* by Peter Norris and Keith Hayward, produced by the Chiltern Aviation Society.

The Newcomers

The population of Ruislip-Northwood rose from 9,113 in 1921 to 16,035 in 1931 and then incredibly fast to 47,000 by 1939, the fastest rate of growth in the country and nearly all in Ruislip and Eastcote. How did the newcomers view their new environment?

Professional and business men and people connected with the arts moved into King's End and the Ruislip Park Estate. Often they were not particularly well off but felt that they had a position to keep up. Mrs Mansford in King's End, for example, took in a lodger in order to be able to pay for a maid! These "squatters" grew to love the "village atmosphere" (which of course their very presence was beginning to dispel) even though they disliked the mud in the High Street around the entrance to Wilkins Farm, which meant that they had to leave pairs of wellingtons at the station when they travelled to town.

The Ruislip and Eastcote Association was inaugurated on 11th February 1919 at a public meeting held at the Church Rooms in Bury Street. Mr Brassington was elected Chairman; Mr Upcroft, Treasurer and Mr Paige, Secretary. Committee members were elected to represent specific areas: Eastcote, Messrs Powell and Sidney; Ruislip Manor, Messrs Fogarty and Cattle; Ruislip Common, Mr Huxley; Ruislip Village, Messrs Speed, Lees and Shatford-Ewer. Ruislip Manor at the time meant Manor Way and Windmill Way.

For several years the new association was concerned with improving urban amenities as its Minute Books show. An early objective was the improvement of train services. The Manor Halt had been closed during the War, but re-opened with gratifying swiftness on 1st April 1919, following a request from the Association to the Metropolitan Railway Company, but no trains stopped. A further letter on the 11th April asking that trains should stop there between 7.34am-9.34am and 5.00pm-7.00pm soon rectified the matter.

The new suburban residents were greatly disturbed by the damage done to their gardens by the thousands of trippers who poured into Ruislip in the summer months to the various tea gardens at the Poplars, Orchard Bungalow, King's End Farm and Eastcote Pavilion. One hundred warning notices were printed "....*any person detected in damaging flowers, fruit or growing crops or trespassing on private property will be prosecuted*". The Association's Secretary wrote to Scotland Yard about it.

The Goodliest Place in Middlesex

There was an outcry for a public hall, as the Assembly Room at The George (i.e. The Old George demolished 1939) was rather small and the tin Church Rooms in Bury Street (near the present Youth Centre) were somewhat inaccessible on winter evenings when people had to walk there along extremely muddy and unlit roads. Despite these difficulties the Association enlivened the winter months with entertainments. There were lantern-slide lectures by Mr Mansford on such topics as Westminster Abbey and by Dr Fountain on astrology. Mr Jeffrey Farnol, the well-known historical novelist, gave a talk. A subcommittee set up in 1923 to form a self supporting musical society gave rise to the still flourishing Ruislip Operatic Society.

As early as 1921 Ruislip Manor representatives complained of feeling socially ostracised by the Village. Like Northwood twenty years earlier, the various parts of the southern district were developing along rather different lines and gradually formed their own ratepayers or residents' associations to meet their own special needs.

During the 1920s, the Ruislip Associations' Minutes first mention the threats to "the village atmosphere". Plans were being made to widen Bury Street, to demolish all the ancient buildings at Manor Farm and the end of the High Street and to build in the southern and eastern parts of Park Wood, in accordance with the Soutar Town Plan. A new era began as the word "conservation" as well as "improvement" was heard on the lips of the newer residents.

Saving of the Woods and Manor Farm[22]
Throughout 1929, discussions took place within the Association about the need to preserve the village centre around the church and the desirability of having Park Wood maintained as a public open space. Mr Menzies of the Royal Society of Arts was invited to visit Ruislip in January 1930 to point out those buildings most worthy of conservation. He chose Manor Farm, the Great Barn and Little Barn, the Old Post Office (now Wendy's World), the Old Bell (now R.S.P.C.A. shop) and the Priest's House (now Priory Restaurant and offices adjoining).

The next step undertaken by Mr J. Hooper of the Ruislip Association was to approach King's College. In November 1930 he and the vicar, the Rev Cornwall-Jones attended the Audit Dinner at the College and spoke at length with the Bursar, J. Maynard Keynes about the state of the woods and future plans. Ruislip residents had many complaints: the woods had been ruthlessly cut, no tree remaining larger than eight inches in diameter; no replanting had taken place and the butt ends and roots had not been cleared. The authorities excused their management on the grounds that the woods were due to be built over.

The College was amenable to the idea of Park Wood becoming an open space and would have liked to end its 500 year-old association with Ruislip with a "gracious act", by giving Park Wood, Manor Farm and the Old Post Office to the U.D.C. However, the College was governed by the Universities' and Colleges' Act and considered as a trustee of its lands. Therefore a sale had to be negotiated. Final agreement was reached in February 1931; Park Wood was sold for £27,300 and Manor Farm and the Old Post Office were included as a gift. Legal expenses on top brought the cost to £28,100. Middlesex County Council was persuaded to contribute 75% of the cost on the grounds that the woods were used by many outsiders and railway day trippers ("Visit Ruislip Woods in

Bluebell Time" exhorted the Metropolitan Railway adverts). R.N.U.D.C. paid the other 25% and agreed to maintain the wood under lease as an open space. The terms of the 999 year lease of one guinea per annum were that no building was to be put up without permission of the County Council and no trees or woodlands cut down without written permission. The southern portion of the wood, where building preparations had already begun, were exempted from the sale, and Broadwood Avenue, Sherwood Avenue and Park Avenue and cul de sacs off were developed in the years which followed. Dormywood is a redevelopment of the garden of a large house called Woodlands which was built in Park Avenue in 1931.

Negotiations were not always entirely amicable. Exception was taken to a sarcastic reference to the College in Mr Horder's preface to Cattle's *Short History of Ruislip* published in 1931 in which he had wondered *"What prayers would be needed to prevent irresponsible building from destroying the last vestiges of the Manor of Ruislip".* Mr Keynes considered this *"impertinent and somewhat offensive to the College".* It was omitted from the second edition.

However, all was peace and friendship when the handing over ceremony took place on Saturday, 23rd July 1932. The Earl of Crawford and Balcarres, Chairman of the Council for the Preservation of Rural England declared the woods open from a platform set up on the ridge overlooking the Reservoir. Mr Maynard Keynes was present and later at a tea in the Great Barn he was presented by Mrs Smedley with a commemorative parchment. Five trees were planted to mark the occasion, one by 94 year-old Mrs Tobutt, the oldest inhabitant (she lived to be over a hundred). Unfortunately none of these remains today.

The *Advertiser and Gazette* waxed lyrical *"The woodland scene was a fitting prelude when the great chief of the ardent band that seeks to retain our Ruritania was there to declare that this ancient fairyland is to be retained by the people for ever".* The tea was followed by *"Rustic games and harmony on the lawn of the Manor House".* A massed camp fire and community singing ended the evening.

All the speakers at the ceremonies in 1932 assumed that Copse Wood was about to be built over but new ideas about the need for a green belt around London and space to breathe were prevalent.

The southern section of Copse Wood, 155 acres, was bought in conjunction with the M.C.C. and L.C.C. for £23,250 in 1936, the contract being signed on 11th May. Much of the northern portion was already developed, but the College was ready to dispose of the section still wooded in 1938. A letter from R. F. Kahn of King's College to Mr J. Hooper says that the College wished it to be added to the rest of Copse Wood as perpetual open space. The M.C.C. was unwilling to proceed in the matter without the co-operation of the U.D.C. and R.N.U.D.C. Committee declined to make the relevant recommendation. That area, the north west corner of Copse Wood, has been in private ownership, ever since.

Mad Bess Wood was also acquired by the Ruislip Northwood Urban District Council in conjunction with Middlesex County Council and London County Council in 1936. 186 acres were purchased for £28,000 by compulsory purchase order from Sir Howard Stransom Button.

The Goodliest Place in Middlesex

After the outbreak of World War II effective management of the woods ceased until 1979 when the London Borough of Hillingdon set up a Woodlands Advisory Working Party composed of relevant Council officials, representatives of interested local organisations and the Nature Conservancy Council. After consideration of various possibilities for the future, a long term management plan was introduced. This advocated the reintroduction of coppicing in the oak-hornbeam areas and a thinning cycle for the rest of the woodlands.

Recent Years
The Second World War marked the end of the period of very rapid growth.
Since then the land zoned for industrial use has been developed as the South Ruislip Industrial Estate, but only a small proportion of residents work locally. Many still run to the various stations each morning, though probably not with *"the shaving lather still on their faces"*, as was said of the new suburbanites in the early years of this century.

Broadly speaking many of the ideas of the town planners had been brought into effect by about 1960. Most of the streets were lined with trees, and were arranged with corner houses on larger plots so that a spacious park-like atmosphere was created. Nearly every house had a garden of fairly generous proportions, enhancing this effect. The towers of the various churches rose above the roof tops of the surrounding houses. A garden suburb had come into existence which was better than the planners had intended as it retained some ancient buildings and most of the woodland.

During the past twenty years the space around houses has been seized and built upon by land-hungry developers, changing the character of once low-density housing areas. Redevelopment has affected the whole of the ancient parish, but Northwood has suffered most. Walking around its footpaths and alleys in 1985 has been like touring a vast building site, as the large gardens of the early suburban houses are filled in with small estates.

Many of the houses built since the late 1970s have made use of traditional materials like brick and tile and therefore fit into the landscape more comfortably than those of the 1960s and early 70s with their steel and large areas of glass, and in many cases have been arranged around attractive brick paved courts. Unfortunately, no matter how pleasant a house may be to look at, nowadays the occupiers have at least one car and the traffic problem has increased on a scale never envisaged by the early planners.

Monolithic office blocks of unacceptable height have penetrated shopping and residential areas in late years, while retail shops are being slowly driven away. Office blocks and high buildings are at present the greatest threat to the neighbourhood.

From a local historian's point of view the saddest developments are those where the green areas around old buildings have been built up with houses which have been allowed to obscure and swamp the original dwellings. The environment of an ancient building is almost as important as the old house itself.

The old parish of Ruislip is still one of the pleasanter places to live near London which is why there is such pressure on the land. Planners should remember that as the green spaces and trees go, so it will lose its attractiveness.

REFERENCES
1. G.L.R.O. DRO 19 C1/4.
2. Uxbridge Library: Ruislip Parish Council Minutes.
3. Et seq. Ibid.
4. Uxbridge Library: R.N.U.D.C. Minute Book.
5. W. Thompson: *Town Planning in Practice*.
6. Ibid.
7. Uxbridge Library: British Freehold Investments Syndicate Brochure 1909.
8. P. Massey: *Ruislip-Northwood: The development of the suburb with special reference to the period 1887-1914*.
9. Uxbridge Library: Middlesex and Bucks Advertiser. Feb. 18 1911.
10. Uxbridge Library: Ruislip Parish Council Minutes.
11. H. Mansford: Journal R.N.E.L.H.S. 1986.
12. Uxbridge Library: Middx. & Bucks. Advertiser July 1932.
13. Brochures of Ruislip Manor Ltd. 1910 and 1915 – personal possession.
14. The Builder Jan. 6 1911. W. Thompson. "The Town Planning Act in Working with an account of the Ruislip Scheme". E. R. Abbot and F. M. Elgood "The Ruislip-Northwood Scheme".
15. Ruislip Manor Cottage Society Brochure – personal possession.
16. Advertising Booklet – personal possession.
17. Advertising Booklet – personal possession.
18. Uxbridge Library: Documents re: Ruislip Manor.
19. P. Norris & K. Hayward *History of Northolt Airport*.
20. H. Mansford in Journal R.N.E.L.H.S. 1986.
21. Reminiscence – Mrs. Alice Hood.
22. Information from Ruislip Residents Association Scrap Book and Minute Books. E. M. Bowlt & C. Bowlt *History of Ruislip Woods*.

INDEX

Abbey of Bec *see* Bec, Abbey of
Abbott, John (Bourne Farm) 141
Acacia Avenue (Eastcote) 224, 252, 254
Acol Crescent (Sth Ruislip) 28
Acre Way (Northwood) 236
Addison Close (Northwood) 236
Addison Way (Northwood) 236
Aelmer (Ickenham) 40
Agriculture 36-37, 155, 195-6, 205; *see also* arable land, crops, farming, Glebe land, labourer, meadow land, pasture land, sellions
Aldershearne (Field) 117
Alderton Field *see* Tybber Field
Aldred, Gilbert (Ruislip customal) 58, 59, 60, 66
Allotment Gardens (Harrys Croft) 71, 105
Allotments Society Ltd, Ruislip – Northwood Cooperative Smallholding 90
Almshouses, Ruislip 133, 169, 171, 172-178; 17thC-20thC residents 172-178; conversion and restoration 177-178 *see also* Church House
Anderson, Mary (Rose Cottage) 94
Anderson, W 143
Anderson Field *see* Tybber Field
Andrews, T ('The Woodman') 94
Andrews, Thomas 71
Apprentices 184
Arable land 106, 117-20, 142, 194; 11thC 36; 13thC 37, 47, 49, 51-2; 15thC 70; 16thC 77, 100, 103, 105; 17thC 135; 18thC 92, 103; 19thC 193, 195 *see also* Glebe land
Archaeology 41, 52, 108
Arlington Drive (Ruislip) 79, 89
Arnall, Henry (Woodbine Cottage) 94
Arnold, Roger (North House) 122, 124, 232
Arnolde, Roger 16thC, 121, 123
Ascot *see* Eastcote
Ascotte *see* Eastcote
Ashby, George (Philpots) 121, 123
Ashby, Robert (Breakspears) 99, 101
Ashby Farm, (Northwood) 111, 112, 123
Ashman occ. 159
'Ashtree Cottage' (Old Barn House) 147
Assart (clearing from woodland) 61
Assize (Court) 63
Atkinson, Brian (Marlpit) 117
Augustine, Vicar of Ruislip 15

Babb, John Humphrey (Highgrove) 167, 195, 196
Bailey *see* Motte-Bailey Castle
Baker occ. 73; shop 164
Baker, Edith (Hayden Hall) daughter of L. J. Baker 21
Baker, John Law (Eastcote Lodge) 227, 230
Baker, Lawrence Ingham 148, 230, 247, 248
Baker, Lawrence James (Hayden Hall) 21, 25, 87, 148, 227, 229, 230
Balding, Thomas 194
Baldwyn, John 71
Ball, George (builder) 259
Ballantyne, Ann (wall paintings, St. Martin's Church) 14

Bankes, Henry (Kingston Lacy) 133
Bankes, Sir John (Corfe Castle) 133
Bankes, Lady Mary (Corfe Castle) 133
Baptisms, Ruislip Parish Register 1689–the present 152, 154, 155, 156, 160; illegitimate births 185
Barclays Bank (Ruislip) 214
Barn Mead (Northwood) 29
Barnett, Ralph (Park Hearne) 122
Barns (Ruislip) *see* Great Barn; (Northwood) 207, 234, 237
'The Barns' (Eastcote) 112, 224, 225, 257
Barnsley, George Derek (Vicar) 23, 25, 90
Barringer, John (High St., Ruislip) 115
'Barringers' (Ruislip) 73, 122
Bastardy 154-5
Batchworth Heath 29, 199; roundabout 132
Batchworth Lane (Northwood) 237, 238
Bates Field (Ruislip) 71, 103, 105, 106
Batescroft Field (Ruislip) 71
Battle of Britain House (Ruislip) 87, 88, 146
Bayne, Robert (author 'Moor Park') 29
Beancroft Field (Bencroft) 70
Bec, Abbey of 13, 15, 23, 42, 43-67, 75, 106, 169
Bedford, John, Duke of 13, 15, 64, 69
Bedford, Joseph (Park Farm, Eastcote) 200
Beech Avenue (Eastcote) 224, 254
Bees Club, (Ruislip) 89
Beggarmen 154
'Bell Inn' (Ruislip) 198 *see also* 'Old Bell'
'Belhammonds' (Harefield Park now Harefield Hospital) 80
Bellair Restaurant, (Northwood) 241
Bells, St. Martins 13, 14
Belton Estates (builders) 259
Bencroft (Beancroft) Field 70
Bennett, R. D. Grange – Vicar *see* Grange – Bennett, R. D.
Bequests c17, c18 (Ruislip) 158-9
Berminton, William de (Vicar) 15
'The Berries', Ruislip 108
Bettz, Thomas 14
Birde, Edmund 123
Bishop Ramsey School (Ruislip) 232
Bishops of London 13, 14, 18, 23, 29
Bisuthe, Gilbert 60, 62, 63
'Black Bull' (Ruislip) 259
Black Death 121
The 'Black Horse' (Eastcote) 112, 179, 227
'Black Pots' (Ruislip) 85
Blacksmith occ. 71, 159, 160
Black Spots (Field) (Ruislip) 85
Blackstaff, William (Brill Cottage) 94
Blaydon Close (Ruislip) 105
Blencowe, Rev. William 167, 196, 203, 216
Bodimead, Matthew 153, 155, 156
Boon Days 57, 58, 60
Bordars 36, 38, 52
Boundaries 11, 35, 38, 59, 88, 94, 107, 108, 209; St. Catherines 75, 85, 90
Bourbrigg field (Ruislip) 70

267

Bourne Cottage (Northwood) 244
Bourne End Road (Northwood) 238
Bourne Farm (New House) (Sth Ruislip) 141, 145, 146, 147, 207, 208, 210, 211, 252, 254
Bourne Farm Cottages (Sth Ruislip) 145, 147
Bourne Field (Sth Ruislip) 49, 99, 100, 103, 105, 106, 117, 141, 142
Bourne Grange (Sth Ruislip) 49
Bourne Grove (meadow) (Sth Ruislip) 120
Bourne Wyck (meadow) (Sth Ruislip) 100, 120
Bowers, H. L. builder 259
Bowman, Thomas, 98
'Brackenbridge' (Sth Ruislip) 211
Bradefer, Richard 70
Brakespear, Nicholas 62
Brasses, St. Martin's Church 125, 128, 129
Braun, Hugh 38
Bray, John *sen* 194, 200
Bray, W. J. (Kings End) 248
'Breakspear Arms' (Ruislip) 88
Breakspear Estate (Ruislip) 95
Breakspear Garage (Ruislip) 79, 81, 92, 94
Breakspear Road, 79, 82, 85, 87, 89, 90, 94, 202; North 81, 88, 92, 94; triangle 87, 88
'Breakspears' (Harefield) 99, 121
Brickmaker occ. 78, 159
Brick Making occ. 78, 122, 241
Brickett Close (Ruislip) 94
Brickfield 219, 241
Bricklayer occ. 159
Bricks & Tiles 122
Brickwall Lane (Hook Lane) (Ruislip) 70, 105, 117, 258
Brickworker occ. 159
Bridle Road (Eastcote) 199
Bright, Jeremiah 154
Bright, Thomas, vicar Ruislip 154
Brill, Christopher 206
Brill, George 194
Brill, 'Shorty' 94
Brill, Thomas 185
'Brill Cottage' (Ruislip) 79, 81, 82, 92, 94
British Freehold Investments 224, 252, 257
British Legion 189, 214, 218 *see also* Park House, Ruislip
Broadwood Ave (Ruislip) 38, 263
Brook Close (Ruislip) 105
Brook Drive (Ruislip) 105
Brook Mead Shot, 117, 118
Brooks, Edward 161
Brooman occ. 159
Brun, Richard (Ruislip Customal) 51
Buckingham, William (The Ferns) 92
Bugbaird, Ralph 184
Bugbeard, William (Black Pots) 85
'The Buildings' *see* Brackenbridge
Burbidge, John died 1795 first gov. old workhouse Oct 1789, 187
Burials, Ruislip Parish register 1695-1705; 1709-the present 152-156; register 183
Burne Jones, Sir Edward 31
Burns, William architect 29
Bury Avenue (Ruislip) 93

Bury Farm (Ruislip) 88, 89, 108, 112, 113, 164
'Bury House' (Ruislip) 42, 52, 73, 75, 92, 132, 146; estates 19thC 213, 225-6
Bury Street (Ruislip) Barn 128; Bury Farm 112; Bury House 225; Church room 232, 262; Dog gravestones 93 c15, 71; Mill House 107; Old House 129, 138, 142, 164, 196; Pound 101; Ruislip Park 37, 38, 41, 105, 108; Vicarage 23, 25, 139; Widening 262; Woodmans Farm 164, 194
Bury Street Farm (Ruislip) 89, 147
Butcher occ. 159
Buttes Mead (field) (Ruislip) 122
Button, Sir Howard Stransom (Franklin House) 88
'Bye-Way Cottage' (Ruislip) 112, 216
'Byeway House' (Ruislip) 216
Byron, C vicar 23

Cambridge *see* Kings College, Cambridge
'Cambridge Villas' (Eastcote) 225
Campbell Close (Eastcote) 232
'Camross' (Northwood) 237
Canal Feeder Ruislip 90, 92, 94, 199, 205 *see also* Reservoir, Ruislip
Cannon Brook (Ruislip) 94
Cannon's Bridge (Ruislip) 57, 81, 82, 108, 121
Cannons Bridge Farm (Ruislip) 108, 196
Canon, Roger (Cannon Bridge) 57
Carew, Frank Murray Maxwell Hallowell 240-242
'Carew Arms' (Northwood) 242
Carew Road (Northwood) 240
Carley, Austin (Brill Cottage) 94
Carmen, Lilian Minnie (Hayden Hall) 221
Carnegie, David (Eastbury) 236, 238, 240
Carpenter *see* 25, 51, 159, 160
Carrier occ. 159
Carters occ. 51
'Case is Altered' (Eastcote) 110, 166, 194
Casemore, A. 177, 178
Castle *see* Motte-Bailey Castle
Catholicism, Papists 17, 18, 77
Catlins Lane (Popes End Lane, Eastcote) 75, 107, 108, 111, 122, 164, 166, 194
'Cavendish' (Tile Kilns) 90
Cavendish Avenue (Sth Ruislip) 28
Cavendish Land Company 88
Cecil, Robert (1st Earl Salisbury) 99, 103
Censor's Wood *see* Mad Bess Wood
Census 1801 – 155, 193; 1841 – 242; 1851 – 144, 174, 225, 227, 242; 1861 – 174-5, 242; 1871 – 175, 219; 1881 – 90, 148, 175-6
Chalk mine (Northwood) 117, 240
Chandos, Lady (Hayden Hall) 164
Chandos, Lord William (Hayden Hall) 164, 166
Chantries, St Martins Church 14
Chantry Priest 14
Chapel of Ease (Northwood) 20
Chapels *see* Eastcote; Northwood; Ruislip Common; Wesleyan 223
Charles I 133
Cheesemonger occ. 159

Cheney Street (Eastcote) 107, 108, 111, 121, 122, 134, 146, 223
Cheney Street Farm (Eastcote) 111, 166, 194, 230, 247
'Chequers', Bucks 125
Chester Road (Northwood) 238, 240
Chestnut Avenue (Northwood) 258
Child, Christopher (St. Catherine's) 79
Child, John (St. Catherine's) 79
Childe, Elena (Terrier 16thC) 121, 123
Childe, Henry (Terrier 16thC) 121
Chimney Sweep occ. 159
Cholera 176
Christian Names, Customal 53-57
Christmas, John & Mathias 125
Christmas, Robert 98, 99, 101
Church Avenue (Ruislip) 216
Church Bridge (Ruislip) 139
Church Field (Ruislip) 99, 103, 105, 117, 142, 198
Church House (Ruislip) 132, 154, 155, 169-71, 172 see also Almshouses, Ruislip
Church Path see Church Ave 216
Church Rooms (Ruislip) 232, 261-2
Church Walks in Middx (Sperling) 15
Churches see Emmanuel; Holy Trinity; Sacred Heart; St. Edmund the King; St. Lawrence; St. Martin's; St. Mary's; St. Paul's; St. Thomas More's
Churchfield Gardens (Ruislip) 128
Churchill, Jenny (Highgrove) 231
Churchill, Sir Winston (Highgrove) 231
Churchyard, Ruislip 128, gate 132 & 157, 167, 171; Charity School 184; Eleanor Warrender buried 232
Circuits Farm see Southcote Farm
Civil Wars 17, 167, 179
Clack Farm (Ruislip) 28, 79, 82, 88, 89, 90
Clack Lane (Ruislip) 23, 51, 58, 108, 110, 122
Clarke (Mr.) Model Pig Farm 90
Clarke, Dr. Adam (Hayden Hall) 20, 226, 227
Clarke, Caroline Louisa daughter of T. T. Clarke of Swakeleys 225
Clarke, Elizabeth widow of John Wesley Clarke 227
Clarke, Henry (St. Catherine's Manor) 76, 79, 101
Clarke, John Wesley (Hayden Hall) 227
Clarke, Katherine (St. Catherine's Manor) 79
Clarke, T. T. (Swakeleys, died 1840) 141, 166, 194, 221, 225
Clarke, T. T. (son of above) 225
Clarke, Rev. Thomas (Swakeleys, died 1796) 80, 165, 166, 225
Clay 37, 55, 70, 78, 90, 117, 122, 219
'Clay Pigeon' (Eastcote) 211
Clay Street (Eastcote) 107, 111
Clayton, Ann (Black Pots) 85
Clayton, Thomas (New Pond Farm) 143
Cleares Lane (Ruislip) 108, 110 see also Ickenham Road
Clifton Arms (Northwood) 242
Coastal Command, Northwood see Eastbury
Coats Hawe 92

Cobbler occ. 159, 160
Cognorth (field) (Sth Ruislip) 103
Coke, Randolf 14, 57, 58, 62
Cogges, John ('Wilkins Farm') 115, 119
Cogges, Richard 'Barrengers' 73, 118
Collet, Thomas 28, 206
Collins, Mary (Fairacre) 221
Collins, Thomas (Brill Cottage) 94
Collins, William 206
Collins, Mrs William, 176
Colne, River 205
Colne Valley Water Company 247, 249
Common Fields 49, 61, 73, 100, 107, 108, 115-117, 118, 119, 120, 124, 129, 134, 135, 137, 185, 194, 195, 196, 198, 199, 200
Common Waste 52, 77, 193, 196, 198, 199, 200, 201; land 207
Common Wood, Ruislip 38, 52, 75, 98, 99, 100, 103, 106, 107, 121, 135
Cook occ. 219
Cook, Joseph 167
Cophawe (field) (Ruislip) 70
Coppice Close (Ruislip) 89
Coppice Wood 77, 78, 138
Copse Wood (Ruislip) 52, 99, 103, 107, 137, 186, 187, 189, 254, 256; conservation 263
Copwell Mead (field) (Ruislip) 71, 103, 105
Copyholds 61, 71, 77, 82, 99, 101, 105, 106, 107, 121, 132, 144
Cordwainer occ. 159
Cordwinder occ. 159, 160
Corfe Castle, Dorset 133
Corn Laws 185
Cornchandler occ. 159
Cornwall-Jones, E. vicar 22, 23, 89, 262
Cornwall Road (Ruislip Manor) 106, 143, 208, 209
Coteford Close (Eastcote) 229, 258
Coteford School (Eastcote) 105, 147
Cottage Society, Ruislip see Ruislip Manor Cottage Society Ltd.
Cottagers' Allotment Charity 206, 207
Cottars 36, 38, 52
Country Park, (Sth Ruislip) 210
Courts see Manor Courts
Court Rolls 60, 61, 62, 119, 165; Ruislip 23, 73, 75
Cow Field (Ruislip) 93
Cowherd occ. 51
Cox, R. H. 88
Cox, Henry Richard (died 1914) (Harefield Place) 87, 88
Cranbourne Road (Northwood) 28
Crematorium (Ruislip) 79, 85, 88, 207
Crescent Rise (Northwood Hills) 236
Crescent Road (Northwood Hills) 236
Croft Gardens (Ruislip) 259
Crofts, Crofters 52, 59, 60, 61, 119
Cromwell, Oliver 133, 167
Crookall (butcher, Ruislip) 232
Crops 46-47, 101, 195
Cross, R. (Lt. Manor Farm) 89
Crosyer, Gilbard 14

269

Croys, Robert (Ruislip Customal) 51
Cuckoo Hill (Eastcote) 111, 129, 225, 248
Cuckoo Hill Farm (Eastcote) 111, 134, 146, 147, 194
'Cuckoos' 'Cucowes' Farm *see* Mistletoe Farm
Currys (Ruislip High St) 214
Customal 13, 14, 51-53, 58, 59, 60, 69, 71, 117, 121

Dairymaid occ. 219
Dame School (Ruislip) 183
'Danemead' 225
Davies, Captain A. Morris (Clack Farm) 90
Davis Estates Limited 28, 259
De Blois, Mr. (Almshouses) 178
Dean, John 203
'Deanes' *see* Hayden Hall
Deane, family 15, 125-150; family tree 126, 7
Deane, Rev. Charles 21
Deane, Francis Henry (1814-1892) 21, 125, 144-145, 207, 208, 209
Deane, Rev. George 196
Deane, Henry 138
Deane, Jane 138, 139
Deane, Philadelphia 138, 139
Deane, Ralph, drowned at Eton 1826, 144
Deane, Ralph 1782-1852 92, 138-144, 194, 195, 196, 206, 207, 208, 214
Deane, Ralph Hawtrey 1848-1924 32, 145-146, 189, 252, 254
Deane, Ralph Hawtrey 1884- 125, 146-147
Deane Estate Office (South Ruislip) 207; estate 211; lands 259
Deane Cottage (Eastcote) 145
Demesne 37, 45, 47, 59, 61, 62, 64, 70, 71, 100, 101-106, 107, 117, 120, 124, 125, 132, 142, 143, 144, 145, 194, 230, 254-5, 257; lessees 97, 98, 99
Denbigh Close (Ruislip) 106
Dene Road (Northwood) 111, 234, 236, 240
Denville, Alfred M.P. 244
Denville Hall (Northwood) *see also* Northwood Hall
Derby, Lady Alice, Dowager Countess 14, 164, 165
Dickett's Mead (Meadow) (Sth Ruislip) 120
Diphtheria 248
Ditchers occ. 203
Dogs' Cemetery (Ruislip) 93
Dogs' Gravestones (Ruislip) 93
Dog Sanatorium (Ruislip) 93
Doharty's Map 1750 23, 70, 100, 101, 103, 105, 106, 115, 132, 137, 143
Domesday, priest 25; Ruislip entry 35-42, 52, 105
Dormywood (Ruislip) 263
Dovecot (Eastcote House) 132
Dowager Queen of Sweden *see* Sweden, Dowager Queen
Down Barns 107; Manor 58, 73
Down Barnes Farm 73, 88, 210, 261
Down Barnes Road (West End Rd, Sth Ruislip) 199, 200
Down Barnes Shot 117

Drainage 199, 247, 248, 249, 251, 252; ditches 82, 250; Ruislip High Street 255
Dressmaker occ. 176
Drew, Thomas F. 92, 93
Drovers occ. 45, 51
Duck, John 159
Duck, Robert 159
Ducks Hill (Ruislip/Northwood) 42, 73, 75, 85, 87, 111, 112, 115, 144, 146, Old Workhouse 185, 186, 198, gravel pit 200, 202, 242, 244
Ducks Hill Farm (Youngwood Farm) (Northwood) 73, 87, 111, 112, 122, 123, 164, 194
Dune, Sir Roger de la (Down Barns) 57, 58, 73
Dwellings, distribution 1565 108

Earthbanks 37, 38
Earthwork 38
East Field (Eastcote) 105, 115, 117, 119, 121
Eastbury (Northwood) 29, 213, 232, 236; 237-242, 247, 257
Eastbury Farm (Northwood) 237, 238
Eastcote 11, 25, 63, 75, 113, 121, 122, 123, 182, 185, 199, 214, 223, 227; chapel 226; development 32, 252-4, 259; drainage 248, 249; fields 105, 115, 117, 118, 119, 120; Highgrove 166; Hopkyttes 125, 128; Manor 60, 107
Eastcote Chapel 21, 223, 225, 226 & 7
Eastcote Conservation Panel 148
Eastcote Cottage (Plocketts, Plucketts) 25, 111, 134, 164, 194, 227
Eastcote Cottage (Fairacres) 200, 218-221; sales cat. 1869 218, 221; estates c19, 213
Eastcote Cricket Club 231
Eastcote Fields 122, 137
Eastcote High Road (Eastcote) 52, 108, 110, 112, 113, 194, 229
Eastcote House (Hopkyttes) 14, 17, 137-8, 144-7, 157-8, 167, 194, 213-4, 247; coach house 148; description 136, 144; Francis Deane 21; Hawtreys 17, 80, 99, 112; Hopkyttes 125, 128-9; 132-5; tenants 148; walled garden 148
Eastcote Lane (Sth Ruislip) 211
Eastcote Lodge 148, 227, 230-231 247, 248; estates 19thC 213
Eastcote Park 218
Eastcote Pavilion 261
Eastcote Road 22, 51, 57, 105, 107, 111, 176, 178, 258; Almshouses 133, 169; Coach House 132; Ruislip Park 37; Town Plan 256; Vicarage 25
Eastcote Roadside 146
Eastcote Station 252
'Ebenezer Cottage' (Tile Kilns) 90
Ebury *see also* Grosvenor
Ebury, Baron (Moor Park) 29
Ebury, Lady (Moor Park) 21
Ebury, Lord (Moor Park) 21, 241
Eden, Catherine 17
Eden, Elizabeth and John 17
Edgell, Harry 214, 216, 218
Edith Road (Northwood) 240
Edlin, Edmund 161
Edlin, John 13
Edlin, William Turner 211

270

Education, the poor 183-4 *see also* under names of schools
Edward I 64
Edward II 64
Edward III 64, 76
Edward IV 69
Edward VI 14, 17, 107, 151
Edwards, Captain Bennett (Hayden Hall) 231
Egerton Close (Eastcote) 218
Elgood, Sir Frank (architect) 31, 250, 251, 252, 255
Elizabeth I 124, 151
Elizabethan Poor Law 1601 11, 169
Elm Avenue (Eastcote) 224, 252, 254
Elm Mead 117
Elmbridge Drive (Ruislip) 105
Elthorne, 11, 18, 60
Embankments 75, 77, 78, 108
Emmanuel Church (Northwood) 31
Empy, Edward (Northwood House) 234
Enclosure 19, 27, 37, 38, 49, 52, 77, 89, 100, 103, 105, 106, 113, 115, 124, 135, 137, 138, 139, 141, 142, 143, 144, 161, 169, 221; Act 1804 196; Award 1814 203; Commissioners 211, 218; effects on farms 207-211, landscape 203-205, the poor 205-207; Enclosure 1769 80-85; fields 185; old enclosure 193, 194, 203, 209, 214, 255; procedure 197-8; roads 199, 200; Ruislip parish 193-211; sale of land 198-199; workhouse 187
Enclosure Map 1806 24, 49, 58, 75, 76, 82, 85, 100, 117, 144, 166, 199, 218, 227, 234, 242
Enfranchisement 82
English Houses Ltd. 89, 92
Environs of London, 1800 15
Epidemics *see* Black death; Cholera; Diphtheria; Measles; Plague; Smallpox; Typhus
'Epsoms' (Kings End) 119, 120
Estates c19, 213-245
Eve, Sir Harry Trelawney *see* Trelawney, Sir Harry Eve
Evelyn Ave (Ruislip) 105
Everett, Thomas Marsh (vicar) 21, 24, 25, 176; marriage 230; 247, 248
'Eversholt Villa' (Eastcote) 225
Eversley Crescent, Ruislip 259
Ewer, Edwin 247, 248
Ewer, Henry James (Manor Farm) 41, 90, 209, 214, 248, 250
Ewer, James d. 1814 82, 94, 186, 201, 202; diary 20, 187, 205
Ewer, Mary (wife of James) 82
Ewer, Richard 20thC (New Pond Farm, Manor Farm) 209
Ewer, Richard 16thC (Mill House) 157
Express Dairies Northwood 199, 236
Extents, Ruislip 45-51, 61, 70

Fairacres (Eastcote) 200 *see also* 'Eastcote Cottage'
Fairfield Avenue (Ruislip) 92
The Fairway (Sth Ruislip) 32, 259
Farming 27, 49, 64, 70, 98, 141, 161, 195, 203

Farms *see* Ashby Farm; Bourne Farm; Bury Farm; Bury Street Farm; Cannons Bridge Farm; Cheney Street Farm; Circuits Farm (Southcote Farm); Clack Farm; Cuckoo Hill Farm; Down Barns Farm; Ducks Hill Farm; Eastbury Farm; Field End Farm; Fore Street Farm; Four Elms Farm; Glebe Farm; Grace's Farm; Green Hills Farm; Green Lane Farm; Hayden Hall Farm; Hill Farm; Home Farm (Northwood); Hundred Acres Farm; Ivy Farm; Joel Street Farm; Kewferry Farm; Kiln Farm; King's End Farm; Knowle's Farm; Little Manor Farm; Little New Pond Farm; Lodge Farm; Manor Farm; Maze Farm; Mistletoe Farm; Model Farm; Myrtle Farm; New Farm (Northwood); New Pond Farm; Northwood Farm; Old Pond Farm (Ruislip); Park Farm; Primrose Hill Farm; Prior's Farm; Rabourne Mead Farm; Rose Hill Farm; St. Catherine's Farm; Southcote Farm; Southill Farm; Starvall Farm; Warren Farm; Whittleborough Farm; Wilkins Farm; Willow Farm; Woodman's Farm; Youngwood Farm
Farthings Close (Eastcote) 158, 221, 225
Feasey, Albert Charles (Southcote Farm) 92
'Fells' (Northwood House) 234
Fenwick, R. Vicar St. Martins 23
Fern *see* Ferne
Fern, Thomas (fl. 1577) 25
Ferne family 181
Ferne, John the Miller (Northwood 16thC) 112; of Rickmansworth 120
Ferne, M. Thomas (will 1521) 14
'The Ferns' (Breakspear Garage) 92
Field End (Eastcote) 32, 106, 111, 122, 124, 134, 135, 146, 157, 158
Field End, Ruislip 73, 110, 132
Field End Cottage, Ruislip 112, 147
Field End Farm (Eastcote) 111, 119, 135, 137, 146
Field End Farm (Ruislip) 70, 73, 194, 254
Field End Green (Eastcote) 108
Field End Green (Ruislip) 107
Field End House Farm (Eastcote) 106, 146, 158, 166, 194; estates 19thC 213; 221-225; chapel 227; 252
Field End Lodge (Eastcote) 146, 147
Field End Road (Eastcote) 21, 107, 108, 112, 122, 134, 146, 147, 164, 199, 203, 218, 223, 230, 254; Shops 259
Field End Villas (Eastcote) 21, 223, 225
Field Ends 193
Fields *see under* common fields and names of fields
'Findon' (Southill Lane) 229, 230
Fine Bush Lane (Harefield) 81, 82, 87, 88
First Fell (Field) (Northwood) 234
Fisher, Hugo 123
Fitzneal, Richard (1189-98) 13
'Flag Cottage' (Eastcote) 111, 230
Flag Walk (Eastcote) 230
Fore Street (Eastcote) 37, 38, 52, 105, 107, 110, 112, 134, 147, 218, 227, cottages 229-230, 258

271

Fore Street Farm (Eastcote) 112, 146, 147, 194
Forester occ. 75, 159
Forge (Ruislip) 71
Forge Green (Eastcote) 145
'Forrers' (High St. Ruislip) 121
Foster's Mead (Ruislip) 121
Four Elms Farm (Eastcote) 110
Fox Holes Shot 117
Foxlee, R. A. (Little Manor Farm) 89, 207
Franklin, Lady Mary (Hayden Hall) 165, 166, 172
Franklin, Sir Thomas (Hayden Hall) 165, 166, 172
Franklin, Elizabeth (Hayden Hall) 166
Franklin House 88 *see also* Battle of Britain House
Freeman 38, 57
'French Grove' (Northwood) 242
Frenchmen 36, 41
Friars: French 64, 66; Ogbourne 64
'Frith Lodge' (Northwood) 236, 238
Frithwood – Woodland 238
Frog Lane (Eastcote) 146
Fuller, Lt. Gen. Sir Joseph ('Highgrove') 231
Fullers Hedge 117, 120
Furst, Mr. & Mrs. (Clack Farm) 90
Further Horse Close (meadow) (Ruislip) 103

Gamekeepers' Cottages (Ducks Hill) 87
Garden Estates Limited 255-6
Gardener occ. 159
Garrett, Mrs 'The Grange' 237
Gas Mains Highgrove Estate – Ruislip Village 1903 251
The 'Gate' (Northwood) 242
Gate Hill (Gyot Hill) (Northwood) 73, 108, 111, 115
Gate Hill Farm (Gyett Hills) 73, 132, 164, 187, 195, 238
Gateway Close (Northwood) 31
'The George' (Ruislip) 93, 111, 121-2, 198, 214; Assembly Room 262; demolition 115; pump & well 174, 249, 251
George V 226
George, Ernest architect 25
Giddy Street (Eastcote) Gyddye, Gyddy 107, 110, 121, 227
Girl Guides (Eastcote & Pinner) 232
Glacier Club (Ruislip) 89
Gladman, James (Six Bells) 85
Glebe Avenue (Sth Ruislip) 211
Glebe Farm (Sth Ruislip) 28, 210, 261
Glebe Land 15, 24, 25, 28, 88, 89, 90, 200, 210, 230 *see also* Arable land
Glenfield Crescent (Ruislip) 92
Glover, Rev. Richard 94, 225
Goatherd occ. 51
Gold, Thomas 78, 79
Golder, Henry 203
Golf Course (Northwood) 38, 99, 141, 207
Golf Course (Haste Hill) 99, 207
Golf Course (Ruislip) 71, 105, 108, 110, 122

Gooderson, Mrs (Ruislip) Shop 111, 115, 216, 218
Goodman, John (Mistletoe Farm) 225
Goodman's Cottages 225, 248
Goose Acre 117
Goose Acre Shot 105
Gooseherd occ. 51
Goschen, Kenneth (Sigers) 32
Grace, John (Northwood) 234
Grace's Farm (Northwood) 234
The 'Grail' (Eastcote) 224
Grand Junction Canal 108, 199, 203
Grand Union Canal 205
'The Grange' (Northwood) 29, 111, 122, 123, 164, 166, 189, 194, 195; estate 19thC 213; haunting 236; 232-237, 238
Grange-Bennett, R. D. (vicar) 23, 25, 90
Grangewood School (Eastcote) 38
Gravel, soil 37, 55, 70
Gravel Pits (Northwood) 185, 200; plan for road 254-5
Graveyard *see* Churchyard, Ruislip
Gray, W. A. G. vicar 22, 250
Great Barn (Ruislip) 51, 64, 70, 128; conservation 262-3; dating 49; Town Plan 256
Great King's End (Ruislip) 110, 216, 255
Great Manor (Ruislip) 201, 202
Great Mead (field) (Eastcote) 223, 254
Great Windmill Field (Ruislip) 117
Greatrex, Walter 93
'Green Close' (Northwood) 29, 234, 236
'Green Cottage' (Ruislip) 164
'Green End' (Northwood) 111, 123, 234
Green Hills Farm (Northwood) 234, 240
Green Lane (Northwood) 108, 111, 115, 134, 203, 234, 241, 247
Green Lane Farm (Northwood) 234
Green Walk (Ruislip) 258
Groom occ. 219
Grosvenor, later Ebury (Moor Park) Lord Robert & Lady 21; inherited Moor Park 1846, 29; 241; Thomas George, died St. Petersburg 1886; 31
The Guardians (Union House Ux.) 188, 189, 190
Guineville, William de (Proctor-General) 13, 51
Gurney, John 28
Guts Pond (bottom of Fore St. Eastcote Road) 248
Guy, Waldo Emerson (architect) 189
Gyddye Street *see* Giddy Street.
Gyett Hill 132
Gyot Hill *see* Gyett Hills

The Hale (Hale End Close) 57
Hale family 166-167; meaning of name 57
Hale, John (Hale End) 118
Hale, Martha (Highgrove House) 167
Hale End (Highgrove) 108, 111, 118, 166, 167
Hale End Close (Eastcote) 57, 232
Half Mile Lane (Northwood) 31, 241
Hall, B. S. (High St, Ruislip) 110
Hallowed Road (Northwood) 241
'Hammonds' Shot 117

272

Hampton Hall Farm (Rickmansworth) 132
Hanwell Lunatic Asylum (St. Bernard's Hospital) 189
Harding Housing Association 178 *see also* Almshouses
Harefield 15, 36, 38, 93, 99, 108; parish 81, 88, 92
Harefield Hospital 80
Harefield Lane (Harefield) 81, 82
Harefield Park 80
Harefield Place 87, 101, 164, 165
Harker, Henry (Church House, Ruislip) 171
Harker's House (Church House, Ruislip) 132, 171
Harlyn Drive (Northwood Hills) 227
Harman, George (Harman Brewery) 94
Harmondsworth: Court roll 23; prior 62; St. Catherine's 73, 75, 76; vill 41; 77
Harnett, John (Hayden Hall) 227
Harriot, Henry will 1659, 157, 158
Harrow Station: opened 252; Harrow & Uxbridge Railway Company 224, 250
Harrys Croft (Harris Croft, Ruislip) 38, 71, 103, 105
Harte, Matthew 120
Harwood, William died 1827, 234
Haste Hill (Northwood) 27, 28, 38, 52, 200, 203
Hatch End Station 223
Hatchments (St. Martins Church, Ruislip) 166
'Hawe Denes' Popes End 122
Hawkins Long (Ruislip) 132, 171 *see also* Hill Farm
Hawthorn Avenue (Eastcote) 224, 252
Hawtrey Family (Eastcote House) 17, 64, 73, 76, 125-150; family tree 158; 209
Hawtrey, Charles 1663-1698 157
Hawtrey, John died 1593, 25, 27, 99, 157, 167, 171
Hawtrey, Mary *see* Bankes, Lady Mary
Hawtrey, Mary wife of Ralph Hawtrey 133; Lady Franklin 166
Hawtrey, Ralph 1494-1574 15, 100, 121, 124, 125
Hawtrey, Ralph d. 1638 99, 157; 171
Hawtrey, Ralph 1626-1725 135-136, 166, 172
Hay Carts 143
Hay Dealer occ. 94, 207
Hayden Hall 87, 132, 148, 158, 167, 221, 226-30; cricket ground 231; estate 19thC 213, 227; lodge 229; owners 164-166
Hayden Hall Farm (Eastcote) 112, 119, 195, 227
Haydon, John 70, 123
Hayward occ. 51
Headstone Manor & Estates Limited of Watford 28
Hearth Tax 155, 164
Heathfield Rise (Ruislip) 171
Hedgers occ. 203
Hedges 82, 98, 100, 117, 203, 205
Henry IV 64, 69
Henry V 66, 69
Henry VI 66, 69
Henry VIII, 76
Herbage 59, 60
Heriot 59

Herlwyn (Herluin) 43
Herridge, Joseph (Northwood Farm) 142
Hesdin, Ernulf de 13, 15, 35, 36, 40, 41-42, 43, 75
Hewitt, Cecil 49, 128
Hides of Land Hydes 25, 36, 40, 41, 51, 58, 59, 60, 61, 73, 75; Hyde 106, 119
High Street, Northwood 31, 234, 238, 240, 241
High Street, Ruislip 58, 105, 107; 16thC 110, 115, 119, 122; 169, 176, 198-9, 255, 258, 261-2; Crookalls 232; Park House/British Legion 214-218
Highfield Crescent (Northwood) 238
Highfield Road (Northwood) 238
Highgrove House 57, 166-7, 216, 231-2, 251; estate 19thC 213; Hume-Campbells 21; Sales Catalogue 1834 167; Second world war 232
Highgrove Lodge 248
Highgrove Swimming Pool 232
Highgrove Way (Eastcote) 232
The Hill (part of Hawtrey estate) 134
Hill, Daniel 145, 203
Hill, Guy atte 73
Hill, Joseph (The Woodman) 94
Hill, Walter 62, 63
Hill, William 57, 206
Hill Corner (part of Hawtrey Deane estate) 146
Hill Farm (Orchard Close) 110, 161, 171, 194
Hill Field 73, 105, 117
Hilliard Family 210; land 238
Hilliard, Edward jun. and sen. 194
Hillingdon, London Borough 90, 92-4, 210; conservation of woods 264; Grange 237; Highgrove 232
Hillingdon, Lord coat of arms 211
'Hillingdon Court' 88, 207, 210
'Hillingdon House' 87, 88
Hillingdon Workhouse 176, 189 *see also* Uxbridge Union
Hillmorton, Thomas (Northwood) 242
'Hillmorton House' (Northwood) 242
Hills Lane (Northwood) 241
Hills Lane (Ruislip) 58, 108, 110, 199 epidemic
Hillside Gardens (Northwood) 236
Hodgekins Horse Pool Shot 117
Hog Field Meadow (Eastcote) 223, 224
Hogs Back, Northwood 206, 236
Holders Lane *See* Howletts Lane
'The Holt' (Almshouses) 178
Holy Trinity (Northwood) 29, 236; Eastbury 237; parish 11; windows 31
Home Farm, Northwood *see* Park Farm
'Homeside' Fore Street 229, 230
'The Homestead', Eastcote 112, 195, 227
Hook Lane *see* Brickwall Lane
Hooper, George 178, 231
Hooper, J. 262, 263
Hope, Susanna (St. Catherine's Farm) 92
'Hope Cottages' (Breakspear Road) 87
'Hopkyttes' *see* Eastcote House
'Horn End', Eastcote 111, 121, 247
Hornbeam 25, 78, 138
Horse Crofts 103, 105, 106
Horseman, Richard 61

273

Horsemanhole (field) (Ruislip) 70
'Horsens' 146 *see also* (Battle of Britain House)
Howard, Simeon (Ducks Hill Farm) 73
Howletts Lane (Ruislip) 79, 81, 82, 89, 92, 93, 94, 137, 164
Hudson, John (died 1696) 159
Hume Way (Eastcote) 232
Hume-Campbell, Sir Hugh and Lady Juliana (Highgrove) 21, 231
Hundred Acres 234, 236, 261
Hundred Acres Farm (West End Road) 88, 210
Hundred Acres Farm (Northwood) 199, 206, 234, 236; development 259
Hundred Acres House (Sth Ruislip) 210
Hundreds 11, 35-6, 60; Elthorne 11; Isleworth 18
Hyde *see* Hides

Ickenham 11, 35, 36, 40, 75, 108
Ickenham Road (Cleares Lane) 105, 108, 110, 112, 115, 214, 216, 255
Ideal Cinema (Eastcote) 259
Ideal Homes: Estate Office 232
Inns *see* Bell Inn; Black Bull; Black Horse; Black Pots; Breakspear Arms; Carew Arms; Case is Altered; Clay Pigeon; Clifton Arms; The Gate; The George; Iron Bridge; Maxwell House; Northwood Hotel; Old Bell; The Orchard; The Plough; Prince Albert; Red Lion; The Ship; Six Bells; The Swan; True Lovers Knot; The Woodman
Institute, Ruislip 232
The 'Ironbridge' 'Northwood' 242
Ive, Ramsey (Six Bells) 88
Ives, Samuel (Southcote Farm) 90
Ivy Farm (Eastcote) 110, 146, 218

Jacketts Lane (Spratts Lane) (Northwood) 81, 108, 242, 244
James, Charles 196
Joel, John (Green Lane Farm) 234
Joel Street (Gowle) (Eastcote) 107, 108, 110, 112, 119, 121, 134, 199, 202, 206, 221, 226, 227, 229; development 259
Joel Street Farm (Eastcote) 110, 112, 164, 195, 221, 225, 234
Johnson, J. M. 90
Joiner occ. 71, 159
Jones, E. Cornwall- *see* Cornwall-Jones, E.
Jones, Sir Edward Burne *see* Burne Jones, Sir Edward
Jones, Val (Priors Farm) 49
'Joy Cottage' 221
Joyner *see* Joiner

Kaduna Close (Eastcote) 121, 231
Katherine End *see* St. Catherine's Manor
'Keepers' Cottages' 229, 230
Keswick Gardens (Ruislip) 108
Kewferry Farm (Northwood) 29, 115, 195, 199
Kewferry Hill (Northwood) 244
Keynes, J. Maynard 262
Kiln Farm 'Northwood' 111, 122, 123, 194, 199, 234

Kiln Pond 219
King, Gregory demographer 181
King Edward's Road (Ruislip) 23, 216, 257
King, Laurance Edward OBE; FRIBA; FSA (St. Mary's, Sth Ruislip) 32
Kings College 25, 27, 69, 73, 97, 124-5, 214, 221, 230; Bury House 226; Deanes 141, 142, 143, 144, 145; Enclosure 194, 196, 199, 200, 201, 203, 207, 208, 209; Hawtreys 132-5; land development 250; 252; 254-9; Manor of Ruislip 64, 66; M.F. conservation 262; Reservoir 203; Rogers 137; Ruislip Park 216; Woods 262; Workhouse 186
Kings College Road (Ruislip) 105
Kings End (Ruislip) 57, 108, 177, 196, 247-8, 255, 261; 'Epsoms' 119, 120; 'The Neat' 122; 'Walden' 257 *see also* Great & Little Kings End
King's End Avenue (Ruislip) 255
Kings End Farm (Ruislip) 214, 261
Kings End Street (Ruislip) 107, 110
Kingsmill, H. 21
King's' Wythy Shot 105, 117
Kingston Lacy 133
Kirby, Daniel 28, 206, 234
Kirk, William (St. Catherine's Farm) 93
Kirton, John (St. Catherine's Farm) 92
Kirton, William 112, 123
Knowles Farm (Northwood) 194, 234

Labourers 25, 157, 160, 176, 181
Lady Bankes Junior School (Ruislip Manor) 133, 259
Ladygate Lane (Ruislip) 27, 66, 76, 81, 90, 92, 128, 249
Lamb, Gilbert 60
Lancaster, John of *see* Bedford, Duke of
Land Roll *see* Terrier
Langley, Thomas 13, 64, 69
'Lantern House' (Tile Kiln Lane) 90
'Laurel Cottage' (Joel Street) 119, 121, 227
The 'Laurels' (White House Ruislip) 224 *see also* 'White House' Ruislip
Lavender, Hannah and Henry 176
Lawrence, William (Field End House Farm) 223
Lay – Patron 15
Lay – Rectors 15, 128
Le Hither Horse Close (field) (Ruislip) 103
'Lea Cottage' (Northwood) 236
Leaholme Way (Ruislip) 90
Lekford, John de (vicar) 15
Leving, William 70
Lewin, John 79, 80, 81, 82, 85
Lewin, Sarah 79, 85, 194
Lewin, Susannah 79, 85
Lidgould, Rev. John 167
The Lido (Ruislip) *see* Reservoir, Ruislip
Light Acre field 117
Lime Grove (Eastcote) 224, 252, 254
Lincoln Road (Northwood) 28
Linden Avenue (Ruislip) 224, 254
Little Barn *see* Manor Farm Library
Little King's End (Ruislip) 110, 161, 216
Little Manor *see* St. Catherine's Manor

Little Manor Farm 28, 79, 88-90, 92
Little New Pond Farm (Sth Ruislip) 143; farm 209
Little Windmill Field 117
Lively, Robert 203
Living, John (Ashby Farm) 123
Livinge, William 13
Loam 90, 117
Local Government Act 1894 247-8
Lodge, Manor Farm 142
Lodge (Park House) (Ruislip) 214
Lodge Farm (Northwood) 238, 247, 248
London Bible College (Northwood) 194, 237
Long, Edward 28
Long, W. (Cheney Street Farm) 247
Long Field (Ruislip) 92, 93, 94
Long Marsh *see* Well Green
Long Mead (field) (Eastcote) 223, 224, development 252
Lords of the Manor 61, 62, 77, 80, 97, 106, 120, 125, 151, 194, 195, 205
Lot Mead (field) (Eastcote) 120
Lovell, Y. J. (builder) 89
Lower Fell (field) (Northwood) 234
Lowys 92
Lowyshill 75, 76, 79
Lulham, John (Southcote Manor House) 76, 85
Lychgate, St. Martin's Church 22
Lyon, John 119
Lyon, Thomas 25
Lysons, Rev. Daniel 15, 103, 138
Lyvinge, John 25

Mad Bess Wood 42, 75, 81, 82, 87, 88, 229, 230; conservation 263
Malmesbury Close (Eastcote) 221
Maltster occ. 159
Maltman occ. 159
Mann, Joseph (Bourne Farm) 141
Manor Close (Ruislip) 258
Manor Courts 11, 47, 61-64, 71, 98, 100, 101, 129, 143, 223
Manor Farm (Ruislip) 13, 25, 49, 64, 99, 101, 103, 106, 110, 115, 135, 137, 158, 196, 209, 248; admin. centre 214; conservation 262; dovecot 132; enclosed lands 193; estate 38; lodge 142; moat 41; Town Plan 256, 262
Manor Farm House 101, 157; conservation 263; description 1750 143; restoration 106
Manor Farm library: conservation 262; dog gravestones 93; Hayden Hall Shield 231; letters (Grange) 236
Manor House (Ruislip) priory 70; Ruislip Park House 214
Manor of Ruislip 35-42, 58, 60, 64, 69-73, 79, 97-124, 125, 128; Extent 45, 46; Settlement 107
Manor of The More *see* Moor Park
Manor Homes (Ruislip Manor) 259 & 260
Manor Road (Ruislip) 216
Manor Senior Upper School (Ruislip) 232
Manor Way (Ruislip) 258, 259, 261
Manorial Rights 98

Mansford, Frederick Mansford F.R.I.B.A. 1871-1946 (Kings End) 177, 255
Mansion House *see* Manor Farm
Markets 59
Marl 55, 70, 117
Marl Pit Field (Ruislip) 55, 70, 99, 103, 105, 106, 115, 117, 142, 198
Marlborough Ave (Ruislip) 76, 89
Marleward, William 63
Marlward, Robert 60
Marriages, Ruislip Parish Register 1694-1717; 1744-the present 152, 155
Marsh, Mrs (Eastbury) 29
Marsh, Thomas 157, 158
Marsh-Everett, Thomas *see* Everett, Thomas Marsh-
Martin, Charles (Southcote Farm) 90
Martin, Henry Pine (Gate Hill Farm) 195
Martins Lane *see* Ladygate Lane
Matheson, Daniel 206
Matheson, Samuel (Northwood Hotel) 248, 250
'Maxwell House' (Northwood) 242
Maxwell Road (Northwood) 240, 242, 247; council offices 250
'May Lodge' (Northwood) 238
Maze Farm, Northwood 198, 242
Mead Way (Ruislip) 71, 105
Meadow Close (Ruislip) 105
Meadowland 28, 37, 38, 77, 92, 98, 103, 104, 106, 107, 115, 120, 121, 142, 143
Mealman occ. 159
Measles 153
Measurement, standard unit (Ruislip) 103, 118
Melthorne Court (Northwood) 240
Messuage 55, 61, 73, 77, 85, 92, 99, 107, 112, 113, 118, 119, 120, 121, 122, 123, 129, 167, 218
Methodism 18, 20
Metropolitan Railway, Eastcote Halt 32, 146, 238, 263
Midcroft (Ruislip) 259
Middle Horse Close (Ruislip) 103
Middlesex 11, 37, 38, 40, 41, 57; Court 60; Rocques Map 1754 79, 80; report by John Middleton 1798 195
Middlesex County Council 28, 88, 93, 177; Hayden Hall 231; Highgrove 232; 262, 263
Middlesex Land Registry 1809 85
Middlesex Sessions Records 1617 171
Middleton, John 195, 196, 205
Middleton Drive (Eastcote) 221
Militia 184
'Mill House' (Ruislip) 107, 108, 132, 157, 186, 201, 202
Millar, Charles W. 28
Miller occ. 51, 112, 121
Millpond (Sitteclack) 58, 75, 108
Mills 23, 51, 71
Mills, Sir Charles Sen. (Hundred Acres Farm) 28, 88, 89, 90, 210
Mills, Charles Henry 210
Mistletoe Farm (Eastcote) 111; estates c19, 213; 225
Mitchell, James (Highgrove) 167

275

Moats 41, 70; Down Barns 73; Ladygate Lane 76; Manor Farm 49, 106; Southcote 85, 89, 92
Model Farm (Eastcote) 211
Model Pig Farm (Ruislip) 90, 93
Mole-Catcher occ. 206
Monuments, St. Martin's Church 125-8, 136, 166, 216
Moor Park (Manor of the More): Lady Ebury 21; Lord Robert Grosvenor 29; 73, 111, 115, 132, 155
Moore, Joseph 141, 145
The Moors (wet place) Hither, Further, Batts, Osier, Alder, Grazing, Flag 103, 105
More, Roger 98
Morford, Walter ('The Laurels') 224; (Field End House Farm) 252
Morford Close (Eastcote) 259
Morford Way (Eastcote) 147, 259
Morris, L. E. 129
Mortimer, E. C. (vicar) 23, 25
Motte-Bailey Castle 41, 106
Mount Vernon Hospital (Northwood) 244
Mounted Police Station (Ruislip) 216
Murdons (Clack Lane) 122
Murrray Road (Northwood) 240, 247, 249
Musgrave, Christopher 166
Musgrave, Joseph 165, 166
Mushroom Farm (Ruislip) 108
Myrtle Avenue (Eastcote) 252, 254
Myrtle Cottage, Joel Street estates 19thC 213, 221
Myrtle Farm (Eastcote) 221

Names: Ruislip customal 52-57; 15thC 69
Nash, Dr. Walter Llewllyn, 'The Grange' 236
National School (Ruislip) 144, 176, 184, 226, 227
The Neat (meadow) (Ruislip) 122
Nelham, James 73
Nelham, John 118
Nelham, Richard 120
Nelham, Robert 115
'New Cottages' (Eastcote) 229, 230
New Farm (Northwood) 145, 146, 147, 207
New Farm Cottages (Northwood) 145, 147
New Farm House (Northwood) 147
New Farm Lane (Northwood) 145
New Field Shot 105, 106
'New House' (South Ruislip) see Bourne Farm
New Pond Farm (Ruislip) 106, 143, 208-209, racecourse 255; development 259
New Pond Playing Fields (Ruislip) 106
New River Company 234
New Street (Ruislip) 107
New Street Lane (Ruislip) 107
New Years Green Lane (Harefield) 92
Newdigate, Amphilisia, John, Sebastian, (Harefield) 17
Newdgate, John (Harefield) 101
Nicholas, George (Ruislip) 115
Nicholas, John (Field End Farm) 119
Nicholas, Robert (Green End) 123
Nicholas, William 120, 123

Nicholson, Sir Charles (architect) 32
Nicknames, Ruislip customal 54, 57
Non-Conformity 17
Norfolk Terrace (Northwood) 241
Normans, St. Martin's Church 12; lord of Ruislip 13; 41, 43
'North House' (Northwood) 122, 232
North Ridings Wood 81, 82, 87
Northall see Northolt
Northcote 113
Northdown Close (Ruislip) 208
Northolt 11; 36, 41, 107; racetrack 210, 255
Northolt Aerodrome 28, 210, 260-1
Northolt Junction Station (South Ruislip Station) 32, 252
Northolt Manor 73
Northolt Road (Sth Ruislip) 146, 199, 230
Northwood 20, 21, 25, 29, 49, 60, 63, 69, 73, 107, 108, 113, 115, 122-124, 132, 141, 182; development 28, 232, 240, 247, 248, 252; drainage 248, 249; gravel cart 200; gravel pits 185, 193; population 11, 31, 242, 250; urban district 249-251
Northwood Cemetery 28
Northwood Chapel 20, 29
Northwood Farm 142, 207, 254
Northwood Grange 49
Northwood Hall see also Denville Hall 29, 242-244; Boys School 244, 248
Northwood Hills, 31, 38; Circus 199; development 259
Northwood Hills Station opening 31, 259
Northwood Hotel, 242, 248
'Northwood House' 29, 189, 234, 236-7
Northwood Park estate 19thC 213, 242-244
Northwood Station 28, 31, 238, 241, 249
Northwood Way (Northwood) 236
Norton, Daniel (Northwood Hall) 29, 242, 244, 248
Norwood see Northwood
Nurse Children 153-154, 183
Nurses occ. 176, 219
Nursery, Ruislip Depot 92

'Oak Cottage' (Ruislip) 81, 94
Oak Grove (Eastcote) 224, 254
The Oaks (Ruislip) 115, 216
Occupations, Ruislip Customal 53, 54, 55-57
Ogbourne, Bailiwick 44, 64, 66
Ogbourne Priory 44, 45
Old Barn Hotel (Ruislip) 110, 194, 199 see also Sherleys Farm
Old Barn House (Eastcote) 111, 147, 166, 194
'Old Bell' (Ruislip) 115; conservation 262 see also Bell Inn, Ruislip
Old Cheyne Cottage (Eastcote) 112, 194
Ye Old Cottage (Ruislip) 112
The Old House (Ruislip) 108, 129, 138, 142, 164, 196
Old Orchard (White House) (Ruislip) 122 see also 'White House' Ruislip
Old Pond Farm (Ruislip) 143, 209
'Old Shooting Box' (Eastcote) 110, 146, 194

276

Open Fields *see* Common Fields
The Orchard (Ruislip) 214
Orchard Bungalow (Ruislip) 261
Orchard Close (Ruislip) 122, 161, 171, 194
Orchard Cottage (Ruislip) 110, 113, 196
Orchard End Hawtrey estate 17thC 134
Ordnance Survey Maps 1865 76; 1866 85, 94, 234
Osborne, Thomas 123
Osmond, James 107
'Outlook' St. Martin's parish magazine 22
Outwood (Common Wood) 38, 52
Overseers of the Poor 132, 135, 154, 169, 172, 179, 181-3, 185, 187; accounts 189, 202, 205

Packe, Christopher (vicar) 19, 20, 21, 24, 28, 29, 88; guardian Uxbridge Union 188
Page, William (Old Workhouse) 189
Page, W. J. (builder) 238
Paget's, family 78, 79
Paget, Henry died 1568 77
Paget, Thomas, 77
Paget, William died 1563 77; fourth lord 79
Pannage 58, 59, 60
Papists 17
Parish Chest, St. Martin's 151
Parish House (Ruislip) *see* Almshouses, Ruislip
Parish Priest 11, 12, 15, 36
Parish Registers 151-153
Park (Ruislip) *see* Ruislip Park
Park Ave (Ruislip) 71, 105, 263; 'Woodlands' 263
Park Farm (Eastcote) 111, 122, 164, 200
'Park Farm' (Northwood) (Philpots Tile House) 111, 115, 121, 123, 195, 242, 244
Park Hearne (Ruislip) 52, 108, 122, 199; reservoir 203
'Park House' (Ruislip) (British Legion) 189, 214-218, 224, 257
Park Way (Ruislip) 258
Park Wood 23, 27, 28, 37, 38, 108, 132, 135, 137, 139, 142, 199, 200, 221, 256, 258; conservation 262-4; reservoir 203
Parker, James 121, 122, 123
Parker, Thomas Champress (St. Catherine's Farm) 89, 93
Parochial Church Council 23; (Almshouses Ruislip) 177, 178
Parson *see* Parish Priest
Parsons Bridge (Ruislip) 139
Parsons, William (The Grange) 234
Parsonage House (Northwood) 29
Partridge, Henry H. (Southcote Farm) 90, 92
Pasture Land 28, 36, 37, 77, 88, 92, 105, 106, 113, 115, 121, 135, 142, 206
Paupers 20; Poor Law 169; Settlement 179-183; Education 183-4, 189-90; Apprenticeship 184; Costs 184-190; Food/work 190
The Pavement (Northwood) 207
'Peteridge' *see* 'Petridge'
Peto, Harrison Ainsworth (architect) 25, 48
Peto, Helen Agnes 230
Peto, Sir Samuel Morton (1808-89) ('Eastcote House') 148

'Petridge', later ('Laurel Cottage', Joel Street) 119, 121; Peteridge 227
Pew, Box St., Martin's Church 14
'Philpots Tile House' (Park Farm Northwood) 121, 242
Pig Farm *see* Model Pig Farm
Pig Keeping occ. 51, 100
Pintold Shot 105
Pinn, river 23, 25, 27, 38, 41, 75, 90, 105, 107, 108, 122, 142, 193, 221, 229; church bridge 139; drains 247, 248; enclosed meadowland 103; recreation 256; water mill 51, 58
Pinn Fields 41, 105
Pinn Way (Ruislip) 41, 71, 105
Pinner Hill 207; estate 221, 234
Pinner Road (Northwood) 28, 31, 145, 199, 234
Pinner Station (Hatch End) 223
Plague 14thC 61
'Plocketts' *see* 'Eastcote Cottage'
Plough – land 36, 58, 59, 60
'The Plough' (Ruislip) 52, 108
Ploughmen occ. 51
'Plucketts' *see* Eastcote Cottage
Police Station (Ruislip) 216, 218
Polish War Memorial (Sth Ruislip) 28
Pond Green (Ruislip) 73, 194
Ponds 206, 219, 248
Poor House (Ruislip) 132 *see also* Almshouses, Ruislip
Poor Law: Elizabethan 11, 132, 169, 172; 1662 – 179, 181; 1834 – 184
Poor Rate 141, 169, 185
Poor Relief 181-183
Poors field (Ruislip) 38, 52, 99, 115, 200-203, 205, 206; Little 207
Popes End 122, 134, 225
Popes End Lane *see* Catlins Lane
'Poplar Cottage' (Eastcote) 221
'The Poplars' (Ruislip) 257, 261
Population: Eastcote 32; Harefield 38; Ickenham 38; Northwood 11; Ruislip 13, 38, 51, 121; table 16thC-19thC 155; table 1801-51, 205; Gregory King 17thC 181; Parish increase c19, 214, 1964 256; Ruislip-Northwood 261-2
Post Office: Ruislip 214, 216; Sth Ruislip 254, 262
Potsherds 52, 108
Potter Street (Northwood Hills) 134, 199; Hill 199
The Pound (Ruislip) 100
Poverty (Ruislip) 169-191
Powell, Thomas (St. Catherine's Farm) 92
Pratt, Frank ('Frith Lodge') 236
Priest's House (Ruislip) conservation 262
Primrose Hill (Ruislip) 110, 164
Primrose Hill Farm (Ruislip) 194
'Prince Albert' (Tile Kilns) 90
Prior; Ogbourne 13, 44; Ruislip 45, 51
Prior, Edward 232
Priors Farm (Sth Ruislip) 49, 144, 146, 147, 194, 209
Priors Field (Sth Ruislip) 49, 120, 209
Priory, Ruislip 13, 43-45, 49, 66, 70, 71, 98, 106

277

Proctor-General 13, 44, 45, 51, 61, 62, 64
Protestantism 17, 18
Prowtings builders 178
Public Health 155, 176, 181, 182, 183 *see also* Drainage, Sanitation
The Pump (Ruislip) 93, 174, 249, 251
Puritanism 17, 18
Pycot, William & Isobel (Southcote) 75

Quainton, Dean 23

Rabourne Mead Farm (Eastcote) 211
Railway 89; improvement 261 *see also* Stations
Raisins Hill (Eastcote), Raisuns Hill, Raisons Hill, Raysons Hill 57, 108, 110, 135, 146, 194, 195, 227
Raisins Hill *see* Raisins Hill
Raisuns Hill *see* Raisins Hill
'Ramin', Eastcote 110, 113, 164
Rate Books 85, 93, 167, 193, 194, 218, 221, 223, 234; 1827 – 216; 1847 – 94; 1855 – 29; 1902 – 146
Rates: Elizabethan 169; 17thC, 18thC, 19thC 184; Ruislip 185, 186
Rawhedge (field) Ruislip 70, 117
Raysons Hill *see* Raisins Hill
Rectors, Ruislip 15-23, 128, 138, 139, 200
Rectory (Ruislip) 15, 25, 27, 125, 128, 132, 138, 139, 141, 142, 145; barn 129; lands Sth Ruislip 144, 207
'Red Lion' (Ruislip) 216
'Redbournes' (Eastcote) 226
Redding family (Reding) (Redinge) 73, 120, 158, 181
Redding, George 17thC 183
Redding, John 16thC (Field End) 106
Reding (Redinge) (Redding) *see also* Redding family
Reding family *see* Redding
Reding, Robert de 13thC 106
Redinge (Reding) (Redding) *see also* Redding family
Redinge family *see* Redding
Redinge, Roger 14thC (Northwood Grange) 49, 97
Redinge, Joanna 16thC 121
Redinge, John (Field End) will 1671 157, 158
Redinge 17thC (Eastcote Cottage) 132
Redinge, John 17thC (Manor Farm) 106
Redland shot 117
'Redwood' (Northwood) 236
Reeve 51, 62
Reeves Mead (Ruislip) 103, 105
Reformation 17
Reginald Road (Northwood) 238
Rents, Manor of Ruislip 16thC 122-124
Reservoir (Ruislip) 38, 81, 108, 203, 205, 240, 248; recreation 256; 263
Reservoir Road (Ruislip) 52, 108; gravel carrying 200
The 'Retreat' (Eastcote) 224
'Retreat Cottage' (Eastcote) 221, 225

Richard II 64, 75
Rickmansworth Road (Northwood) 49, 111, 194, 199; gravel pit 200; 203, 240, 244
The Ridgeway (Ruislip) 105
Ridley, Nicholas 14
Ripple Tea Rooms (Northwood) 241
Rivee Brook 105
Rivers *see* Colne, Pinn *see also* brooks – Cannon, Rivee, Roxbourne, Yeading; *streams* Roxbourne
Road Making occ. 203, 205
Roads 89, 199-200, 254; *see also* under name of roads
Robarts family 236
Roberts, Howard (grocer) 88
Roberts Mead (Ruislip) 103, 105
Robins, John (Black Horse) 112
Robins, Richard 115
Robinson, George 92, 93, 94, 227, 234
Rochester Road (Northwood) 28
Rocques Map of Middx 1754 79, 80, 81, 82, 107
Roman Catholicism *see* Catholicism
Rogers, Elizabeth 1722-1803 80, 82, 92, 128, 137, 138, 196
Rogers, family 15, 125-150, family tree 126, 127
Rooke Acres 117
'Rose Cottage' (Breakspear Road) 79, 81, 82, 87, 94, 202
'Rose Hall Cottage' (West End Road) 211
Rose Hall Farm (Willow Gdns) 211
'The Rosery' (Eastcote) 145
Rothwell Field (Ruislip) 70
Rouen, Holy Trinity 42, 75, 76
Roumieu, Rev. J. J. 21, 25, 206
Rouse, Clive F. S. A. 14
Rovers Den (Almshouses Ruislip) 178
Rowe, John ('The Grange') (Northwood House) 195, 234
Rowe, John Paul ('Northwood House') 234
Rowland-Brown, Miss *see* Garrett, Mrs.
Roxbourne 129
Roxbourne Brook 49, 117, 120
Roxbourne Field 105, 106, 115, 117, 120
Roxbourne Mead 120
Roxbourne stream 71, 107
Roy Road (Northwood) 238
Royal Commission on Historical Buildings 128
Ruddy Developments 28
Ruislip 17thC, 18thC 151-168; Social class (17 156-7; 19thC 213-244; 20thC 247-264
Ruislip & Eastcote Association inauguration 261; 262
Ruislip & Ickenham Station (West Ruislip) 252
Ruislip Building Company Limited 255-6
Ruislip Castle 41
Ruislip Common 176, 186
Ruislip Common Chapel 21
Ruislip Court (Manor Farm) 25, 64, 66, 98, 99, 106
Ruislip Depot & Nursery 92
Ruislip District Council *see* R.N.U.D.C.
Ruislip excavations 41
Ruislip Gardens station 70

278

'Ruislip Holt' (house) 28
Ruislip Manor 11; development 259, 260, 262; Halt 255, 257, 261; station 117
Ruislip Manor Cottage Society Limited 257-259
Ruislip Manor Limited 255-6, 257, 258
Ruislip Manor Station 117; Halt 255, 261
Ruislip Northwood & Eastcote L.H. Society Hayden Hall 231
R.N.U.D.C. 22, 28, 36, 88, 92, 106, 177, 205-207, 210, 211, 221; Eastcote House 148; Grange 237; Hayden Hall 164, 231; Highgrove 232; Kings College 262, 263; Ruislip District Council 248, 249; R.N.U.D.C. formation 1904 – 250-251; 256, 257; Town Plan 251-254
Ruislip Nursing Home (Cornwall Road, New Pond Farm) 209
Ruislip Operatic Society 262
Ruislip Parish 11-33, 42, 51, 73, 135, 138, 141, 144, 169, 172, 179, 200, 211, 214; enclosure 193-211; pensioners 181-3, 185; population 155-156; vestry/parish council 20thC – 247-250
Ruislip Park 25, 36, 37-38, 66, 98, 99, 103, 105, 108, 132, 134, 135; estates 19thC 213, 218, 261
Ruislip Rugby Club 57
Ruislip Station opening 250, 252
Ruislip Valuation 41
Ruislip Village 35, 36, 38; conservation 262
Ruislip Village Trust 178, 251
Rush Shot 105, 117
Rythe Shot 105
Ryves, John (St. Catherine's) 79

Sacred Heart Church (Ruislip) 232
St. Benedict, rule of 43
Saint Bernard's Hospital (Hanwell Lunatic Asylum) 189
St. Catherine's Farm (Catlins Lane) 75, 108, 111, 122, 164, 194
St. Catherine's Farm (Howletts Lane) 79, 81, 92-93, 137, 164
St. Catherine's Manor 62, 73, 75-95; sale 85; 108, 155, 158, 185, 194; enclosure 1769- 201; 230
St. Catherine's Road (Ruislip) 93
'St. Cloud' (Ruislip) 216
'St. Edmund The King' (Northwood Hills) 31
St. Edmund Avenue (Ruislip) 108
Saint George, Joan & John 49
St. George's, Windsor *see* Windsor, St. George's
St. Helen's School (Northwood) 237
St. Lawrence Church (Eastcote) 32, 146
St. Margaret's Road (Ruislip) 89, 92
St. Martin of Tours 14
St. Martin's Approach (Ruislip) 38, 41; dove cot 132
St. Martin's Church 11, 12-33, 40, 66, 79, 115, 261; brasses 125, 128, 129; chantries 14; churchyard 167, 232; hatchment 166; monuments 125, 128, 133, 216; parish chest 151; parish registers 151-153; windows 12, 14, 15 *see also* vestry
St. Martin's Churchyard Cottages *see* Almshouses, Ruislip

St. Mary's Church (Sth Ruislip) 32
Saint Michael's School (Eastcote) 231
St. Paul's Church (Ruislip Manor) 32, 259
St. Thomas More's Church (Eastcote) 158, 221, 224
St. Vincent's Orthopaedic Hospital (Northwood Hills) 28
Salisbury Road (Eastcote) 218, 219, 221
Salter, Samuel (Six Bells) 85, 216
Salters Mede meadow (Eastcote) 129
Sand, soil 37, 55, 70, 117; pit 117; mining 241
Sanders, John 107, 115, 120, 121, 124
Sandman occ. 159
Sandy Lane (Northwood) 238
Sanitation: Ruislip Sewerage Farm 92, 248, 249, 250, 258; Uxbridge Rural Sanitation Authority 247; Water 174, 176, 178, 204, 205
Sanson, Thomas 143
Sanson's Hill Wood 82
Saxons 11, 35, 38, 60; hall 41; lord 40; names 57
Scaffold, William (Prince Albert) 90
Schools *see* Bishop Ramsey School; Coteford School; Dame School; Grangewood School; Lady Bankes School; Manor Senior Upper School; Mrs Willis School; National School; St. Helen's School; St. Michael's School; Whiteheath Junior School
Scott, Gilbert 19thC (St. Martins Church restoration) 13, 15, 145
Scrope, Thomas (Hayden Hall) 165
Scrope, Gervase (Hayden Hall) 165, 166
Scrope, George (Hayden Hall) 166
Scrope, Frederick James (Hayden Hall) 165
Second Fell (field) (Northwood) 234
Second World War Home Guards 93, 214
Sellions (Strips) 25, 52, 118-122, 193, 200
Servants 17thC, 18thC 161
Seven Acres, meadow Ruislip 103, 105
Seymour, Henry 79
Seymour, Robert (St. Catherine's) 79
Shackell, John 194
Sharps Lane (Ruislip) 27, 28, 71, 107, 110, 112, 122, 194, 214, 216; well 251
Sharvell Lane (Sth Ruislip) 73
Shenley Avenue (Ruislip) 259
Shepherd, Robert (Mistletoe Farm)
Shepherd, William 18thC 85
Shepherd, William Hulbert (St. Catherine's) 85, 194
Shepherds occ. 51
Sherleys Farm (Ruislip) *see* Old Barn Hotel
Sheriff *see* Shire Reeve
Sherwood Avenue (Ruislip) 263
The 'Ship' (Joel Street) 227
Shire Reeve (Sheriff) 60
Shots – smaller fields 117-120, 193
Shovelmaker occ. 159
Shower, Sir Bartholomew 73
Sigers, Eastcote 32, 57, 112, 194, 218
Silver Street Green (Ruislip) 52, 75, 108
Sitteclack (Sithelack) millpond 58, 75, 108
Sitwell, Elizabeth (Hayden Hall) 166
Sitwell, George (Hayden Hall) 165, 166

279

'Six Bells' Ruislip 81, 82, 85, 88, 186, 202
Slipere, William (Ruislip Customal) 51
Small, Francis J. (Little Manor Farm) 89
Small Shot 117
Small Stone Acres (shot) 117
Smallholding & Allotments Society Ltd, Ruislip-Northwood Co-op 90
Smallpox 153, 182, 251
Smedley, Mrs. 263
Smith occ. 51, 121
Smith, John (demesne farmer) 16thC 25, 98, 100, 101
Smith, Robert Masson 20thC 224
Smith, Thomas (vicar) 27, 71
Smith's Shop (Ruislip High Street) 115, 142 *see also* Smithy, Ruislip
Smithy (Ruislip) 71, 115
Smythe, John 77
'Snail Holes' (Northwood) 242
Snake Hedge 117
Soames, Daniel Wilshin 238
Soames, Nathaniel 29, 189, 206, 234, 236
Soil *see* chalk, clay, gravel, loam, marl, sand
Somerset, John 69
Soutar, A. & J. (Town Plan) 256-8, 262
South Drive (Ruislip) 259
South Ruislip 11, 28, 88; Bourne Farm 207; development 254, 259, 260; enclosure 200; industrial estate 264; rectory lands 141, 144; station 32
South Ruislip Station (Northolt Junction) 32, 252
Southbourne Gardens (Eastcote) 223, 224
Southcote (Ruislip) 57, 58, 75-76, 77, 79, 81, 82, 85, 157, 158, 194
Southcote, Roger de & Avicia 57, 75
Southcote Farm (Ruislip) 76, 79, 81, 82, 90-92, 201; Sewerage Works 249
Southcote Rise (Ruislip) 122
Southern Estates Ltd. 206, 209, 259
Southill Farm (Eastcote) 112, 121, 164, 194
Southill House (Old Shooting Box, Eastcote) 146
Southill Lane (Ruislip) 107, 112, 227, 229
Spastics day centre 28
Spelthorne 18
Sperling (author) 15
Spratts Lane *see* Jackets Lane
Stackmakers occ. 51
Stain Hill (Eastcote) 223, 224; development 252
Standale Grove (Ruislip) 93
Standale Wood (Ruislip) 82
Stanford Close (Ruislip) 76, 89
Stanley Road (Northwood) 236
Starvall Farm (Eastcote) 211
Station Approach (Sth Ruislip) 28, 207, 210; Post Office 254
Stations *see* Eastcote; Harrow; Northolt Junction; Northwood; Northwood Hills; Pinner (Hatch End); Ruislip; Ruislip & Ickenham; Ruislip Gardens; Ruislip Manor; South Ruislip; Uxbridge; West Ruislip
Statues, St. Martin's Church 13
Steane Field (Stone) (Eastcote) 105; Stene 115; 117, 119, 120

Steel, Jeremiah (Hundred Acres Farm) (Northwood) 199
Stene Field *see* Steane Field
Stent, William (Woodbine Cottage) 94
Steven Elmes (close) 16thC 129
Stiles, Peter & John 94
Stockden, Joanna & John 121
Stone, Orlando guardian Ux. Union 188
Stony Field (Eastcote) 219
Stowe Crescent (Ruislip) 90
Stubbs, Francis (Eastcote Cottage) 200, 218
Suicides, Ruislip 153
The 'Sun & Ship' *see* The 'Ship'
'Sunnyside' (Joel Street) 121, 227, 230
Surnames 52-53, 54, 55-57, 120-121
'Swakeleys' 80, 141, 166, 194
'The Swan' (Ruislip High Street) 110, 115, 122, 214, 251
Sweden, Dowager Queen 231
Swineherd occ. 51
Swyncombe 59
Swyncombe, Peter de 45, 57
'Symbotes' (Northwood) 242

Tailor (Taylor) occ. 71, 159
Taylor *see* Tailor
Taylor, A. J. A. (builder) 259 & 260
Teasdales 88
Telling, W. A. (builder) 236, 237, 259
Tenants (Ruislip) 51-62, 71, 77, 78; rights 99-101; 107, 120, 121, 124, 128, 145, 151
Terrier c16, 23, 25, 73, 101, 106, 107, 111, 115, 117, 118, 119, 120, 121, 124, 129, 155, 165; 1837 – 85
Teulon, S. S. (church architect Holy Trinity) 29
Thackers Common (Northwood) 237
Thatch (roofing) 55
The 'Thorns' (Northwood) 248
Thurlstone Road (Ruislip Manor) 32
Tile House (Philpots) Northwood 121
Tile Kiln 58, 78, 82, 159
Tile Kiln Hamlet 90, 108
Tile Kiln Lane (Ruislip) 78, 79, 82, 90, 94
Tile Kilns (Ruislip) 81, 185
Tilemaking occ. 78, 90, 122, 159, 241
Tileman (Tiler/Tyler) 51, 55, 71, 159
Tiler *see* Tileman
Tiles & Bricks 122
Timber-Framed Buildings 29, 78, 94, 112, 113, 128, 136, 164, 167, 171, 178, 242, 256
Timberlake, Ezekial 183
Timberlake, Ralph (Hill Farm) 161
Tithe Collectors 51
Tithes 11, 13, 20, 25, 27, 28, 135, 138, 141; allotments – Enclosure 200; great & small tithes 15, 128, 134; Ruislip tithes 139
Tithing Barn *see* Great Barn
Tithings 47, 63
'Tivoli House' 244 *see also* Northwood Hall
Tobutt, 'Granny' 176, 263
Tobutt, Henry 92
Toovey, K. (vicar) 23, 25
Torcross Road (Ruislip Manor) 100

280

Town Plan 254, 255, 256-7; Outline Plan 1910 257
Tradesmen *see* Occupations
Travellers 154
'Treetops' 225
Trelawney-Eve, Sir Harry 89, 93
True Lovers' Knot (Northwood) 156, 242
Truesdale, Elizabeth (Bury House) 225
Truler, Ralph 13
Truler, Randolf 57
'Tudor Cottage' (Ruislip) 110
Tudor Lodge Hotel (Eastcote) 111
Turner, Robert (Highgrove) 167
Turnpike Road (Northwood) 234
Twenty Acres (Ruislip) 103, 105
Tybber Field (Ruislip) (Alderton) (Anderson) 105, 115; meaning 117, 119, 120
Tyler *see* Tileman
Typhus 153

Underwood (woodland) 78, 79, 87, 98, 115, 138, 203
Unemployment 19thC 185
Union House (Uxbridge) *see* Uxbridge Union House
Uxbridge Station opened 252
Uxbridge Union House 188, 189, 247
St. Vaast, Sir William de, Prior of Ogbourne, died 1404 13, 64, 69

Vagrants 154
Vestry 11, 89, 172; funds 182; meeting 11, 182, 185; minutes 20, 151; parish 144; parish council 20thC 247-250; workhouse 1789 – 186, 187, 188
The Vicarage (Ruislip) 18; house 23-25, 27, 88, 90, 107, 108, 139, 177, 225, 230
'Vicarage Cottage' (Ruislip) 24
Vicarage Close (Ruislip) 28
Vicars & Rectors (Ruislip) 15-23; list 16; 25, 27, 28, 66, 88, 128, 138 & 139, 200
Victualler occ. 159, 160
Villeins 36, 38, 61, 66
Village Sweet Shop (Ruislip) 115
Village Tea Shop (Ruislip) 110
Vills 41, 60, 117, 120, 248
Vincent, John (Northolt) 120
Virgate 36, 41, 51, 52, 58, 60, 61, 71, 119

Waggons 58, 59
Walaxton *see* Walleston
'Walden' (Kings End) 255, 257
Wall Paintings (St. Martin's Church) 12, 14
Wallaston *see* Walleston
Walleston family 16thC 15, 27, 120-122, 128-129
Walleston, John 16thC 13, 115, 120, 121-122, 123, 124, 128
Walleston, William 16thC 115, 121, 128
Walleston, Winifred wife of Ralph Hawtrey 16 125, 128
Wallington Crescent (Ruislip) 90
Wallis, J. H. (Brill Cottage) 94
Wallison *see* Walleston
War Memorial (Ruislip) 101

War Office (Eastcote) 224
Warren Farm (Ruislip) 94-95
Warrender, Eleanor 129, 231, war service, founded Sacred Heart Church & founded E. & P. Girl Guides 232
Warrender, Col. Hugh 231
Warrender Park (Eastcote) 232
Warrender Way (Ruislip) 232
H.M.S. Warrior (Northwood) 29, 238
Watercourses 120
Waterfurrows 117
Waterlow, Daniel Sydney (The Thorns N'wood) 248
Watermill 46, 51
Watford Road (Northwood) 238
Watson, Thomas (Hayden Hall) 165
Wattle 59, 113
Weatherley, Ralph (Ruislip Workhouse) Old Workhouse 187
Weatherley, William 186
Weaver occ. 181
Weedon, E. ('New Farm' Northwood) 207
Weedon, Councillor G. T. ('The Poplars' Ruislip) 257
Weedon, John ('Brill Cottage') 94
Weedon, Samuel 206
Weedon, William 203
Welch, James 28
Well Field (Eastcote) 105, 115, 119, 120
Well Green (Long Marsh Eastcote Road) 108, 111, 125, 129
Well Mead (Well Hooke) 120
Wells 174, 249, 251
Welsted, Henry died 1651 79, 157, 158
Welsted, Catherine died 1634 79
Welsted, Mary died 1688 79
Welsted, Henry died 1651 79
West Coat Common *see* Westwood
West End Road (Ruislip) 27, 28, 70, 71, 73, 88, 105, 108, 112, 143, 144, 198, 199, 203, 209, 210, 211, 255, 261
West Ruislip Station (Ruislip & Ickenham) 252
West Wood Common 201
Westbury Close (Ruislip) 232
Westcote 25, 63, 105, 113, 115, 118, 119, 120, 124, 132, 199, 214, 225; field names 117; poor 181, 182; rents 123; size 107
Westcote Common 92
Westcote Fields (Ruislip) 120, 121
Westcote Wood Close (Ruislip) 82
Western Avenue (Sth Ruislip) 28
Wesleyan Chapel (Eastcote) 223
Westwood 75, 76, 79; common 78, 80; house 237
Wetherlye, Thomas 122
Wheeler, Stephen 25
Wheelwright occ. 159, 160
Wheler, William 123
White, William 60, 73
White Butts (Ruislip) 70; Bridge 261
White Butts Shot 105, 106
White Chapel Close (Farthings Close) 225
'White Cottage' (Eastcote) 110, 195, 227

281

'White Cottage' (Sharps Lane) (The Laurels) 257 see also 'White House' Ruislip
White Hill, Ruislip 186, 244
'White House' (Ruislip) (Old Orchard) 110, 122, 194, 216
Whiteheath Ave (Ruislip) 92
Whiteheath Junior School 76, 92
Whitehorne, George (vicar) 17
Whiteslands 73
Whittingrove Field (Ruislip) 105, 115, 117, 120
Whittleborough Farm (Whitwells) (Northwood) 238
Whitwells Farm (Northwood) 238
Whyteleaf Close (Ruislip) 90
Whytes 73
Widdicutts see Withycrofts
Wieland, George (Eastbury Estate) 242
Wilchin, Elizabeth, George, John (Highgrove) 167
Wilkins Farm (Ruislip) 111, 115, 119, 194, 247, 248, 261
Willbesouths (Westcote) 57, 132
Willis, Old Bett Willis (School) 88
Willow Farm (Ruislip) 81
Willow Gardens (Ruislip) 106, 211
Wills: St. Martin's Church 13, 14; will makers 156-161
Wilshin, Daniel (Pinner) 187
Wilshin, Daniel (1783-1864) 142, 143
Wilshin, Jason (Rose Hall Ruislip) 211
Wilshin, Jason (1759-1823) 142, 196, 199
Wilshin, John (floreat 1700) 156
Wiltshire Lane (Wylcher) (Eastcote) 25, 107, 112, 129, 146, 195, 218, 221, 227
Wiltshire Street (Eastcote) 107, 110, 200
Wimpeys (builders) 90
Winchester, Agnes 16thC 121
Winchester, Isabel (daughter of Agnes) 16thC 121
Winchester, Joanna (daughter of Agnes) 16thC 121
Winchester, John (Northwood) 16thC 123
Winchester, William (Kiln Farm N'wood) 16thC 122, 124
Winchester Road (Northwood) 28
Windmill 46, 51, 117
Windmill Field (Ruislip) 122
Windmill Field, Great & Little (Ruislip) 70, 99, 100, 103, 105, 117
Windmill Hill (Ruislip) 51, 70, 256, 259
Windmill Way (Ruislip) 258, 261
Windmylnhill see Windmill Hill
Windows, St. Martin's Church 12, 14, 15
Windsor College 66
Windsor, Dean & Canons 13, 15, 17, 19, 21, 23, 29, 69, 88, 89, 125, 128, 132, 134, 135, 138, 141, 145, 200, 208
Windsor, St. George's 13, 17, 19, 69

Windsor, Warden & Canons 13
Wingfield, Augustine (St. Catherine's) will 1664 – 157
Winston Churchill Hall (Ruislip) 70, 71, 105
Winter, Cordelia (Field End House Farm) 223
Winter, Cornelius (Field End House Farm) 221
Winter, W. C. (Field End House Farm) 223
Withy Lane (Ruislip) 108
Withycrofts (Ruislip) Withycutts/Widdicutts 103, 105, 106, 255
Withycutts see Withycrofts
Wlward Wit 35, 36, 40
'Wood Cottages' (Fore Street) 230
Wood Dealer occ. 25
Wood Lane (Ruislip) 73, 105, 107, 108, 255
Wood Rise (Eastcote) 227
Woodbine Cottage (Ruislip) 79, 82, 93, 94
Woodland 36, 37, 52, 75, 77, 78, 79, 87, 88, 107, 144, 193
'Woodlands' (Park Avenue) 263
Woodlands Advisory Working Party 264
Woodlea Grove (Northwood) 236
Woodley, William (Six Bells) 85
Woodman family (Clack Farm) 90
Woodman, Alfred, George, Mary, Spencer 90 (Clack Farm)
Woodman, Augustus 19thC (Clack Farm) 89
Woodman, 'Curly' 85
Woodman, Francis, Martha 94 ('Woodbine Cottage')
The 'Woodman' (Eastcote) 110
The 'Woodman', Ruislip 81, 94
Woodman's Farm (Ruislip) 108, 111, 113, 164, 194
Woodmen occ. 78
Woodroffe, George (Hayden Hall) 165, 166, 227
Woods see Common Wood; Mad Bess Wood (Censors Wood); North Ridings Wood; Outwood; Park Wood; Sanson's Hill Wood; Standale Wood; Westcote Wood Close; Youngwood
Woodville Gardens (Ruislip) 122
Woolworth (Ruislip): (Wilkins Farm) 115, 119, 194; Ruislip Manor 117
Woodward occ. 51, 79, 94
Workhouse/Old Workhouse Ruislip 146, 174, 186-190, 202, 206; diet 1835 – 188; inventory 188; restoration 189; sale 1838 – 144
World War II 94, 95
Wylchers Street see Wiltshire Lane
Wythy Lane 202
Wythies (Poors Field) (Ruislip) 202, 206, 207
Yeading Brook 49, 70, 105, 106, 107, 117, 199, 259, 261
Yeoman see Farming
Young Wood (Ruislip) 87, 200, 202
Youngwood Farm (Ducks Hill Farm) 79, 81, 82, 88, 201